AMARTYA SEN'S WORK

CU00832948

This unique volume is the first to examine Nobel Laureate, Amartya Sen's ideas through the lens of gender. Renowned for his humanitarian approach to economics, his contributions have been crucial to the development of several aspects of feminist economics and gender analysis. This book outlines the range and usefulness of his work from a gender perspective while also exploring some of its silences and implicit assumptions.

The result is a collection of groundbreaking and insightful essays which cover major topics in Sen's work, such as the capability approach, freedom, social choice, justice, agency, "missing women", and development and well-being. Perspectives have been drawn from both developing and developed countries, with most of the authors applying Sen's concepts to cultural, geographic and historical contexts which differ from his original applications.

Significant highlights include a wide-ranging conversation between the book's editors and Sen on many aspects of his work, and an essay by Sen himself on why he is disinclined to provide a definitive list of capabilities.

Previously published in *Feminist Economics*, these multidisciplinary essays make for a compelling read for both economists and scholars from other disciplines, as well as for policymakers and practitioners.

Bina Agarwal is Professor of Economics at the Institute of Economic Growth, University of Delhi. She is also Vice President of the International Economic Association, and Past President of IAFFE.

Jane Humphries is a Professor of Economic History and Fellow of All Souls College, University of Oxford.

Ingrid Robeyns is a post-doctoral research fellow in the department of Political Science at the University of Amsterdam.

AMARTYA SEN'S WORK AND IDEAS
A Gender Perspective

Edited by
Bina Agarwal, Jane Humphries &
Ingrid Robeyns

Routledge
Taylor & Francis Group

LONDON AND NEW YORK

First published 2005
by Routledge, an imprint of Taylor & Francis
2 Park Square, Milton Park, Abingdon, Oxon OX14 4RN

Simultaneously published in the USA and Canada
by Routledge
270 Madison Ave, New York, NY 10016

Routledge is an imprint of the Taylor & Francis Group

Transferred to Digital Printing 2008

Typeset in NewBaskerville by Elite Typesetting Techniques Ltd,
Eastleigh, Hampshire, UK

British Library Cataloguing in Publication Data
A catalogue record for this book is available
from the British Library

Library of Congress Cataloging in Publication Data
A catalog record for this book has been requested

ISBN 0-415-37253-4 (hbk)
ISBN 0-415-37320-4 (pbk)

Publisher's Note
The publisher has gone to great lengths to ensure the quality of this reprint
but points out that some imperfections in the original may be apparent.

CONTENTS

This book was previously published as a special issue of the journal, *Feminist Economics*, the official journal of the International Association for Feminist Economics (IAFFE). All contributions have been subjected to the journal's rigorous peer review process and comply with the journal's editorial policies, as overseen by the editor, Diana Strassmann, and the journal's editoral team, including the associate editors, the editorial board, numerous volunteer reviewers, and the journal's in-house editorial staff and freelance style editors. The special issue and book have been made possible by the generous financial support of Rice University and the Ford Foundation.

Jon Chase, Harvard News Office

AMARTYA SEN

Amartya Sen is Lamont University Professor at Harvard University and was until recently the Master of Trinity College, Cambridge. Born in Santiniketan, India, in 1933, Amartya Sen studied at Presidency College in Calcutta, India, and at Trinity College, Cambridge. He is an Indian citizen. Before joining Harvard in 1987, he was the Drummond Professor of Political Economy at Oxford University and a Fellow of All Souls College. Prior to that he was Professor of Economics at Delhi University and at the London School of Economics. He has served as President of the Econometric Society, the Indian Economic Association, the American

Economic Association, and the International Economic Association. He is also Honorary Advisor of OXFAM.

Amartya Sen's research has ranged over a number of fields in economics, philosophy, and decision theory, including social choice theory, welfare economics, theory of measurement, development economics, moral and political philosophy, and the economics of peace and war. His books have been translated into many languages, and include *Collective Choice and Social Welfare* (1970), *On Economic Inequality* (1973, 1997), *Poverty and Famines* (1981), *Choice, Welfare and Measurement* (1982), *Resources, Values and Development* (1984), *On Ethics and Economics* (1987), *The Standard of Living* (1987), *Inequality Reexamined* (1992), and *Development as Freedom* (1999), among others. His most recent book, *Rationality and Freedom*, published by Harvard University Press as a Bellknap Book, will be followed by a companion volume, *Freedom and Justice*, also to be published as a Bellknap Book.

Amartya Sen has received honorary doctorates from major universities in North America, Europe, and Asia. Among the awards he has received are the Bharat Ratna (the highest honor awarded by the President of India); the Frank E. Seidman Distinguished Award in Political Economy; the Senator Giovanni Agnelli International Prize in Ethics; the Alan Shawn Feinstein World Hunger Award; the Edinburgh Medal; the Brazilian Ordem do Merito Cientifico (Grã-Cruz); the Presidency of the Italian Republic Medal; the Eisenhower Medal; Honorary Companion of Honour (UK); and the Nobel Prize in Economics in 1998.

EXPLORING THE CHALLENGES OF AMARTYA SEN'S WORK AND IDEAS: AN INTRODUCTION

Bina Agarwal, Jane Humphries, and Ingrid Robeyns

Nobel Laureate Amartya Sen is renowned for his humanitarian approach to economics. His contribution has also been crucial to the development of several aspects of feminist economics and gender analysis. Many of his writings have addressed gender concerns directly, but even when not explicitly feminist, his work has often engaged with themes that are central to feminist economics and philosophy. Indeed, the International Association for Feminist Economics (IAFFE) has claimed him as "a feminist economist." This volume is meant as a tribute to a brilliant economist and a fine man. It is also intended as a contribution to scholarship and future research on gender. It both builds on Sen's ideas *and* engages with them critically. It outlines the range and usefulness of his work for gender analysis but does not shy away from exploring some of its silences and implicit assumptions.

This challenging project was conceptualized in June 2000, first as a special issue of the journal *Feminist Economics* (Vol. 9, No. 2/3, 2003), and subsequently as this book. The book contains all the papers published in the journal's special issue plus a subsequent paper by Sen on why he is disinclined to provide a fixed list of capabilities. In planning the volume, we sought to identify all the major topics and concepts in Sen's work, such as justice, freedom, social choice, agency, functionings and capabilities, missing women, famines, inequality and poverty measures, the human development approach, and culture and identity. The final set of papers, which covered most but not all of these subjects, were discussed at a workshop at All Souls College, Oxford, UK, in September 2002. The workshop aimed at facilitating wide-ranging and in-depth interactions between Sen and the authors, as well as among the authors themselves and others invited. The discussions were interactive, spirited, and challenging. Amartya Sen joined us for the full duration of the workshop, and commented on all the presentations. After the workshop, with a final round of revisions, the papers took the form in which they appeared in the journal and are now included in this volume.

Although at the project's initiation we had hoped to cover the full gamut of Sen's work, we were only partially successful. For a start, we found that although a large number of scholars and policy-makers have engaged with Sen's ideas, relatively few have done so from a gender perspective. Also, there appears to be a natural clustering of research, and not just feminist research, around Sen's capability approach and his concept of freedom (especially as enunciated in his 1999 book, *Development as Freedom*), with relatively few writers engaging with other dimensions, such as social choice theory or famines, or applying his concepts empirically. Our attempts to invite papers on some of these relatively neglected issues, or to locate more authors in developing countries, also had limited success. Nonetheless, we are happy with the coverage achieved. We are also pleased that Sen agreed to answer some questions we posed about aspects of his work, as well as about the intellectual and personal trajectories that propelled him to focus on gender inequality and explore the field of feminist economics. We hope the readers of this volume will find our dialogue with him ("Continuing the Conversation") illuminating.

The contributions contained here are both theoretical and empirical. Where possible, the authors have applied Sen's concepts to cultural, geographic, and historical contexts that are different from his original applications. Perspectives have been drawn from developing as well as developed countries. Our authors include both established scholars and younger researchers and come from across the globe. Several live in more than one country.

I. SOCIAL CHOICE THEORY

The first chapter in this volume provides a gender perspective on a theoretical area of economics – social choice theory – which, in a sense, served as the launching pad for Amartya Sen's academic career, and which contains the seeds of many of the ideas he was to develop later. It is also an area of work (embodied in his 1970 book *Collective Choice and Social Welfare*) highlighted at length in his Nobel Prize citation. Sen's writings on social choice have, however, received little attention from feminist economists. An exception is Fabienne Peter, who engages with this field in her article, "Gender and the Foundations of Social Choice: The Role of Situated Agency." In examining the relationship between gender and the theory of social choice, Peter poses two questions: how can insights from social choice theory benefit the study of women's well-being and gender inequality, and how can social choice theory benefit from insights from women's studies and gender studies? In pursuing these questions, Peter uses different aspects of Sen's work to provide, she argues, a fuller account of the role of gender in social choice than he has done so far.

Peter points out that conventional and narrowly interpreted social choice theory is preoccupied with solving the problem of aggregating individual preferences, and does not lend itself easily to exploring themes such as women's agency, women's participation in democratic institutions, democracy and difference, universalism vs. relativism, and the tensions between an ethics of impartial justice and an ethics of care. She notes that Sen rejects the notion that social evaluation should be based on purely subjective assessments of individual welfare because, among other things, people's overt preferences may be adapted to adverse circumstances. He also emphasizes the importance of people's agency. This emphasis, Peter argues, brings to the fore a broader conception of social choice, and shifts the focus from problems of aggregating individual preferences to participation and inclusion in democratic decision-making. Hence, in contrast to much of social choice theory, it calls attention to fair procedures. Treating people as agents means giving them a chance to be heard, and to be involved in collective evaluations and decisions. The challenge for social evaluation of policy alternatives is to take seriously women's evaluations as situated agents, and to identify ways of enhancing their participation in policy discourse. This would also strengthen the role of freedom in social evaluation. Peter suggests that research in social choice theory and related fields should investigate avenues that make social choice and evaluation more responsive to situated agency and thus to issues of participation and inclusion, building on but moving beyond the foundations for this laid by Sen's work.

As Peter's chapter illustrates, Sen's early work on social choice already embodied preliminary aspects of his capability approach (and relatedly his ideas on agency and freedom). Today this dimension of Sen's work has developed a life of its own. The capability approach is currently being examined, applied, and discussed in a wide range of disciplines and subfields. And of all his contributions, this is the one that has most engaged feminist scholars, as is clearly reflected in this volume: the majority of our authors, in one way or another, focus on Sen's capability approach. Indeed several authors, such as Martha Nussbaum, Ingrid Robeyns, Vegard Iversen, and Marianne Hill, have made it their primary focus.

II. THE CAPABILITY APPROACH

Justice, entitlements, and lists

Martha Nussbaum is undoubtedly the most notable among feminist scholars who have engaged with, critiqued, and extended Sen's capability approach. In fact today an entire body of literature is devoted to Nussbaum's version of the capability approach, parallel to Sen's own formulation. Nussbaum's chapter in this volume – "Capabilities as Fundamental Entitlements: Sen and Social Justice" – discusses Sen's writings on the capability approach and her own development of those ideas, outlining in the process both the usefulness of the approach for examining gender and social justice, and some of the limitations of its current version. Nussbaum notes that Sen has made a major contribution to the theories of social justice and gender justice by arguing that capabilities are the relevant space of comparison for justice-related issues. She agrees with Sen that the capability approach as a framework for examining social justice is superior to utilitarianism, resource-focused analysis, the social contract tradition, or even some accounts of human rights. At the same time, she argues that to make the capability approach more useful for exploring social justice, Sen needs to take a more definite stand on which capabilities are important in our ethical judgments and our conceptions of justice. According to her, without such a list, the capability approach cannot offer valuable normative guidance on gender justice. Nussbaum also holds that Sen's treatment of freedom needs to be more specific. Freedom, she argues, can have both good and bad dimensions, and not all freedoms are of equal worth. Nussbaum proposes a list of ten capabilities for which she claims a degree of universal relevance, although she also emphasizes that the list could be modified by context.

The argument that we need a definite "list of capabilities" is extended further by Ingrid Robeyns in her chapter "Sen's Capability Approach and Gender Inequality: Selecting Relevant Capabilities." Like Nussbaum, Robeyns begins with a positive appreciation of Sen's capability approach for gender analysis, but goes on to argue that the approach also has the drawback of being "underspecified." For applying the approach to concrete questions, additional theoretical specifications are needed. Robeyns proposes a method for selecting the relevant capabilities, and applies this method to an analysis of gender inequality in affluent societies. In particular, she emphasizes the importance of *process* in specifying a list, such as taking account of the existing literature in the field and having a public discussion on it, to give the list academic and political legitimacy. According to her, the list should fulfill a number of criteria. In particular, it should be exhaustive, non-reducible, and sensitive to context. On some counts, her list is similar to previous lists such as that of Nussbaum; but on other counts it is quite different, as indicated in the comparative table she provides. Robeyns also briefly discusses how inequalities in capabilities can be judged if information is only available at the level of achieved functionings.

Robeyns' emphasis on public discussion and context specificity in making a list of capabilities is in keeping with Sen's own insistence on these aspects, in his response to a question we posed to him – as a follow up to our earlier "conversation" piece – why doesn't he provide a list of capabilities? In

"Capabilities, Lists, and Public Reason: Continuing the Conversation" Sen answers that the problem is not with providing a list *per se*, but with insisting on one fixed canonical list, based only on theory and usable for every purpose. Capability assessment, he notes, can be used for different purposes (varying from poverty evaluation to the assessment of human rights or of human development), and public reasoning and debate are necessary for choosing relevant capabilities and weighing them against each other, in each context. Any list should thus be context-specific and flexible.

Intrahousehold inequality and social power

Sen's capability approach receives attention from a somewhat different angle, namely that of social power, in the chapters by Vegard Iversen and Marianne Hill. Iversen, in his chapter "Intra-household Inequality: A Challenge for the Capability Approach?", examines the extent to which Sen's work has taken account of intra-household inequality when evaluating people's well-being. He emphasizes the importance of being sensitive to the role of domestic power imbalances when interpreting central concepts of the capability approach, such as agency, freedom, and choice. Drawing on literature on household behavior in developing countries, he examines these concepts through a feminist lens, and argues that when evaluating well-being more attention should be paid to the existence of alternative types of power within the realm of the household. He points to the interdependence between individual capabilities which affects well-being outcomes. For instance, in a marriage, a woman's well-being will depend not only on her own capabilities but also on those of her spouse. To illustrate this interdependence, he draws especially on recent literature on intra-household bargaining. In this context, he also calls attention to the central relevance of nonmaterial capabilities, such as "bargaining skills," in determining well-being outcomes. Such skills matter, along with a person's individual characteristics, resource endowments, and so on. Because of interdependencies and power relations (with material, nonmaterial, and agency constituents), Iversen argues, one household member's opportunities for achieving well-being will be influenced by the fall-back position and bargaining skills of other household members. According to him, taking these features into account poses a challenge for the capability approach.

A plea for more attention to social power is also central to Hill's chapter "Development as Empowerment." She begins with the observation that Sen's capability approach, while valuable as a starting point, also needs to take into account the impact of social power on human capabilities. Because social power is primarily mediated through social institutions, the latter deserve special attention by scholars aiming to take the capability approach forward. The approach, Hill argues, pays inadequate attention to the role of institutional power in generating or sustaining gender inequalities. And until the analytical frameworks being developed to extend the capability approach address the issue of social power, the analysis of well-being will be incomplete, and decisions made to enhance human capabilities will systematically fall short. She focuses especially on democratization as a way to begin incorporating power into the capability framework, but notes that there are significant differences between Sen and several other authors in their understanding of what democratization would imply. Democratization, she emphasizes, should be a process which allows recognition of the interests of those who are subordinate, oppressed, or for other reasons lack voice. To take this process forward, she argues, will require, among other things, extending more social power to those currently disadvantaged, and changing practices that are deeply embedded in institutions such as the family, the firm, and the state.

Since the issue of power is so central to studying gender inequality, and given that many feminist scholars (including several of our authors) have argued that Sen does not directly address this issue in examining gender, it is useful to highlight his response to it in our dialogue with him. Sen argues that it is not possible to discuss gender inequality as extensively as he has done without recognizing the centrality of power asymmetries. He emphasizes that even if he does not often use the word "power", the concept itself is embedded in all his writings on gender, including his assessment of gender inequality in terms of real "capabilities"; his work on "cooperative conflict" which shows how one form of power asymmetry can lead to other forms of power asymmetries; and his discussions on women's agency, empowerment, and freedom. Sen's response provides the basis for an interesting debate, including on how the issue of power is discussed in different disciplines. In any case, the capability approach, whether or not it adequately captures the complexity of gendered power relations, provides the single most significant dimension around which chapters tend to cluster in this volume.

III. FREEDOM AND DEMOCRACY

The second major clustering of chapters is around the concept of "freedom." While this concept is embedded in Sen's definition of capability, in terms of an individual's freedom to achieve valuable functionings, Sen takes it further in his book *Development as Freedom*. Indeed, according to Des Gasper and Irene van Staveren, Sen takes the concept of freedom too far, and makes it overarching. Nussbaum, as noted, had also commented on Sen's concept of freedom, finding it not specific enough, and not allowing for the possibility of freedom having both good and bad dimensions. Gasper and van Staveren, while drawing on Nussbaum, take this discussion in a somewhat different direction, arguing that the *language* of freedom itself, as used in *Development as Freedom*, could be misleading. According to them, the concept of freedom, as elaborated in Sen's book, has been overextended, in that all the capabilities that human beings could acquire are to be understood as freedom. This, according to them, can lead to confusion since freedom does not have this overarching meaning in everyday parlance. They argue that freedom needs to be seen as one value among a number of other significant values, such as justice, respect, friendship, and care – hence the title of their chapter "Development as Freedom – and as What Else?" Indeed they feel Sen has, in some sense, downsized his notion of capability in giving so much importance to the language of freedom, ignoring the baggage that comes with the term. They emphasize, in particular, the values of justice and caring which they see as related to freedom, but which cannot be subsumed within it. Too much of a burden of caring labor (which falls particularly in women's domain as unpaid caregivers), for example, can limit women's freedom. Too much freedom could be read as independence from household and community. They stress the need for an alternative language to the language of freedom – one that also incorporates the importance of other values. They argue that this would provide a more pluralistic understanding of capabilities.

Sen's notion of freedom, especially as elaborated in *Development as Freedom*, is also the starting point of Christine Koggel's discussion in her chapter "Globalization and Women's Paid Work: Expanding Freedom?" In particular, she engages with Sen's emphasis on women's agency as central for development, and the importance he gives to increasing women's freedom to work outside the home as a way of strengthening their agency. She seeks to problematize the effect of paid employment on women's lives, and asks whether increasing such employment as a strategy for expanding women's agency does in fact achieve that end. She notes that the impact of paid work on women's agency can depend on a complex range of local and global factors which affect opportunities, earnings, and the work environment. Drawing on empirical studies of women workers linked to the global market either as home-based workers producing items for export, or as employees in export factories in free trade zones, Koggel stresses that often the conditions of work seriously limit the ability of paid work to enhance women's well-being. She argues that further levels of complexity thus need to be added to Sen's account of freedom, by examining how global forces of power interact with local systems of oppression in ways that limit women's freedom.

A different perspective on the issue of freedom is obtained in Stanley Engerman's chapter, "Slavery, Freedom, and Sen." Implicit in Sen's writings on the capability approach, and explicit in *Development as Freedom*, is the idea that all good things tend to go together. In contrast, Engerman argues that there can be important tradeoffs between different dimensions of well-being in societies and contexts where people live at the edge of subsistence.

Using slavery as an illustration, Engerman suggests that in many historical contexts individuals were forced to make complex and difficult choices between physical survival and freedom, one of the starkest being under slavery. Faced with such a tradeoff, there were slaves who decided to remain in slavery. Such choices provide one important explanation for the contested phenomenon of "voluntary slavery." Apart from examining differences in gender roles under slavery and after emancipation, Engerman also applies this analogy to the more general situation of women today, where women might end up accepting an oppressive family situation, or staying in abusive marriages, for their own and their children's material well-being. To overcome such painful tradeoffs and correct these adverse outcomes, Engerman stresses the importance of creative and more extensive state intervention on a range of counts.

Another aspect of state functioning is examined in Elizabeth Anderson's chapter "Sen, Ethics, and Democracy," in which she emphasizes the issue of public discussion and democratic choice. Anderson builds on Sen's concept of "positional objectivity" to highlight how value judgments, made from particular social positions, can be consistent with shared universal values such as democracy. She also explores at considerable length various elements in Sen's treatment of democracy: for instance, as a means by which the government can respond to people's needs, as a practice that includes public discussions among ordinary citizens which helps them learn from each other, as a way of defining needs and preference formation, and as a way of sorting out differences in initial positions. Anderson notes, however, that in practice democracy can fail to correct chronic deprivations in capabilities among significant sections of citizens, such as women, the poor, and the lower castes. She then makes a persuasive case for enhancing the representation of such groups, in particular of women, in democratic political bodies, arguing that this can be seen (among other things) as a way of mobilizing local positional knowledge for shared ends. For example, women elected to local offices might focus government energies on previously neglected basic needs, such as safe drinking water – needs which are not just specific to women's interests but which speak to the larger social good.

IV. DEVELOPMENT AND WELL-BEING

The last three chapters in this volume discuss some aspects of Sen's work which impinge particularly on the effects of development policies on women's well-being: the issue of women's agency in reproductive choice, the question of the "missing women," and the comparison of countries in terms of their level of human development.

The complexities involved in assessing well-being and agency, highlighted conceptually in several chapters in this volume, are explored empirically by

Austraberta Nazar Beutelspacher, Emma Zapata Martelo, and Verónica Vázquez García. In their chapter "Does Contraception Benefit Women?: Structure, Agency, and Well-Being in Rural Mexico" they apply Sen's work on well-being and agency to evaluate the Mexican government's family planning policies in rural Chiapas. They critique the popular and simplistic assumption that fertility-reducing family planning policies, such as those set in place by the government, necessarily enhance women's well-being. They demonstrate empirically that several factors intervene to determine whether or not greater contraception use and a reduction in overall fertility rates improve women's well-being, one of the most important being whether or not women themselves are party to the decision. In situations where women have relatively little education and few possibilities of well-paid work outside the home, rural women do not see having fewer children as necessarily a benefit. If allowed the choice by the state and by their husbands, many would have preferred to have more children. The authors thus lay particular stress on women's subjective perception of well-being. They note that their empirical analysis provides further support for the significance Sen places on agency and choice, in exercises for evaluating the impact of public policies on individual well-being.

The issue of reproductive choice takes a rather different turn in Stephan Klasen and Claudia Wink's chapter. In 1990, in a dramatically titled article "More Than a 100 Million Women Are Missing," which appeared in the *New York Review of Books*, Sen focused international attention on the fact that in a large part of the developing world there are fewer females than males, not because of natural causes but because of a major bias against females, leading to excess female mortality. While none have disputed Sen's argument, there has been debate about the appropriate method for arriving at exact estimates of the missing women. Stephan Klasen has been a major contributor to this debate on methodology and estimates. In their chapter "Missing Women: Revisiting the Debate," he and Wink focus again on the debate and compare different methodologies for measurement. They present alternative estimates of the number of women missing, that is, the number of females who would have been alive today had there been no bias against females, and both sexes had been treated equally. They also provide estimates of sex ratios (defined by them as male/female ratios) based on recent data. Their careful empirical work shows that in aggregate terms discrimination against females still persists, and the absolute number of missing women has been increasing over time. However, there are notable regional variations both in the levels and in the direction of shifts over time. While in some countries (and in some regions within countries) there has been substantial improvement, in others there has been only moderate improvement, and yet others have seen a deterioration. The spread of female education and job opportunities for women has helped reduce gender bias, but the spread of new technologies for identifying an unborn child's sex and associated sex-selective abortions has tended to worsen the gender imbalances in sex ratios.

Finally, Sakiko Fukuda-Parr's chapter gives an historical account of Sen's contributions to the human development approach to assessing a country's development, as adopted by the United Nations Development Program (UNDP) over a decade ago. In her chapter titled "The Human Development Paradigm: Operationalizing Sen's Ideas on Capabilities," she highlights the importance and influence of Sen's work and ideas in the framing of the human development paradigm. The chapter identifies the three key elements of this paradigm: namely, the explicit philosophical basis of its concept of well-being, its evaluative aspect, and its agency aspect. This paradigm and the associated *Human Development Reports* (HDRs) brought out by the UNDP have provided an increasingly important alternative to standard assessments of development and welfare. The Human Development Indices are today widely discussed and used as broad evaluative measures. The chapter also traces the evolution of the HDRs over time, from their earlier emphasis on public services to the more recent emphasis on people's political empowerment. Gender analysis, Fukuda-Parr argues, has been central to the evolution of the human development approach, both in developing indices, such as the Gender-Related Development Index and the Gender Empowerment Index, and in its impact on the human development paradigm itself. A gender perspective has particularly helped in highlighting significant aspects of this paradigm, such as the role of collective agency in promoting development.

V. CONVERSATION AND CONCLUSION

The volume concludes with a dialogue with Sen himself. In this we have sought to ask several of the questions that were on our minds (and we presume have been on the minds of many others), but which have seldom been posed to him directly. This covers both personalized questions about the factors that led him to examine gender concerns and the impact of feminist writings on his work, and more general questions about his approach to issues of power, identity politics, and environmental sustainability. His followup piece also elaborates on the question of capability lists, as noted earlier. His responses flag additional topics for research and provoke further questions, which could provide the basis for future conversations.

***

In recent years, a number of edited volumes have appeared, containing papers that engage with Sen's work, in particular with his capability approach to evaluating human well-being. But none have examined the wide gamut of his ideas through the specific lens of gender. This makes this volume, in many senses, unique. We recognize of course that some of the work presented here is still exploratory in nature, and that papers on some aspects of Sen's writings, such as that on famines (and more generally food entitlements), and inequality and poverty indices, do not feature in this collection. But, as noted earlier, the gaps largely reflect the limited feminist scholarship on these aspects of his work. And what we see included here reflects the overwhelmingly greater interest in his work on capabilities, freedom, agency, and democracy.

While working on this volume, we have felt privileged in having had the chance to engage with Sen and our authors on the significant ideas with which Sen has challenged the intellectual world. We thank Sen too for his stimulating interactions at the September 2002 workshop at All Souls, and for his detailed responses to the issues we raised in our dialogue with him. We are also grateful to all the authors for their wide-ranging intellectual engagement, their careful responses to the reviewers' comments, and their good humor and patience in dealing with our detailed editorial inputs. Special thanks go to Diana Strassmann, the editor of *Feminist Economics*, who devoted enormous time and energy both to making the journal's special issue possible, and to the subsequent process of converting it into a book. In addition, we are indebted to Tracy Roberts and her colleagues at Taylor and Francis for facilitating the book's publication. Several others whose inputs we gratefully acknowledge are Jean Shackelford, Barbara Krohn, Cheryl Morehead, Anna Mueller, and Amy Storrow, as well as the many experts (too numerous to name individually) who gave generously of their time and energy in reviewing the papers submitted for this volume. Finally, we thank the Ford Foundation (New York), the Swedish International Development Agency (SIDA, Stockholm), Rice University, the British Academy (UK), and All Souls College, Oxford, for their financial support for various aspects of this project.

GENDER AND THE FOUNDATIONS OF SOCIAL CHOICE: THE ROLE OF SITUATED AGENCY

Fabienne Peter

OVERVIEW

Amartya Sen defends a rich conception of social choice theory against tendencies to limit social choice theory to the formal investigation of rules of collective deci-sion-making. His understanding of social choice theory makes the field a natural candidate for exploring gender issues in the evaluation of democratic policy. Not surprisingly, Sen has applied the insights he developed from his study of social choice to the evaluation of gender inequality, in particular to women's well-being in the context of the family. I focus on Sen's distinction between well-being and agency, and argue that from the perspective of women's movements and related social movements, the role of agency has so far been unduly neglected in social choice theory.

INTRODUCTION

Kenneth Arrow catalyzed research on social choice, as is well known, with his Impossibility Theorem (Kenneth Arrow 1963).[1] Before Arrow's contribution, it was standard practice in welfare economics to assume a "benevolent dictator" in charge of implementing socially desirable policies. Arrow posed the important question: how can the benevolent dictator – or any public official – gain democratic legitimacy? He sought a collective decision-making mechanism so that individual preferences about policy alternatives could be aggregated into a social preference ordering, and thus pave the way for grounding the social evaluation of policy alternatives in democratic values and procedures. As Arrow explained in a recent re-evaluation, "the real purpose [of social choice theory] was to analyze policy decisions" (Kenneth Arrow 1997: 3). Unfortunately, the Impossibility Theorem showed that in Arrow's axiomatic world, democratic choices could be arbitrary and lack legitimacy, which exposed a serious difficulty in democratic policy evaluation. Not surprisingly, the implications of this strong and robust result have been overwhelming, not only in economics but also in philosophy and related disciplines.

In a sense, one would expect a longstanding association between social choice theory and research linked to the emancipatory goals of women's movements, as well as to related social movements. Even according to a standard textbook definition, "Social Choice Theory is the study of systems and institutions for making collective choices, choices that affect a group of people" (Jerry S. Kelly 1988: 1). Such groups of people, one suspects, are often heterogeneous, comprised of women and men (and dependent children); are structured by gender and other forms of social hierarchies; and contain subgroups which are unequal with respect to having their voices heard and how they are affected by the group's choices. In spite of this potential affinity with gender issues, searching for the keywords "gender" and "women" in *Social Choice and Welfare* – the principal journal in the field – produces no results. A search in other publications yields little more.[2] This silence is all the more surprising since social choice theory, unlike other fields in economics, does not shy away from the normative dimensions of economic analysis. Kelly, for example, adds to his definition of social choice that it "is breaking off [from philosophy] to provide progress on political philosophy questions about how societies ought to be making collective choices" (Kelly 1988: 1).

We can explain the silence insofar as social choice theory is equated with finding solutions for problems related to the aggregation of individual preferences as they arise in Arrow's formulation of social choice. The very foundations of such a narrow interpretation of social choice theory do not fit in easily with themes like women's agency and women's participation in democratic institutions, democracy and difference, universalism vs. relativism, and the tensions between an ethics of impartial justice and an ethics of care for others.[3] Insofar as social choice theory targets the aggregation of expressed preferences, it cannot deal with the issue of inclusion or exclusion in participation. And if the utilitarian legacy in social choice theory allows nothing but individual preferences as inputs into social choice and the evaluation of social policies, then debates about the scope and substance of justice and equality are beside the point. With only a narrow interpretation of social choice theory, the silence on gender thus appears not only unfortunate, but structural.

Luckily, this situation does not characterize quite all of social choice theory. Amartya Sen's work is one notable exception. To Sen, the affinity between the problem of social choice and gender has been obvious for a long time, and he has written on the relevance of social choice theory for evaluating gender inequalities in the family and beyond (Amartya Sen 1990, 1995b). Sen's broad understanding of the subject of social choice theory – identifying as its main problem the necessity of reconciling the social evaluation of policy decisions with "the diversity of preferences, concerns, and predicaments of the different individuals *within* the society" (Amartya Sen 1999a: 349) – underlines the field's potential for exploring gender issues in democratic policy evaluation.

Sen does not condemn the formal study of aggregation mechanisms with which the field is sometimes associated; rather he sees the use of axiomatic methods as a "mixed pattern of virtues and vices" (Amartya Sen 1997a: 15). In a similar vein, to criticize this literature is not the goal of my chapter. Instead, I want to ask – constructively – how gender can and should be taken into account. This is a foundational issue, and I shall thus refrain from quarreling with particular axioms.

At a general level, two questions can be asked about the relationship between gender issues and social choice theory. First, how can insights from social choice theory benefit the study of women's well-being and gender inequality? Second, and more conjecturally, how can social choice theory benefit from insights in the fields of women's and gender studies? I shall pursue both questions.

I. SEN'S INFORMATIONAL INTERPRETATION OF SOCIAL CHOICE

Sen has never lost sight of the motivation behind Arrow's work: to explore the possibilities for democratic social evaluation. In general, Sen's work has been much influenced by Arrow's theorem, and in its early stages a focal point of Sen's research has been to understand what drives Arrow's impossibility result (see Amartya Sen 1970a, 1979).

To set the stage, let me briefly review Arrow's result. An Arrowian social welfare function is a mechanism that would aggregate individual preference orderings over alternative social states to a social preference ordering over these states, thus enabling rational social choice. A social state stands for a full description of all the economic, political, and social circumstances. A social welfare function should satisfy the following four (normative) conditions in order to be called minimally democratic. Unrestricted Domain (condition U) requires that all possible profiles of individual preferences should be admitted. Independence of Irrelevant Alternatives (condition I) requires that social choice should not be affected by individual preferences over alternatives that are not in the subset from which the choice is to be made; only individual preferences over pairs of alternatives in the subset should determine social choice. According to the weak Pareto principle (condition P), if all individuals judge an alternative x to be better than an alternative y, the social preference ordering should also regard x as better than y. Non-Dictatorship (condition D) rules out dictatorial social choice; social choice should not be determined by the preferences of a single individual. The Impossibility Theorem establishes that if the number of alternatives is at least three and the number of individuals at least two, the four conditions are inconsistent. The only social welfare function that yields a (transitive) social preference ordering and that satisfies P, I, and U is dictatorial.[4]

As Sen has made clear, the first three conditions have the secondary effect of defining the informational basis of social choice. Indeed, exploring the pertinence of the informational assumptions in social choice is probably one of Sen's most important long-term projects in the field. Conditions U, I, and P together imply a variety of what is called *welfarism*.[5] Welfarism is a form of consequentialism, requiring that only the individual preferences over alternative social states (or the utility they draw from these states) matter in ethical judgments and social evaluation. This privileging of utility information over nonutility information, such as considerations of needs, rights, liberties, etc., in social choice theory, stems from the utilitarian roots of welfare economics.[6]

Amartya Sen (1977b, 1995a) distinguishes between two separate dimensions of social choice theory: the *social welfare judgment* dimension and the *collective decision-making* dimension. The first offers a systematic approach to the questions of welfare economics, whereas the second is associated with the study of collective decision-making rules that can be traced back to Cusanus, Borda, and Condorcet. Sen has worked on both, but with an emphasis on the former because, for many social problems, collective decision-making mechanisms such as the majority rule do not, by themselves, cut deep enough.[7] This is especially true for pure distributional problems. Sen illustrates the argument with the classic cake division example. If there are three people, majority rule cannot distinguish between the following two cases: (a) the case where two of the three people already have most of the cake and take away more cake from the third, who has practically nothing, and (b), the case where two of them have very little and get some more from the third person, who has the bigger part of the cake (Sen 1995a). The example shows that an adequate assessment of the situation would require more information than majority rule alone can process: aggregating expressed preferences through a voting rule does not exhaust the domain of social evaluation.

What happens to the impossibility result if we broaden the informational basis of social choice to accommodate cardinally measurable utility and/or interpersonal comparability of utility? An early theorem showed that cardinal measurability alone does not change anything (Sen 1970a). But if we modify Arrow's framework to allow for interpersonal comparisons, a variety of nondictatorial social welfare functions become available. With interpersonal comparisons, we can derive consistent social welfare judgments from information about individual welfare. Moreover, this important result sheds light on the working of the Impossibility Theorem itself: Sen concludes that "The impossibility theorem can be seen as resulting from combining a version of welfarism ruling out the use of non-utility information with making the utility information remarkably poor" (1979: 539).

II. WELL-BEING, AGENCY, AND GENDER

Sen's research on social choice did not come to a halt with the above result. Quite the contrary: he puts much effort into criticizing ordinal, interpersonally noncomparable individual preferences as the sole informational input to social choice and into exploring alternative informational frameworks. The first problem with preference-based social evaluation is the neglect of what lies behind preferences. Often, overt preferences may be a result of the situation in which people live. This is especially bothersome if people have adapted their preferences to adverse circumstances.[8] Sen rejects the notion that social evaluation should be based on purely subjective assessments of individual welfare. While not denying that there are important differences in individual notions of well-being, he argues that they should not keep us from seeking objective mainstays for social evaluation, since for many exercises of social evaluation, a broad consensus can be expected about the main elements of well-being. Against welfarism in general, whether it refers to subjective preferences or objective measures of utility, Sen argues that for the social evaluation of well-being, nonutility information such as individual rights often matter (Sen 1979).

Finally, Sen rejects the exclusive focus on well-being, no matter how it is measured. In particular he suggests that beyond information on well-being, information on people's *agency* should also be taken into account (Amartya Sen 1985). He defines agency as the ability to set and pursue one's own goals and interests, of which the pursuit of one's own well-being may be only one. Other ends may include furthering the well-being of others, respecting social and moral norms, or acting upon personal commitments and the pursuit of a variety of values (Amartya Sen 1977c). It is fundamentally different to view a person as an agent and not just as a "patient" – who does or does not have well-being (Amartya Sen 1995c: 103). A person's actions come to the fore: how she acts or refuses to act, and her motives for choosing one action over another. In contrast to the outcome-based structure of the received view of individual rational choice and social choice, agency highlights how acts themselves may have value.[9] Speaking in the language of Sen's informational interpretation of social choice theory, the evaluation of the agency aspect requires a broader informational basis than the social evaluation of well-being alone. It requires paying attention to the specific motivations and constraints under which people act: "A person's agency aspect cannot be understood without taking note of his or her aims, objectives, allegiances, obligations, and – in a broad sense – the person's conception of the good'' (Sen 1985: 203). Taking agency seriously as one of the constitutive features of the person also strengthens the role of *freedom* in social evaluation – "what the person is free to do and achieve in pursuit of whatever goals or values he or she regards as important'' (Sen 1985: 203). The notion of freedom Sen invokes is a positive one. It focuses on what a person is actually able to do and achieve. Standard rational choice theory, by contrast, is linked to a negative conception of freedom (freedom as noninterference) when it views a person as free to choose as long as there is no duress or deceit.[10]

Sen does not limit himself merely to criticizing the preference framework. With the capability approach, he offers a highly productive alternative informational basis for social evaluation. As is well known, the capability approach has a two-stage structure: first, the identification of valuable functionings, and, second, asking which functionings a person can achieve if she wants to do so. The set of functionings a person is able to achieve to a satisfactory degree is her capability.[11] The capability approach brings to bear all the features that Sen finds lacking in preference-based social evaluation. It is nonwelfarist; it can accommodate both well-being and agency considerations; it puts social evaluation on an objective basis, which makes interpersonal comparisons possible; and it embodies a positive notion of freedom by asking which valuable functionings are within a person's range of opportunities.[12]

In "Gender and Cooperative Conflict," Sen (1990) applies this strand of his work to the evaluation not just of social states in general, but of the institution of the family in particular. In line with feminist theorists who have argued that gender inequalities in the family are linked to inequalities in the public sphere (Susan Moller Okin 1989; Anne Phillips 1991), Sen thus recognizes that the realm of the family and of gender relations falls within the scope of social choice theory and indeed of justice more generally.

I shall briefly summarize Sen's contribution to the economics of the family since it can serve both as an illustration of his theoretical arguments and of their bearing upon gender issues in social choice. It focuses on the bargaining models, which are becoming increasingly common in economic analyses of family behavior and well-being. Sen argues that while conventional bargaining models of the family are an improvement over the earlier single-utility models, they remain unsatisfactory because they are restricted to individual preferences. They fail to take into account the formation of beliefs and preferences under the influence of social norms and social experience in general. With regard to beliefs, Sen argues that married women tend to devalue their contribution to the household – to perceive their work as being worth less than it actually is and less than that of the breadwinner husband. Such perceptions fit in with, and reinforce, general social perceptions of the relative worth of market and nonmarket work and, ultimately, of the relative worth of gendered contributions to the social good. With regard to preferences, Sen argues that women's already low bargaining power is compounded by their tendency to value the well-being of their family members more than their own, to silently accept their fate, and to engage reluctantly in hard bargaining.

The example of gender relations in the family illustrates the problem of adaptive preferences, the insufficiency of subjective evaluation, and the need to take into account nonutility information as well as information on people's agency. Sen suggests that instead of relying on narrow preference-based evaluation, the socially entrenched division of roles in families should be evaluated in terms of an objective measure, such as capability. Compared to the preference framework, the capability approach has the advantage of not taking overt preferences and actual choices – which may simply be a result of one's circumstances – as the ultimate expression of what a person's interests are. And whereas conventional (preference-based) bargaining analysis bears the risk of cloaking the mechanisms which perpetuate gender inequalities, Sen's emphasis on objective criteria for women's well-being has the advantage of not being blind to restricted agency, thus providing a corrective force.

There is, however, something of a tension between the solution Sen suggests in "Gender and Cooperative Conflict" and the agenda of contemporary women's movements and gender theory. The latter often highlight the active role of women's agency in bringing about social change. Sen, by contrast, seems to focus on low well-being and restricted agency, and on the potential of an objective framework of social evaluation such as capability to correct for this situation. Insofar as "Gender and Cooperative Conflict" can be read in this way, using the capability approach primarily to evaluate women's well-being does not seem quite sufficient to lift women out of their status as "patients." Bina Agarwal (1997: 22–25) queries Sen's reading of women's actions as necessarily indicating false perceptions and provides substance for an alternative reading based on women's covert actions. She argues that women's overt compliance with social norms does not necessarily mean they have accepted the legitimacy of intrahousehold inequality; it might merely reflect their lack of options. She thus comments on Sen's proposal that she would "place much less emphasis than Sen does on women's incorrect perceptions of their self-interest, and much more on the external constraints to their acting overtly in their self-interest" (Agarwal 1997: 25). Too much emphasis on the manifest restriction of agency bears the danger of denying women's agency altogether. In more recent work, Sen acknowledges this shift of perspective towards the potential of women's agency and, as argued above, the capability approach can in principle accommodate an agency-oriented approach.[13] Nevertheless, his issue, as well as its bearing on the conception of social choice theory, needs to be explored in greater detail.

First, however, I will examine Sen's famous Liberal Paradox (Amartya Sen 1970b). The Paradox also turns on the limitations of preference-based evaluation and thus stands squarely within Sen's overall research project on social choice and related topics. While Sen has not, to my knowledge, directly drawn any implications of the paradox for gender and social choice, exploring the Liberal Paradox offers an interesting twist on this issue, as discussed below.

III. SEN'S LIBERAL PARADOX AND INTERDEPENDENCE

The Liberal Paradox uses a slightly modified version of Arrow's axiomatic framework to describe a possible conflict between liberty and rights on the one hand, and efficiency – or purely preference-based evaluation of outcomes – on the other, presenting a further argument against preference-based evaluation.

The Liberal Paradox requires highly differentiated social states to keep track of the different actions of individuals. Individual liberty, then, becomes the right to determine certain social states irrespective of what others think or want. In the language of social choice theory, such rights make individuals decisive. Preference-based evaluation is interpreted in the same way as in Arrow's original framework – Sen uses conditions U and P. Sen's theorem says that social evaluation based on respecting liberty rights may clash with the overall evaluation of social states in terms of individual preferences about these social states.

Sen gives an example to illustrate the paradox. There are two people – Prude and Lewd – and the question is, who gets to read *Lady Chatterley's Lover*? There are three alternatives: Prude reads it (x), Lewd reads it (y), or no one reads it (z). In Sen's example, Prude strongly dislikes the book and would most prefer that no one read it. However, he would prefer to read it himself rather than have Lewd read it. His preference ordering is thus (z, x, y). Lewd likes the book, but gets even more pleasure from thinking about uptight Prude reading the book. He thus prefers that Prude read it to reading it himself to no one reading it (x, y, z). The paradox is the following: if the choice is between x and z, between Prude reading the book and no one reading it, one could argue from a perspective of liberal rights that society should leave it up to Prude to decide whether or not he wants to read the book (Prude should be decisive). Since he prefers z to x, society should also prefer z to x. If the choice is between y and z, similarly, Lewd should be decisive and society should prefer y to z. This leads to the social preference ordering (y, z, x). This preference ordering is, however, Pareto inferior, as both Prude and Lewd prefer x to y – hence the paradox.

The Paradox reveals the difficulty of meaningfully combining considerations of rights with respect for preferences in social choice (Amartya Sen 1976). Sen interprets the paradox to mean that social evaluation should be based on an informational framework which, unlike preference-based evaluation, can accommodate reasoned tradeoffs between the rights and good consequences. According to Sen, since consequences may matter, it is wrong for social evaluation to focus exclusively on rights, just as it is wrong to insist on outcome-based evaluation irrespective of individual rights. The capability approach offers such an extended consequentialist framework.

The Liberal Paradox arises only if there are preferences regarding the choices of others. The Paradox does not arise with completely independent individuals whose only concern is with their own benefits. In Sen's example, both Lewd and Prude have preferences about each other's actions. Sen argues that such an assumption is entirely justifiable given the many forms of interactions between individual agents in day-to-day living. Amartya Sen (1986b: 232) says: "Given the complex interdependencies that operate in a society, tying together the lives of different people, it may be impossible to isolate their environment sufficiently to guarantee that each has all the controls over his or her personal life." Many feminist critics of some strands of liberalism and economics have targeted precisely this neglect of interdependencies. For Carol Gilligan, for example, interdependence is the core of an "ethics of care": "Care is grounded in the assumption that self and other are interdependent. ... The self is by definition connected to others."[14]

Although interdependence is a central assumption in the Liberal Paradox, it is not examined further. To better work out this dimension, consider the following variation of Sen's original example. Take again two people and one possible action, for instance eating the last piece of chocolate. (Assume it cannot be divided without creating a mess.) There are thus three alternatives: Anthony eats the chocolate (x), Gina eats the chocolate (y), and no one eats it (z). Assume Anthony believes that chocolate is bad for Gina's health, as he has explained to her many times before. Since he knows how much she likes chocolate, he would not want to eat it either, but would rather throw it away. His most preferred alternative is thus z. If Gina insists that he have the chocolate, he would eat it, however. His preference ordering is thus (z, x, y). Gina is unconvinced that chocolate would harm her health. But although Gina likes chocolate very much, she would not want to eat the last piece before making sure that Anthony does not want it. If they both want it, Gina prefers Anthony to have it – she thus ranks x above y. What she would least want is to throw away the chocolate. Her preference ordering is thus (x, y, z). Let us proceed as in Sen's original example. If the choice is between x and z, according the perspective of liberal rights would again demand that Anthony be decisive and, since he prefers z to x, that society should also rank z above x. If the choice is between y and z, Gina should be decisive and, since she prefers y to z, society should also rank y above z. This leads to the social preference ordering (y, z,

x). Again we have a conflict with the Pareto criterion, as both Anthony and Gina prefer x to y.

This time, the paradox is not the only problem, however. First, look at the rights-based social preference ordering. In Sen's original example, this ordering makes some sense, given the story. It makes sense that a rights framework should enable Lewd, who has a taste for it, to read the book and regard this case as better than the case where no one reads the book and better than the case where Prude, who hates the book, has to read it.[15] In the chocolate example, the ordering makes no sense whatsoever. Why, given that both equally like chocolate, should y be ranked first and x last? Should these two states not be regarded as indifferent from a liberal point of view? And why should a rights system identify y as the best social choice given that, as we know, Gina would prefer to forgo the pleasure of eating chocolate for Anthony's sake? Should it not be Gina's right to give away the chocolate if she wanted to?

Abandoning rights-based evaluation and switching to preference-based evaluation would not be an adequate solution either, since the preference-based approach does not contain enough information to properly assess the situation. In particular, it neglects the agency aspect of a person, and with that, the value people assign to their actions above and beyond the outcomes that result from these actions. To go back to the example, it is important to Anthony that Gina does not harm her health, and he will only eat the chocolate if she insists that he do so. For Gina, it is important to express her care for Anthony by leaving the piece of chocolate to him. Assume that after a dinner together, they decide that Anthony should eat the chocolate. If, instead, a third party were to assign the chocolate to Anthony, we would have the same outcome in terms of who gets to eat the chocolate, but the crucial role of interdependent agency in this example would be neglected. Anthony would not enjoy the chocolate in the same way as if Gina had given it to him, and Gina might feel left out.[16]

Of course, not too much should be inferred from a simple example. Nevertheless, in comparison with Sen's original example, this one shows how interdependence bears on an evaluation of the situation. To illustrate the point further, suppose that the rankings in the example are now the result of a different story. Suppose that Anthony is Gina's older brother, and Gina has been brought up to leave the best things to him, while he is accustomed to enjoying them without concern for his sister's well-being. When Anthony does not feel like eating the chocolate, he either saves it for some other day, or he gives it to a friend. It does not occur to him to leave the chocolate for his sister. His preference ranking is thus still (z, x, y) and Gina's preferences also remain unchanged (x, y, z). In this case, we would be skeptical about the result if Anthony were to get the piece of chocolate, even if Gina left it for him.

What are the implications of such an application of Sen's Paradox? I see several aspects, all related to the problem of interdependence. First, my interpretation reinforces Sen's point about the importance of agency in social evaluation. The examples illustrate how in deciding who gets to eat the chocolate, what matters is not only who actually gets the chocolate but also the nature of their relationship. Seyla Benhabib (1987) distinguishes between the standpoint of the "generalized other" and the standpoint of the "concrete other." While the former predominates in liberal theory, she advocates the standpoint of the "concrete other" as a necessary complement to moral evaluation.[17] The latter, Benhabib (1987: 87) argues:

> requires us to view each individual and every rational being as an individual with a concrete history, identity, and affective – emotional constitution. ... Our relation to the other, is governed by the norms of *equity* and *complementary reciprocity*: each is entitled to expect and to assume from the other forms of behavior through which the other feels recognized and confirmed as a concrete, individual being with specific needs, talents and capacities. ... The moral categories that accompany such interactions are those of responsibility, bonding, and sharing.

Taking people seriously as agents means taking their relationships and commitments to other people seriously, as well.[18] This, too, echoes demands in feminist moral and political philosophy. Virginia Held (1993: 169) explains the scope of an ethics of care as follows:

> Most of those trying to clarify the alternative ethic of care question the individualistic assumptions of much moral theory. A relationship of care or trust between a mother and a child, for instance, cannot be understood in terms of the individual states of each taken in isolation. And the values of relationships cannot be broken down into individual benefits and burdens, we need to assess the worth of relationships themselves.

From the Liberal Paradox one can conclude that neither the language of good outcomes, nor the language of rights are, by themselves, suitable tools for social evaluation. Considering interdependence, relationships, and personal commitments shows that both types of language are together insufficient, as long as good consequences are interpreted independently of agency: valuing specific relationships and commitments to other people creates some tension both with the universal impartial character of rights and with outcome-oriented, agency-independent evaluation.

A final aspect of interdependence draws attention to how relationships may enrich one's life as well as have potential for oppression. Some interdependencies between persons carry positive value, others negative. To include the evaluation of relationships and commitments in social evaluation should not be limited to their positive sides, but extend to their darker sides as well.

We can classify the three cases in the following way. In Sen's original example, our intuition is that Prude's agency should not extend to preventing Lewd from reading the book, just as Lewd's agency should not extend to compelling Prude to read it. The condition of minimal liberty captures this intuition. In the first example about Anthony and Gina, the reasons behind their preferences about x and y are such that, intuitively one feels, their agency should not be restricted. Neither the principle of minimal liberty nor the preferences framework (which contains information only about outcomes) speak to this situation. The second story about Anthony and Gina draws attention to cases in between. Preference-based evaluation – insofar as it is based on overt choices – may reinforce oppressive relations. Rights-based evaluation protects Gina because it prevents Anthony from deciding whether or not Gina should get the piece of chocolate. The question remains, however, whether the solution has to be to "feed" Gina the chocolate – thus treating her as a "patient." Taking her seriously as an agent would require gearing the evaluation of the situation towards her own assessment of it – even if barely audible in the established forums of democratic evaluation.

In sum, while the Liberal Paradox hinges on interdependence, the informational constraints within which it operates do not allow an evaluation of this interdependence. We have thus reached another juncture at which a broader informational basis for social choice is called for. We need to find ways of rendering social evaluation responsive to the interests of those whose agency is restricted. The challenge is to make restricted agency an object of social evaluation without, at the same time, treating those whose agency is restricted as objects of social evaluation.

IV. SITUATED AGENCY AND PARTICIPATORY SOCIAL EVALUATION

Agency brings to the fore a broader conception of social choice. The focus shifts from problems of *aggregation* of unexamined individual preferences to *participation* and *inclusion* in democratic decision-making.

This implies, first, that compared with much of social choice theory, more attention should be paid to fair procedures. Taking people seriously as agents entails giving them a chance to be heard, and to be involved in collective evaluations and decisions. To be sure, this aspect of democratic decision-making is not entirely new to social choice theory and welfare economics. Kotaro Suzumura, for example, a leading social choice theorist, urges his peers to explore the procedural aspects of social choice (Kotaro Suzumura 1999a, 1999b, 2000).[19] Similarly, Sen's recent writings (Amartya Sen 1999a, 1999b, 1999c) underline the importance of fair procedures in social choice.

A second aspect of democratic social evaluation needs to be emphasized: what Sen calls the informational aspect. Sen (1999c) stresses that democracy has constructive value, along with its intrinsic and instrumental values that are connected to fair procedures – the values of rights and liberties, accountability, etc. Social choice theory largely limits its analysis of collective decision-making to preferences that exist independently of the decision-making process. In contrast, the broader conception of democratic decision-making discussed here takes into account the point that the needs, aims, and assessments that flow into the social evaluation of policy alternatives cannot be identified independently of public deliberation. They emerge from a process of public exchange, of contestation, and of learning about the different situations in which people live. Sen (1999c: 3) characterizes this aspect of democracy as follows:

> the practice of democracy gives the citizens an opportunity to learn from each other, and to re-examine their own values and priorities, along with those of others. Even the idea of "needs" (including the understanding of "economic needs") requires public discussion and exchange of information, views and analyses. . . . Political rights and civil rights, especially those related to the guaranteeing of open discussion, debate, criticism and dissent are central to the process of generating informed and reflected choices.[20]

From a gender perspective, several issues in democratic evaluation and decision-making demand particular attention. First, there is the question of the autonomy of agents. Some have argued that the respecting individual autonomy clashes with taking into account morally significant differences among people and their relationships to each other. Barbara Herman (1991) addresses this criticism from the angle of Kantian ethics. She argues that:

> much of the critique of the Kantian conception of autonomy confuses autonomy and agency. Autonomy is the condition of the will that makes agency possible. If we were not rational beings we would not have wills that could be interfered with. . . . Agency is situated. The empirical and contingent conditions of effective agency set the terms of permissibility because it is through effective agency that autonomy is expressed.
>
> (Herman 1991: 795)

There are two implications of this argument. Keeping autonomy and agency apart makes the recognition of situated, often restricted agency compatible with equal moral autonomy: while effective agency may be limited, there is an aspect of a person's agency-capability which remains untouched. In addition, since autonomy can only be expressed through situated agency, the situatedness (and restrictedness) of agency is no longer seen as a hindrance for social evaluation, but its focal point.

27

There is some controversy in contemporary gender theory about the extent to which emancipatory politics requires the conception of an individual agent capable of self-reflection, self-determination, and autonomy and the extent to which agency is merely a result of the cultural (including gender) constitution of the subject. Nancy Fraser – rightly, in my opinion – rejects such a dichotomy as false. With an argument that implicitly evokes Herman's distinction between autonomy and agency, she points out that acknowledging the situatedness of agents need not imply robbing people of their autonomy.[21] In any case, the controversy relates primarily to the *interpretation* of the constitution of persons and their agency, a topic I cannot address here, but the role of agency in bringing about social change is not in dispute.[22]

Related to this is whether the requirement to treat individuals as "concrete" and not only as "generalized" others (Benhabib 1987) may create some tension with the ideal of impartiality often advocated in ethics, in theories of justice, and also in social choice theory.[23] Both deontological (Kantian) ethics and consequentialist ethics have been repeatedly criticized for failing to respect the agent-relativity of moral judgments.[24] And feminist theorists often point to the failure of Western moral thought to take this aspect of people's lives seriously.[25] Amartya Sen (1983, 1993b) does not accept this line of criticism: properly interpreted, he claims, consequential evaluation can be reconciled with agent-relativity. The key is to recognize that one's own actions and how one treats others may be part of the consequences of a certain decision.

Herman (1991) and other Kantian scholars also reject this objection. Herman asks how treating others as specific persons can be reconciled with the universal character of Kantian ethics and the ideal of impartiality. She argues that the concrete situation of others enters into our deliberations about the right way of acting. The Kantian norm of treating others as ends can thus only be followed if there is some understanding of whom and what we are dealing with.[26]

Here it does not matter so much how agent relativity can be accommodated within different ethical theories, whether its best place is in consequentialist or Kantian ethics, or whether an alternative approach – such as communitarianism (Michael Sandel 1981) or a distinctively feminist theory – are necessary. What is essential, however, is that this feature of moral evaluation has become a recognized concern throughout the theoretical spectrum, and tensions with such ideals as impartiality are by now primarily viewed as a problem for theory interpretation rather than for the evaluation of ethical conduct, justice, and legitimacy.

Earlier, I argued that Sen's analysis underrates the positive role women's agency can play in bringing about policies towards social change. This can now be qualified as follows. It need not be denied that the agency of women Sen discusses – their ability to have their concerns heard and to express their assessment of desirable changes – is restricted. But limited effective agency does not imply impaired moral autonomy, absence of agency-capability, and thus absence of judgment. What may, in terms of manifest behavior, seem like submission may hide more subtle strategies of resistance (for examples, see especially, Agarwal 1997). Limited though these strategies may be, given these women's situations, they can nevertheless form grounds for policy change. The challenge for social evaluation of policy alternatives is to register and take seriously the interpretations and evaluations of these women as situated agents, thus identifying the means by which their participation in policy discourses can be enhanced and their effectiveness reinforced.[27]

V. CONCLUDING REMARKS

At the beginning of this chapter I asked two questions: how could the study of women's well-being and gender inequality benefit from results of social choice theory, and how could social choice theory benefit from insights from women's and gender studies. I have explored these questions on the basis of Sen's contributions to social choice and related topics, with the goal of pulling together the different strands of his work that speak to the foundations of social choice theory from a gender perspective.

What, then, are the answers to these two questions? First, I have argued that Sen's informational interpretation of social choice theory and his efforts to explore the appropriate informational basis of social choice are particularly promising for the analysis of gender issues in democratic policy evaluation. This strand of his work not only offers a cogent critique of basing social evaluation on individual preferences but, along with the capability approach, also offers a full-fledged alternative informational framework for social evaluation. In addition, Sen has worked out the difference between information on people's well-being and information on individual agency, arguing that the latter has too often been neglected in social choice theory and welfare economics. For the line of reasoning I have tried to develop in this chapter, the distinction between well-being and agency has been particularly important. This brought me to the second question. In response, I suggest that research in social choice theory and related fields should investigate avenues that make social choice and social evaluation more responsive to situated agency and thus to issues of participation and inclusion. Sen's work provides the necessary foundations for such an endeavor, but much work remains.

ACKNOWLEDGMENTS

I have received very helpful comments from Ingrid Robeyns, Hans Bernhard Schmid, and three anonymous referees. I have also greatly benefited from the feedback received from the participants at the Oxford Workshop (September 11–13, 2002) on Sen's Work and Ideas, in particular from Amartya Sen and Bina Agarwal.

NOTES

[1] For comprehensive surveys of social choice theory, see Amartya Sen (1970a, 1986a, 1995a). See also the two volumes edited by Kenneth Arrow, Amartya Sen, and Kotaro Suzumura (1997).

[2] Search in "Econlit," August 2001. In *Social Choice and Welfare*, there are a few contributions to population issues – focusing on the question of how a social planner should choose the optimal size of the population – but there is no mention of the role of women and of gender relations in producing that population.

[3] See, among others, Seyla Benhabib (1987), Nancy Fraser (1989), Iris Marion Young (1990, 2000), Seyla Benhabib, Judith Butler, Drucilla Cornell, and Nancy Fraser (1995), Seyla Benhabib (1996), and Martha Nussbaum (2000). For an empirical analysis of the gender gap in political participation, see Nancy Burns, Kay Lehman Schlozman, and Sidney Verba (2001).

[4] For a proof, see Sen (1995a). For the original proof, see Arrow (1963, 51f.) or Amartya Sen (1970a: Ch. 3).

[5] To be precise, they imply "strict-ranking welfarism": nothing but individual preferences should count for social choice as long as these preferences are strict, i.e., of the "better-than" form, and not merely of the "at-least-as-good" form (see Amartya Sen 1979: 540f.). The term "welfarism" was coined by Sen (1977a).

[6] According to Amartya Sen and Bernard Williams (1982), utilitarianism can be broken down into welfarism, consequentialism, and sum-ranking. With only ordinal, interpersonally noncomparable utility information as in Arrow's framework, sum-ranking is ruled out. The other two aspects of utilitarianism are, however, preserved. For discussions on some of the limitations of welfarism and consequentialism in social choice theory and welfare economics, see Kotaro Suzumura (1999a, 2000).

[7] On the problem of collective decision-making, see e.g. Amartya Sen (1969, 1993a). Moreover, one can discern a shift of emphasis in his most recent work towards the importance of democratic processes and values. I shall comment on this below.

[8] On adaptive preferences, see Jon Elster (1982), Sen (1990), and Nussbaum (2000).

[9] Sen (1985: 204) writes: "The importance of the agency aspect ... relates to the view of persons as responsible agents. Persons must enter the moral accounting by others not only as people whose well-being demands concern, but also as people whose responsible agency must be recognized."

[10] Recently, there have been some efforts in social choice theory to measure freedom (e.g., Walter Bossart, Prasanta K. Pattanaik, and Yongshen Xu 1994).

[11] On the capability approach, see for example Amartya Sen (1992).

[12] Martha Nussbaum's interpretation of the capability approach, in contrast to Sen's interpretation, downplays the role of the agency dimension. According to Nussbaum (2000: 14), the role of agency is already safely packed into the distinction between capability and functioning. Such an interpretation assigns, however, a very limited role to agency: agency is allowed to play in the achievement of functionings given a

set of capabilities, but not in the definition of the relevant capabilities. For this reason, I follow Sen's interpretation of the capability approach.

[13] Sen (1995c: 103) writes: "Over the last couple of decades, an important evolution has begun to alter the basic nature of the women's movements in developing countries. Not long ago, the tasks faced by these movements were primarily aimed at working toward achieving better treatment for women – a more square deal. The concentration was mainly on women's well-being – and it was a much needed corrective. The objectives have, however, gradually evolved and broadened from this 'welfarist' focus to incorporate – and emphasize – the active role of women's agency. No longer as the passive recipient of welfare-enhancing help, women are increasingly seen ... as active agents of change: the dynamic promoters of social transformations that can alter the lives of both women and men." See also Amartya Sen (1999b).

[14] Carol Gilligan (1987: 24). I am not quoting Gilligan to suggest that care is a distinctively feminine quality, but rather to note that she brought this issue into moral reasoning.

[15] Brian Barry (1986) argues against such an interpretation of liberalism.

[16] Preference-based evaluation will fare better if assumptions on individual choice are relaxed to accommodate menu- and chooser-dependent preferences; on this, see Amartya Sen (1997b).

[17] Seyla Benhabib (1987: 87) notes: "The standpoint of the generalized other requires us to view each and every individual as a rational being entitled to the same rights and duties we would want to ascribe to ourselves. ... Our relation to the other is governed by the norms of *formal* equality and reciprocity: each is entitled to expect and to assume from us what we can expect and assume from him or her."

[18] For Sen, this is one of the elements that impose "agent-relativity" on moral and social evaluation (see Amartya Sen 1982, 1983, 1993b). I shall return to this issue in the next section.

[19] Kotaro Suzumura (1999b: 4) demands that social evaluation "should be based on an extended conceptual framework which goes far beyond the informational basis of 'income, wealth, and welfare' used in the conventional framework of welfare economics and social choice. ... It stands to reason to go even beyond consequentialism as such, and pay more explicit attention to procedural considerations. This is a useful step to take in order to accommodate such important aspects of individual advantages as the right of participation in the public decision-making procedure which circumscribes people's live chance, the right of autonomy in making the best and effective use of opportunities, and procedural justice in the treatment of persons and nations." In Fabienne Peter (2001), I explore the consequences for social evaluation of shifting the focus from "aggregation" to "participation."

[20] On contested needs, see also Fraser (1989).

[21] See the debate between Seyla Benhabib and Judith Butler and comments by Drucilla Cornell and Nancy Fraser in Seyla Benhabib, Judith Butler, Drucilla Cornell and Nancy Fraser (1995).

[22] For a recent re-evaluation of the debate between Butler and Benhabib, see Fiona Webster (2000).

[23] In social choice theory, impartiality is often captured in the so-called axioms of anonymity and of neutrality. Anonymity requires that the social preference ordering should not change with a permutation of a profile of individual preferences. Neutrality requires that if individual preference orderings for two pairs of alternatives are the same, the social preference ordering should rank these two pairs in the same way.

[24] Cf. Bernard Williams (1973, 1981); Annette Baier (1986).

[25] Cf. Carol Gilligan (1982); Iris Young (1990); Virginia Held (1993).

[26] Herman (1991: 788) notes: "Commitment to treat others as ends ... does not by itself guide deliberation. As I come to understand more of what is involved in friendship and intimacy, so I also come to see more of what the moral requirement amounts to. ... Where power and/or inequality mix with intimacy, questions of exploitation and abuse are raised. Such questions are not part of the concept of treating persons as ends. They are what we discover treating persons as ends amounts, given what human relationships tend to be like, or what particular relationships involve. Absent such knowledge, moral judgment is not possible."

[27] For an in-depth study – both empirical and conceptual – of the factors that constrain women's agency, of the consequences of participatory exclusion on women's lives, and of the possibilities of enhancing women's participation in public decision-making, see Bina Agarwal (2001).

REFERENCES

Agarwal, Bina. 1997. " 'Bargaining' and Gender Relations: Within and Beyond the Household." *Feminist Economics* 3(1): 1–51.

——. 2001. "Participatory Exclusions, Community Forestry, and Gender: An Analysis for South Asia and a Conceptual Framework." *World Development* 29(10): 1623–48.

Arrow, Kenneth J. 1963. *Social Choice and Individual Values*, 2nd edn New Haven and London: Yale University Press.

——. 1997. "The Functions of Social Choice Theory," in Kenneth Arrow, Amartya Sen, and Kotaro Suzumura (eds.) *Social Choice Re-Examined* Vol. 1, pp. 3–9. London: Macmillan.

——, Amartya Sen, and Kotaro Suzumura (eds.). 1997. *Social Choice Re-Examined* (2 Volumes): London: Macmillan.

Baier, Annette. 1986. "Trust and Anti-Trust." *Ethics* 96: 231–60.

Barry, Brian. 1986. "Lady Chatterley's Lover and Doctor Fisher's Bomb Party," in Jon Elster and Aanund Hylland (eds.) *Foundations of Social Choice Theory*, pp. 11–43. Cambridge, UK: Cambridge University Press.

Benhabib, Seyla. 1987. "The Generalized and the Concrete Other," in Seyla Benhabib and Drucilla Cornell (eds.) *Feminism as Critique*, pp. 77–95. Cambridge, UK: Polity Press.

——. 1996. *Democracy and Difference*. Princeton: Princeton University Press.

——, Judith Butler, Drucilla Cornell, and Nancy Fraser (eds.). 1995. *Feminist Contentions*. New York: Routledge.

Bossart, Walter, Prasanta K. Pattanaik, and Yongsheng Xu. 1994. "Ranking Opportunity Sets: An Axiomatic Approach." *Journal of Economic Theory* 63(2): 326–45.

Burns, Nancy, Kay Lehman Schlozman, and Sidney Verby. 2001. *The Private Roots of Public Action: Gender, Equality, and Political Participation*. Cambridge, MA: Harvard University Press.

Elster, Jon. 1982. "Sour Grapes: Utilitarianism and the Genesis of Wants," in Amartya Sen and Bernard Williams (eds.) *Utilitarianism and Beyond*, pp. 219–38. Cambridge, UK: Cambridge University Press.

Fraser, Nancy. 1989. "Talking about Needs: Interpretive Contests as Political Conflicts in Welfare-State Societies." *Ethics* 99(2): 291–313.

Gilligan, Carol. 1982. *In a Different Voice*. Cambridge, MA: Harvard University Press.

——. 1987. "Moral Orientation and Moral Development," in Eva Feder Kittay and Diana T. Meyers (eds.) *Women and Moral Theory*, pp. 19–33. Totowa, NJ: Rowman & Littlefield.

Held, Virginia. 1993. *Feminist Morality*. Chicago: University of Chicago Press.

Herman, Barbara. 1991. "Agency, Attachment, and Difference." *Ethics* 101(4): 775–97.

Kelly, JerryS. 1988. *Social Choice Theory*. Berlin: Springer.

Nussbaum, Martha. 2000. *Women and Human Development*. Cambridge, UK: Cambridge University Press.

Okin, Susan Moller. 1989. *Justice, Gender, and the Family*. New York: Basic Books.

Peter, Fabienne. 2001. "Rawlsian Justice, Legitimacy, and Deliberative Social Evaluation." *Revue de Philosophie Economique* 2: 23–50.

Phillips, Anne. 1991. *Engendering Democracy*. Cambridge, UK: Polity Press.

Sandel, Michael. 1981. *Liberalism and the Limits of Justice*. Cambridge, UK: Cambridge University Press.

Sen, Amartya. 1969. "Quasi-Transitivity, Rational Choice and Collective Decisions." *Review of Economic Studies* 36: 381–93.

——. 1970a. *Collective Choice and Social Welfare*. San Francisco: Holden-Day.

——. 1970b. "The Impossibility of a Paretian Liberal." *Journal of Political Economy* 78: 152–7.

——. 1976. "Liberty, Unanimity, and Rights." *Economica* 43: 217–45.

——. 1977a. "On Weights and Measures: Informational Constraints in Social Welfare Analysis." *Econometrica* 45: 1539–72.

——. 1977b. "Social Choice Theory: A Re-Examination." *Econometrica* 4: 53–89.

——. 1977c. "Rational Fools." *Philosophy and Public Affairs* 6: 317–44.

——. 1979. "Personal Utilities and Public Judgements; Or: What's Wrong with Welfare Economics?" *Economic Journal* 89: 537–58.

——. 1982. "Rights and Agency." *Philosophy and Public Affairs* 11: 3–39.

——. 1983. "Evaluator Relativity and Consequential Evaluation." *Philosophy and Public Affairs* 12: 113–32.

——. 1985. "Well-Being, Agency and Freedom." *Journal of Philosophy* 82: 169–221.

——. 1986a. "Social Choice Theory," in Kenneth Arrow and M. D. Intriligator (eds.) *Handbook of Mathematical Economics*, pp. 1073–181. Amsterdam: North-Holland.

——. 1986b. "Foundations of Social Choice Theory," in Jon Elster and Aanund Hylland (eds.) *Foundations of Social Choice Theory*, pp. 213–48. Cambridge, UK: Cambridge University Press.

——. 1990. "Gender and Cooperative Conflict," in Irene Tinker (ed.) *Persistent Inequalities*, pp. 123–49. New York and Oxford, UK: Oxford University Press.

——. 1992. *Inequality Re-Examined*. Oxford, UK: Clarendon Press.

——. 1993a. "Internal Consistency of Choice." *Econometrica* 61: 459–521.

——. 1993b. "Positional Objectivity." *Philosophy and Public Affairs* 22(2): 126–45.

——. 1995a. "Rationality and Social Choice." *American Economic Review* 85: 1–24.

——. 1995b. "Gender Inequality and Theories of Justice," in Martha Nussbaum and Jonathan Glover (eds.) *Women, Culture, and Development*, pp. 259–73. Oxford, UK: Clarendon Press.

——. 1995c. "Agency and Well-Being: The Development Agenda," in Noeleen Heyzer, Sushma Kapoor, and Joanne Sandler (eds.) *A Commitment to the World's Women*, pp. 103–12. Washington, DC: Unifem.

——. 1997a. "Individual Preference as the Basis of Social Choice," in Kenneth Arrow, Amartya Sen, and Kotaro Suzumura (eds.) *Social Choice Re-Examined* Vol. 1: pp. 15–37. London: Macmillan.

——. 1997b. "Maximization and the Act of Choice." *Econometrica* 65(4): 745–79.

——. 1999a. "The Possibility of Social Choice." *American Economic Review* 89(3): 349–78.

——. 1999b. *Development as Freedom*. New York: Knopf.

———. 1999c. "Democracy and Social Justice." Paper presented at the Seoul Conference on Democracy, Market Economy and Development. On-line. Available http://www.idep.org/conference/program/particpants/Amartya_Sen/Amartya_Sen_e_paper_fulltext.htm (Accessed April 2003).

——— and Bernard Williams (eds.). 1982. *Utilitarianism and Beyond*. Cambridge, UK: Cambridge University Press.

Suzumura, Kotaro. 1999a. "Consequences, Opportunities, and Procedures." *Social Choice and Welfare* 16: 17–40.

———. 1999b. "Inclusion, Justice, and Poverty Reduction: From the Viewpoint of Contemporary Social Choice Theory." Deutsche Stiftung für Internationale Entwicklung: Villa Borsig Workshop Series. On-line. Available http://www.dse.de/ef/poverty/suzumura.htm (Accessed April 2003).

———. 2000. "Welfare Economics Beyond Welfarist-Consequentialism." *Japanese Economic Review* 51(1): 1–32.

Webster, Fiona. 2000. "The Politics of Sex and Gender: Benhabib and Butler Debate Subjectivity." *Hypathia* 15(1): 1–22.

Williams, Bernard. 1973. "A Critique of Utilitarianism," in J. J. C. Smart and Bernard Williams (eds.) *Utilitarianism: For and Against*, pp. 75–150. Cambridge, UK: Cambridge University Press.

———. 1981. *Moral Luck*. Cambridge, UK: Cambridge University Press.

Young, Iris Marion. 1990. *Justice and the Politics of Difference*. Princeton, NJ: Princeton University Press.

———. 2000. *Inclusion and Democracy*. Oxford, UK: Oxford University Press.

CAPABILITIES AS FUNDAMENTAL ENTITLEMENTS: SEN AND SOCIAL JUSTICE

MarthaC. Nussbaum

OVERVIEW

Amartya Sen has made a major contribution to the theory of social justice, and of gender justice, by arguing that capabilities are the relevant space of comparison when justice-related issues are considered. This chapter supports Sen's idea, arguing that capabilities supply guidance superior to that of utility and resources (the view's familiar opponents), but also to that of the social contract tradition, and at least some accounts of human rights. But I argue that capabilities can help us to construct a normative conception of social justice, with critical potential for gender issues, only if we specify a definite set of capabilities as the most important ones to protect. Sen's "perspective of freedom" is too vague. Some freedoms limit others; some freedoms are important, some trivial, some good, and some positively bad. Before the approach can offer a valuable normative gender perspective, we must make commitments about substance.

I. THE CAPABLITIES APPROACH AND SOCIAL JUSTICE[1]

Throughout his career, Amartya Sen has been preoccupied with questions of social justice. Inequalities between women and men have been especially important in his thinking, and the achievement of gender justice in society has been among the most central goals of his theoretical enterprise. Against the dominant emphasis on economic growth as an indicator of a nation's quality of life, Sen has insisted on the importance of *capabilities*, what people are actually able to do and to be.[2] Frequently his arguments in favor of this shift in thinking deal with issues of gender.[3] Growth is a bad indicator of life quality because it fails to tell us how deprived people are doing; women figure in the argument as people who are often unable to enjoy the fruits of a nation's general prosperity. If we ask what people are actually able to do and to be, we come much closer to understanding the barriers societies have erected against full justice for women. Similarly, Sen criticizes approaches that measure well-being in terms of utility by pointing to the fact that women frequently exhibit "adaptive preferences," preferences that have adjusted to their second-class status (Amartya Sen 1990, 1995). Thus the utilitarian framework, which asks people what they currently prefer and how satisfied they are, proves inadequate to confront the most pressing issues of gender justice. We can only have an adequate theory of gender justice, and of social justice more generally, if we are willing to make claims about fundamental entitlements that are to some extent independent of the preferences that people happen to have, preferences shaped, often, by unjust background conditions.

This critique of dominant paradigms in terms of ideas of gender justice is a pervasive feature in Sen's work, and it is obvious that one central motivation for his elaboration of the "capabilities approach" is its superior potential for developing a theory of gender justice. But the reader who looks for a fully formulated account of social justice generally, and gender justice in particular, in Sen's work will not find one; she will need to extrapolate one from the suggestive materials Sen provides. *Development as Freedom* develops one pertinent line of thought, arguing that capabilities provide the best basis for thinking about the goals of development (Amartya Sen 1999). Both when nations are compared by international measures of welfare and when each nation strives internally to achieve a higher level of development for its people, capabilities provide us with an attractive way of understanding the normative content of the idea of development. Thinking of development's goal as increase in GNP per capita occluded distributional inequalities, which are particularly central when we are thinking about sex equality. It also failed to dissaggregate and separately consider important aspects of development, such as health and education, that are demonstrably not very well correlated with GNP, even when we take distribution into account. Thinking of development's goal in terms of utility at least has the merit of looking at what processes do for people. But utility, Sen argues, is inadequate to capture the heterogeneity and noncommensurability of the diverse aspects of development. Because it fails to take account of the fact of adaptive preferences, it also biases the development process in favor of the status quo, when used as a normative benchmark. Finally, it suggests that the goal of development is a state or condition of persons (e.g., a state of satisfaction), and thus understates the importance of agency and freedom in the development process.

All these failings, he stresses, loom large when we confront the theory with inequalities based on sex: for women's lives reflect a striving after many different elements of well-being, including health, education, mobility, political participation, and others. Women's current preferences often show distortions that are the result of unjust background conditions. And agency and freedom are particularly important goals for women, who have so often been treated as passive dependents. This line of argument has close links with the feminist critique of Utilitarianism and dominant economic paradigms (e.g. Elizabeth Anderson 1993; Bina Agarwal 1997). It also connects fruitfully with writings by activist-scholars who stress the importance of women's agency and participation (e.g. Martha Chen 1983; Bina Agarwal 1994).

Not surprisingly, I endorse these arguments. But I think that they do not take us very far in thinking about social justice. They give us a general sense of what societies ought to be striving to achieve, but because of Sen's reluctance to make commitments about substance (which capabilities a society ought most centrally to pursue), even that guidance remains but an outline. And they give us no sense of what a minimum level of capability for a just society might be. The use of capabilities in development is typically comparative merely, as in the *Human Development Reports* of the UNDP. Thus, nations are compared in areas such as health and educational attainment. But concerning what level of health service, or what level of educational provision, a just society would deliver as a fundamental entitlement of all its citizens, the view is suggestive, but basically silent.

A different line of argument pursued by Sen in works from "Equality of What?" to *Inequality Reexamined* seems more closely related to concerns of social justice. This argument begins from the idea of equality as a central political value (Amartya Sen 1992). Most states consider equality important, Sen argues, and yet they often do not ask perspicuously enough what the right space is within which to make the relevant comparisons. With arguments closely related to his arguments about the goals of development, Sen argues that the space of capabilities provides the most fruitful and ethically satisfactory way of looking at equality as a political goal. Equality of utility or welfare falls short for the reasons I have already summarized. Equality of resources falls short because it fails to take account of the fact that individuals need differing levels of resources if they are to come up to the same level of capability to function. They also have differing abilities to convert resources into actual functioning.

Some of these differences are straightforwardly physical: a child needs more protein than an adult to achieve a similar level of healthy functioning, and a pregnant woman more nutrients than a nonpregnant woman. But the differences that most interest Sen are social, and connected with entrenched discrimination of various types. Thus, in a nation where women are traditionally discouraged from pursuing an education it will usually take more resources to produce female literacy than male literacy. Or, to cite Sen's famous example, a person in a wheelchair will require more resources connected with mobility than will the person with "normal" mobility, if the two are to attain a similar level of ability to get around (Amartya Sen 1980).[4]

Sen's arguments about equality seem to have the following bearing on issues of social justice and public policy: to the extent that a society values the equality of persons and pursues that as among its social goals, equality of capabilities looks like the most relevant sort of equality to aim at. And it is clear that equality is a central goal for women who pursue social justice; once again, then, the arguments have particular force and relevance in the context of feminism. But Sen never says to what extent equality of capability *ought* to be a social goal,[5] or how it ought to be combined with other political values in the pursuit of social justice. Thus the connection of his equality arguments with a theory of justice remains as yet unclear.

In this chapter I shall suggest that the capabilities approach is indeed a valuable way to approach the question of fundamental entitlements, one that is especially pertinent to issues of sex equality.[6] I shall argue that it is superior to other approaches to social justice in the Western tradition when we confront it with problems of sex equality. It is closely allied to, but in some ways superior to, the familiar human rights paradigm, in ways that emerge most vividly in the area of sex difference. And it is superior to approaches deriving from the Western notion of the social contract, because of the way in which it can handle issues of care, issues that are fundamental to achieving sex equality, as recent feminist work has demonstrated.[7]

I shall argue, however, that the capabilities approach will supply definite and useful guidance, and prove an ally in the pursuit of sex equality, only if we formulate a definite list of the most central capabilities, even one that is tentative and revisable, using capabilities so defined to elaborate a partial account of social justice, a set of basic entitlements without which no society can lay claim to justice.

II. CAPABILITIES AND RIGHTS

The capabilities that Sen mentions in illustrating his approach, and those that are part of my more explicit list, include many of the entitlements that are also stressed in the human rights movement: political liberties, the freedom of association, the free choice of occupation, and a variety of economic and social rights. And capabilities, like human rights, supply a moral and humanly rich set of goals for development, in place of "the wealth and poverty of the economists," as Marx so nicely put it (Karl Marx 1844). Thus capabilities have a very close relationship to human rights, as understood in contemporary international discussions. In effect they cover the terrain covered by both the so-called "first-generation rights" (political and civil liberties) and the so-called second-generation rights (economic and social rights). And they play a similar role, providing both a basis for cross-cultural comparison and the philosophical underpinning for basic constitutional principles.

Both Sen and I connect the capabilities approach closely to the idea of human rights, and in Martha Nussbaum (2001a: Ch. 1) I have described the relationship between the two ideas at some length (see also Martha Nussbaum 1997). The human rights approach has frequently been criticized by feminists for being male-centered, and for not including as fundamental entitlements some abilities and opportunities that are fundamental to women in their struggle for sex equality. They have proposed adding to international rights documents such rights as the right to bodily integrity, the right to be free from violence in the home, and from sexual harassment in the workplace. My list of capabilities explicitly incorporates that proposal, and Sen's would appear to do so implicitly.[8] But the theoretical reasons for supplementing the language of rights with the language of capabilities still require comment.

Capabilities, I would argue, are very closely linked to rights, but the language of capabilities gives important precision and supplementation to the language of rights. The idea of human rights is by no means a crystal-clear idea. Rights have been understood in many different ways, and difficult theoretical questions are frequently obscured by the use of rights language, which can give the illusion of agreement where there is deep philosophical disagreement. People differ about what the *basis* of a rights claim is: rationality, sentience, and mere life have all had their defenders. They differ, too, about whether rights are prepolitical or artifacts of laws and institutions. They differ about whether rights belong only to individual persons, or also to groups. They differ about whether rights are to be regarded as side-constraints on goal-promoting action, or rather as one part of the social goal that is being promoted. They differ, again, about the relationship between rights and duties: if A has a right to S, then does this mean that there is always someone who has a duty to provide S, and how shall we decide who that someone is? They differ, finally, about what rights are to be understood as rights *to*. Are human rights primarily rights to be treated in certain ways? Rights to a certain level of achieved well-being? Rights to resources with which one may pursue one's life plan? Rights to certain opportunities and capacities with which one may make choices about one's life plan?

The capabilities approach has the advantage of taking clear positions on these disputed issues, while stating clearly what the motivating concerns are and what the goal is. The relationship between the two notions, however, needs further scrutiny, given the dominance of rights language in international feminism.

Regarding fundamental rights, I would argue that the best way of thinking about what it is to secure them to people is to think in terms of capabilities. The right to political participation, the right to religious free exercise, the right of free speech – these and others are all best thought of as secured to people only when the relevant capabilities to function are present. In other words, to secure a right to citizens in these areas is to put them in a position of capability to function in that area. To the extent that rights are used in defining social justice, we should not grant that the society is just unless the capabilities have been effectively achieved. Of course people may have a prepolitical right to good treatment in this area that has not yet been recognized or implemented; or it may be recognized formally and yet not implemented. But by defining the securing of rights in terms of capabilities, we make it clear that a people in country C don't really have an effective right to political participation, for example, a right in the sense that matters for judging that the society is a just one, simply because this language exists on paper: they really have been given a right only if there are effective measures to make people truly capable of political exercise. Women in many nations have a nominal right of political participation without having this right in the sense of capability: for example, they may be threatened with violence should they leave the home. In short, thinking in terms of capability gives us a benchmark as we think about what it is really to secure a right to someone. It makes clear that this involves affirmative material and institutional support, not simply a failure to impede.

We see here a major advantage of the capabilities approach over understandings of rights – very influential and widespread – that derive from the tradition within liberalism that is now called "neoliberal," for which the key idea is that of "negative liberty." Often fundamental entitlements have been understood as prohibitions against interfering state action, and if the state keeps its hands off, those rights are taken to have been secured; the state has no further affirmative task. Indeed, the US Constitution suggests this conception directly: for negative phrasing concerning state action predominates, as in the First Amendment: "Congress shall make no law respecting an establishment of religion, or prohibiting the free exercise thereof; or abridging the freedom of speech, or of the press; or the right of the people peaceably to assemble, and petition the Government for a redress of grievances." Similarly, the Fourteenth Amendment's all-important guarantees are also stated in terms of what the state may not do: "No State shall make or enforce any law which shall abridge the privileges or immunities of citizens of the United States; nor shall any State deprive any person of life, liberty, or property, without due process of law; nor deny to any person within its jurisdiction the equal protection of the laws." This phraseology, deriving from the Enlightenment tradition of negative liberty, leaves things notoriously indeterminate as to whether impediments supplied by the market, or private actors, are to be considered violations of fundamental rights of citizens (Martha Nussbaum forthcoming a).

The Indian Constitution, by contrast, typically specifies rights affirmatively.[9] Thus for example: "All citizens shall have the right to freedom of speech and expression; to assemble peaceably and without arms; to form associations or unions; ... [etc.]" (Art. 19). These locutions have usually been understood to imply that impediments supplied by nonstate actors may also be deemed to be violative of constitutional rights. Moreover, the Indian Constitution is quite explicit that affirmative action programs to aid the lower castes and women are not only not incompatible with constitutional guarantees, but are actually in their spirit. Such an approach seems very important for gender justice: the state needs to take action if traditionally marginalized groups are to achieve full equality. Whether a nation has a written constitution or not, it should understand fundamental entitlements in this way.

The capabilities approach, we may now say, sides with the Indian Constitution, and against the neoliberal interpretation of the US Constitution.[10] It makes it clear that securing a right to someone requires more than the absence of negative state action. Measures such as the recent constitutional amendments in India that guarantee women one-third representation in the local *panchayats*, or village councils, are strongly suggested by the capabilities approach, which directs government to think from the start about what obstacles there are to full and effective empowerment for all citizens, and to devise measures that address these obstacles.

A further advantage of the capabilities approach is that, by focusing from the start on what people are actually able to do and to be, it is well placed to foreground and address inequalities that women suffer inside the family: inequalities in resources and opportunities, educational deprivations, the failure of work to be recognized as work, insults to bodily integrity. Traditional rights talk has neglected these issues, and this is no accident, I would argue: for rights language is strongly linked with the traditional distinction between a public sphere, which the state regulates, and a private sphere, which it must leave alone.

The language of capabilities has one further advantage over the language of rights: it is not strongly linked to one particular cultural and historical tradition, as the language of rights is believed to be. This belief is not very accurate, as Sen has effectively argued: although the term "rights" is associated with the European Enlightenment, its component ideas have deep roots in many traditions (Amartya Sen 1997; Martha Nussbaum 2000a). Nonetheless, the language of capabilities enables us to bypass this troublesome debate. When we speak simply of what people are actually able to do and to be, we do not even give the appearance of privileging a Western idea. Ideas of activity and ability are everywhere, and there is no culture in which people do not ask themselves what they are able to do and what opportunities they have for functioning.

If we have the language of capabilities, do we also need the language of rights? The language of rights still plays, I believe, four important roles in public discourse, despite its unsatisfactory features. First, when used as in the sentence "A has a right to have the basic political liberties secured to her by her government," it reminds us that people have justified and urgent claims to certain types of urgent treatment, no matter what the world around them has done about that. It imports the idea of an urgent claim based upon justice. This is important particularly for women, who may lack political rights. However, the capabilities approach can make this

41

idea of a fundamental entitlement clear in other ways, particularly, as I shall be arguing, by operating with a list of capabilities which are held to be fundamental entitlements of all citizens based upon justice.

Rights language also has value because of the emphasis it places on people's choice and autonomy. The language of capabilities, as both Sen and I employ it, is designed to leave room for choice, and to communicate the idea that there is a big difference between pushing people into functioning in ways you consider valuable and leaving the choice up to them. Sen makes this point very effectively in *Development as Freedom* (Sen 1999). But we make this emphasis clear if we combine the capabilities analysis with the language of rights, as my list of capabilities does at several points, and as the Indian Constitution typically does.[11]

III. ENDORSING A LIST

One obvious difference between Sen's writings and my own is that for some time I have endorsed a specific list of the Central Human Capabilities as a focus both for comparative quality-of-life measurement and for the formulation of basic political principles of the sort that can play a role in fundamental constitutional guarantees.

The basic idea of my version of the capabilities approach, in *Women and Human Development* (2000a), is that we begin with a conception of the dignity of the human being, and of a life that is worthy of that dignity – a life that has available in it "truly human functioning," in the sense described by Marx in his 1844 *Economic and Philosophical Manuscripts*. With this basic idea as a starting point, I then attempt to justify a list of ten capabilities as central requirements of a life with dignity. These ten capabilities are supposed to be general goals that can be further specified by the society in question, as it works on the account of fundamental entitlements it wishes to endorse (Nussbaum 2000a: Ch. 1). But in some form all are part of a minimum account of social justice: a society that does not guarantee these to all its citizens, at some appropriate threshold level, falls short of being a fully just society, whatever its level of opulence. Moreover, the capabilities are held to be important for each and every person: each person is treated as an end, and none as a mere adjunct or means to the ends of others. And although in practical terms priorities may have to be set temporarily, the capabilities are understood as both mutually supportive and all of central relevance to social justice. Thus a society that neglects one of them to promote the others has shortchanged its citizens, and there is a failure of justice in the shortchanging (Martha Nussbaum 2001b). (Of course someone may feel that one or more of the capabilities on my list should not enjoy this central status, but then she will be differing with me about what ought to be on the list, not about the more general project of using a list to define a minimal conception of social justice.)

The list itself is open-ended and has undergone modification over time; no doubt it will undergo further modification in the light of criticism. But here is the current version.

The Central Human Capabilities

1. Life. Being able to live to the end of a human life of normal length; not dying prematurely, or before one's life is so reduced as to be not worth living.

2. Bodily Health. Being able to have good health, including reproductive health; to be adequately nourished; to have adequate shelter.

3. Bodily Integrity. Being able to move freely from place to place; to be secure against violent assault, including sexual assault and domestic violence; having opportunities for sexual satisfaction and for choice in matters of reproduction.

4. Senses, Imagination, and Thought. Being able to use the senses, to imagine, think, and reason – and to do these things in a "truly human" way, a way informed and cultivated by an adequate education, including, but by no means limited to, literacy and basic mathematical and scientific training. Being able to use imagination and thought in connection with experiencing and producing works and events of one's own choice, religious, literary, musical, and so forth. Being able to use one's mind in ways protected by guarantees of freedom of expression with respect to both political and artistic speech, and freedom of religious exercise. Being able to have pleasurable experiences and to avoid nonbeneficial pain.

5. Emotions. Being able to have attachments to things and people outside ourselves; to love those who love and care for us, to grieve at their absence; in general, to love, to grieve, to experience longing, gratitude, and justified anger. Not having one's emotional development blighted by fear and anxiety. (Supporting this capability means supporting forms of human association that can be shown to be crucial in their development.)

6. Practical Reason. Being able to form a conception of the good and to engage in critical reflection about the planning of one's life. (This entails protection for the liberty of conscience and religious observance.)

7. Affiliation.
A. Being able to live with and toward others, to recognize and show concern for other human beings, to engage in various forms of social interaction; to be able to imagine the situation of another. (Protecting this

capability means protecting institutions that constitute and nourish such forms of affiliation, and also protecting the freedom of assembly and political speech.)

B. Having the social bases of self-respect and nonhumiliation; being able to be treated as a dignified being whose worth is equal to that of others. This entails provisions of nondiscrimination on the basis of race, sex, sexual orientation, ethnicity, caste, religion, national origin.

8. Other Species. Being able to live with concern for and in relation to animals, plants, and the world of nature.

9. Play. Being able to laugh, to play, to enjoy recreational activities.

10. Control Over One's Environment.

A. Political. Being able to participate effectively in political choices that govern one's life; having the right of political participation, protections of free speech and association.

B. Material. Being able to hold property (both land and movable goods), and having property rights on an equal basis with others; having the right to seek employment on an equal basis with others; having the freedom from unwarranted search and seizure. In work, being able to work as a human being, exercising practical reason, and entering into meaningful relationships of mutual recognition with other workers.

Because considerations of pluralism have been on my mind since the beginning, I have worked a sensitivity to cultural difference into my understanding of the list in several ways.

First, I consider the list as open-ended and subject to ongoing revision and rethinking, in the way that any society's account of its most fundamental entitlements is always subject to supplementation (or deletion).

I also insist, second, that the items on the list ought to be specified in a somewhat abstract and general way, precisely in order to leave room for the activities of specifying and deliberating by citizens and their legislatures and courts that all democratic nations contain. Within certain parameters it is perfectly appropriate that different nations should do this somewhat differently, taking their histories and special circumstances into account. Thus, for example, a free speech right that suits Germany well might be too restrictive in the different climate of the United States.

Third, I consider the list to be a free-standing "partial moral conception," to use John Rawls's phrase: that is, it is explicitly introduced for political purposes only, and without any grounding in metaphysical ideas of the sort that divide people along lines of culture and religion.[12] As Rawls says: we can view this list as a "module" that can be endorsed by people who otherwise have very different conceptions of the ultimate meaning and purpose of life; they will connect it to their religious or secular comprehensive doctrines in many ways.

Fourth, if we insist that the appropriate political target is capability and not functioning, we protect pluralism here again.[13] Many people who are willing to support a given capability as a fundamental entitlement would feel violated were the associated functioning made basic. Thus, the right to vote can be endorsed by believing citizens who would feel deeply violated by mandatory voting, because it goes against their religious conception. (The American Amish are in this category: they believe that it is wrong to participate in political life, but they endorse the right of citizens to vote.) The free expression of religion can be endorsed by people who would totally object to any establishment of religion that would involve dragooning all citizens into some type of religious functioning.

Fifth, the major liberties that protect pluralism are central items on the list: the freedom of speech, the freedom of association, the freedom of conscience.[14] By placing them on the list we give them a central and nonnegotiable place.

Sixth and finally, I insist on a rather strong separation between issues of justification and issues of implementation. I believe that we can justify this list as a good basis for political principles all round the world. But this does not mean that we thereby license intervention with the affairs of a state that does not recognize them. It is a basis for persuasion, but I hold that military and economic sanctions are justified only in certain very grave circumstances involving traditionally recognized crimes against humanity (Martha Nussbaum 2002). So it seems less objectionable to recommend something to everyone, once we point out that it is part of the view that state sovereignty, grounded in the consent of the people, is a very important part of the whole package.

Where does Sen stand on these questions? I find a puzzling tension in his writings at this point. On the one hand, he speaks as if certain specific capabilities are absolutely central and nonnegotiable. One cannot read his discussions of health, education, political and civil liberties, and the free choice of occupation without feeling that he agrees totally with my view that these human capabilities should enjoy a strong priority and should be made central by states the world over, as fundamental entitlements of each and every citizen (although he says little about how a threshold level of each capability would be constructed). In the case of liberty, he actually endorses giving liberty a considerable priority, though without giving an exhaustive enumeration of the liberties that would fall under this principle. His role in the formulation of the measures that go into the *Human Development Reports*, moreover, clearly shows him endorsing a group of health- and education-related capabilities as the appropriate way to measure quality of life across nations.

On the other hand, Sen has conspicuously refused to endorse any account of the central capabilities. Thus the examples mentioned above remain in limbo: clearly they are examples of some things he thinks very important, but it is not clear to what extent he is prepared to recommend them as important goals for all the world's people, goals connected with the idea of social justice itself. And it is equally unclear whether there are other capabilities not mentioned so frequently that might be equally important, and, if so, what those capabilities might be. The reason for this appears to be his respect for democratic deliberation.[15] He feels that people should be allowed to settle these matters for themselves. Of course, as I have said above, I do too, in the sense of implementation. But Sen goes further, suggesting that democracy is inhibited by the endorsement of a set of central entitlements in international political debate, as when feminists insist on certain requirements of gender justice in international documents and deliberations.

In *Development as Freedom* things become, I believe, even more problematic. For Sen speaks throughout the work of "the perspective of freedom" and uses language, again and again, suggesting that freedom is a general all-purpose social good, and that capabilities are to be seen as instances of this more general good of human freedom. Such a view is not incompatible with ranking some freedoms ahead of others for political purposes, of course. But it does seem to go in a problematic direction.

First of all, it is unclear whether the idea of promoting freedom is even a coherent political project. Some freedoms limit others. The freedom of rich people to make large donations to political campaigns limits the equal worth of the right to vote. The freedom of businesses to pollute the environment limits the freedom of citizens to enjoy an unpolluted environment. The freedom of landowners to keep their land limits projects of land reform that might be argued to be central to many freedoms for the poor. And so on. Obviously these freedoms are not among those that Sen considers, but he says nothing to limit the account of freedom or to rule out conflicts of this type. Indeed, we can go further: any particular freedom involves the idea of constraint: for person P is only free to do action A if other people are constrained from interfering with A.[16]

Furthermore, even if there were a coherent project that viewed all freedoms as desirable social goals, it is not at all clear that this is the sort of project someone with Sen's political and ethical views ought to endorse. The examples I have just given show us that any political project that is going to protect the equal worth of certain basic liberties for the poor, and to improve their living conditions, needs to say forthrightly that some freedoms are central for political purposes, and some are distinctly not. Some freedoms involve basic social entitlements, and others do not. Some lie at the heart of a view of political justice, and others do not. Among the ones that do not lie at the core, some are simply less important, but others may be positively bad.

For example, the freedom of rich people to make large campaign contributions, though defended by many Americans in the name of the general good of freedom, seems to me not among those freedoms that lie at the heart of a set of basic entitlements to which a just society should commit itself. In many circumstances, it is actually a bad thing, and constraint on it a very good thing. Similarly, the freedom of industry to pollute the environment, though cherished by many Americans in the name of the general good of freedom, seems to me not among those freedoms that should enjoy protection; beyond a certain point, the freedom to pollute is bad, and should be constrained by law. And while property rights are certainly a good thing up to a point and in some ways, the freedom of large landowners in India to hold property under gender-discriminatory ceiling laws – laws that some early Supreme Court decisions have held to enjoy constitutional protection – is not part of the account of property rights as central human entitlements that a just society would want to endorse. To define property capabilities so broadly is actually a bad thing, because giving women equal access to land rights is essential to social justice (see generally Agarwal 1994).

To speak more generally, gender justice cannot be successfully pursued without limiting male freedom. For example, the "right" to have intercourse with one's wife whether she consents or not has been understood as a time-honored male prerogative in most societies, and men have greatly resented the curtailment of liberty that followed from laws against marital rape – one reason why about half of the states in the US still do not treat nonconsensual intercourse within marriage as genuine rape, and why many societies the world over still lack laws against it. The freedom to harass women in the workplace is a tenaciously guarded prerogative of males the world over: the minute sexual harassment regulations are introduced, one always hears protests invoking the idea of liberty. Terms like "femi-nazis" are used to suggests that feminists are against freedom for supporting these policies. And of course in one sense feminists are indeed insisting on a restriction of liberty, on the grounds that certain liberties are inimical both to equalities and to women's liberties and opportunities.

In short, no society that pursues equality or even an ample social minimum can avoid curtailing freedom in very many ways, and what it ought to say is: those freedoms are not good, they are not part of a core group of entitlements required by the notion of social justice, and in many ways, indeed, they subvert those core entitlements. Of other freedoms, for example the freedom of motorcyclists to drive without helmets, a society can say, these freedoms are not very important; they are neither very bad nor very good. They are not implicit in our conception of social justice, but they do not subvert it either.

In other words, all societies that pursue a reasonably just political conception have to evaluate human freedoms, saying that some are central and some trivial, some good and some actively bad. This evaluation also affects the way we will assess an abridgment of a freedom. Certain freedoms are taken to be entitlements of citizens based upon justice. When any one of these is abridged, that is an especially grave failure of the political system. In such cases, people feel that the abridgment is not just a cost to be borne; it is a cost of a distinctive kind, involving a violation of basic justice. When some freedom outside the core is abridged, that may be a small cost or a large cost to some actor or actors, but it is not a cost of exactly that same kind, one that in justice no citizen should be asked to bear. This qualitative difference is independent of the cost, at least in terms of standard subjective willingness-to-pay models. Thus, motorcyclists may mind greatly a law that tells them to wear a helmet. In terms of standard willingness-to-pay models, they might be willing to pay quite a lot for the right to drive without a helmet. On the other hand, many citizens probably would not think that not being able to vote was a big cost. In terms of standard willingness-to-pay models, at least, they would not pay much for the right to vote, and some might have to be paid for voting. And yet I would want to say that the right to vote is a fundamental entitlement based upon justice, whereas the right to drive without a helmet is not (Nussbaum 2001b).

Sen's response to these questions, in public discussion (Bielefeld, July 2001), has been to say that freedom per se is always good, although it can be badly used. Freedom, he said, is like male strength: male strength is per se a good thing, although it can be used to beat up women. I am not satisfied by this reply. For so much depends on how one specifies the freedoms in question. Some freedoms include injustice in their very definition. Thus, the freedom to rape one's wife without penalty, the freedom to hang out a sign saying "No Blacks here," the freedom of an employer to discriminate on grounds of race or sex or religion–those are freedoms all right, and some people zealously defend them. But it seems absurd to say that they are good per se, and bad only in use. Any society that allows people these freedoms has allowed a fundamental injustice, involving the subordination of a vulnerable group. Of other freedoms, for example, the freedom of the motorcycle rider to ride without a helmet, we should not say, "good in itself, bad only in use," we should say "neutral and trivial in itself, probably bad in use." Once again, attention to the all-important issue of content is vital.

Thus Sen cannot avoid committing himself to a core list of fundamental capabilities, once he faces such questions. If capabilities are to be used in advancing a conception of social justice, they will obviously have to be specified, if only in the open-ended and humble way I have outlined. Either a society has a conception of basic justice or it does not. If it has one, we have to know what its content is, and what opportunities and liberties it takes to be fundamental entitlements of all citizens. One cannot have a conception of social justice that says, simply, "All citizens are entitled to freedom understood as capability." Besides being wrong and misleading in the ways I have already argued, such a blanket endorsement of freedom/ capability as goal would be hopelessly vague. It would be impossible to say whether the society in question was just or unjust.

Someone may now say, sure, there has to be a definite list in the case of each nation that is striving for justice, but why not leave the list-making to them, and to their processes of public discussion? Of course, as I have already said, in the sense of *implementation,* and also in the sense of *more precise* specification, I do so. So, to be a real objection to my proposal, the question must be, why should we hold out to all nations a set of norms that we believe justified by a good philosophical argument, as when feminists work out norms of sex equality in documents such as CEDAW, rather than letting each one justify its own set of norms? The answer to this question, however, is given in all of Sen's work: some human matters are too important to be left to whim and caprice, or even to the dictates of a cultural tradition. To say that education for women, or adequate healthcare, is not justified just in case some nation believes that it is not justified seems like a capitulation to subjective preferences, of the sort that Sen has opposed throughout his career. As he has repeatedly stated: capabilities have intrinsic importance. But if we believe that, we also believe that it is right to say to nations that don't sufficiently recognize one of them: you know, you too should endorse equal education for girls, and understand it as a fundamental constitutional entitlement. You too should provide a certain level of healthcare to all citizens, and view this as among their fundamental constitutional entitlements. Just because the US does not choose to recognize a fundamental right to healthcare, that doesn't make the US right, morally justified. A very important part of public discussion is radical moral statement and the arguments supporting those statements. Such statements may be justified long before they are widely accepted. Such was true of the statements of Gandhi, of Martin Luther King, Jr., of early feminists. Where feminist demands are not yet widely accepted, it is true of those demands today: although public debate has not yet accepted them, they are a part of that debate right now, and a part that has already presented adequate moral justification for basic human entitlements.

In short: it makes sense to take the issue of social justice seriously, and to use a norm of justice to assess the various nations of the world and their practices. But if the issue of social justice is important, then the content of a conception of justice is important. Social justice has always been a profoundly normative concept, and its role is typically critical: we work out an account of what is just, and we then use it to find reality deficient in various ways. Sen's whole career has been devoted to developing norms of justice in exactly this way, and holding them up against reality to produce valuable criticisms. It seems to me that his commitment to normative thinking about justice requires the endorsement of some definite content. One cannot say, "I'm for justice, but any conception of justice anyone comes up with is all right with me." Moreover, Sen, of course, does not say that. He is a radical thinker, who has taken a definite stand on many matters, including matters of sex equality. He has never been afraid to be definite when misogyny is afoot, or to supply a quite definite account of why many societies are defective. So it is somewhat mysterious to me why he has recently moved in the direction of endorsing freedom as a general good. Certainly there is no such retreat in his practical policies regarding women. In recent writing such as "The Many Faces of Misogyny" he is extremely definite about what is just and unjust in laws and institutions, and one can infer a rich account of fundamental human entitlements from his critique (Amartya Sen 2001). But then it would appear that he cannot actually believe that the content of an account of fundamental entitlements should be left up for grabs.

Such leaving-up-for-grabs is all the more dangerous when we are confronting women's issues. For obviously enough, many traditional conceptions of social justice and fundamental entitlements have made women second-class citizens, if citizens at all. Women's liberties, opportunities, property rights, and political rights have been construed as unequal to men, and this has been taken to be a just state of affairs. Nor have traditional accounts of justice attended at all to issues that are particularly urgent for women, such as issues of bodily integrity, sexual harassment, and, as my next section will describe, the issue of public support for care to children, the disabled, and the elderly.

Some supporters of a capabilities approach might be reluctant to endorse a list because of concerns about pluralism.[17] But here we may make two points that pertain specifically to the norm of respect for pluralism. First, the value of respect for pluralism itself requires a commitment to some cross-cultural principles as fundamental entitlements. Real respect for pluralism means strong and unwavering protection for religious freedom, for the freedom of association, for the freedom of speech. If we say that we are for pluralism, and yet refuse to commit ourselves to the nonnegotiability of these items as fundamental building blocks of a just political order, we show that we are really half-hearted about pluralism.

I am sure that Sen would agree with this. I am sure, too, that he would say the same about other items on my list, such as health and education: if a nation says that they are for human capabilities, but refuses to give these special protection for all citizens, citing reasons of cultural or religious pluralism, Sen will surely say that they are not making a good argument, or giving genuine protection to pluralism. Instead, they are, very often, denying people (often, women in particular) the chance to figure out what culture and form of life they actually want. So they are actually curtailing the most meaningful kind of pluralism, which requires having a life of one's own and some choices regarding it. And that goal surely requires a certain level of basic health and education.

But then we are both, in effect, making a list of such entitlements, and the only question then must be what shall go on the list, and how long it will be.

The second argument is one that derives from the Rawlsian idea of political liberalism, and I am not certain that Sen would endorse it. The argument says that classical liberalism erred by endorsing freedom or autonomy as a general good in human life. Both earlier liberals such as John Stuart Mill and modern comprehensive liberals such as Joseph Raz hold that autonomy and freedom of choice are essential ingredients in valuable human lives, and that society is entitled to promote freedom across the board. Rawls, and I with him, hold that this general endorsement of freedom shows deficient respect for citizens whose comprehensive conceptions of the good human life do not make freedom and autonomy central human values. People who belong to an authoritarian religion cannot agree with Raz or Mill that autonomy is a generally good thing. Mill responds, in Chapter 3 of *On Liberty,* by denigrating such people (he understands Calvinists to be such people) (John Stuart Mill 1859). Presumably the Millean state would denigrate them too, and would design education and other institutions to disfavor them, although their civil liberties would not be restricted. Rawls and I agree that this strategy shows deficient respect for a reasonable pluralism of different comprehensive conceptions of the good life. We should respect people who prefer a life within an authoritarian religion (or personal relationship), so long as certain basic opportunities and exit options are firmly guaranteed.

I hold that this respect for pluralism is fostered both by making capability and not functioning the appropriate political goal and also by endorsing a relatively small list of core capabilities for political purposes. Thus we say two things to religious citizens. We say, first, that endorsing the capabilities list does not require them to endorse the associated functioning as a good in their own lives, a point I have stressed earlier in this section. And we say, second, that the very fact that it is a short list shows that we are leaving them lots of room to value other things in mapping out their plan of life. We do not ask them to endorse freedom as a general good – as we might seem to do if we talk a lot about freedom but fail to make a list. Instead, we just ask them to endorse this short list of freedoms (as capabilities) for political purposes and as applicable to all citizens. They may then get on with the lives they prefer.

The expectation is that a Roman Catholic citizen, say, can endorse this short list of fundamental liberties for political purposes, without feeling that her view of Church authority and its decisive role in her life is thereby being denigrated. Even an Amish citizen, who believes that all participation in public life is simply wrong, can still feel that it's all right to endorse the capabilities list for political purposes, because no general endorsement of autonomy as an end tells her that her life is less worthwhile than other lives. And, as I argued in Nussbaum (2000a: Chs. 1 and 3), even a woman who believes that the seclusion of women is right may endorse this small menu of liberties and opportunities for all women, though she herself will use few of them – and she will feel that the conception is one that respects her, because it does not announce that only autonomous lives are worthwhile.

I am not certain whether Sen is in this sense a comprehensive liberal like Raz, or a political liberal like Rawls and me. But to the extent that he finds Rawls's arguments on this score persuasive, he has yet a further reason to endorse a definite and relatively circumscribed list of capabilities as political goals, rather than to praise freedom as a general social good.

The question of how to frame such a list, and what to put on it, is surely a difficult one, in many ways. But I have argued that there is no way to take the capabilities approach forward, making it really productive for political thought about basic social justice, without facing this question and giving it the best answer one can.

IV. CAPABILITIES AND THE SOCIAL CONTRACT TRADITION[18]

One further issue, fundamental to concerns about gender justice, will help us to see both why the capabilities approach is superior to other approaches to social justice within the liberal tradition, and why a definite list of entitlements is required if the approach is to deliver an adequate conception of justice. This is the all-important issue of care for people who are physically and/or mentally dependent on others: children, the disabled, the elderly. This is a central issue for gender justice, because most of the caregiving for such dependents is done by women, often without any public recognition that it is work. The time spent on this caregiving disables women from many other functions of life, even when a society has in other respects opened those functions to them. For this reason a large body of feminist writing has developed pursuing this issue; and the 1999 *Human Development Report* devoted special attention to it as an issue of gender justice. To appreciate why this problem has not been adequately addressed, and why the capabilities approach does better, we must now contrast it with approaches familiar within the social contract tradition.

Insofar as the capabilities approach has been used to articulate a theory of social justice, or part of such a theory, it has been in dialogue from the start with the ideas of John Rawls and the Western liberal social contract tradition (John Rawls 1971, 1996). In "Equality of What?" Sen already argued for the capabilities approach by contrasting it with Rawls's approach, which defines justice in terms of the distribution of "primary goods," prominently including wealth and income (Sen 1980). My account of capabilities in *Women and Human Development* takes the argument further, comparing capabilities to Rawlsian primary goods at several points and endorsing the idea of an overlapping consensus (Nussbaum 2000a: Ch. 1). Sen and I both argue that Rawls's theory would be better able to give an account of the relevant social equalities and inequalities if the list of primary goods were formulated as a list of capabilities rather than as a list of things.[19]

But there is another problem that ought to trouble us, as we ponder the social contract tradition as a source of basic principles of justice, particularly with women's lives in view. All well-known theories in the social contract tradition imagine society as a contract for mutual advantage. They therefore imagine the contracting parties as rough equals, none able to dominate the others, and none asymmetrically dependent upon the others. Whatever differences there are among the different founders of that tradition, all accept the basic Lockean conception of a contract among parties who, in the state of nature, are "free, equal, and independent."[20] Thus for Kant persons are characterized by both freedom and equality, and the social contract is defined as an agreement among persons so characterized. Contemporary contractarians explicitly adopt this hypothesis. For David Gauthier, people of unusual need are "not party to the moral relationships grounded by a contractarian theory."[21] Similarly, the citizens in Rawls's Well Ordered Society are "fully cooperating members of society over a complete life" (John Rawls 1980: 546; 1996: 183).

Life, of course, is not like that. Real people begin their lives as helpless infants, and remain in a state of extreme, asymmetrical dependency, both physical and mental, for anywhere from ten to twenty years. At the other end of life, those who are lucky enough to live on into old age are likely to encounter another period of extreme dependency, either physical or mental or both, which may itself continue in some form for as much as twenty years. During the middle years of life, many of us encounter periods of extreme dependency, some of which involve our mental powers and some our bodily powers only, but all of which may put us in need of daily, even hourly, care by others. Finally, and centrally, there are many citizens who never have the physical and/or mental powers requisite for independence. In short, any real society is a caregiving and care-receiving society, and must therefore discover ways of coping with these facts of human neediness and dependency that are compatible with the self-respect of the recipients and do not exploit the caregivers. This, as I have said, is a central issue for gender justice.

In this area a Kantian starting point, favored by Rawls and other modern contractarians, is likely to give bad guidance. For Kant, human dignity and our moral capacity, dignity's source, are radically separate from the natural world. Morality certainly has the task of providing for human neediness, but the idea that we are at bottom split beings, both rational persons and animal dwellers in the world of nature, never ceases to influence Kant's way of thinking about how these deliberations will go.

What is wrong with the split? Quite a lot. First, it ignores the fact that our dignity is just the dignity of a certain sort of animal. It is the animal sort of dignity, and that very sort of dignity could not be possessed by a being who was not mortal and vulnerable, just as the beauty of a cherry tree in bloom could not be possessed by a diamond. Second, the split wrongly denies that animality can itself have a dignity; thus it leads us to slight aspects of our own lives that have worth, and to distort our relation to the other animals.[22] Third, it makes us think of the core of ourselves as self-sufficient, not in need of the gifts of fortune; in so thinking we greatly distort the nature of our own morality and rationality, which are thoroughly material and animal themselves; we learn to ignore the fact that disease, old age, and accident can impede the moral and rational functions, just as much as the other animal functions. Fourth, it makes us think of ourselves as a-temporal. We forget that the usual human lifecycle brings with it periods of extreme dependency, in which our functioning is very similar to that enjoyed by the mentally or physically handicapped throughout their lives. Feminist thought has recognized these facts about human life more prominently, at any rate, than most other political and moral thought.

Political thought in the Kantian social contract tradition (to stick with the part of the tradition I find deepest and most appealing) suffers from the conception of the person with which it begins. Rawls's contracting parties are fully aware of their need for material goods. Here Rawls diverges from Kant, building need into the foundations of the theory. But he does so only to a degree: for the parties are imagined throughout as competent contracting adults, roughly similar in need, and capable of a level of social cooperation that makes them able to make a contract with others. Such a hypothesis seems required by the very idea of a contract for mutual advantage.

In so conceiving of persons, Rawls explicitly omits from the situation of basic political choice the more extreme forms of need and dependency that human beings may experience. His very concept of social cooperation is based on the idea of reciprocity between rough equals, and has no explicit place for relations of extreme dependency. Thus, for example, Rawls refuses to grant that we have any duties of justice to animals, on the grounds that they are not capable of reciprocity (TJ 17, 504–5); they are owed "compassion and humanity," but "[t]hey are outside the scope of the theory of justice, and it does not seem possible to extend the contract doctrine so as to include them in a natural way" (TJ 512). This makes a large difference to his theory of political distribution. For his account of the primary goods, introduced, as it is, as an account of the needs of citizens who are characterized by the two moral powers and by the capacity to be "fully cooperating," has no place for the need of many real people for the kind of care we give to people who are not independent (see Eva Kittay 1999).

Now of course Rawls is perfectly aware that his theory focuses on some cases and leaves others to one side. He insists that, although the need for care for people who are not independent is "a pressing practical question," it may reasonably be postponed to the legislative stage, after basic political institutions are designed:

So let's add that all citizens are fully cooperating members of society over the course of a complete life. This means that everyone has sufficient intellectual powers to play a normal part in society, and no one suffers from unusual needs that are especially difficult to fulfill, for example, unusual and costly medical requirements. Of course, care for those with such requirements is a pressing practical question. But at this initial stage, the fundamental problem of social justice arises between those who are full and active and morally conscientious participants in society, and directly or indirectly associated together throughout a complete life. Therefore, it is sensible to lay aside certain difficult complications. If we can work out a theory that covers the fundamental case, we can try to extend it to other cases later.

(Rawls 1980: 546)

This reply seems inadequate. Care for children, the elderly, and the mentally and physically handicapped is a major part of the work that needs to be done in any society, and in most societies it is a source of great injustice. Any theory of justice needs to think about the problem from the beginning, in the design of the most basic level of institutions, and particularly in its theory of the primary goods.[23]

What, then, can be done to give the problem of care and dependency sufficient prominence in a theory of justice? The first thing we might try, one that has been suggested by Eva Kittay in her fine book, is to add the need for care during periods of extreme and asymmetrical dependency to the Rawlsian list of primary goods, thinking of care as among the basic needs of citizens.

This suggestion, if we adopt it, would lead us to make another modification: for care is hardly a commodity, like income and wealth, to be measured by the sheer amount of it citizens have. As Sen has long suggested (see Section I above), we would do well to understand the entire list of primary goods as a list – not of things but of central capabilities. This change would not only enable us to deal better with people's needs for various types of love and care as elements of the list, but would also answer the point that Sen has repeatedly made all along about the unreliability of income and wealth as indices of well-being. The well-being of citizens will now be measured not by the sheer amount of income and wealth they have, but by the degree to which they have the various capabilities on the list. A woman may be as well off as her husband in terms of income and wealth, and yet unable to function well in the workplace, because of burdens of caregiving at home (see Joan Williams 2000).

If we accepted these two changes, we would surely add a third, relevant to our thoughts about infancy and old age. We would add other capability-like items to the list of basic goods: for example, the social basis of health, adequate working conditions, and the social basis of imagination and emotional well-being, items that figure on my list (Nussbaum 2000a: Ch. 1).

55

Suppose, then, we do make these three changes in the list of primary goods: we add care in times of extreme dependency to the list of primary goods; we reconfigure the list as a list of capabilities; and we add other pertinent items to the list as well. Have we done enough to salvage the contract doctrine as a way of generating basic political principles? I believe that there is still room for doubt. Consider the role of primary goods in Rawls's theory. The account of primary goods is introduced in connection with the Kantian political conception of the person, as an account of what citizens characterized by the two moral powers need. Thus, we have attributed basic importance to care only from the point of view of our own current independence. It is good to be cared for only because care subserves moral personality, understood in a Kantian way as conceptually quite distinct from need and animality. This seems like another more subtle way of making our animality subserve our humanity, where humanity is understood to exclude animality. The idea is that because we are dignified beings capable of political reciprocity, therefore we had better provide for times when we are not that, so we can get back to being that as quickly as possible. I think that this is a dubious enough way to think about illnesses in the prime of life; but it surely leads us in the direction of a contemptuous attitude toward infancy and childhood, and, a particular danger in our society, toward elderly disability. Finally, it leads us strongly in the direction of not fully valuing those with lifelong mental disabilities: somehow or other, care for them is supposed to be valuable only for the sake of what it does for the "fully cooperating." They are, it would seem, being used as means for someone else's ends, and their full humanity is still being denied.

So I believe that we need to delve deeper, redesigning the political conception of the person, bringing the rational and the animal into a more intimate relation with one another, and acknowledging that there are many types of dignity in the world, including the dignity of mentally disabled children and adults, the dignity of the senile demented elderly, and the dignity of babies at the breast. We want the picture of the parties who design political institutions to build these facts in from the start. The kind of reciprocity in which we humanly engage has its periods of symmetry, but also, of necessity, its periods of more or less extreme asymmetry – and this is part of our lives that we bring into our situation as parties who design just institutions. And this may well mean that the theory cannot be a contractarian theory at all.

We thus need to adopt a political conception of the person that is more Aristotelian than Kantian, one that sees the person from the start as both capable and needy– "in need of a rich plurality of life-activities," to use Marx's phrase, whose availability will be the measure of well-being. Such a conception of the person, which builds growth and decline into the trajectory of human life, will put us on the road to thinking well about what society should design. We don't have to contract for what we need by producing; we have a claim to support in the dignity of our human need itself. Since this is not just an Aristotelian idea, but one that corresponds to human experience, there is good reason to think that it can command a political consensus in a pluralistic society. If we begin with this conception of the person and with a suitable list of the central capabilities as primary goods, we can begin designing institutions by asking what it would take to get citizens up to an acceptable level on all these capabilities. Although Sen refrains from specifying a political conception of the person, I believe that this suggestion is squarely in line with his ideas.

In *Women and Human Development* I propose that the idea of central human capabilities be used as the analogue of Rawlsian primary goods, and that the guiding political conception of the person should be an Aristotelian/Marxian conception of the human being as in need of a rich plurality of life activities, to be shaped by both practical reason and affiliation (Nussbaum 2000a: Ch. 1). I argue that these interlocking conceptions can form the core of a political conception that is a form of political liberalism, close to Rawls's in many ways. The core of the political conception is endorsed for political purposes only, giving citizens a great deal of space to pursue their own comprehensive conceptions of value, whether secular or religious. Yet more room for a reasonable pluralism in conceptions of the good is secured by insisting that the appropriate political goal is capability only: citizens should be given the option, in each area, of functioning in accordance with a given capability or not so functioning. To secure a capability to a citizen it is not enough to create a sphere of noninterference: the public conception must design the material and institutional environment so that it provides the requisite affirmative support for all the relevant capabilities. Thus care for physical and mental dependency needs will enter into the conception at many points, as part of what is required to secure to citizens one of the capabilities on the list.

Although Sen has not commented explicitly on issues of mental disability and senility, I believe that the view I have just mapped out is squarely in line with his emphasis on freedom as goal. We see, then, here again, that the capabilities approach solves some problems central to a theory of social justice that other liberal theories seem unable to solve well; the capability-based solution seems to be an attractive way of thinking about fundamental entitlements.

But now we must observe that the capabilities approach does these good things only in virtue of having a definite content. The capabilities approach provides us with a new way of understanding the *form* of "primary goods," and that is one part of the work that it does in providing a more adequate theory of care. But getting the *form* right was not all that had to be done: we also had to add the need for care in times of acute dependency to the existing list of primary goods.[24] And then, I argued, we would also need to add other capabilities as well to the list, in areas such as healthcare, work conditions, and emotional well-being. My own list of capabilities provides

57

for these things already, in areas such as emotions, affiliation, and health. A shift from the space of resources to the space of capabilities would not go far in correcting the deficiencies of the Rawlsian framework unless we had a list with a definite content, one that prominently includes care. Moreover, I also argued that we need to associate the list with a specific political conception of the person, one that conceives of dignity and animality as related rather than opposed. This is another piece of definite content, one that suffuses the capabilities list as I conceive it.

The capabilities approach is a powerful tool in crafting an adequate account of social justice. But the bare idea of capabilities as a space within which comparisons are made and inequalities assessed is insufficient. To get a vision of social justice that will have the requisite critical force and definiteness to direct social policy, we need to have an account, for political purposes of what the central human capabilities are, even if we know that this account will always be contested and remade. Women all over the world are making critical proposals in public discussion, proposals that embody their radical demand for lives with full human dignity. While we await the day when the world as a whole accepts such ideas, the capabilities list is one way of giving theoretical shape to women's definite, and justified, demands.

ACKNOWLEDGMENTS

I would like especially to thank Amartya Sen and the other participants of the Oxford workshop (September 11 – 13, 2002) on Sen's Work and Ideas, as well as the editors of this volume, for their most helpful comments.

NOTES

[1] I develop related arguments similar to those developed in this paper, but with a focus on constitutional and legal issues, in Martha Nussbaum (forthcoming a).

[2] See Amartya Sen (1980, 1982, 1985, 1992, 1999).

[3] See for example Amartya Sen (1990, 1995, 1999).

[4] Although Sen tends to treat this example as one of straightforward physical difference, it should not be so treated, since the reasons why wheelchair persons cannot get around are thoroughly social – the absence of ramps, etc. (for elaboration, see Nussbaum 2001a) See also Martha Nussbaum (forthcoming b), where I point out

that all societies cater to the disabilities of the average person. Thus we do not have staircases with steps so high that only giants can climb them.

A further problem not mentioned by Sen, but relevant to his critique of Rawls: even if the person in the wheelchair were equally well off with regard to economic well-being, there is a separate issue of dignity and self-respect.

[5] Obviously the case for this depends very much both on what capability we are considering and on how we describe it. Thus, equality of capability seems to be important when we consider the right to vote, the freedom of religion, and so on; but if we consider the capability to play basketball, it seems ludicrous to suppose that society should be very much concerned about even a minimum threshold level of it, much less complete equality. With something like health, much hangs on whether we define the relevant capability as "access to the social bases of health" or "the ability to be healthy." The former seems like something that a just society should distribute on a basis of equality; the latter contains an element of chance that no just society could, or should, altogether eliminate. So the question whether equality of capability is a good social goal cannot be well answered without specifying a list of the relevant capabilities, another point in favor of the argument I advance in Section V.

[6] One way of using it, discussed elsewhere, is as a basis for constitutional accounts of fundamental entitlements of all citizens (see Nussbaum, 2000a; forthcoming a).

[7] See especially Eva Kittay (1999), Nancy Folbre (1999, 2001), Joan Williams (2000), Mona Harrington (1999). Earlier influential work in this area includes: Martha Fineman (1991, 1995), Sarah Ruddick (1989), Joan Tronto (1993), Virginia Held (1993), Robin West (1997). For an excellent collection of articles from diverse feminist perspectives, see Held (1995). See also Martha Nussbaum (2000b). And, finally, see *Human Development Report 1999.*

[8] See his reply to letters concerning Amartya Sen (2001).

[9] Not invariably: Art. 14, closely modeled on the equal protection clause of the US Fourteenth Amendment, reads: "The State shall not deny to any person equality before the law or the equal protection of the laws within the territory of India."

[10] Of course this account of both is in many ways too simple; I refer primarily to the wording of the documents here, not to the complicated jurisprudential traditions stemming from them.

[11] On a difference with Sen concerning the role of rights as "side-constraints," see Martha Nussbaum (1997).

[12] For the relation of this idea to objectivity, see Martha Nussbaum (2001c).

[13] See my discussion of this issue in Nussbaum (2000a: Ch. 1); and for a rejoinder to perfectionist critics, see Martha Nussbaum (2000c).

[14] I am very skeptical of attempts to add group cultural rights to the list, because every group contains hierarchy; see Martha Nussbaum (forthcoming c).

[15] This is what Sen said in response to the present paper at the conference on his work at the Zentrum für interdiziplinarische Forschung in Bielefeld at which it was first presented, in July 2001.

[16] Thus, I do not see that we can coherently frame the notion of an increase or decrease in freedom, without specification of whose freedom, and freedom to do what. See John Rawls (1971: 202): "liberty can always be explained by a reference to three items: the agents who are free, the restrictions or limitations which they are free from, and what it is that they are free to do or not to do."

[17] Sen stated at the Bielefeld conference that this is not his concern.

[18] For a detailed discussion, see Nussbaum (2000b).

[19] For the idea of "overlapping consensus," see discussion above, Section III: the idea is that the values in the political conception can be viewed as a "module" that can be

attached to different comprehensive conceptions. Rawls's list of primary goods is actually heterogeneous, including liberties, opportunities, and powers alongside income and wealth; recently Rawls has added still other capability-like items to the list, such as access to healthcare and the availability of leisure time.

[20] John Locke (1698: Ch. 8).

[21] David Gauthier (1986: 18), speaking of all "persons who decrease th[e] average level" of well-being in a society.

[22] For one particularly valuable treatment of this theme, see James Rachels (1990).

[23] See Kittay (1999: 77): "Dependency must be faced from the beginning of any project in egalitarian theory that hopes to include all persons within its scope." For a remarkable narrative of a particular life that shows exactly how many social structures play a part in the life of a mentally handicapped child from the very beginning, see Michael Bérubé (1996).

[24] In terms of the capabilities list, I argue in current work-in-progress that both the capabilities of the cared-for and those of the caregiver are multiple, and should be understood to include many of the existing capabilities on the list. Getting care when one needs it is a "primary good" in Rawls's sense, in that it is one of the essential prerequisites for being able to carry out one's plan of life.

REFERENCES

Agarwal, Bina. 1994. *A Field of One's Own: Gender and Land Rights in South Asia.* Cambridge, UK: Cambridge University Press.

——. 1997. "'Bargaining' and Gender Relations: Within and Beyond the Household." *Feminist Economics* 3(1): 1–51.

Anderson, Elizabeth. 1993. *Value in Ethics and Economics.* Cambridge, MA: Harvard University Press.

Bérubé, Michael. 1996. *Life As We Know It: A Father, A Family, and An Exceptional Child.* New York: Vintage.

Chen, MarthaA. 1983. *A Quiet Revolution: Women in Transition in Rural Bangladesh.* Cambridge, MA: Schenkman Publishing Co., Inc.

Fineman, Martha. 1991. *The Illusion of Equality.* Chicago: University of Chicago Press.

——. 1995. *The Neutered Mother, the Sexual Family and Other Twentieth Century Tragedies.* New York: Routledge.

Folbre, Nancy. 1999. "Care and the Global Economy." Background paper prepared for *Human Development Report 1999.*

——. 2001. *The Invisible Heart: Economics and Family Values.* New York: The New Press.

Gauthier, David. 1986. *Morals By Agreement.* New York: Oxford University Press.

Harrington, Mona. 1999. *Care and Equality.* New York: Knopf.

Held, Virginia. 1993. *Feminist Morality: Transforming Culture, Society, and Politics.* Chicago: University of Chicago Press.

—— (ed.). 1995. *Justice and Care: Essential Readings in Feminist Ethics.* Boulder, CO: Westview Press.

Kittay, Eva. 1999. *Love's Labor: Essays on Women, Equality, and Dependency.* New York: Routledge.

Locke, John. 1698. *The Second Treatise of Government.* In *Two Treatises of Government,* ed. Peter Laslett. Cambridge, UK: Cambridge University Press, 1960.

Marx, Karl. 1844. *Economic and Philosophical Manuscripts of 1844.* In Karl Marx, *Early Writings,* trans. and ed. T. Bottomore. New York: McGraw-Hill, 1964.

Nussbaum, Martha. 1997. "Capabilities and Human Rights." *Fordham Law Review* 66: 273–300.

——. 2000a. *Women and Human Development: The Capabilities Approach.* Cambridge, UK: Cambridge University Press.

——. 2000b. "The Future of Feminist Liberalism." Presidential Address delivered to the Central Division of the American Philosophical Association. *Proceedings and Addresses of the American Philosophical Association* 74: 47–79.

——. 2000c. "Aristotle, Politics, and Human Capabilities: A Response to Antony, Arneson, Charlesworth, and Mulgan." *Ethics* 111: 102–40.

——. 2000d. "Animal Rights: The Need for a Theoretical Basis." *Harvard Law Review* 114(5): 1506–49 (A review of Wise 2000.).

——. 2001a. "Disabled Lives: Who Cares?" *The New York Review of Books* 48: 34–7.

——. 2001b. "The Costs of Tragedy: Some Moral Limits of Cost–Benefit Analysis," in Matthew D. Adler and Eric A. Posner (eds.). *Cost–Benefit Analysis: Legal, Economic, and Philosophical Perspectives,* pp. 169–200. Chicago: University of Chicago Press.

——. 2001c. "Political Objectivity." *New Literary History* 32: 883–906.

——. 2002. "Women and the Law of Peoples." *Philosophy, Politics, and Economics* 1(3): 283–306.

——. 2003. "The Complexity of Groups." *Philosophy and Social Criticism* 29: 57–69.

——. Forthcoming a. "Constitutions and Capabilities," In M. Krausz and D. Chatterjee (eds.) *Globalization, Development and Democracy: Philosophical Perspectives.* Oxford: Oxford University Press.

——. Forthcoming b. *Hiding from Humanity: Disgust, Shame, and the Law.* Princeton, NJ: Princeton University Press.

Rachels, James. 1990. *Created from Animals: The Moral Implications of Darwinism.* New York: Oxford University Press.

Rawls, John. 1971. *A Theory of Justice.* Cambridge, MA: Harvard University Press.

——. 1980. *Kantian Constructivism in Moral Theory: The Dewey Lectures.* The *Journal of Philosophy* 77: 515–71.

——. 1996. *Political Liberalism.* Expanded Paperback Edition. New York: Columbia University Press.

Ruddick, Sarah. 1989. *Maternal Thinking.* New York: Beacon Press.

Sen, Amartya. 1980. "Equality of What?" in S. M. McMurrin (ed.) *Tanner Lectures on Human Values.* Salt Lake City: University of Utah Press. Reprinted in Sen 1982, pp. 353–69.

——. 1982. *Choice, Welfare and Measurement.* Oxford, UK: Blackwell.

——. 1985. *Commodities and Capabilities.* Amsterdam: North-Holland.

——. 1990. "Gender and Cooperative Conflicts," in Irene Tinker (ed.) *Persistent Inequalities,* pp. 123–49. New York: Oxford University Press.

——. 1992. *Inequality Reexamined.* New York and Cambridge, MA: Russell Sage and Harvard University Press.

——. 1995. "Gender Inequality and Theories of Justice," in M. Nussbaum and J. Glover (eds.) *Women, Culture and Development,* pp. 259–73. Oxford: Clarendon Press.

——. 1997. "Human Rights and Asian Values." *The New Republic* (July 14/21): 33–40.

——. 1999. *Development as Freedom.* New York: Knopf.

——. 2001. "The Many Faces of Misogyny." *The New Republic* (September 17): 35–40.

Tronto, Joan. 1993. *Moral Boundaries: A Political Argument for an Ethic of Care.* New York: Routledge.

West, Robin. 1997. *Caring for Justice.* New York: New York University Press.

Williams, Joan. 2000. *Unbending Gender: Why Family and Work Conflict and What to Do About It.* New York: Oxford University Press.

Wise, Steven. 2000. *Rattling the Cage: Toward Legal Rights for Animals.* Cambridge, MA: Perseus Books.

SEN'S CAPABILITY APPROACH AND GENDER INEQUALITY: SELECTING RELEVANT CAPABILITIES

Ingrid Robeyns

OVERVIEW

This chapter investigates how Amartya Sen's capability approach can be applied to conceptualize and assess gender inequality in Western societies. I first argue against the endorsement of a definitive list of capabilities and instead defend a procedural approach to the selection of capabilities by proposing five criteria. This procedural account is then used to generate a list of capabilities for conceptualizing gender inequality in Western societies. A survey of empirical studies shows that women are worse off than men on some dimensions, better off on a few others, and similarly placed on yet others, while for some dimensions the evaluation is unclear. I then outline why, for group inequalities, inequalities in achieved functionings can be taken to reflect inequalities in capabilities, and how an overall evaluation could be arrived at by weighting the different capabilities.

INTRODUCTION

Much of Amartya Sen's work has focused on inequality and poverty. In his earlier writings, Sen (1973) criticized the existing literature on inequality measurement in welfare economics for being too concerned with complete rankings of different social states. Sen argued that we should not assume away complexities or ambiguities, and that often we can only make partial comparisons. For example, we might be able to say that person 1 (or country 1) is definitely better off than persons 2 and 3, but we might not be able to rank the well-being of 2 and 3. Sen has also criticized the inequality literature in welfare economics for being exclusively focused on income (Amartya Sen 1985, 1987, 1992, 1993, 1995, 1998). Instead, Sen argues, we should focus on the real freedoms that people have for leading a valuable life, that is, on their capabilities to undertake activities such as reading, working, or being politically active, or of enjoying positive states of being, such as being healthy or literate. This line of Sen's work, known as the capability approach, postulates that when making normative evaluations, the focus should be on what people are able to be and to do, and not on what they can consume, or on their incomes. The latter are only the means of well-being, whereas evaluations and judgments should focus on those things that matter intrinsically, that is, on a person's capabilities.

It is immediately clear that the capability approach has enormous potential for addressing feminist concerns and questions. Ever since its inception, the women's movement has focused on many issues that are not reducible to financial welfare, such as reproductive health, voting rights, political power, domestic violence, education, and women's social status. In this chapter I want to ask how the capability approach can be used to study one core and overarching feminist concern, namely gender inequality. More precisely, I will outline how gender inequality can be conceptualized and assessed from a capability perspective. What precisely do we measure, and how much gender inequality can we observe?

Sen has claimed that "the question of gender inequality ... can be understood much better by comparing those things that intrinsically matter (such as functionings and capabilities), rather than just the means [to achieve them] like ... resources. The issue of gender inequality is ultimately one of disparate freedoms" (Sen 1992: 125). However, Sen's capability approach does not provide a ready-made recipe that we can apply to study gender inequality. It only provides a general framework, and not a fully fleshed-out theory. One of the crucial questions that Sen has not answered is which capabilities are relevant for assessing inequality. In other words, Sen has not proposed a well-defined list of capabilities.

It could be argued that there are already a number of studies that measure gender inequality in capabilities. Indeed, some studies on aggregated or macro gender inequality indices effectively assess inequality in capabilities or capability-like dimensions (Jane Humphries 1993; UNDP 1995; A. Geske Dijkstra and Lucia Hanmer 2000). This literature certainly comes close to defining gender-sensitive multidimensional inequality or well-being indices that are in line with Sen's capability approach. However, these indices generally compare countries, not individuals. We need to conduct similar studies that compare individuals within countries instead of average levels between countries. This chapter is a step in that direction.

I. A BRIEF DESCRIPTION OF SEN'S CAPABILITY APPROACH

The capability approach advocates that we focus on people's capabilities when making normative evaluations, such as those involved in poverty measurement, cost-benefit analysis, efficiency evaluations, social justice issues, development ethics, and inequality analysis. What are these capabilities? Capabilities are people's potential functionings. Functionings are beings and doings. Examples are being well fed, taking part in the community, being sheltered, relating to other people, working on the labor market, caring for others, and being healthy. The difference between a functioning and a capability is similar to the difference between an achievement and the freedom to achieve something, or between an outcome and an opportunity. All capabilities together correspond to the overall freedom to lead the life that a person has reason to value. Sen stresses the importance of "reason to value" because we need to scrutinize our motivations for valuing specific lifestyles, and not simply value a certain life without reflecting upon it. By advocating that normative evaluations should look at people's capabilities, Sen criticizes evaluations that focus exclusively on utilities, resources, or income. He argues against a utility-based evaluation of individual well-being because such an evaluation might hide important dimensions and lead to misleading interpersonal or intertemporal comparisons. A person may be in a desperate situation and still be contented with life if she has never known differently. A utilitarian evaluation will only assess her satisfaction and will not differentiate between a happy, healthy, well-sheltered person, and an equally happy, but unhealthy and badly sheltered person who has mentally adapted to her situation. This is especially important from a gender perspective because utility seems to have a gendered dimension. For example, Andrew Clark (1997) has shown that British women have a higher job satisfaction or utility from doing paid work than men, even after controlling for personal and job characteristics. Women who are worse off than men in objective terms might still have the same utility level. Clark examined several possible explanations for this gender differential and concluded that women's higher job-related utilities were caused by their lower expectations.

The capability approach also rejects normative evaluations based exclusively on commodities, income, or material resources. Resources are only the *means* to enhance people's well-being and advantage, whereas the concern should be with what matters intrinsically, namely people's functionings and capabilities. Resource-based theories do not acknowledge that people differ in their abilities to convert these resources into capabilities, due to personal, social or environmental factors, such as physical and mental handicaps, talents, traditions, social norms and customs, legal rules, a country's public infrastructure, public goods, climate, and so on. In traditional welfare economics, income (and sometimes expenditure) is the most widely used variable, and there is little discussion on whether other variables should be used (Frank Cowell 1995; Alissa Goodman, Paul Johnson, and Steven Webb 1997; D. G. Champernowne and Frank Cowell 1998). Economic historians have long looked at other dimensions, such as height, mortality, and political freedoms. Welfare economists who measure individual well-being have also begun to pay more attention to other indicators, but income remains the dominant focus.

The focus on capabilities does not deny the important contribution that resources can make to people's well-being. Indeed, inequalities in resources can be significant causes of inequalities in capabilities and therefore also need to be studied. For example, Bina Agarwal (1994: 1455) has argued that "the gender gap in the ownership and control of property is the single most critical contributor to the gender gap in economic well-being, social status, and empowerment." A complete analysis of gender inequality should not only map the gender inequalities in functionings and capabilities, but also analyze which inequalities in resources cause gender inequalities in capabilities and functionings. This is especially important for assessing which policies can reduce gender inequalities, because intervening in the distribution of resources will be a crucial (although not the only) way of affecting the distribution of capability well-being. This chapter has the more limited aim of assessing gender inequality in capabilities, without investigating the corresponding resources that cause these inequalities, or the policies that can rectify them.

One important aspect of Sen's capability approach is its underspecified character. The capability approach is a framework of thought, a normative tool, but it is *not* a fully specified theory that gives us complete answers to all our normative questions. It is not a mathematical algorithm that prescribes how to measure inequality or poverty, nor is it a complete theory of justice. The capability approach, strictly speaking, only advocates that the evaluative space should be that of capabilities. However, it does not stipulate which capabilities should be taken into account, or how different capabilities should be aggregated in an overall assessment. Applying the capability approach implies that we choose the relevant capabilities and indicate how important each will be in an overall judgment. In addition, normative frameworks always depend on explanatory or ontological views of human nature and society, and Sen's capability approach does not defend one particular world-view. If we interpret all of Sen's work as being one integrated body of thought, as Sabina Alkire (2002: 87) does, then many theories of human nature and society would be excluded (e.g., strong libertarian or communitarian theories), but there will still remain a range of theories (e.g., most strands of liberal theories) that are compatible with the capability approach.[1]

II. SOME STRENGTHS AND WEAKNESSES OF THE CAPABILITY APPROACH

Why make normative assessments in the space of capabilities, and why would this framework be attractive for an analysis of gender inequality? In this section, I will discuss three strengths and one weakness of the capability approach for normative assessments in general and for gender inequality analysis in particular.

The first advantage is that functionings and capabilities are properties of individuals. Hence the capability approach is an ethically (or normatively) individualistic theory. This means that each person will be taken into account in our normative judgments. Ethical individualism implies that the units of normative judgment are individuals, and not households or communities. At the same time, the capability approach is not ontologically individualistic. It does not assume atomistic individuals, nor that our functionings and capabilities are independent of our concern for others or of the actions of others. The social and environmental conversion factors also allow us to take into account a number of societal features, such as social norms and discriminatory practices. In sum, the ethically individualistic and ontologically nonindividualistic nature of the capability approach is a desirable characteristic for well-being and inequality analysis (Ingrid Robeyns 2001b). This is also attractive for feminist research, because ethical individualism rejects the idea that women's well-being can be subsumed under wider entities such as the household or the community, while not denying the impact of care, social relations, and interdependence between family or community members.

The capability approach is therefore a major improvement over standard well-being approaches in welfare economics or political philosophy. In the latter, accounts of inequality and well-being often use implicit assumptions about gender relations within the family which are unrealistic and deny or ignore intra-household inequalities (Susan Okin 1989; Diemut Bubeck 1995). In welfare economics generally, inequality theories are ethically individualistic, but this principle gets lost in applied work. Individuals and families are often sloppily equated as in assumptions that partners pool their incomes, or that they receive equal shares of the benefits. There is by now a substantial literature on intra-household allocations, but this literature has had little significant impact on inequality measurement in welfare economics.[2] As Frances Woolley and Judith Marshall (1994: 420) have argued: "standard approaches to inequality measurement presume that there is no inequality within the household." But this standard assumption turns out to be unrealistic, as not all partners share the total household income equally (Jan Pahl 1989; Shelley Phipps and Peter Burton 1995; Shelly Lundberg, Robert Pollak, and Terence Wales 1997). Moreover, Woolley and Marshall (1994) and Phipps and Burton (1995) have shown that assumptions about the degree of sharing within the household significantly affect inequality and poverty measurement. And even if household income were shared completely, it is problematic to assume that it does not matter in a well-being assessment whether a person has earned this money herself, or obtained it from her partner. Conceptualizing and measuring gender inequality in functionings and capabilities helps avoid these problems, since it focuses on the lives that individuals can and do choose to live, and not on their average household income.

The second advantage of the capability approach is that it is not limited to the market, but looks at people's beings and doings in both market and nonmarket settings. The inclusion of nonmarket dimensions of well-being in our normative analysis will reveal complexities and ambiguities in the distribution of well-being that an analysis of income or wealth alone cannot capture. This is especially important for gender inequality research. Feminist economists have long been arguing that economics needs to pay attention to processes and outcomes in both the market economy and the nonmarket economy (e.g., Nancy Folbre 1994, 2001; Susan Himmelweit 2000). Inequality comparisons based only on the market economy, such as comparisons of income, earnings, and job-holdings, exclude some important aspects of well-being such as care labor, household work, freedom from domestic violence, or the availability of supportive social networks. They also miss the fact that women spend much more time outside the market than men. These aspects matter particularly in gender-related assessments of well-being and disadvantage.

The third strength of the capability approach is that it explicitly acknowledges human diversity, such as race, age, ethnicity, gender, sexuality, and geographical location as well as whether people are handicapped, pregnant, or have caring responsibilities. Sen has criticized inequality approaches that assume that all people have the same utility functions or are influenced in the same way and to the same extent by the same personal, social, and environmental characteristics:

> Investigations of equality – theoretical as well as practical – that proceed with the assumption of antecedent uniformity ... thus miss out on a major aspect of the problem. Human diversity is not a secondary complication (to be ignored or to be introduced "later on"); it is a fundamental aspect of our interest in equality.
>
> (Sen 1992: xi)

Again, this characteristic of the capability approach is important for gender inequality analysis. Sen's concern with human diversity contrasts strikingly with the tendency in standard welfare economics to neglect intra-household inequalities in nonmarket labor and total work loads. Equality is ultimately measured in "male terms" with an exclusive focus on the market dimensions. Feminist scholars have argued that many theories of justice claim to address the lives of men *and* women, but closer scrutiny reveals that men's lives form the standard and gender inequalities and injustices are assumed away or remain hidden, and are thereby indirectly justified. For example, many theories of justice simply *assume* that families are just social institutions where love, justice, and solidarity are the rule. This assumption renders these theories inadequate *in their very design* for understanding or analyzing intra-household inequalities. Susan Okin (1989: 10–13) has called this "false gender neutrality." As these theories use gender-neutral language, we might be tempted to see them as including the concerns of both men and women. But they ignore the biological differences between the sexes, and the impact that gender has on our lives through gendered social institutions, gender roles, power differences, and ideologies: "Thus gender-neutral terms frequently obscure the fact that so much of the real experiences of 'persons,' so long as they live in gender-structured societies, *does* in fact depend on what sex they are" (Okin 1989: 11). By conceptualizing gender inequality in the space of functionings and capabilities, there is more scope to account for human diversity, including the diversity stemming from people's gender.

However, these positive features notwithstanding, the capability approach also has one major drawback, which stems from its underspecified character. Capability egalitarianism, strictly speaking, only advocates that when making inequality assessments we should focus on capabilities. But every evaluative assessment, implicitly or explicitly, endorses additional social theories, including accounts of the individual, social, and environmental conversion factors, and a normative theory of choice. We get quite divergent normative results, depending on which social theories we add to the capability framework. If the social theories are racist, homophobic, sexist, ageist, Eurocentric, or biased in any other way, the capability evaluation will be accordingly affected. For example, gender discrimination in the market can reduce a person's capability set. Or mechanisms that form gendered preferences, such as socialization, can have an impact on the different choices that women and men make from their capability sets. If someone denies the existence of gender discrimination and gendered preference formation, or claims that they have no normative significance, then she will come to different conclusions about gender inequality in capabilities.[3] Thus, a major concern for feminists is that the capability approach is vulnerable to androcentric interpretations and applications. In the remainder of this paper, I present a feminist capability perspective on gender inequality. This implies that the view of social and human nature that I endorse is one that does not assume away people's interconnectedness, or the importance of care and interpersonal interdependencies, or the gendered nature of society.

However, viewing social and human nature from a feminist perspective is not sufficient for applying the capability approach to gender inequality. Because of its underspecified nature, Sen's capability approach needs at least three additional specifications before we can apply it. First, we have to select which capabilities are important for evaluating gender inequality and should therefore be included in a list of relevant capabilities. Second, we have to take a stand on whether to look at gender inequality in functionings or in capabilities. Third, to make an overall evaluation, we need to decide how to weight the different functionings or capabilities. In this chapter I am concerned mainly with the selection of capabilities, and will discuss the other two issues only briefly.

III. THE NEED FOR A DEFINITE LIST

Martha Nussbaum (1988: 176; 2003) has argued that Sen should endorse one definite list of valuable capabilities, if he wants to apply the capability approach to social justice and gender inequality. Nussbaum (1995, 2000, 2003) has herself drawn up such a list of capabilities that she defends as universally valid. Although she concedes that her list would need further elaboration and adaptation by context, she argues that such a specification is an essential first step.

I disagree with Nussbaum's claim that Sen should endorse *one definite* list of capabilities. It is crucial to note that Nussbaum's and Sen's versions of the capability approach have different theoretical assertions, and their approaches entail different conceptions of what the list should be doing. As Sabina Alkire (2002: 54) notes: Nussbaum's list is "a list of normative things-to-do"; it has a highly prescriptive character and she makes strong universalistic claims regarding its scope. Nussbaum has also used the capability approach to develop a universal theory of the good: it applies to all social justice issues, and to the world as a whole. This does not imply, she argues, that her list is insensitive to culture and context. It is formulated at a highly abstract level, and for each country or community it can then be made more specific. Hence, in Nussbaum's theory, there is one universal general list that can be translated into more detailed and specific lists to suit the context (Nussbaum 2000).

Sen's capability approach, by contrast, makes broader and less specified claims. Given the intrinsic underspecification of Sen's capability approach, there cannot be one catch-all list. Instead, each application of the capability approach will require its own list. For Sen, a list of capabilities must be context dependent, where the context is both the geographical area to which it applies, and the sort of evaluation that is to be done. Applications of Sen's capability approach can be very diverse. They can be academic, activist, or policy-oriented. They can be abstract and philosophical, or applied and down-to-earth. They can be theoretical or empirical. They can concern social, political, economic, legal, psychological, or other dimensions of advantage, taken together or individually or in any combination. They can be specified for the global or the local context. And so forth.

The differences in Sen's and Nussbaum's capability approaches, and their different views on the desirability of one definite list can be better understood by keeping in mind their respective academic fields and expertise. Sen's roots lie in the field of social choice, and he therefore believes that we should search for fair and consistent democratic procedures to draw up the list. Nussbaum, on the other hand, has done a lot of work on the philosophy of the good life and, more recently, on constitutional design, and in this context it is much more important that a scholar proposes and defends a fully-fleshed out list of capabilities. As Fabienne Peter (2003) concludes from her analysis of the relevance of Sen's contribution to social choice theory for gender issues, "taking people seriously as agents entails giving them a chance to be heard, and to be involved in collective evaluations and decisions." For a collective evaluation or for making a decision from a capability perspective, this certainly includes being heard and being involved in the selection of capabilities.

Suppose now that we apply Sen's capability approach to a particular question, and we end up with exactly the same list as Nussbaum's. Would this then confirm that Nussbaum is correct in defending one particular list? I think not. First, even if the actual list drawn up by someone using Sen's capability approach is the same as Nussbaum's, the underlying assumptions of what this list *is*, and what it is supposed to *do*, remain different. The theoretical status of the lists will remain distinct, even if both lists contain exactly the same elements.

Second, the *process* that generates a list is important and this could affect a list's political or academic legitimacy. Amartya Sen has repeatedly emphasized that in matters of social choice and distributive justice, processes matter a great deal. Indeed, we should be concerned not only with culmination outcomes (the outcome narrowly defined, here the items on the list), but also with the comprehensive outcome, which includes aspects of the choice process, including the identity of the chooser (Amartya Sen 1997). Suppose that a social scientist applies the capability approach to gender inequality assessment, or a village council uses the capability approach to decide on priorities for the allocation of its funds, and they end up using Nussbaum's list of capabilities. In terms of the comprehensive outcome, it would still be important that the social scientist or the village council go through a democratic process for drawing up a list of priorities. This will give a legitimacy to the outcome that simply copying Nussbaum's list will lack. In other words, even if the application of Sen's capability approach leads us to a list identical to Nussbaum's, the process by which Nussbaum's list is generated might lack the political legitimacy needed for policy design. Similarly, when the capability approach is applied to particular research questions concerning gender inequality, we might prefer lists that are derived from, embedded in, and engage with the existing literature in that field. In this sense, Nussbaum's list, even when proposing the same dimensions, might lack academic legitimacy.[4]

Summing up, if we want to respect Sen's capability approach as a general framework for normative assessments, then we cannot endorse one definite list of capabilities without narrowing the capability approach.[5] Note that

71

this does not contradict the claim that to use Sen's capability framework for specified purposes, be they theoretical or empirical, we must select capabilities. I now turn to the question: how can this selection be made without violating the basic tenets of Sen's approach?

IV. FIVE CRITERIA FOR THE SELECTION OF CAPABILITIES

The fact that the capability approach is not a fully fleshed-out theory means that its further specifications can be diverse. For each such specification, we will need a relevant list of functionings and capabilities. How should this selection be made, and what type of list is appropriate? When drawing up a list of functionings, I suggest that the following five criteria should be met.

1. *The criterion of explicit formulation*: The most basic criterion is that the list should be explicit, discussed, and defended. To political and moral philosophers this might seem an obvious requirement, as can be seen from Nussbaum's (1995, 2000) very careful and elaborate defense of her list. But this is not a common practice in welfare economics. Existing applications in welfare economics operate almost exclusively at the level of quantitative empirical analysis, and use whatever functionings can be found in the available data sets, without defending an *a priori* list of functionings. Moreover, few of the existing applications discuss the capabilities that would have been appropriate, but for which no information is available.

2. *The criterion of methodological justification*: When drawing up a list, we should clarify and scrutinize the method that has generated the list and justify this as appropriate for the issue at hand. I will propose such a method for gender inequality research in Section V.

3. *The criterion of sensitivity to context*: The level of abstraction at which the list is pitched should be appropriate for fulfilling the objectives for which we are seeking to use the capability approach. This criterion thus proposes a pragmatic approach towards drawing up a list by acknowledging that it is important to speak the language of the debate in which we want to get involved. For example, in philosophical discussions the list will be specified at a highly abstract level, whereas for political, social, or economic discussions the list will be less abstract. And even within the latter discussions the level of abstraction can vary: the context of legal rights will require a list at a higher level of abstraction than one measuring socio-economic inequality.

4. *The criterion of different levels of generality*: The fourth criterion is related to, but distinct, from the third. It states that *if* the specification aims at an empirical application, or wants to lead to implementable policy proposals,

72

then the list should be drawn up in at least two stages. The first stage can involve drawing up a kind of "ideal" list, unconstrained by limitations of data or measurement design, or of socio-economic or political feasibility. The second stage would be drawing up a more pragmatic list which takes such constraints into account. Distinguishing between the ideal and the second-best is important, because constraints might change over time, for example as knowledge expands, empirical research methods become more refined, or the reality of political or economic feasibility changes. Care labor is a case in point in the context of gender inequality. Few, if any, empirical data sets have information on capabilities related to care labor; however, listing these capabilities in an ideal list strengthens the case for collecting data on care, which will then alter the analysis and perhaps the policies. Gender biases in the social sciences partly explain why many data sets contain so little information on who provides caring labor, and where, when, how much, why, and under what circumstances. Without this multi-stage procedure, the list could automatically reproduce the existing biases. The use of this procedure could help reduce such biases stemming from the social situatedness of researchers and policy-makers.

5. *The criterion of exhaustion and non reduction*: The last criterion is that the listed capabilities should include all important elements. Moreover, the elements included should not be reducible to other elements. There may be some overlap, provided it is not substantial. This does not exclude the possibility that a subset might have such an important status that it requires being considered on its own, independent of the larger set.

To sum up, the selection of capabilities requires careful attention, as there is a potential danger here of strengthening existing androcentric and other biases. I have defended a procedural approach and provided some selection criteria.

V. SELECTING CAPABILITIES FOR GENDER INEQUALITY ASSESSMENT

For the conceptualization of gender inequality in post-industrialized Western societies,[6] I propose the following list of capabilities at the ideal level:

1 *Life and physical health*: being able to be physically healthy and enjoy a life of normal length.
2 *Mental well-being*: being able to be mentally healthy.
3 *Bodily integrity and safety*: being able to be protected from violence of any sort.

4 *Social relations*: being able to be part of social networks and to give and receive social support.

5 *Political empowerment*: being able to participate in and have a fair share of influence on political decision-making.

6 *Education and knowledge*: being able to be educated and to use and produce knowledge.

7 *Domestic work and nonmarket care*: being able to raise children and to take care of others.

8 *Paid work and other projects*: being able to work in the labor market or to undertake projects, including artistic ones.

9 *Shelter and environment*: being able to be sheltered and to live in a safe and pleasant environment.

10 *Mobility*: being able to be mobile.

11 *Leisure activities*: being able to engage in leisure activities.

12 *Time-autonomy*: being able to exercise autonomy in allocating one's time.

13 *Respect*: being able to be respected and treated with dignity.

14 *Religion*: being able to choose to live or not to live according to a religion.

Below I will defend these capabilities as important for an evaluation of gender inequality in Western societies, as required by the criterion of explicit formulation. But before doing that, I will justify the method and show how I respect the criterion of context. It is also important to keep in mind that this method might be appropriate for a range of measurement and evaluative problems, but probably not for political or policy decisions. For the latter purpose much more would need to be said on the importance and type of public debate, and hard issues would need to be discussed, such as deciding on the list where deep disagreements exist.

Methodologically, I have followed four steps to generate this list. The first step is unconstrained brainstorming. The second step is to test a draft list by engaging with existing academic, political, and grassroots literature and debates on gender inequality. This step aims to root the list in the local contexts and experiences of those whom the list concerns. Those drafting the list have to be especially careful to include information stemming from groups with whom they are less familiar. Given that the method is much more inductive than deductive, and accesses knowledge in different spheres of life, constructing this list is likely to be a substantial project. The last two steps are more formal. The third step involves engaging with other lists of capabilities (discussed in detail below). And the fourth and last step involves debating the list with other people (an aim toward which this article will hopefully contribute).

Let me now compare my list with the lists of others (the third step of my methodology). My comparison is with the lists proposed by Sabina Alkire and Rufus Black (1997), Martha Nussbaum (1995, 2000, 2003), and the Swedish approach to the quality of life measurement (Robert Erikson and Rune Åberg 1987; Robert Erikson 1993). Table 1 presents these different lists and their dimensions.

The Swedish approach to welfare, developed since 1965, has generated an important list. This approach stipulates that a person's standard of living is her "command over resources in the form of money, possessions, knowledge, mental and physical energy, social relations, security, and so on" (Erikson 1993: 72–3). As can be seen, this approach differs from the capability approach in that it focuses on material and nonmaterial resources, and achieved functionings. In contrast, I deliberately exclude economic resources, as these do not constitute a capability. The Swedish list is also narrower and more directed towards the material dimensions of life. Another difference with the capability approach is that it does not distinguish between real opportunities and achievements. It is also gender-biased, as it does not include care and household work, or time-autonomy. Nevertheless, this list can function as a useful sounding board when the capability approach is applied to general well-being measurements in welfare states. These studies also give detailed guidelines on how the items on the list can be translated into quantitatively measurable variables.

Alkire and Black (1997) argue that the elements on a list should be the most basic reasons that people have for acting, that is, reasons for doing or not doing certain things. They argue that one should compare lists to see whether some of the dimensions overlap. Only those dimensions that cannot be reduced to another dimension should be kept, so as to arrive at a list of completely nonreducible dimensions. By comparing the work of Germain Grisez, Joseph Boyle, and John Finnis (1987) with Nussbaum's (1995), Alkire and Black end up with a list that contains the dimensions listed in Table 1: life; knowledge and appreciation of beauty; work and play; friendship; self-integration; coherent self-determination; transcendence; and being able to live with concern for and in relation to animals, plants, and the world of nature. But applying the criterion of context makes it immediately clear that this list will not be very helpful in an academic and/ or political discussion on gender inequality at the individual level. Many items of this list are too abstract and vague for our purpose. It is a list of very general capabilities, as opposed to the more specific capabilities that I propose for the assessment of gender inequality.

A widely published list of capabilities is that proposed by Nussbaum (1995: 83–5; 2000: 78–86; 2003). Her list has ten dimensions: life; bodily health; bodily integrity; sense, imagination and thought; emotions; practical reason; affiliation; other species; play; and control over one's environment. My list overlaps considerably with Nussbaum's. At the same time, there are several differences. First, Nussbaum's interpretation of functionings and capabilities is different from Sen's, and my list follows Sen's conceptualiza-

Table 1 Comparison of several lists

Authors	Swedish approach (1987)	Alkire and Black (1997)	Nussbaum (1995, 2000, 2003)	Robeyns (this paper)
Aim/scope of the list	Quality of life measurement in Sweden	Universal	Universal	Gender inequality in Western societies
Level of abstraction	Low	High	High	Low
Dimensions	1. Mortality 2. Physical and mental health and healthcare use 3. Employment and working hours 4. Working conditions 5. Economic resources 6. Educational resources 7. Housing conditions 8. Political resources 9. Family and social integration 10. Leisure and recreation	1. Life 2. Knowledge and appreciation of beauty 3. Work and play 4. Friendship 5. Self-integration 6. Coherent self-determination 7. Transcendence 8. Other species	1. Life 2. Bodily health 3. Bodily integrity 4. Senses, imagination, and thought 5. Emotions 6. Practical reason 7. Affiliation 8. Other species 9. Play 10. Control over one's environment	1. Life and physical health 2. Mental well-being 3. Bodily integrity and safety 4. Social relations 5. Political empowerment 6. Education and knowledge 7. Domestic work and nonmarket care 8. Paid work and other projects 9. Shelter and environment 10. Mobility 11. Leisure activities 12. Time-autonomy 13. Respect 14. Religion

tion. For Sen, capabilities are real opportunities, but for Nussbaum they also include talents, internal powers, and abilities. This implies that for Nussbaum Sen's conversion factors are integrated in the concept of capability itself. The question then is: should we use Sen's conceptualization of capabilities, or Nussbaum's? For policy-related issues and debates in the social sciences, and especially for the measurement of individual advantage and the design of socio-economic policy proposals, the criterion of context would, in my view, favor the use of Sen's conceptualization. Nussbaum's list will be more appropriate in other discussions, mainly those concerning moral philosophical principles that might result in legal rights and political declarations, or in qualitative analyses of how people can cultivate their capabilities.

The second difference between Nussbaum's list and mine is that, even if we take from Nussbaum's list only those capabilities that are real opportunities, our lists differ in what is included. For instance, I explicitly include the functioning of time-autonomy, which means that my conceptualization of gender inequality includes inequalities in time allocation, leisure time, time-related stress, and so forth. This is an important social issue in some Western societies, and below I discuss some studies of gender inequalities in time use.

Third, the elements that are included in both lists are labeled and categorized differently. The difference here reflects the criterion of context: I have tried to categorize capabilities in a way that links them with the existing (mainly empirical) literature on gender inequalities in the social sciences.

Finally, as highlighted earlier, Nussbaum's list differs *in character* from other lists. In addition, she takes it for granted that the government will have to deliver minimum levels of the capabilities on her list. This belief in the government stands in sharp contrast to some critical theory, which sees the government as part of the problem of injustices (Nivedita Menon 2002). In formulating my list I steer clear of both positions. Rather, my concern is to highlight aspects of gender inequality and disadvantage, without outlining by what process these might be reduced, be it through government policy or otherwise. This is in line with Sen's capability approach, which allows for an analytical distinction between the distribution of well-being on the one hand and policies of redistribution and rectification on the other. Thus, even if some of the same capabilities figure in Nussbaum's list and mine, their character and normative assertions are distinct.

It is interesting to note that even though these lists have been drawn up by scholars from different backgrounds and with different aims, they show considerable overlap. The overlap is especially in the selected dimensions, albeit the levels of abstraction and generality of these dimensions differ substantially. Life, physical and mental health, knowledge/education, work, play/leisure, and social relations (family/friendship/affiliation) can be found in all the lists, even though they are labeled and grouped differently. All of these capabilities are in some way also included in the United Nations Declaration of Human Rights, which suggests that at a high level of abstraction there is probably a core set of capabilities that will always be considered important. Also, as Mozaffar Qizilbash (2002) concludes, many of the existing lists are reconcilable. I agree with Qizilbash that it is context and strategic reasons that play the major role in determining the length and content of different lists, rather than fundamental differences in the accounts of well-being or advantage. Nevertheless, for the mentioned reasons of agency and legitimacy, it will remain important to involve the affected people in the selection of capabilities and not to impose on them a list they simply have to accept, especially when the capability approach is used in political and policy contexts.

VI. GENDER INEQUALITY IN CAPABILITIES AND ACHIEVED FUNCTIONINGS

The criterion of explicit formulation and justification of the list requires that I present the list and defend it. So far I have only listed the selected capabilities. In this section I will seek to justify why these capabilities are relevant for gender inequality analysis. I will also present evidence on gender inequality in these capabilities, although the evidence will be illustrative and not meant to provide a complete assessment of gender inequality. I can only scratch the surface of the relevant issues and of the empirical studies. Moreover, much of the evidence is aggregative and rather general in character, thereby obscuring other social differences such as between generations, races, classes, and so forth. For some capabilities there is reliable information; for others there is intense debate on prevalence and incidence as well as their gender dimensions. It therefore cannot be stressed enough that more detailed analysis will be required before any definite conclusions can be drawn. In addition, most of the statistics and figures presented here will be about achieved functionings and not about capabilities. This raises the crucial question of how much actual achievements can reveal about an individual's capabilities, which will be discussed below.

Some capabilities described below could also be interpreted as a resource for other capabilities. For example, belonging to a supportive community or family is a valuable state of being in itself, but it can also be seen as an important resource for mental health. However, as long as a capability is important in its own right, it does not matter if it is also simultaneously a resource for other capabilities.

1. *Life and physical health*: The capability of life and physical health has two dimensions: being able to be born, and once born, being able to live a life

of normal length in good health.[7] As far as I know, there are no indications of a gender bias in the chances of being born in Western societies[8] (in contrast, say, to countries where the net economic benefits of having a son might exceed those of having a daughter and lead to sex-selective abortion).

It is also well known that there is a substantial gender difference in life expectancy at birth. In 1999, in the UK, life expectancy at birth was 74.7 for men relative to 79.7 for women. Data for other Western countries are similar (World Health Organization 2000: 163). Is this gender gap in women's favor an unjust inequality? Amartya Sen (2001) has argued that any discrimination against women in the health system that would level down their life expectancy would violate fairness in the process of redistributing health services. In other words, Sen is not exclusively interested in outcomes (strict equality in achieved functionings) but holds that "it would be morally unacceptable to suggest that women should receive worse health care than men so that the inequality in the achievement of health and longevity disappears" (Sen 2001: 8). In addition, we could argue that society should compensate men for their shorter life expectancy *only* insofar as this inequality is reducible to their sex and gender, and not to their own life style choices. But this seems difficult to implement. Also, insofar as this gender gap is reducible to biologically intrinsic differences between men and women that cannot be altered by human intervention, it could be argued that we should regard this inequality as ethically irrelevant. But to the extent that men's lower life expectancy is linked to social causes, such as suicide or high-risk social behavior (excessive drinking, fast driving, participating in armed battles, and so on), we should try to intervene so as to expand men's capability of life. Gender identities might also explain this gender gap. According to Ian Banks (2001), men do care about their health but find it often difficult to express their fears and worries, and therefore often seek no help until a disease has progressed. If hegemonic notions of masculinity make it more difficult for men to go to see a doctor, then there is a case for making health services more accessible to boys and men.[9]

The second major aspect is gender differences in morbidity. Research using general health indicators finds that women experience more ill-health than men. However, some recent research has moved away from overall health indicators and shown that if we look at more specific health indicators, and disaggregate by class and age, gender inequalities are less clear (Kate Hunt and Ellen Anandale 1999; Eero Lahelma, Pekka Martikainen, Ossi Rahkonen, and Karri Silventoinen 1999; Sara Arber and Myriam Khlat 2002.)

2. *Mental well-being.* Mental well-being relates mainly to the absence of any negative mental states of being and doings, such as not being able to sleep,

worrying, or feeling depressed, lonely, or restless.[10] Studies show that women have worse mental health than men (Lahelma *et al.* 1999; R. Fuhrer, S. A. Stansfeld, J. Chemali, and M. J. Shipley 1999). As Lesley Doyal (2000) argues, in most parts of the developed world, anxiety and depression are more common among women than men, but there is no evidence that this is biologically caused. David Goldberg and Paul Williams (1988: 81), for instance, when comparing men and women who live in "comparable social circumstances" found no significant differences.[11] Fuhrer *et al.* (1999: 84) argue that "[w]omen, as opposed to men, are socially and biologically channeled towards nurturing others, part of which includes giving social support. The difficulties implicit in fulfilling demands of support from others as well as the undervaluing of this role may contribute to the greater prevalence of psychological distress in women compared to men." Lone mothers may be particularly vulnerable to mental suffering (Myriam Khlat, Catherine Sermet, and Annick Le Pape 2000).

3. *Bodily integrity and safety*: Bodily integrity and safety are important states of being. This capability is adversely affected when people experience all sorts of personal violence, such as attacks on the street, domestic violence, rape, sexual assault, or stalking.[12] This capability also has a gender dimension: studies suggest that women bear a greater incidence of and more severe sexual violence than men, while men experience more physical violence of other kinds. For women, the most common place of violent attacks is their home and the most likely offender is their partner, whereas for men this is not the case (Rosemarie Bruynooghe, Sigrid Noelanders, and Sybille Opdebeeck 2000). Men and women are equally likely to suffer verbal abuse or physical violence within their homes, but women are more likely to be injured (Catriona Mirrlees-Black 1999). In the USA, almost 13 percent of women have experienced rape, compared to 3.3 percent of men (Brian Spitzberg 1999). Women also experience twice as much stalking (Keith Davis and Irene Hanson Frieze 2000).

However, the reporting ratio of these crimes varies, which could bias the estimates of gender inequality. While some criminologists conclude that women are less likely to be victims of violence, others argue that the true victimization rates are unknown because of biases in reporting (William Smith and Marie Torstensson 1997). In addition, domestic violence could be argued to be more devastating for victims than violence outside the home, as it might leave victims without a safe place to live, with no one to trust, and anxieties about the safety of their children. In conclusion, assessing this capability will be difficult, and existing findings remain somewhat inconclusive on the corresponding gender inequality.

4. *Social relations*: Forming, nurturing, and enjoying social relations is an important capability. Social relations, in the limited way I am using the

term, concerns two main aspects: social networks and social support. The social networks dimension relates to the number of people in one's network, the frequency of contacts, group membership, and so forth. The social support dimension focuses on the type and amount of support that one receives. In Western societies, men have more extensive networks in the political, economic, and legal arenas, which they can use to perpetuate their advantages in economic and public life. Women tend to have better informal networks and social support (Allison Munch, J. Miller McPherson, and Lynn Smith-Lovin 1997; Fuhrer *et al.* 1999). In Britain, an analysis based on the data of the British Household Panel Survey showed that women meet their friends more often than men, and they are less likely to have no one to help them if they are depressed, from whom to borrow money, or who can help out in a crisis or provide comfort when they are very upset (Robeyns 2002: 122–6).

5. Political empowerment: In all countries fewer women than men hold positions of political power. Data on women in Parliament provide a rough but easily available proxy for this capability. In October 2002, the percentage of women in the lower houses of Western Parliaments ranged from 14 in the USA to 45 in Sweden (Inter-Parliamentary Union 2002). But gender inequality in political power is not limited to dimensions for which statistics are available. For example, female politicians often complain about the masculine culture in politics that includes playing power games, using an aggressive tone in discussions, interrupting one another, talking for longer than needed, and so on. Of course, men who do not conform to dominant masculine identities might feel equally uncomfortable in such an environment.

6. *Education and knowledge:* Girls and boys have equal access to formal education, but gendered social norms and traditions continue to make it more difficult for girls to acquire knowledge and obtain degrees. Some parents are still less likely to encourage their daughters to do well at school and at higher education compared with sons, as many think that a good job is more important for men than for women, and a good education can help young men secure better jobs. And while it has convincingly been argued that we cannot easily generalize for all boys and girls, and that class backgrounds often matter more than gender (Robert Connell 1989), teachers and lecturers pay more attention to the needs and wishes of boys than of girls. Molly Warrington and Michael Younger (2000: 495) conclude for England that "[girls] still feel alienated from traditionally 'male' subjects such as science. Career aspirations are still highly gendered, and boys are frequently found to be dominating the classroom environment and monopolizing a teacher's time."

In recent years, less attention has been paid to the gendered character of schools, colleges, and universities, or to the gendered social norms and expectations that are making it more difficult for girls and women to pursue advanced studies or studies in areas that are perceived as men's domain. Instead, most public attention has been paid to the apparent under-achievement of boys in schools. However, this alleged underachievement is not unambiguously supported by evidence. A recent study of 15-year-olds in OECD countries found that girls consistently outperformed boys in reading skills. In half of the countries males did better in mathematics (OECD 2001). For science the gender differences were small and balanced out. Large gender differences are not inevitable. They are large in some countries and small or insignificant in others. In any case, a capability analysis of educational equality should go beyond these performances and investigate the gendered hurdles to educational achievements, such as sexist behavior and sometimes even sexual harassment by teachers, gender differences in expectations and encouragement given by parents, a male-dominated class atmosphere, and so forth.

7. *Domestic work and nonmarket care.* This capability involves raising children and taking care of other dependents, especially the elderly, and it is highly gendered: women do more nonmarket care for children as well as for the frail, the elderly, and the sick. But the largest inequality is in household work.

Is domestic work and nonmarket care an important capability? Obviously these activities are crucially important for the receivers; they affect their functionings of life and health, education and knowledge, bodily integrity and safety, social relations, and leisure activities. Thus, analyzing the supply of labor for domestic work and nonmarket care through a capability lens supports the claim that they are extremely important (Folbre 1994, 2001; Himmelweit 2000).

But how do nonmarket care and domestic work affect the caregiver? The answer will be mixed: some aspects of this capability will be valuable, others less so, and still others plainly negative. Some of these functionings will be valuable and enjoyable if done out of choice and for short periods, but could become burdensome and monotonous if they are mandatory and have to be done for extended periods. For example, cooking a meal once a week on a relaxing Sunday is a different experience from cooking meals five days a week, under time pressure, and after a full working day. The same can be said of caring for the ill, the elderly, or children – it becomes a different experience if undertaken every day rather than occasionally.

This capability, together with the capability to undertake paid work, do pose interpretation difficulties because they cannot unambiguously be seen as contributing to the well-being of the worker. This will be discussed below.

8. *Paid work and other projects:* This functioning is again highly gendered and mirrors to a large extent the gender inequality in domestic work and nonmarket care. On average, women are less active in the labor market than men and do worse jobs. To investigate this gender inequality we have to look at labor market participation, employment rates, unemployment rates, annual hours of work, and working conditions – all aspects that have been studied extensively (e.g., Francine Blau 1998; Jill Rubery, Mark Smith, and Colette Fagan 1999). Also, given that the capability approach should not be restricted to the market economy, we also need to include projects that do not necessarily involve paid work, like artistic creations or the organizing of a social or community event. For example, it should not be made more difficult for a female than a male artist to display her paintings or sculptures in an art gallery.

9. *Shelter and environment:* Being sheltered and enjoying a safe and pleasant environment can be conceptualized as functionings and capabilities, although we would probably first think of shelter and environment as resources. Both conceptualizations are possible, but more theorizing is needed for conceptualizing them as functionings and capabilities. Rachel Bratt (2002) argues that housing is important for people's well-being. At the instrumental level, good housing is positively related to good mental and physical health. But housing also counts intrinsically as "the physical space that is most intimately associated with one's identity" (Bratt 2002: 19), and thereby has a substantial impact about how one feels about oneself and even about one's personal empowerment. How can shelter and environment be a relevant dimension of gender inequality? Most quantitative empirical studies of housing and neighborhood conditions do not find a significant gender inequality (Sara Lelli 2001; Robeyns 2002), although Enrica Chiappero Martinetti (2000) finds for Italy that on average women live in slightly better housing than men. To fully assess gender inequality in shelter, we have to investigate aspects such as the extent to which men and women have equal access to space within the house they share, or equal decision-making power over constructing or furnishing a house, or whether neighborhoods provide facilities for childcare or spaces for children to play in, and so on.

10. *Mobility:* Relative to other capabilities, being mobile is an instrumental capability. But it can also be valuable in itself, since it enables movement between geographical locations. There are indications that this capability has a gendered dimension. For example, public transport does not always accommodate the needs of people caring for small infants. Many railway stations and train carriages are not designed to accommodate parents (often mothers) traveling with pushchairs. If women are disproportionately responsible for infants (which is the case), or if women have to rely more on

83

public transport than men, or if they are more responsible for caring for the old and the sick who might be in wheelchairs, then this creates a gender inequality in mobility. Also, in many old European cities sidewalks are sometimes too narrow for a pushchair, making it more difficult for parents of infants to be mobile than for people without small children, again resulting in a gender inequality since typically women are responsible for infants. These direct constraints on women's mobility are in addition to the constraints created by their responsibility for the care of children, the aged, and the ill – a responsibility that tends to keep them more confined to the home than men.

11. *Leisure activities*. Material affluence gives people the opportunity to enjoy leisure activities, such as watching TV, reading, walking, doing physical exercise, playing games, practicing the arts, and so on. These activities are an important means of relaxation, creativity, and pleasure; hence, they are intrinsic aspects of well-being.

Based on 1999 time budget data for Flanders, Ignace Glorieux, Suzanna Koelet and Maarten Moens (2001) find that on a weekly basis men spend 6 hours and 46 minutes longer on leisure activities than women. However, time-inequalities do not tell us the full story. Based on an international comparison, Michael Bittman and Judy Wajcman (2000) argue that on average men and women tend to have similar quantities of free time, but there is a gender gap in how leisure is experienced and enjoyed. On the basis of Australian data, Bittman and Wajcman (2000: 181 – 3) argue that on average men enjoy higher quality leisure than women do because men's leisure is less interrupted by work, or combined with unpaid work or childcare.

12. *Time-autonomy*. The list of capabilities proposed in this chapter includes the three main activities on which people spend their time (market work and projects, domestic work and nonmarket care, and leisure activities). But it is still argued that the core of gender inequality is the gender division of labor, in other words the gender division of time and responsibilities for market work, nonmarket work, and leisure. The allocation of time within the household is usually a collective and not an individual decision and is influenced by many individual, household, and community characteristics (Bubeck 1995; Agarwal 1997; Ingrid Robeyns 2001a). Feminist scholars have argued repeatedly that the current gender division of labor is unjust and generally to women's disadvantage.

Another aspect of the quality of time spent on an activity is the way people experience that activity. Shelley Phipps, Peter Burton, and Lars Osberg (2001) have shown that women in dual-career households face more time-pressure than their husbands. Even if their total work hours (paid and unpaid) are equal, the fact that women are more often responsible for domestic work that cannot be postponed generates more stress for them. The authors also argue that women's time stress tends to increase because they have to cope with different sets of responsibilities and are subject to social norms that lay more responsibilities on them for the way the household is run or family members are publicly presented.

A full assessment of gender inequalities in time autonomy would also have to investigate whether women and men have the same freedom to go where they please, when they please; whether they are subject to the same social restrictions and expectations; and so on. For example, women are often expected to spend more time keeping their elder parents company than their male relatives. Or they are expected to be on a constant stand-by in case a relative needs help or falls ill, or to take care of their grandchildren.

13. *Being respected and treated with dignity*: Another capability that warrants inclusion in our list is being respected and treated with dignity. Some feminists have argued that the root of our gendered society is the fact that women are systematically devalued and not considered fully human. Some radical feminists, for instance, give the example of pornography, prostitution, or other acts that treat women as sexual objects (Catharine MacKinnon 1982). Gender differences in the respect accorded to women and men can also be deduced from the limited individual and public recognition that care and domestic work receives. For example, in some European countries, fathers who took paternity leave have reported that they underestimated the importance and pressures of domestic work, and that due to their paternity leave they now have much more respect for this work (Vincent Duindam 1999). However, fathers who take substantial paternity leave are still few. People who do domestic work still receive little respect for their work, in part because such work is culturally perceived as "feminine."

14. *Religion*: Men and women should have the same freedom to practice or not to practice a religion. In addition, men and women should have the same freedom to debate and determine how their religion develops and to shape religious practices. But several religions reserve the right to interpret the holy books and to make religious statements only for men. Also in several religions women cannot become religious leaders, such as Catholic priests or Muslim Imams. Androcentric or misogynist rules are often imposed on women because they are so interpreted by male religious leaders, even if such rules are not an intrinsic part of the religion. Rather they are cultural practices that have become closely intertwined with religion over time. And while it is generally difficult for both men and women to leave a religious community into which they were born, the costs of women-unfriendly religious practices or of rigid religious identities are usually higher for women.

It is difficult to say to what extent there is significant gender inequality in this capability in Western societies, as these societies have become widely secularized. Many people in Western societies do not actively practice any religion, or belong to branches of Christianity (the predominant religion in the West) that have become more women-friendly over time. But other religious groups also exist in the West, and their share is increasing. Today, virtually all Western societies include some conservative-orthodox groups of most religions, including Christianity, Judaism, and Islam, all of which are judged to contain some women-unfriendly practices. There is, in fact, a growing scholarly and public debate on the unequal gender implications of religious practices.

Obviously an in-depth analysis of gender inequality in capabilities would have to study this capability in detail, since for some citizens in Western societies their religious capability is important but highly gendered. Such an analysis will need to acknowledge not only religion as a capability in itself (that is, the freedom to practice a religion in the way a person wants, or to not practice it at all), but also as a potential locus of gender inequalities. Moreover, there are important interdependencies between the capability of religious practice and other capabilities. As a result, there can be tradeoffs between practicing a religion and developing other capabilities that women might value, such as having the freedom of reproductive choice, undertaking paid work, or engaging in politics.

VII. CAPABILITIES OR ACHIEVED FUNCTIONINGS?

Let us now suppose that the empirical evidence discussed in the previous section gives us a reliable picture of the nature and size of gender inequalities in achieved functionings. What does this tell us about gender inequality in capabilities?

One possible answer would be that in Western societies, men and women are equal before the law, and thus have equal opportunities. Women have less favorable outcomes in some dimensions because their preferences are different. For instance, it could be argued that women would have a stronger preference for children than men (Victor Fuchs 1988). Hence, we should not aim at equality of outcomes, but should respect women's choices. As long as women have the same legal rights as men, their capability sets are thus equal and gender inequality is not an issue of ethical concern.

I dispute this position, which is based on implicit assumptions that are by no means obvious. An alternative position would be that for group inequalities (such as those based on race, caste, gender, or nationality) inequality in achieved functionings implies inequality in capabilities, except if one can give a plausible reason why one group would systematically choose different functionings from the same capability set. This is an application of Anne Phillips's (1999, 2003) more general claim that for group inequalities, equality of opportunities and equality of outcomes converge. In other words, if we observe inequalities in outcomes between men and women, we deduce that they did not have equal opportunities in the first place. Underlying this reasoning is the assumption that the distribution of preferences between groups is identical, that is, we are as likely to find a man as a woman with a given set of preferences. The burden of proof should fall on those who claim that women would *systematically* prefer different options than men, *if they had the same real opportunities*. The observation that given existing social conditions women are more likely than men to choose domestic and care labor over paid work does not mean that this is what they would choose if they had the same capabilities as men, precisely because the real opportunities for women to have a good job under good conditions are fewer than for men.

Ultimately, we are interested in evaluating group inequalities in the space of capabilities, and not in achieved functionings. But given that we have little direct information about people's capability levels, we could start by taking group inequality in achieved functionings as indicative of inequalities in capabilities. This could later be refined and adapted in the face of new evidence or compelling arguments.

It might be helpful to make a distinction between three types of capabilities. Type 1 would include physical and mental health, bodily integrity and safety, shelter and environment, and respect. I think there would be little dispute over the claim that most people would consider these achieved functionings as intrinsically desirable. The fact that there are gender inequalities in some of these dimensions cannot plausibly be attributed to different preferences. No woman wants to be depressed, and no man wants to be attacked on the street.

Type 2 would include education and knowledge, mobility, leisure activities, time-autonomy, and religion. Here people are likely to disagree on what the optimal level of achieved functioning is, due to their different life plans. For example, not everybody wants to study until they are in their late 20s or early 30s to earn a PhD degree. Hence, if there is full equality in educational capability we would expect to see inequalities in achieved educational functioning. But there is no reason to expect that there would be *group-based* inequalities in achieved functionings that are due to innate differences. Gender inequalities in these achieved functionings thus point to gender inequalities in capabilities.

The difficulty lies in the third type of capabilities, which encompass social relations, political empowerment, domestic work and nonmarket care, and paid work. If we believe that these different outcomes in terms of functionings are explained by men's and women's different natures, and intrinsically different choices, then these inequalities are not of ethical concern. At most we could argue that the corresponding material rewards of women's and men's social position are not justified. For example, housewives should be financially protected and care labor should be better rewarded. According to this view, the fact that men and women are living segregated and gendered lives would not bother us from a justice point of view.[13] Indeed, some have even argued that today an injustice is done against women because they are not sufficiently supported in their traditional domestic roles, which is what they ultimately want (James Tooley 2002). In contrast, if we hold that gender differences are socially constructed and imposed on men and women, then the conclusion would be that the gender inequalities in achieved functionings are unjust, and the main ethical concern would be to abolish gender as we know it. There is no consensus over whether gendered choices are due to nature or to social upbringing. But as long as there is no consensus, we have to conclude, in line with John Stuart Mill (1869), Bubeck (1995) and Phillips (2003), that we do have convincing evidence that coercive social processes restrict and mold us. We do not know what men and women would choose if they were liberated from their gender roles and thus *genuinely* free to choose. But we do know that at the moment our choices are constrained unequally because the constraints on choices are structured along gender lines (Folbre 1994; Robeyns 2001a). Thus, the burden of proof falls on those who claim that women are "essentially" different.

VIII. WEIGHTS, AGGREGATIONS, AND OVERALL JUDGMENTS

How, if at all, should we weight the different capabilities in order to aggregate them into an overall evaluation? Obviously, we gain most insights into the nature and size of gender inequality if we look at inequalities in capabilities at the more disaggregated level. But one cannot conclude that women in general are worse off than men, or vice versa, without aggregating the functionings. In addition, for policy decisions and overall judgments, we need to decide whether all capabilities are equally important or whether we should give them different weights.

Can we draw a tentative and provisional conclusion on the nature and size of gender inequality in achieved functionings and thus, in capabilities? On gender differences in achieved functionings, the evidence on social interaction is inadequate to arrive at a firm conclusion. For life expectancy, housing, and bodily integrity, similarly, there is no strong evidence of gender inequality. For domestic and care work, and paid work, the evaluation is disputed, since both types of work can be either a burden or a pleasure. But for mental health, political empowerment, education and knowledge (except for language skills), leisure, time-autonomy, mobility, respect, and religion, the arguments and studies discussed above suggest that women's well-being is less than men's. This means that we can only conclude that women are equally well off or better off than men if we attach more weight to the functionings of reading skills and spending time in domestic and care work than we attach to all other functionings. Some people might value these functionings strongly, and therefore might not judge women's well-being to be worse than men's. But most people are unlikely to value domestic work and care as indisputably positive. Indeed, it is quite likely that most people would weight all other functionings taken together as more important than those in which women excel. In other words, my overall judgment would be that women in Western societies are worse off than men, since taken together the dimensions in which women are worse off are more important than those in which men lose out. Ultimately, making an overall judgment implies making a normative choice regarding the weights that should be assigned to different capabilities.

IX. CONCLUSION

In this chapter I have investigated how we can use the capability approach to study gender inequality. After arguing against the view that Sen's capability approach needs one definite list of capabilities, I proposed a methodology to select relevant capabilities. This methodology was applied to generate a list of capabilities for the study of gender inequality in Western societies and consisted of four steps. The first step was unconstrained brainstorming. The second was an engagement with the existing socio-economic literature and debates on gender inequality. Third, the generated list was compared with other lists. Fourth and finally, the list was debated at seminars and conferences, in informal discussions, and in feminist activist networks. In addition I took account of arguments in anti-feminist literature. To illustrate gender inequality in these dimensions, some empirical findings were discussed. Comments on the list and on the empirical findings led to subsequent revisions – a process which is likely to continue into the future.

I also argued that when looking at group inequalities, the default position should be that group inequalities in achieved functionings mirror inequalities in capabilities, unless there is a plausible reason to expect one group to systematically choose different functionings from its capability set relative to another group. Finally, I offered a tentative answer to the question whether in overall terms one can say that on average men are more advantaged than women. As noted, ultimately the answer depends on the weights that one attaches to the different functionings.

It is obvious that this is not a completed research project. There is much work to be done on furthering the capability approach to gender inequality analysis. On the empirical side we need carefully collected micro-data on all these capabilities. On the theoretical side, we need to further our understanding of the gendered nature of preference formation and the constraints on choice. Once we have a deeper analytical understanding of these phenomena, we can ask how we should deal with them in a normative framework. Progress on this front is especially important since many nonfeminist political philosophers and welfare economists tend to deny or ignore the gendered dimension of capabilities, which affects their normative conclusions.

ACKNOWLEDGMENTS

More people have commented on earlier versions of this chapter than I can possibly acknowledge here. Special thanks to Bina Agarwal and Jane Humphries who gave detailed and thought-provoking comments that led to substantial improvements, and to Serena Olsaretti, Roland Pierik, Amartya Sen, and Frances Woolley for other crucial comments. I also benefited from comments that I received at the Workshop on Amartya Sen's Work and Ideas held at All Souls College, Oxford (September 11–13, 2002), at the School of Development Studies, University of East Anglia, and at St. Edmund's College, Cambridge. I remain solely responsible, however, for the arguments and positions taken in the chapter. I am grateful for the financial support provided by the Cambridge Political Economy Society Trust, which supported my PhD research on which this article is based, and the Netherlands Organization of Scientific Research (NWO) for subsequent research funding.

NOTES

[1] A good introduction to these theories can be found in Will Kymlicka (2002).

[2] For references to this literature, see Bina Agarwal (1997).

[3] For a more detailed analysis of this problem, see Robeyns (2001b).

[4] This, of course, does not only hold for Nussbaum's list, but for any list with universal claims.

[5] Scholars who endorse Nussbaum's capability theory instead of Sen's approach, might argue that the fact that Sen only offers an approach and not a fully fleshed-out theory is exactly the problem, as it does not sufficiently inform us about how to apply it. I think such a claim would be unwarranted. Indeed, the application developed by Alkire (2002) on poverty reduction in small-scale NGO projects in Pakistan, and the measurement of gender inequality in achieved functionings for Britain (Ingrid Robeyns 2002: Ch. 7) illustrate that it is perfectly possible to use Sen's framework to address normative questions and come to definite evaluations.

[6] Some of these aspects would be common to developing countries, but to contextualize my discussion I have chosen to concentrate on developed countries and their relevant literature.

[7] This raises the issue of abortion, which lies beyond the scope of this paper.

[8] Over the past few decades, the male-to-female birth ratio declined significantly in some developed countries. But this is attributed to general factors such as chronic exposure to environmental toxins, including those from smoking, rather than to gender bias (Misao Fukuda, Kiyomi Fukuda, Takashi Shimizu, Claus Yding Andersen, and Anne Grete Byskov 2002).

[9] Obviously race is another important determinant of mortality. For example, African-American men have significantly worse age-specific survival rates than white American men, or men from China or parts of India (Sen 1998).

[10] Mental well-being should also include serious mental disorders. However, in the illustrative empirical overview of this article, I do not discuss gender differences in mental disorders.

[11] Goldberg and Williams do not give a precise description of these "comparable social circumstances," but their discussion focuses only on comparing men and women who are holding the same job.

[12] Focusing on capability and not on achieved functionings implies that we do not need to be concerned about persons who have this capability but deliberately put their achieved functioning at risk. Boxers or rugby players are cases in point.

[13] However, from an efficiency point of view it might in that case still be better if highly talented women would work on the labor market instead of staying at home.

REFERENCES

Agarwal, Bina. 1994. "Gender and Command Over Property: A Critical Gap in Economic Analysis and Policy in South Asia." *World Development* 22(10): 1455–78.

——. 1997. " 'Bargaining' and Gender Relations: Within and Beyond the Household." *Feminist Economics* 3(1): 1–51.

Alkire, Sabina. 2002. *Valuing Freedoms. Sen's Capability Approach and Poverty Reduction.* Oxford, UK: Oxford University Press.

—— and Rufus Black. 1997. "A Practical Reasoning Theory of Development Ethics: Furthering the Capabilities Approach." *Journal of International Development* 9(2): 263–79.

Arber, Sara and Myriam Khlat. 2002. "Introduction to: Social and Economic Patterning of Women's Health in a Changing World." *Social Science and Medicine* 54: 643–7.

Banks, Ian. 2001. "No Man's Land: Men, Illness and the NHS." *British Medical Journal* 323: 1058–60.

Bittman, Michael and Judy Wajcman. 2000. "The Rush Hour: The Character of Leisure Time and Gender Equity." *Social Forces* 79(1): 165–89.

Blau, Francine. 1998. "Trends in the Well-Being of American Women, 1970–1995." *Journal of Economic Literature* 36: 112–65.

Bratt, Rachel. 2002. "Housing and Family Well-Being." *Housing Studies* 14(1): 13–26.

Bruynooghe, Rosemarie, Sigrid Noelanders, and Sybille Opdebeeck. 2000. "Vreedzame Samenleving Nog Niet in Zicht. Geweld als Maatschappelijk Probleem voor Mannen en Vrouwen," in *CGSO-jaarboek*. Gent: CGSO.

Bubeck, Diemut. 1995. *Care, Gender and Justice.* Oxford, UK: Clarendon Press.

Champernowne, D. G. and Frank Cowell. 1998. *Economic Inequality and Income Distribution.* Cambridge, UK: Cambridge University Press.

Chiappero, Martinetti Enrica. 2000. "A Multidimensional Assessment of Well-Being based on Sen's Functioning Theory." *Rivista Internazionale di Scienza Sociali* 108(2): 207–39.

Clark, Andrew. 1997. "Job Satisfaction and Gender: Why Are Women so Happy at Work?" *Labour Economics* 4: 341–72.

Connell, Robert. 1989. "Cool Guys, Swots and Wimps: The Interplay of Masculinity and Education." *Oxford Review of Education* 15(3): 291–303.

Cowell, Frank. 1995. *Measuring Inequality.* Hemel Hempstead, UK: Prentice-Hall/Harvester Wheatsheaf.

Davis, Keith and Irene Hanson Frieze. 2000. "Research on Stalking: What Do We Know and Where Do We Go?" *Violence and Victims* 15(4): 473–87.

Dijkstra, A. Geske and Hanmer, Lucia C. 2000. "Measuring Socio-Economic Gender Inequality: Toward an Alternative to the UNDP Gender-Related Development Index." *Feminist Economics* 6(2): 41–75.

Doyal, Lesley. 2000. "Gender Equity in Health: Debates and Dilemmas." *Social Science and Medicine* 51: 931–9.

Duindam, Vincent. 1999. "Men in the Household: Caring Fathers," in Linda McKie, Sophia Bowlby, and Susan Gregory (eds.) *Gender, Power and the Household.* London: Macmillan.

Erikson, Robert. 1992. "Descriptions of Inequality: The Swedish Approach to Welfare Research," in Martha Nussbaum and Amartya Sen (eds.) *The Quality of Life.* Oxford, UK: Clarendon Press.

—— and Rune Åberg. 1987. *Welfare in Transition. A Survey of Living Conditions in Sweden 1968–1981.* Oxford, UK: Clarendon Press.

Folbre, Nancy. 1994. *Who Pays for the Kids? Gender and the Structures of Constraint.* New York: Routledge.

——. 2001. *The Invisible Heart. Economics and Family Values.* New York: The New Press.

Fuchs, Victor. 1988. *Women's Quest for Economic Equality.* Cambridge, MA: Harvard University Press.

Fuhrer, R., S. A. Stansfeld, J. Chemali, and M. J. Shipley. 1999. "Gender, Social Relations and Mental Health: Prospective Findings from an Occupational Cohort (Whitehall II Study)." *Social Science and Medicine* 48: 77–87.

Fukuda, Misao, Kiyomi Fukuda, Takashi Shimizu, Claus Yding Andersen, and Anne Grete Byskov. 2002. "Parental Periconceptional Smoking and Male:Female Ratio of Newborn Infants." *The Lancet* 359: 1407–8.

Glorieux, Ignace, Suzanna Koelet, and Maarten Moens. 2001. "Tijdsbesteding van de Vlamingen: een tijdsbudget-onderzoek bij een repressatieve steekproef van Vlamingen," in Ministerie van de Vlaamse Gemeenschap (ed.) *Vlaanderen gepeild! De Vlaamse Overheid en Burgeronderzoek,* pp. 157–84. Brussels: Ministerie van de Vlaamse Gemeenschap.

Goldberg, David and Paul Williams. 1988. *A User's Guide to the General Health Questionnaire.* London: NFER-Nelson.

Goodman, Alissa, Paul Johnson, and Steven Webb. 1997. *Inequality in the UK.* Oxford, UK: Oxford University Press.

Grisez, Germain, Joseph Boyle, and John Finnis. 1987. "Practical Principles, Moral Truth and Ultimate Ends." *American Journal of Jurisprudence* 32: 99–151.

Himmelweit, Susan (ed.). 2000. *Inside the Household: From Labour to Care.* Basingstoke, UK: Macmillan.

Humphries, Jane. 1993. "Gender Inequality and Economic Development," in Dieter Bös (ed.) *Economics in a Changing World. Vol. 3: Public Policy and Economics Organization,* pp. 218–33. Basingstoke, UK: Macmillan.

Hunt, Kate and Ellen Annandale. 1999. "Editorial: Relocating Gender and Morbidity: Examining Men's and Women's Health in Contemporary Western Societies." *Social Science and Medicine* 48: 1–5.

Inter-Parliamentary Union 2002. Women in National Parliaments. World Classification. Available at http://www.ipu.org/wmn-e/classif.htm (accessed November 5, 2002).

Khlat, Myriam, Catherine Sermet, and Annick Le Pape. 2000. "Women's Health in Relation with their Family and Work Roles: France in the Early 1990s." *Social Science and Medicine* 50: 1807–25.

Kymlicka, Will. 2002. *Contemporary Political Philosophy*. Oxford, UK: Oxford University Press.

Lahelma, Eero, Pekka Martikainen, Ossi Rahkonen, and Karri Silventoinen. 1999. "Gender Differences in Illhealth in Finland: Patterns, Magnitude and Change." *Social Science and Medicine* 48: 7–19.

Lelli, Sara. 2001. "Factor Analysis vs. Fuzzy Sets Theory: Assessing the Influence of Different Techniques on Sen's Functioning Approach." Discussion Paper 01.21, Center for Economic Studies, Katholieke Universiteit Leuven.

Lundberg, Shelly, Robert Pollak, and Terence Wales. 1997. "Do Husband and Wives Pool Their Resources? Evidence from the United Kingdom Child Benefit." *Journal of Human Resources* 32(3): 463–80.

MacKinnon, Catharine. 1982. "Feminism, Marxism, Method and the State: An Agenda for Theory." *Signs* 7(3): 515–44.

Menon, Nivedita. 2002. "Universalism without Foundations?" *Economy and Society* 31(1): 152–69.

Mill, John Stuart. 1869. *The Subjection of Women*. Cambridge, MA: MIT Press, reprinted 1970.

Mirrlees-Black, Catriona. 1999. *Domestic Violence: Findings from a New British Survey Self-Completion Questionnaire*. London: Home Office.

Munch, Allison, J. Miller McPherson, and Lynn Smith-Lovin. 1997. "Gender, Children, and Social Contact: The Effects of Childrearing for Men and Women," *American Sociological Review* 62(4): 509–20.

Nussbaum, Martha. 1988. "Nature, Function and Capability: Aristotle on Political Distribution." *Oxford Studies in Ancient Philosophy*, Supplementary Volume: pp. 145–84.

——. 1995. "Human Capabilities, Female Human Beings," in Martha Nussbaum and Jonathan Glover (eds.) *Women, Culture and Development: A Study of Human Capabilities*, pp. 61–104. Oxford, UK: Clarendon Press.

——. 2000. *Women and Human Development. The Capabilities Approach*. Cambridge, UK: Cambridge University Press.

——. 2003. "Capabilities as Fundamental Entitlements: Sen and Social Justice." *Feminist Economics,* this issue.

OECD 2001. *The Programme for International Students Assessment Database,* Executive Summary. Available at http://www.pisa.oecd.org (Accessed June 2002).

Okin, Susan. 1989. *Justice, Gender and the Family*. New York: Basic Books.

Pahl, Jan. 1989. *Money and Marriage*. Basingstoke, UK: Macmillan.

Peter, Fabienne. 2003. "Gender and the Foundations of Social Choice: The Role of Situated Agency." *Feminist Economics,* this issue.

Phillips, Anne. 1999. *Which Equalities Matter?* Cambridge, UK: Polity Press.

——. Forthcoming 2003. "Defending Equality of Outcome." *Journal of Political Philosophy* 11(2).

Phipps, Shelley and Peter Burton. 1995. "Sharing within Families: Implications for the Measurement of Poverty among Individuals in Canada." *Canadian Journal of Economics* 28(1): 177–204.

——, Peter Burton, and Lars Osberg. 2001. "Time as a Source of Inequality within Marriage: Are Husbands More Satisfied with Time for Themselves than Wives?" *Feminist Economics* 7(2): 1–21.

Qizilbash, Mozaffar. 2002. "Development, Common Foes and Shared Values." *Review of Political Economy* 14(4): 463–80.

93

Robeyns, Ingrid. 2001a. "Will a Basic Income do Justice to Women?" *Analyse und Kritik* 23(1): 88–105.

———. 2001b. "Sen's Capability Approach and Feminist Concerns." Presented at the Conference on Sen's Capability Approach. St. Edmund's College, Cambridge, UK.

———. 2002. *Gender Inequality. A Capability Perspective.* Doctoral dissertation, Cambridge University, UK.

Rubery, Jill, Mark Smith, and Colette Fagan. 1999. *Women's Employment in Europe. Trends and Prospects.* London: Routledge.

Sen, Amartya. 1973. *On Economic Inequality.* Reprinted in 1997 by Clarendon Press, Oxford, UK.

———. 1985. *Commodities and Capabilities.* Reprinted in 1999 by Oxford University Press, Delhi.

———. 1987. *The Standard of Living.* Cambridge, UK: Cambridge University Press.

———. 1992. *Inequality Reexamined.* Oxford, UK: Oxford University Press.

———. 1993. "Capability and Well-Being," in Martha Nussbaum and Amartya Sen (eds.) *The Quality of Life*, pp. 30–53. Oxford, UK: Clarendon Press.

———. 1995. "Gender Inequality and Theories of Justice," in Martha Nussbaum and Jonathan Glover (eds.) *Women, Culture and Development: A Study of Human Capabilities*, pp. 259–73. Oxford: Clarendon Press.

———. 1997. "Maximization and the Act of Choice." *Econometrica* 65(4): 745–79.

———. 1998. "Mortality as an Indicator of Economic Success and Failure." *Economic Journal* 108: 1–25.

———. 2001. "Why Health Equity?" Keynote address to the Third International Conference on "The Economics of Health: Within and Beyond Health Care," York, UK, July 23.

Smith, William and Marie Torstensson. 1997. "Gender Differences in Risk Perception and Neutralizing Fear of Crime." *British Journal of Criminology* 37(4): 608–34.

Spitzberg, Brian. 1999. "An Analysis of Empirical Estimates of Sexual Aggression, Victimization and Perpetration." *Violence and Victims* 14(3): 241–60.

Tooley, James. 2002. *The Miseducation of Women.* London: Continuum.

UNDP 1995. Human Development Report. Oxford, UK: Oxford University Press.

Warrington, Molly and Michael Younger. 2000. "The Other Side of the Gender Gap." *Gender and Education* 12(4): 493–508.

Woolley, Frances and Judith Marshall. 1994. "Measuring Inequality Within the Household." *Review of Income and Wealth* 40(4): 415–31.

World Health Organization 2000. The World Health Report 2000. Geneva: WHO.

INTRA-HOUSEHOLD INEQUALITY: A CHALLENGE FOR THE CAPABILITY APPROACH?

Vegard Iversen

OVERVIEW

In this chapter, the author examines the capability approach and how it applies in the context of individuals and families living together on unequal terms. The interpretations of agency, freedom, and choice in Sen's framework are analyzed from a feminist perspective, and the author suggests that these important concepts invite special attention in the presence of domestic power imbalances. Problems with the interpretations embedded in the capability approach are pinpointed and adjustments proposed. Drawing on the vast literature on household behavior in developing countries, the author argues that capabilities have a distinctly interdependent dimension. While the discussion of agency in the capability approach has been either normative or policy-oriented, exercises that seek to evaluate individual well-being should pay more attention to the existence of alternative types of power within the realm of the household.

INTRODUCTION

Amartya Sen's capability approach provides a framework for evaluating the quality of life. This task is immensely important, especially in developing countries.[1] While conventional measures of deprivation are often based on income inadequacy, the capability approach is multidimensional and facilitates interpersonal comparisons of opportunities for achieving well-being. The concepts of functionings and capabilities occupy central space in this endeavor. Functionings reflect the various things a person manages "to do or be in leading a life" (Amartya Sen 1993). There are basic functionings, such as being adequately nourished, having decent shelter, and being able to read and write, as well as more complex functionings, such as achieving self-respect. A person's capability, or well-being freedom, reflects the alternative combinations of functionings he or she can achieve. The phrase "development as freedom" is closely, but not exclusively, associated with an enhancement of well-being freedom (Amartya Sen 1999).

A particularly valuable feature of the capability approach, which gives it an edge over the work of John Rawls (1971) and others, is the acknowledgment that the possession of resources or commodities may be an inadequate indicator of well-being freedom. In judging the well-being of a person, Amartya Sen (1985b: 6) argues, one should avoid limiting the analysis to the characteristics of the goods possessed. Figure 1 provides a representation of the capability approach, reproduced from Ingrid Robeyns (2000). In contrast to Rawls (1971), Sen has shaped his framework to take into account the impact individual characteristics and social arrangements may have on a person's ability to convert resources or commodities such as Rawlsian primary goods into valuable functionings. As a result fundamental disparities in individual opportunities to achieve well-being may exist among persons who possess equal amounts of a prim-ary good. As Figure 1 illustrates and Ingrid Robeyns (2001) has noted, the movement from capability to achieved functionings requires an act of choice.

Notwithstanding these attractive properties of Sen's framework, a central tenet of my argument in this chapter is that in interpersonal comparisons it is necessary to recognize that capabilities often have a distinctly interdependent dimension. Such interdependencies are parti-cularly pronounced within the realm of the household, where extensive conflict often coexists with pervasive cooperation (Amartya Sen 1990a). While sharing and caring distinguishes the domestic from other arenas of exchange, the focus, in this chapter, will be on how domestic power imbalances, often with a gender connotation, generate inequality and mediate opportunities to achieve well-being among household members. This reality poses two types of challenges for the capability approach.

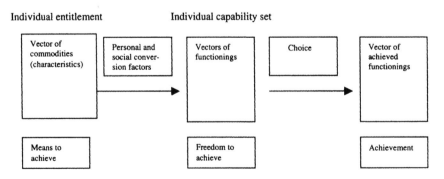

Figure 1 A schematic representation of the capability approach
Source: Robeyns (2000).

First, a framework geared at capability evaluation must rely on articulations of key concepts like agency, freedom, and choice, which are sufficiently sensitive to the presence of domestic power imbalances of this kind. The first part of the chapter therefore examines the robustness of these concepts within the capability approach, at some length. Second, how can the capability approach deal with gendered power imbalances within the household? In the second part of this chapter, I argue that the recent theoretical and empirical literature on household behavior in developing countries can provide valuable guidance to efforts to evaluate individual well-being, by uncovering the material and nonmaterial foundations of power and intra-household inequality, and shedding light on why and how individual capabilities are interconnected.

Following brief reviews of the literature on intra-household allocations and Sen's critique of welfarism, I examine possible inconsistencies between two important areas of Sen's work: namely, whether his ideas and reasoning on gender and intra-household inequality are compatible with the capability approach. In Section II, I focus on the notions of freedom embedded in the capability approach and how these ideas square with domestic power imbalances. Section III underscores the need to recognize and account for the interconnected dimension of individual capabilities. Finally, using a Nash-bargaining framework as a backdrop, I discuss whether the ideas about power and agency in Sen's writings provide a sufficient foundation for interpersonal comparisons.

I. INTRA-HOUSEHOLD DISTRIBUTION

Methodological individualism is a central tenet of the theory of consumer choice, which presumes that observed market behavior will reveal individual preferences. The notion that market behavior mirrors maximization of individual utility functions, subject to well-defined budget constraints, is, of course, tenuous. Most people live together in groups, as members of coveted units of social organization, which are usually multi-person families or households. To be persuasive, interpretations of observed market demand, labor supply, or intra-household resource allocation must accommodate this elementary, yet pivotal fact.

Until recently, most economists were quite content with treating households as if their members had congruent interests (Paul Samuelson 1956; Gary Becker 1965).[2] While accommodating this notion, the assumptions of a joint utility function or that a dictatorial household head determined resource allocation also provided analytical convenience, effectively extending standard consumer theory to collectives of individuals.[3] Over the last two decades, however, reservations about this unitary perspective have intensified among economists and other social scientists.[4] Apart from losing ground in rigorous tests, the unitary paradigm has been much weakened by its failure to persuasively explain systematic intra-household disparities in developing countries.[5]

The Nash-bargaining models of marriage developed by Marilyn Manser and Murray Brown (1980) and Marjorie B. McElroy and Mary J. Horney (1981) introduced economic power and bargaining into the domestic arena. In a Nash-bargain model of marriage, the intra-household allocation of resources is determined by what has broadly been termed the bargaining power of the two spouses.[6] As Nancy Folbre has eloquently argued (1986: 251):

> The suggestion that women and female children "voluntarily" relinquish leisure, education, and food would be somewhat more persuasive if they were in a position to demand their fair share. It is the juxtaposition of women's lack of economic power with the unequal allocation of household resources that lends the bargaining power approach much of its persuasive appeal.[7]

Folbre's (1986) focus on gendered differences in opportunities to achieve well-being within the household is closely tied to the central tenet of the capability approach. While the bargaining literature seeks to unpack the determinants of intra-household inequality by focusing on alternative types of power and their material and nonmaterial foundations, the capability approach is concerned with evaluating opportunities. If an unequal balance of power affects the intra-household distribution of goods and services (or, in the capability approach, "the means to achieve"), it is necessary for interpersonal comparisons of opportunities to account for this.

Compared with its unitary predecessors, the bargaining perspective complicates interpretations of market behavior and intra-household distribution. By considering not only individual interests but also the differential abilities to act on those interests. The focus on power and gender relations makes the bargaining perspective particularly attractive as a backdrop for a discussion of the capability approach.[8]

Central to Sen's development of the capability approach is his critique of welfarism. The foundations for his rejection of welfarism as a basis for evaluating well-being are widely recognized.[9] Apart from being insensitive to distributional concerns, conventional utilitarian ethics interprets utility as a mental state of happiness, as desire-fulfillment or merely as choice (Amartya Sen 1985a, 1985b). These mental state and desire-fulfillment interpretations of utility ignore potentially important aspects of a person's well-being – being happy is only one among numerous relevant dimensions that add to well-being. A core argument against welfarism, according to Robert Sugden (1993: 1947) is that "the informational base of welfarism is too thin to support an acceptable – and perhaps even a coherent – account of the social good."

Sen also rejects individual preferences as foundations for evaluating well-being, since rather than being immutable, preferences are endogenous or adaptive. In short, "our desires and pleasure-taking abilities adjust to circumstances, especially to make life bearable in adverse situations" (Sen 1999: 62).[10] The circumstances that prompt adaptation are, however, less transparent. While destitution is one such circumstance, it is not, in general, clear when and how domestic power imbalances might spur similar adjustments.[11] Philip Pettit (2001), Robeyns (2001), and other scholars recognize that domestic hierarchies may mold preferences, and Sen (1999: 63) mentions "hopelessly subdued housewives in severely sexist cultures" as a candidate category. Below, I propose that domestic hierarchies can deform individual preferences in other ways.

Sen's otherwise powerful critique does not address the individualistic nature of welfarism. In contrast, his seminal contributions to the theoretical and empirical literature on household behavior reveal an acute sensitivity to the modifying influence that the institution of the family may have on individual freedom, agency, and choice. To answer whether the capability approach reflects a similar prudence, we need to revisit Sen's own reasoning on intra-household inequality.[12]

In critiquing the bilateral Nash-bargaining model of marriage, Sen (1990a) argues that the feature that fallback positions or disagreement points alone determine bargaining power and therefore intra-household distribution is based on a too narrow informational base. A theory that aims to explain intra-household inequality should also, according to Sen, accommodate what he terms "the perceived interest response" (and the "perceived contributions response").[13] His focus on how a person might perceive his/her own self-interest is particularly relevant for the present discussion. He notes (1990a: 136):

> Given other things, if the self-interest perception of one of the persons were to attach less value to his or her own well-being, then the collusive solution, if different, would be less favorable to that person, in terms of well-being.

In short, he argues that women in traditional societies may lack a notion of personal welfare because their identities are too closely tied to the interests of the household. This overlap between personal and household interests preserves intra-household inequality. The explanation is simple and may not, on closer inspection, warrant novel theorizing. If a woman in a standard Nash-bargaining model perceives the welfare of other household members as on a par with her own, intra-household distribution would tally with this interest perception.[14]

More importantly, Sen views this ambivalence of female interests as closely associated with a curtailment of the agency aspect of personhood. Sen (1990a: 148–9) notes:

Our actual agency role is often overshadowed by social rules and by conventional perceptions of legitimacy. In the case of gender divisions, these convictions often act as barriers to seeking a more equitable deal, and sometimes militate even against recognizing the spectacular lack of equity in the existing social arrangements.

As an example, consider the situation of a poor woman, Nirmala. If developing the agency aspect of Nirmala's personhood is instrumental to her achievement of equality and well-being within the household, it is reasonable to expect this aspect of her agency to provide information that will be relevant to an evaluation of her opportunities to achieve well-being. For individuals co-residing in households, at least two issues now invite attention. First, the evolution of a distinct identity or self will increase a woman's perception of self-interest and prompt the perceived interest response (or its equivalent in a bilateral Nash bargain). It could perhaps be argued that the presence of a distinct self is integral to or taken for granted in the capability approach and therefore not a matter of concern in evaluative exercises (that is, exercises that seek to measure and/or assess individual well-being and social states). This might well be a reasonable assertion in nontraditional societies. In traditional societies, in contrast, a woman's opportunities for achieving well-being would depend on very basic aspects of her agency. Second, and more interestingly, we may ask what affects Nirmala's ability to take actions that further her interests within the household.

Whereas Naila Kabeer (1999) and other feminist scholars, in addressing gender relations within and beyond the household, have sought to articulate and gain insights into the multiple facets of female agency under the purview of a process of female empowerment, Sen's *theoretical* focus, as indicated by his discussions of agency freedom (Sen 1985a, 1993), has been normative, and concerned with what a person can be or do in line with her perception of the good. In other work, notably Sen (1990a, 1999), the discussions have been more policy-oriented focusing, in particular, on female labor-force participation and literacy, which he sees as means of strengthening women's agency and intra-household bargaining power. While the latter focus undoubtedly has considerable appeal in a policy discourse, it is unlikely to provide an adequate account of those aspects of female agency that merit attention in evaluative exercises.[15] In carrying out such exercises, it may therefore be quite necessary to acquire more in-depth knowledge about the pluralistic aspects of female agency that enable women to mediate intra-household power relations, improving their opportunities for achieving well-being. Section II elaborates on this argument.

II. DEVELOPMENT AS FREEDOM

Sen (1999: 3) perceives "development as a process of expanding the real freedoms that people enjoy." While a conventional well-being evaluation would focus on achievements, Sen (1985a) distinguishes between well-being freedom and agency freedom. Well-being freedom reflects the capability of having various functioning vectors and raises the informational stakes of an evaluative exercise. In other words, it requires the evaluator to have knowledge about opportunities and not just about the more easily detected outcomes. The capability approach evaluates the functionings available for individuals to choose rather than, or in addition to, the functionings they eventually achieve. Flavio Comim (2001) refers to the latter as the counterfactual nature of the capability approach. According to Robeyns (2001: 4):

> The capability approach stipulates that an evaluation of individual or social states should focus on people's real or substantive freedoms to lead the lives they find valuable. This real freedom is called a person's capability. Someone's capability hence refers to her empowerment, the power that she has to be the person she wants to be and to have the kind of life she wants to lead.

Thus, the capability approach focuses on the positive or real freedoms that people enjoy and Robeyns (2001) claims that capability represents an individual's "empowerment." Later, I will examine how these notions about real freedom and empowerment in the capability approach square with ideas about agency in the feminist literature.

Notions of freedom and the capability approach

What are the notions of freedom embedded in the capability approach? Moving from capabilities to functionings, as noted, requires an act of choice (Robeyns 2001). While Mozaffar Qizilbash (2001) points out that choosing itself is a valuable functioning, the act of choosing, or what Sen (1985a) terms "procedural" or "choice-mediated" control, is not granted lexical priority by Sen himself.[16]

Consider, first, the relationship between freedom and choice. If I make a choice between two alternatives, call them A and B, I will exercise direct freedom or choice-mediated control (Sen 1985a). Indirect freedom or effective power is a more subtle notion; it enables me to determine which alternative is chosen – A or B – without my active exercise of choice (Pettit 2001). So if somebody chooses on my behalf, and my preferred choice is A, then A will be chosen by my "representative." Although I am not myself actively involved in choosing, I am still in the driver's seat. I exercise effective power.[17] Note that this distinction between *choice-mediated* control

101

and *effective* power is important in practice since effective power (indirect freedom) is considered adequate for the capability approach (Amartya Sen 2001: 52).

Probing Sen's interpretations of freedom embedded in the capability approach, Pettit (2001) argues that effective power may be contingent on the favors or goodwill of those around you. This leaves the capability approach vulnerable to critique:

> Whatever you obtain as a result of your preferences, then, you obtain by virtue of your good fortune in having masters or betters who look kindly on you; by virtue of your success in securing their complacence; or by virtue of your cunning in managing to avoid their notice. You may be said to have decisive preferences [effective power] but their decisiveness is favor-dependent.
>
> (Pettit 2001: 6).

According to Pettit, an acceptable notion of freedom must not be favor-dependent since "the enjoyment of favor-dependent effective power is quite consistent with the person's living in a position of total subjugation to another...." (Pettit 2001: 7). To resolve this problem, Pettit proposes that a new requirement be added to the capability approach: effective power should not be favor- or context-dependent. This apparently reasonable requirement, and Sen's (2001) reluctance to endorse it, merits attention.

To attract the interest of a feminist audience, replace the phrase "master" in the above quotation with "patriarchal head of household." A failure to accommodate Pettit's requirement would now lead to the endorsement of a notion of freedom in which effective power requires a willingness to "bribe" the master. Such "bribes" could, as noted, involve acts of strong subordination, and therefore undermine the fundamental thrust of a freedom-based concept of well-being. This example has striking parallels with the literature on informal, rural institutions in developing countries. Landlords may have an incentive to safeguard a higher level of well-being (interpreted in a narrow sense) for agricultural laborers, in exchange for the willingness of some laborers to forgo certain aspects of their freedom by committing themselves to providing peak season labor (Pranab Bardhan 1983). Alternatively, in a theory that stresses stronger subordination, Julie Schaffner (1995) adds servility requirements and landlords' interest in "limiting the horizons" of permanent laborers. Servility is manifested in the additional services permanent laborers are expected to provide. These services confer social and political prestige on the landlords.

In the first version of this example, annual contracts protect laborers against the vagaries of spot markets and seasonal fluctuations. One could argue that many voluntary cooperative ventures involve some sacrifices of individual freedom. The second version is the more striking, and here the validity of Pettit's complaint would hinge on the degree of subordination necessary to achieve effective power. In other words, the persuasive power of Pettit's argument is circumstantial, but nevertheless forceful.[18]

Sen argues that in performing well-being evaluations, it is necessary to prioritize certain types of freedom. He thus grants Pettit has a point, noting (2001: 54), "the capability and the republican [Pettit's] approach concentrate on different aspects of freedom and both have importance." Despite recognizing Pettit's point, however, Sen (2001) insists on leaving the capability approach intact. He defends this intransigence by giving an example of a disabled person who can only leave her house with the help of volunteers. The counterfactual is that, in the absence of such assistance, she will be stuck at home. Sen argues that applying Pettit's requirement would render her "unfree" when the assistants are around, while the capability approach would consider her to be free because she is able to leave the house. In my view this example does not do justice to the serious nature of Pettit's concern. The explanation may be that Sen's example stems from an asymmetry between people caused by differences in physical needs, whereas Pettit focuses on asymmetries attributable to social or interpersonal power imbalances.

Given Sen's concern for gendered intra-household inequality, his reluctance to give weight to Pettit's argument is somewhat puzzling; by not doing so, he appears to endorse the view that even strong imbalances in conjugal relations may be immaterial to a freedom-based evaluation of well-being. If taken seriously, the capability approach would be unable to distinguish between a woman who lives in an oppressive household and must go to extraordinary lengths to appease her spouse, and another woman who can readily exercise her preferences. While Sen constantly mentions, as a valuable functioning, the importance of being able to appear in public without shame, his rejection of Pettit's argument seems to imply that addressing conjugal humiliation and servility is a lower priority. It is therefore difficult to see how the capability approach can remain immune to Pettit's complaint.

Effective power and hierarchy

In his discussions of freedom in relation to choice, Sen endorses effective power as adequate for the capability approach. For example, he argues (1985b: 208–9): "It does not matter for effective power precisely how the choices are 'executed.' Indeed the choices may not be directly addressed." His reasons for downplaying procedural or choice-mediated control stem from the practical intricacies of social living: "The contrast between effective power and procedural control is important in practice. It is often not possible to organize society in such a way that people can directly exercise the levers that control all the important aspects of their personal lives" (1985b: 210). In a more recent version of the same argument, he noted, "We live in a world in which being completely independent of the help and goodwill of others may be particularly difficult to achieve, and sometimes may not be the most important to achieve" (Sen 2001: 56).

In these passages, Sen defends effective power as a satisfactory notion of freedom in relation to choice in the capability approach. He is, of course, quite right to affirm that complete independence from others is unrealistic and not always important. However, aside from Pettit's critique, this position may provoke unease for other reasons. While Sen's appeal to indirect freedom may be acceptable in societies in which women have well-developed skills in deliberation and analysis in general, it is likely to be problematic in developing societies characterized by hierarchical domestic realms. For instance, tension may arise from a conflict between indirect freedom and the unfolding of potentially vital aspects of women's agency. Suppose a husband and wife inhabit a society in which the direct execution of choices strengthens individual abilities to deliberate on and make carefully considered and important decisions.[19] If we now superimpose an intra-household structure of authority, in which the husband always makes decisions on the wife's behalf, Sen's defense of indirect freedom as satisfactory for the capability approach may become untenable.

To see why, consider the following account from rural Bangladesh, where Naila Kabeer (2001) found, in a subset of households in her case study, that women were responsible for important managerial decisions within their households, even prior to the introduction by aid organizations of micro credit schemes. These women were particularly competent managers, and their experience of being in charge would be distinctly different from, say, being party to a consultation in which a husband makes a concerted effort to elicit the wife's preference on an important matter. The direct exercise of choice would, in this case, involve much responsibility, while mere consultations over time could mold the maturation of female preferences such responsibility would nourish. By overlooking this possible curtailment of the development of female preferences by the authoritarian household structure, the appeal to indirect freedom would appear to brush aside a concern for female agency associated with learning from responsibility associated with active choice.

One should note, however, that granting lexical priority to choice-mediated control might make the capability approach vulnerable to another important complaint. As an illustration, consider a simple analogy from Gary Becker's Rotten Kid Theorem. According to Becker (1981), a (male) household head, while acting altruistically, will condition income transfers to his partner on her choices. This gives him considerable power over her. Intra-household inequality in resource control is a prerequisite for transfers to occur, and Becker's theory reminds us that there may be good grounds for skepticism about endorsing choice-mediated control as a robust indicator of freedom and agency in developing countries (where transfers could make a critical difference) and elsewhere. Feminist and other analyses must be sensitive to the possibility that apparently autonomous choices can be exercised under serious covert or overt duress.

Note also the commonalities between Pettit's and Becker's arguments. In both cases, it would seem, choosers succumb to "bribes." These bribes take distinctly different forms, in Pettit's case as acts of subordination and in the Beckerian case as resource transfers. While Becker's theory makes it unambiguously difficult to accept choice-mediated control as a robust indicator of freedom, Pettit focuses on what these acts of subordination do to the dignity of the subordinate person. Could Pettit's argument be interpreted to give rise to further suspicion about choice-mediated control as a robust indicator of freedom within households? Under most circumstances the answer would be no, but it could happen if effective power is indeed favor-dependent.

Freedom and agency

In light of the preceding discussion, it is important to carefully deliberate on the aspects of freedom and empowerment that merit attention in evaluations.[20] Naila Kabeer (1999: 438) proposes a pluralistic and multi-dimensional interpretation of agency as

> . . . the ability to define one's goals and act upon them. Agency is about more than observable action; it also encompasses the meaning, moti-vation and purpose which individuals bring to their activity, their sense of agency, or "the power within." While agency tends to be operatio-nalized as "decision-making" in the social science literature, it can take a number of other forms. It can take the form of bargaining and negotiation, deception and manipulation, subversion and resis-tance, as well as more intangible, cognitive processes of reflection and analysis. It can be exercised by individuals as well as by collectiv-ities.

Among other issues, the current discussion is concerned with aspects of agency that affect an individual's opportunities to achieve well-being within the realm of the household. The appeal of the above definition lies in its openness about overt and covert manifestations of agency, in the shape of either genuine overt autonomy in strategic life-choices or more covert talents that correct for women's relative disadvantage within the household. A persuasive framework for well-being evaluation cannot, *a priori*, remain oblivious to such manifestations of abilities to exercise power. The interesting question, then, must be whether or not such skills strengthen real opportunities. I grant that it has yet to be established that overlooking these aspects of female agency indicates a shortfall in the capability approach. As noted above, broad policy debates can afford to be less preoccupied with attention to detail than evaluative exercises. Any conclusions on this matter would need to be guided by balanced theoretical reasoning, and, eventually, by persuasive empirical evidence. In the section below I examine how a person's individual attributes and skills can also affect her agency.

Individual and social heterogeneity

A main goal of the capability approach is capturing the importance of human diversity in judging advantage (Robeyns 2000). The ability to deal with the conversion of commodity characteristics into functionings is a central tenet of Robeyns's (2000) claim that Sen's framework is sensitive to the attributes of individuals (intelligence, metabolism, etc.) and societies (gender roles, institutions, etc.). Let f_i represent a personal utilization function, which reflects one pattern of commodity use individual i can achieve, converting characteristics of commodities into a functioning vector (see Figure 1).

The capacity to convert commodity characteristics into functionings is subject to interpersonal variation; the standard example is the conversion of food into being well nourished, which depends on a person's physical attributes, activity patterns, and other factors. The general point "in judging the well-being of a person [is not] to limit the analysis to the characteristics of the goods possessed (Sen 1985b: 6)." Let F_i be the set of utilization functions available to i. i's capabilities (or freedom) now correspond to i's feasible functioning vectors determined by the personal features represented by F_i and individual endowments of resources or commodities. Note that "commodities" should be interpreted broadly and include publicly provided services, such as healthcare and education. Is this framework sufficiently sensitive to the influence of domestic power imbalances on individual opportunities to achieve well-being? Robeyns (2001: 7–8) argues that the curtailment of freedoms by, say, structural constraints imposed by gender or class can be accommodated by the capability approach: "The point is that the more a person deviates from the model of an unattached healthy worker who has substantial control over his life, the more other factors influence the mapping from income onto well-being." Moreover,

> The conversion of the characteristics of commodities into functionings can also differ between individuals. Some of these differences are individual like those related to physical handicaps: a crippled person will need a wheelchair to be mobile, whereas a healthy person will not ... Other differences between people will be structural, related to gender, class, race and so forth.

While a government-provided adult literacy class may be open to individuals of both sexes, female participation may, by way of illustration, be curtailed by group-dependent constraints such as norm-driven labor obligations. Women, for instance, are expected to do most of the childcare and domestic chores. The conversion of adult literacy classes into the functioning of being able to read and write may therefore require more resources in the hands of women than men. While informative and useful, such an account of the effects of a group-dependent constraint on well-being freedom will be necessary but not quite sufficient to judge individual opportunities.

Severine Deneulin and Frances Stewart (2001) make a different point in claiming that social expectations or cultural conditioning may more directly influence well-being freedom. While a conversion of, say, higher education, into valuable functionings may be feasible for children of different social backgrounds, the exercise of choice has psychological, "cultural," and social connotations:[21] "How can one distinguish between someone refusing to make use of an opportunity because of social conditioning or because he has freely accepted to not make use of that opportunity?" (Deneulin and Stewart 2001: 14).

Deneulin and Stewart examine the issue of access to and funding for a university education. They argue that a gifted boy from a working-class background may be less inclined to opt for a university education than a less-gifted middle-class boy, and that the capability approach is silent on the capability to exercise freedom. In this case, adaptation works in a different fashion and restricts the set of functionings available for choice.

III. INTRA-HOUSEHOLD BARGAINING, INTERDEPENDENT CAPABILITIES, AND BARGAINING SKILLS

As discussed previously, Figure 1 portrays individuals as endowed with well-defined commodity entitlements. Robeyns's (2000) focus of attention is on the individual and social characteristics that influence the conversion of these commodities into functionings, and thus on what you are able to do or be with the goods at your disposal, rather than with the fact that your command over goods may be circumscribed in the first place. It is evident that the principal *source* of disparities in well-being freedom may lie not in unequal abilities to convert goods into functionings, but in unequal abilities to establish command over goods. Sen is, of course, acutely aware of this difference. He notes (1985a: 6):

> There are, of course, cases of joint ownership and even of social ownership. In the case of such jointness and also when the ownership is not joint but the use is (as with a family), there is a further problem of internal division of commodities commanded by the multi-person unit.

Disparities in the command over essential goods and services are a less severe problem in industrial societies, simply because social policy and law enforcement overrule household authority and ensure that, say, primary school attendance is compulsory. This situation contrasts starkly with that in developing countries, where households or families are largely responsible for decisions on children's school attendance, the use of healthcare services, and so on.

By way of illustration, consider a government initiative that provides adult literacy classes, with the focus being on two women, Nirmala and Geetanjali, and their respective functionings of being able to read and write. If we interpret their entitlements in Figure 1 as their general access to the literacy program, the conversion of the program into literacy requires that we account for the structural or group-dependent constraints facing the two women. Suppose, for simplicity, that these constraints are identical. The women's access to literacy may still differ if they have different abilities to negotiate with their spouses on the time they can actually spend in class. It is distinctly possible that Nirmala, because her influence on intra-household decision-making is more circumscribed, will spend less time in the literacy class than her friend, even though the two women attach similar values to literacy. The main source of Nirmala's capability deprivation may thus lie not in the constraints affecting her conversion of class time into literacy, but in the fact that she is unable to negotiate with her spouse more time for attending the literacy class.

Bargaining theories interpret intra-household allocation of resources as outcomes of bargaining processes.[22] The bargaining perspective allows us to distinguish between command over goods and services established by social norms and habits and distributions determined through contestation and bargaining. Theories differ in their hypotheses regarding the sources of bargaining power, but like the empirical literature drawing on the capability approach, they usually emphasize material foundations, such as how much women earn in the labor market or their control over resources.[23] Human capital may impact on bargaining power in a number of different ways.[24]

An overly strong emphasis on the material foundations of power distracts attention from other, potentially significant, manifestations of agency that enable women to mediate intra-household power relations and thereby improve their outcomes. Notice that for Nash-bargaining models, a primary or sole focus on material possessions or economic power is needlessly restrictive.

A simple example will clarify why we need to carefully consider these other aspects of agency in interpersonal comparisons of opportunities. The Nash-bargaining framework will also help illustrate the precise and occasionally unexpected nature of capability interdependencies. As some scholars rightly argue (for example, Kaushik Basu and Luis F. Lopez-Calva

1999), the actions or decisions of one individual might limit the options available to others. One would expect such interdependencies to be particularly stark within the household. This implies not only that the goods and services under your control may depend quite strongly on the characteristics of your partner, but also that the group-dependent constraints facing your partner will have repercussions for you. In short, by affecting the balance of power, possibly in complex ways, group-dependent constraints will influence the intra-household distribution of goods and services; that is, the means to achieve in the capability approach.

Consider an adult, married woman, sharing a residence with her husband. Let the gendered division of agricultural production in rural households in sub-Saharan Africa be our real-world analogy. Rural women are presumed responsible for cultivating food crops while men cultivate cash crops on separate plots. The parties collaborate by exchanging labor.[25] Should cooperation cease, the wife will retain full control over her plot, the resulting noncooperative equilibrium defining her internal threat point in the ensuing bilateral Nash bargain. In the event of breakdown in cooperation, the marital contract will remain intact. Intra-household distribution will now be determined by the noncooperative fallback positions of the parties and their individual abilities to influence the intra-household bargaining process.[26] The latter aspect is captured by what Partha Dasgupta (1993) broadly terms the two parties' bargaining skills, as elaborated below.

The bargaining weights in the Nash-bargaining model can be used as broad and formal representations of bargaining skills, expressing both overt and covert manifestations of such talents. Elizabeth Katz (1997) proposes that the weights capture that people of, say, different ages and genders may have different abilities to convert their fallback positions into bargaining power. Some people might, for instance, be "harder bargainers than others based on personal (and gender-specific) attributes such as 'boldness' and lack of fear of disagreement" (Katz 1997: 32). One may disagree with this description of the constituents of the relevant skills, but the central tenet of her argument is important enough; the bargaining weights reflect the parties' respective "voices" in resolving the conflict of interest over intra-household distribution (Katz 1997: 32).

This emphasis on bargaining skills supports the idea that even in situations of overt sex-role asymmetry, women may have more power than most theorists assume (Janet MacGaffey 1988). Some evidence on domestic violence suggests that educated women from middle-class backgrounds may offer less resistance than poor, illiterate women, who are more likely to fight back. Or, as noted above, while access to loans may have expanded the sphere of decision-making for one group of poor Bangladeshi women in Kabeer's (2001) sample, this group already enjoyed a significant role in household decision-making, emanating from their superior (and possibly innate) managerial skills. It is distinctly possible, and rather plausible, that abilities of this kind may be quite unrelated to education and material possessions, but highly correlated with bargaining skills.

In a similar vein, and without disputing the disadvantages facing working-class women in the spheres of legal, political, educational, and employment opportunities, the oral histories of women in the United Kingdom indicate that the domestic balance of power was often not reflective of these disparities (Elizabeth Roberts 1984).[27] Spanning the time period 1890– 1940, the material Roberts gathered includes a number of interesting verbal accounts, including the following comments from separate individuals (Roberts 1984: 112–13):

> Was it your mother who wanted to move to Newsham Road or was it your father's choice; do you know? Oh, I think my mother's. . . . I don't think he would object, but my mother had all the push. . . .

> Was it your mother who decided to move or was it your father? Well, I should think, knowing the character of them, Mother would arrange it. You felt that she made all that sort of decisions, did she? That's right, she was the leader. There are in every couple and she was the one.

> My mother was the more dominant personality in the family. Although, outside the family father was an extremely powerful personality, as I described, at home Mother generally prevailed.

So the idea that women have no power vis-à-vis men, even in circumstances of structural adversity, should be subject to careful scrutiny. Indeed, people have been known to defy authority even in the face of grave adversity. Examining the history of slavery in the United States, John Hope Franklin and Loren Schweininger (1999) argue that everyday resistance to slaveowners took both overt and covert forms. Open defiance was not uncommon, and slaves refused to work, demanded concessions, rejected orders, and even threatened whites. A similar example is the challenge, by field-based, empirical research, to a classic presumption in orthodox economics – that children have little or no agency. In a careful study of school-age girls in rural Andra Pradesh (India), Masako Ota (2002) provides several insightful accounts of how very young girls adopt individual strategies to protect and promote their school attendance, including persuasion, unruly behavior, and requests to persons of authority (teachers) to argue their case. In my own empirical study from rural Karnataka (India), I found that very young boys (12–14 years) regularly defied the will of their parents and left for Bangalore city to work completely on their own terms (Vegard Iversen 2002).

The determinants of such autonomous behavior, apart from gender, were age, problems at home, peer-group behavior, and caste. Individual and household characteristics thus mattered a great deal for these very strong expressions of the ability to make strategic life-choices, thereby redefining the content of the existing intergenerational contract. In sum, I would argue that while the existing literature, including Sen's own work, on the determinants of female agency, has covered important ground, there is much room for recognizing individual variation. Of course, if on closer inspection the determinants of fallback positions and bargaining skills in the Nash-bargaining framework turn out to be highly correlated, the value added from taking bargaining skills into account may be questioned. Moreover, whereas uncovering such skills may be difficult to translate into policy and advocacy, doing so is likely to be highly relevant for evaluative exercises.

Let us now return to the example of rural Africa, presuming that the spouses have land plots of similar size and soil quality, but that the husband is better educated.[28] Suppose also that the educational advantage has made him a more productive farmer, enabling him to convert his land endowment into more valuable output and therefore a stronger fallback position. Education now interacts with the husband's endowment of land to strengthen his threat point. Rather than being an end in itself, the threat point is a source of power and power has both a natural resource (land) and a human capital (education) foundation.

What is the effect of a group-dependent constraint in this framework? Suppose that the group-dependent constraint, in the event of noncooperation, confines the wife to cultivating only food crops. If the collaborative household output is unaffected by the constraint, the Nash bargain takes the shape of a zero-sum game, in which one party's loss will be another's gain. By restricting the woman's economic options, the group-dependent constraint will now affect the balance of power and therefore the well-being prospects *of both parties*, in this case by improving the husband's prospects and weakening the wife's. To convert the husband's landholding into first a threat point and then into the command over commodities he values, it will be necessary to recognize and account for this interdependence.

The foundation for interpersonal comparisons is as yet incomplete. In the Nash-bargaining framework, the individual's command over the means to achieve will be contingent on economic power as represented by the threat points, and on the aspects of agency captured by the bargaining weights. The key point is that because of interdependencies and power relations (with material, nonmaterial, and agency constituents) my opportunities to achieve well-being as a household member will be influenced by everything that affects my partner's fallback position, as well as her bargaining skills. This has important practical implications since the conversion of my endowment of land into well-being will depend not only on my individual characteristics, resource endowments, the group-dependent constraints I face, and my bargaining skills, but also on my wife's individual characteristics, resource endowments, and the rest. In other words, my individual conversion factors are incomplete without a recognition of this interdependence and without such additional information. This demonstrates the information requirements confronting an opportunity-based well-being measure, in an attempt to accommodate togetherness in its most basic and popular form.

This claim also remains valid for the conversion of the government-funded literacy class into Nirmala's ability to read and write. In other words, the conversion factor will depend not only on Nirmala's individual characteristics and resources, her bargaining skills, and the group-dependent constraints confronting her, but also on everything that affects the threat point, bargaining skills, and other characteristics of her spouse.

IV. CONCLUSION

My discussion has centered on how Sen's capability approach applies in the context of individuals living together on unequal terms. Intra-household inequality is common in developing countries and often distinctly gendered. In such contexts, the concepts of agency, freedom, and choice require special attention and caution.

The new literature on household behavior with a bargaining or game-theoretic foundation provides a sound basis for examining economic and noneconomic sources of power and their impact on the opportunities for women and others to enhance their well-being within the household. While depending on the sufficiency of indirect freedom in the capability approach raises concerns about the override of female agency when active choice is important, an endorsement of choice-mediated control as a salient alternative to indirect freedom would be subject to important caveats, given the frequency of intra-household disparities in resource control.

I argue that the requirement Pettit proposes – that effective power should not be favor- or context-dependent – should prompt an adjustment in the capability approach to accommodate what are reasonable feminist and humanist concerns. Moreover, a failure of the capability approach to encompass those aspects of agency termed bargaining skills may preclude meaningful interpersonal comparisons of opportunities for achieving well-being within families. The Nash-bargaining framework sheds useful light on the interdependence of individual opportunities. As a result, when researchers and policy-makers seek to convert endowments such as a landholding or the access to an adult literacy class into well-being, they must account not only for the individual characteristics of the person concerned, but also for the characteristics (individual resource endowments, bargaining skills, group-dependent constraints) of his or her spouse.

Such accounting is necessary, because the individual opportunities of household members to achieve well-being will be influenced by power relations, which in turn are influenced by each party's material and nonmaterial endowments, broadly conceived.

ACKNOWLEDGMENTS

This chapter has benefited greatly from the comments of the three editors of this volume. I am especially grateful to Bina Agarwal for her extensive and thoughtful comments and editorial input. I would also like to thank Amartya Sen and my fellow participants at the Oxford workshop (September 11–13, 2002) for valuable suggestions.

NOTES

[1] Mozaffar Qizilbash (2001) highlights three aspects of the capability approach: (a) the perception of development and well-being as an expansion of (valuable) capabilities or freedoms, (b) the focus on justice as capability equality, and (c) poverty as basic capability failure. The following discussion will focus on (a) and certain aspects of (b).

[2] While I am aware of the ambiguities and definitional problems underpinning the concept "household," I shall nevertheless use the phrases "household" and "family" interchangeably throughout.

[3] In Gary Becker (1981), common interests is an outcome, driven by resource transfers to reward behavior commensurate with the interests of the household member controlling resources.

[4] Inspired by Kenneth Arrow's impossibility theorem, there is now a comprehensive literature in orthodox economics addressing the problem of preference aggregation.

[5] For excellent overviews of the relevant literature, see Harold Alderman, Pierre Chiappori, John Hoddinott, and Ravi Kanbur (1995), Lawrence Haddad, John Hoddinott, and Harold Alderman (1997), and Jere Behrman (1997). The "neoclassical" restriction of income pooling was rejected in pioneer tests of the neutrality of sources of nonearned income on labor supply (T. Paul Schultz 1990) and intra-household distribution (Duncan Thomas 1990). For further evidence on the latter, see Haddad, Hoddinott, and Alderman (1997).

[6] I adopt the convention of referring to this as the intra-household allocation of resources. By that I mean the intra-household distribution of goods and services, taken to reflect individual commands over or "possessions" of the relevant goods. The terms "commands over" or "possessions of" will be used interchangeably throughout the paper. In the jargon of Figure 1, these goods are the "means to achieve" well-being.

[7] Nancy Folbre's (1986) statement might suggest that economic power is the only type of power that can be analyzed in a bargaining framework. This, I will later argue, conveys too narrow an interpretation of at least some bargaining models.

[8] More recent theories, such as those developed by Shelley Lundberg and Robert A. Pollak (1993) and Michael R. Carter and Elizabeth Katz (1997), go further. The latter portray individual autonomy and interdependence as key attributes of the household economy.

[9] Robert Sugden (1993) reviews and interprets welfarism as the orthodox position in normative economics, pioneered by Adam Bergson and Paul Samuelson.

[10] Welfarism needs to be corrected to reflect "true" interests, which fuels the claim that the capability approach is paternalistic. A distinction between manifest and true preferences is articulated by John Harsanyi (1982).

[11] For evaluation of egalitarian justice, the capability approach is sensitive to the problem of people adjusting to deprivation by developing "compensating abilities" (Mozaffar Qizilbash 1997).

[12] As is well recognized Amartya Sen has done much to bring intra-household inequality and gender to the forefront of analyses and policy debates. Sen (1981) demonstrates that there was a noted gender bias disfavoring girls in the aftermath of the 1978 floods in West Bengal. Again, using anthropometric measures and data from two villages in West Bengal, Amartya Sen and S. Sengupta (1983) find girls under 5 to be nutritionally disadvantaged. See also Sen (1990a, 1990b, 1999) and Jean Dreze and Amartya Sen (1995), among others.

[13] My focus here will be on the perceived interest response. That the bargaining or collusive solution is responsive to, say, an increase in the perceived contributions of individual i means that the increase strengthens i's bargaining power and tilts the intra-household distribution in favor of individual i.

[14] Bina Agarwal (1994, 1997) has argued that maximization of family welfare may reflect women's long-term self-interest. Drawing on evidence on covert resistance, she also questions whether women suffer from a "false conciousness" about their self-interest. Agarwal (1994, 1997) also extends Sen's analytical framework to include the effect of kin and other support systems on bargaining power, the effects of social norms on bargaining sets, etc.

[15] It is also a question of whether the evidence is quite as unambiguous as one is sometimes led to believe. More on that in Section III.

[16] The capabilities involved in choosing may be quite important and include, for any given capability set, (i) capabilities involved in articulating the contents of that set and (ii) capabilities involved in choosing from that set. The latter might include capacities for rational deliberation and capabilities involved in making hard choices (Qizilbash 2001).

[17] Pettit (2001) uses the term "decisive preference" in place of effective power.

[18] Pettit (2001: 7) acknowledges that the issue of degree is relevant, but mainly related to how difficult it is for others to impose their will (conjugal servility) on a person. My argument is that it is the degree of subordination required that determines the force of Pettit's critique.

[19] Or what Qizilbash (2001) terms "hard choices."

[20] Severine Deneulin and Frances Stewart (2001: 13) underscore this separation of the well-being aspect from the agency aspect of personhood for evaluative purposes: "They [functionings achieved] are evaluated as effects, which are divorced from human intentions and the process of realising them."

[21] See Robeyns (2001: 11–12) for a similar example. This is analogous to Bina Agarwal's (1997) observation that within the realm of the household, social norms may constrain bargaining sets or the domain for contestation, by effectively precluding feasible functionings from actual consideration.

[22] "Bargaining" theories are interpreted to include theories with a game- or bargaining-theoretic foundation, including the noncooperative models by David Ulph (1988) and

Frances Woolley (1988), the cooperative Nash-bargaining models introduced by Marilyn Manser and Murray Brown (1980) and Marjorie McElroy and Mary Jean Horney (1981); the gendered spheres model of Shirley Lundberg and Robert A. Pollak (1993); and the conjugal contract model by Michael Carter and Elizabeth Katz (1997).

[23] This, admittedly, is a simplified account. Marjorie McElroy (1990) provides a number of examples of how what she calls Extra Environmental Parameters impact on the threat point of married women, including for instance rights to child maintenance after divorce, the right for rural women to return to the native home in the case of marital breakdown, and so on. See also Agarwal (1994, 1997) who examines both the material and ideological basis of bargaining power.

[24] It is notable that risk-averse individuals are typically penalized in bargaining processes.

[25] Needless to say, this is a stylized representation of the diversity of rural Africa. For discussions, see Ann Whitehead (1994) and Cheryl R. Doss (2001).

[26] Let the Nash objective be given by $N = (U_1 - \bar{U})^a (U_2 - \bar{U})^{1-a}$; a and $1 - a$ represent the bargaining weights. Sen (1985a) interprets agency information to include each person's pursuits and choices. My specification does not include caring or altruism, which would blur the pursuit of self-interest. As noted by Sen (1990a) a person may have objectives and goals other than the achievement of personal well-being, which is distinctly plausible within the realm of the household. Caring for the well-being of other household members is easy to accommodate in a Nash-bargaining model. For expositional ease, I also avoid discussing attitudes towards risk.

[27] While selectivity is a potential problem in all case studies, here accompanied by possible problems of recall, the examples are still illustrative.

[28] I am glossing over the empirical problems associated with the verification of female/male differences in agricultural productivity discussed by Agnes Quisumbing (1996).

REFERENCES

Agarwal, Bina. 1994. *A Field of One's Own: Gender and Land Rights in South-Asia.* Cambridge, UK: Cambridge University Press.

——. 1997. "Bargaining and Gender Relations: Within and Beyond the Household." *Feminist Economics* 3(1): 1–51.

Alderman, Harold, Pierre A. Chiappori, John Hoddinott, and Ravi Kanbur. 1995. "Unitary vs. Collective Models of the Household: Is it Time to Shift the Burden of Proof?" *World Bank Research Observer* 10(1): 1–19.

Bardhan, Pranab. 1984. *Land, Labor and Rural Poverty.* Delhi: Oxford University Press.

Basu, Kaushik and Luis F. Lopez-Calva. 1999. "Functionings and Capabilities," in K. Arrow, A. Sen, and K. Suzumura (eds.) *Handbook of Social Choice and Welfare.* Amsterdam: Elsevier Science/North-Holland.

Becker, Gary. 1965. "A Theory of the Allocation of Time." *Economic Journal* 75(299): 493–517.

——. 1981. *A Treatise on the Family.* Cambridge, MA: Harvard University Press.

Behrman, Jere R. 1997. "Intrahousehold Distribution and the Family," in M. R. Rosenzweig and O. Stark (eds.) *Handbook of Family and Population Economics.* Amsterdam: Elsevier Science.

Carter, Michael R. and Elizabeth Katz. 1997. "Separate Spheres and the Conjugal Contract: Understanding the Impact of Gender-Biased Development," in L. Haddad, J. Hoddinott, and H. Alderman (eds.) *Intrahousehold Resource Allocation in Developing Countries – Models, Methods and Policy.* Baltimore, MD: Johns Hopkins University Press.

Comim, Flavio. 2001. Operationalizing Sen's Capability Approach, Paper prepared for the Conference "Justice and Poverty: examining Sen's Capability Approach," Cambridge 5–7 June 2001.

Dasgupta, Partha. 1993. *An Inquiry into Well-Being and Destitution.* Oxford: Oxford University Press.

Deneulin, Severine and Frances Stewart. 2001. "A Capability Approach for Individuals Living Together." Paper prepared for the conference Justice and Poverty: Examining Sen's Capability Approach. Cambridge, June 5–7.

Doss, Cheryl R. 2001. "Designing Agricultural Technology for African Women Farmers: Lessons from 25 Years of Experience." *World Development* 29(12): 2075–92.

Dreze, Jean and A. K. Sen. 1995. *India: Economic Development and Social Opportunity.* Delhi: Oxford University Press.

Folbre, Nancy. 1986. "Hearts and Spades: Paradigms of Household Economics." *World Development* 14(2): 245–55.

Franklin, John Hope and Loren Schweininger. 1999. *Runaway Slaves: Rebels on the Plantation.* New York: Oxford University Press.

Haddad, Lawrence, John Hoddinott, and Harold Alderman. 1997. *Intrahousehold Resource Allocation in Developing Countries – Models, Methods and Policy.* Baltimore, MD: Johns Hopkins University Press.

Harsanyi, John C. 1982. "Morality and the Theory of Rational Behavior," in A. Sen, and B. Williams (eds.) *Utilitarianism and Beyond.* Cambridge, UK: Cambridge University Press.

Iversen, Vegard. 2002. "Autonomy in Child Labor Migrants." *World Development* 30(5): 817–34.

Kabeer, Naila. 1999. "Resources, Agency, Achievements: Reflections on the Measurement of Women's Empowerment." *Development and Change* 30(3): 435–64.

———. 2001. "Conflicts Over Credit: Re-Evaluating the Empowerment Potential of Loans to Women in Rural Bangladesh." *World Development* 29(1): 63–84.

Kanbur, Ravi and Lawrence Haddad. 1994. "Are Better Off Households More Unequal or Less Unequal." *Oxford Economic Papers* 46(3): 445–58.

Katz, Elizabeth. 1997. "The Intra-Household Economics of Voice and Exit." *Feminist Economics* 3(3): 25–46.

Lundberg, Shelley and Robert A. Pollak. 1993. "Seperate bargaining spheres and the marriage market." *Journal of Political Economy* 101: 988–1010.

McElroy, Marjorie. 1990. "The Empirical Content of Nash-Bargained Household Behaviour." *Journal of Human Resources* 25(4): 559–583.

——— and Mary Jean Horney. 1981. "Nash-Bargained Household Decisions: Toward a generalisation of the Theory of Demand." *International Economic Review* 22(2): 333–49.

MacGaffey, Janet. 1988. "Evading Male Control: Women in the Second Economy in Zaire," in S. B. Stichter, and J. L. Parpart (eds.) *Patriarchy and Class: African Women in the Home and Workforce.* Boulder, CO: Westview Press.

Manser, Marilyn and Murray Brown. 1980. "Marriage and Household Decision-Making: A Bargaining Analysis." *International Economic Review* 21(1): 31–44.

Ota, Masako. 2002. *Between Schooling and Work: Children in Rural Andhra Pradesh.* PhD dissertation, School of Development Studies, University of East Anglia, Norwich, UK.

Pettit, Philip. 2001. "Capability and Freedom: A Defense of Sen." *Economics and Philosophy* 17(1): 1–20.

Qizilbash, Mozaffar. 1997. "A Weakness of the Capability Approach with Respect to Gender Justice." *Journal of International Development* 9(2): 251–62.

———. 2001. "Amartya Sen's Capability View: Insightful Sketch or Distorted Picture?" Discussion Paper No. 2001–4. Economics Research Centre, School of Economic and Social Studies, University of East Anglia, Norwich, UK.

Quisumbing, Agnes. 1996. "Male–Female Differences in Agricultural Productivity." *World Development* 24(10): 1579–95.

Rawls, John. 1971. *A Theory of Justice.* New York: Oxford University Press.

Roberts, Elizabeth. 1984. *A Woman's Place – An Oral History of Working-Class Women.* Oxford, UK: Blackwell.

Robeyns, Ingrid. 2000. "An Unworkable Idea or a Promising Alternative? Sen's Capability Approach Re-Examined." Discussion Paper No. 00.30. Katholieke Universiteit, Leuven.

——. 2001. "Sen's Capability Approach and Feminist Concerns." Paper prepared for the conference Justice and Poverty: Examining Sen's Capability Approach. Cambridge, June 5–7.

Rosenzweig, Mark R. and T. Paul Schultz. 1982. "Market Opportunities, Genetic Endowments and Intrafamily Resource Distribution: Child Survival in Rural India." *American Economic Review* 72(4): 803–15.

—— and T. Paul Schultz. 1984. "Market Opportunities, Genetic Endowments and Intrafamily Resource Distribution: Reply." *American Economic Review* 74(3): 521–2.

Samuelson, Paul. 1956. "Social Indifference Curves." *Quarterly Journal of Economics* 70(1): 1–22.

Schaffner, Julie A. 1995. "Attached Farm Labor, Limited Horizons and Servility." *Journal of Development Economics* 47(2): 241–70.

Schultz, T. Paul. 1990. "Testing the Neoclassical Model of Family Labor Supply and Fertility." *Journal of Human Resources* 25(4): 599–634.

Sen, Amartya K. 1981. *Poverty and Famines.* Oxford, UK: Clarendon Press.

——. 1985a. "Well-Being, Agency and Freedom – The Dewey Lectures." *Journal of Philosophy* 82(4): 169–221.

——. 1985b. *Commodities and Capabilities.* Amsterdam: North-Holland.

——. 1990a. "Gender and Cooperative Conflicts," in I. Tinker (ed.) *Persistent Inequalities: Women and World Development.* New York: Oxford University Press.

——. 1990b. "More than 100 Million Women are Missing." *New York Review of Books* 20: 61–6.

——. 1993. "Capability and Well-Being," in Martha C. Nussbaum and Amartya K. Sen (eds.) *The Quality of Life.* Oxford, UK: Clarendon Press.

——. 1999. *Development as Freedom.* Oxford, UK: Oxford University Press.

——. 2001. "Reply." *Economics and Philosophy* 17(1): 51–66.

—— and S. Sengupta. 1983. "Malnutrition of Rural Children and the Sex Bias." *Economic and Political Weekly,* Annual Number, May, 855–64.

Sugden, Robert. 1993. "Welfare, Resources and Capabilities: A Review of Inequality Reexamined by Amartya Sen." *Journal of Economic Literature* 31: 1947–62.

Thomas, Duncan. 1990. "Intrahousehold Allocations – An Inferential Approach." *Journal of Human Resources* 25(4): 635–64.

Ulph, David. 1988. "A General Non-Cooperative Model of Household Behavior." Mimeo, University of Bristol, UK.

Whitehead, Ann. 1994. "Wives & Mothers: Female Farmers in Africa," in A. Adepoju, and C. Oppung (eds.) *Gender, Work & Population in Sub-Saharan Africa.* London: International Labour Organization.

Woolley, Frances. 1988. "A Non-Cooperative Model of Family Decision-Making." Working Paper No. TIDI/125, London School of Economics, London.

DEVELOPMENT AS EMPOWERMENT

Marianne T. Hill

OVERVIEW

Amartya Sen's capability approach to human welfare recognizes the impact of social institutions on human capabilities. But as an evaluative framework, it does not analyze the role of institutionalized power in causing or perpetuating inequalities in individual opportunities to achieve. Drawing on authors who are receptive to the capability approach and who have examined the political aspects of advancing human capabilities, this chapter presents a view of social power and its exercise that is congruent with the capability approach. This examination of power continues the exploration of intergroup relationships that Sen has advocated, and it can be expected to yield new criteria for policy evaluation as well as new policy options.

INTRODUCTION

Feminist economics recognizes that social relationships, as structured within institutions, largely determine our capability to lead the kind of lives we value. One factor operating at all levels of society that has significant impact on social goals and their achievement is the exercise of social power. But this is a factor that has not received systematic consideration. Until the analytical frameworks being developed as extensions of the capability approach address the issue of social power, the analysis of well-being will be incomplete, and decisions made to enhance human capabilities will systematically fall short. Since social power is exercised largely through institutions, we begin by examining how the capability approach addresses the effect of social institutions on human capabilities, and then turn to the issue of democratization as a way of beginning to incorporate power into the capability framework.

I. SOCIAL INSTITUTIONS AND HUMAN CAPABILITIES

Amartya Sen (1976, 1987, 1992, 1999b) has been the leading theorist of the capability approach to human welfare, an alternative to traditional welfare theory. According to the capability approach, an individual's achieved well-being is evaluated by considering the level of her valued functionings, or the "beings" and "doings" that she can attain. Potential functionings are her capabilities. Examples of functionings could include, say, choosing to have a child, the intentional activity of actually conceiving a child, the enjoyment (or its lack) in conceiving, the process of carrying the growing fetus, the state of being pregnant, and the subsequent activities resulting from, or made possible by, being pregnant (David Crocker 1995: 154). Work activities and the sympathetic enjoyment of other persons and things (such as the beauty of nature) are also functionings. The capability space – that is, the matrix of all attainable functionings – in turn is the proper evaluative framework for measuring a person's advantage, or her ability to achieve well-being. It can also be used in evaluating social arrangements.

This approach takes into account the uniqueness of each person. A young child, for example, needs fewer calories than an adult; a disabled person may require more than usual economic resources to attain a given level of mobility. Since each individual has different needs and abilities, a given set of goods and services will result in a different outcome relative to the set of functionings attainable by each person. What Sen stresses is the outcome in terms of valued functionings, including the ability to choose. Only valued functionings contribute to well-being. Whether or not a functioning is valued will vary according to the individual situation – for example, under some circumstances, pregnancy would reduce rather than increase a woman's well-being.[1]

Part of the difference in attainable outcomes is due to conversion factors. The ability to convert a certain amount of resources into an achieved functioning, such as mobility, depends on personal, social, and environmental factors, as Ingrid Robeyns (2000) notes. Among the social factors are customs and institutions that impact a person's freedom to function, from norms regarding women's responsibilities to laws on workers' rights.

Sen speaks of valued functionings that are attainable as substantive freedoms, and he emphasizes the intrinsic value of the freedom to choose among alternative sets of functionings. However, although the capability approach provides a framework for the evaluation of individual and social welfare, it is not a theory of the social causes of poverty and inequality, nor of the effects of social institutions on human welfare. In fact, we can link criticisms of the capability approach to the need to take on the question of how to advance human welfare through social policy. In particular, we need to expand the capability approach to enable analysis of basic social institutions and processes, from the firm to the family and from the market to public policy-making. The problem is sketched out below.

Social institutions and the capability approach

The capability approach provides not only a framework for evaluating human welfare, but a tool for advancing it. In *Development as Freedom*, Sen (1999a) argues that the capability approach provides an understanding of economic development that gives a firmer foundation to those working towards its achievement.

Contending that development consists of the expansion of substantive freedoms, Sen recognizes the importance of institutions to development: "A variety of social institutions ... contribute to the process of development precisely through their effects on enhancing and sustaining individual freedoms" (1999a: 297). He mentions in particular the role of democratic institutions, civil liberties, and a free press in the formation of social norms, ethics, and goals, and the importance of public deliberation in addressing problems ranging from corruption to the neglect and oppression of women and the poor. Although democratic institutions alone do not ensure that injustices affecting those with less power will be addressed, there are strong arguments that democratic institutions do increase equity.

Sen recognizes, however, an unmet need for a theoretical framework within which to explore intergroup relationships. He notes (1992: 101, 117) that "in fact ... general analyses of inequality must, in many cases, proceed in terms of groups – rather than specific individuals – and would tend to confine attention to intergroup variations." He acknowledges that his own earlier concept, the Sen index, failed to capture dimensions of deprivation linked to inequalities outside of the income space and agrees that much work remains to be done.[2]

Some of the criticisms directed at the capability approach in general and *Development as Freedom* in particular can be seen as expressions of frustration that the analysis behind the approach does not go farther. Amiya Bagchi (2000), for example, laments Sen's silence in his book on the shortcomings of procedural democracy and of today's market economies, in which abuse of monopoly and financial power is common. He argues that Sen's focus remains on the ways in which institutions affect the exchange entitlements of individuals, not on the ways in which relationships of production confine human possibilities. Bagchi calls for a deeper look at institutions, pointing out that the competition for profits has had very negative effects on workers, especially in poor countries. Bagchi's points have merit. Although Sen speaks of the benefits of democratic institutions and of the need for state intervention in the case of externalities and public goods, he does not analyze the class character of the state nor, for that matter, its engendered nature. While he does integrate rights and freedoms into his analysis, he does not locate the origin of rights and freedoms in social relations of dominance and

Sen does not discuss these issues using the language of needs/ interests, and this, according to Hamilton (1999: 545), will delay, perhaps indefinitely, the realization of the conditions required for the implementation of Sen's capability approach. If substantive freedoms involve needs that place demands on society, a social structure that aids the recognition and articulation of needs, and accepts a responsibility for meeting those needs, will further the advancement of human capabilities.

While Sen and Hamilton differ in some respects, overall Sen appears to agree that the deepening of democracy that Hamilton describes could expand the capabilities of those gaining a greater voice. Sen (1999a: 78, 280–98) points out several ways in which democracy advances human freedoms and speaks of the need for "public discussion and a democratic understanding and acceptance" of the social choice process and particularly of the social evaluation criteria. He also states, "The emergence and consolidation of ... [democracy and political and civil] rights can be seen as being *constitutive* of the process of development" (1999a: 288). But Sen uses the language of freedom in the capability approach rather than that of rights. He states that freedom does not place demands on people to try to help others, although he notes that "there may sometimes be a good case for suggesting – or demanding – that others help the person to achieve the freedom in question" (1999a: 231).[5] The differences between Sen and Hamilton appear greatest in terms of their understanding of what democratization implies.

Democratization and empowerment

The democratization that Hamilton advocates refers to increasing participation in all spheres of social life, not only in the articulation of needs, but also in their recognition by society and the collective social response. He argues for increased equity in the distribution of power as it relates to the articulation and satisfaction of needs, stressing local involvement and the devolution of power.

Feminist Nancy Fraser (1989) further develops this understanding of democracy, addressing the role of self-organization. Citing Michel Foucault, she accepts that institutionalized power is "capillary" in nature, circulating everywhere through the social body and sustaining it: "If power is instantiated in mundane social practices and relations, then efforts to dismantle or transform the regime must address those practices and relations" (1989: 26). Equity in the exercise of institutionalized power involves more than increasing the input of individuals into social decision-making; it involves the empowerment of individuals through their self-organization and through increasing their self-determination in all areas of activity. This restructuring of decision-making hierarchies, along with changes in ideology, would accompany the sweeping changes that both Hamilton and Fraser envision.

Fraser (1989: 135) deduces that such emancipatory outcomes in social processes depend on the development of new contexts of interaction, achieved through communication. She stresses the importance of collective identification and denounces the tendency of the state to pre-empt processes of self-definition and self-determination. Individuals rightly should be active co-participants in shaping their life conditions. The advance of individual freedom rests on collective efforts for greater self-determination by persons sharing similar interests.

Nancy Folbre (1994) is another feminist author (among others) who proposes the dismantling of inequitable power structures, stressing particularly those based on gender, race, class, age, sexual orientation, or nation, which she terms "structures of collective constraint." Groups held back by structures of constraint have an especially strong stake in a redistribution of social power.

In terms of the capability approach, what is of concern in this debate about the meaning of democracy and democratization is the nature of the social process which determines the social practices and activities affecting the well-being and freedoms of persons in a society. Democratization, as discussed, involves extending more social power to those currently disadvantaged in this process of social choice. The emphasis here is on deliberative democracy – that is, on conscious, rational individuals acting in concert to advance their true interests as individuals and as groups (the needs of others, including those of future generations and of the environment, will be taken into account during this process according to the values of these agents).

The recognition and articulation of the true interests of those who are subordinate, oppressed, or for other reasons lack voice is a difficult process. It requires changing practices that are deeply embedded in institutions such as the family, the firm, and the state. Democratization involves the creation of new knowledge and values, in effect a paradigm shift, that brings about the meaningful empowerment of groups relegated to subordinate positions. In addition, shifts or changes in power typically meet resistance from those whose sphere of authority is diminished as a result, and the institutional means of handling such conflicts will strongly impact outcomes. A look at theories of power can help to clarify the nature of institutionalized power and the process of democratization.

II. DEMOCRATIZATION: CHANGING IDENTITIES, PRACTICE, AND KNOWLEDGE

Power has been a focus of theorists such as Michel Foucault (1989), Anthony Giddens (1994), Nancy Fraser (1989), Sandra Harding (1995), and Nancy Hartsock (1998), and their work provides insights into power relationships. These theorists analyze how the institutional practices of society reproduce and recreate systemic inequalities in power based on gender, class, race, and other characteristics. They also analyze the resistance to domination that is the base upon which democratization builds new institutional practices.

In contrast to these theories, which focus on institutions, the theory of power most used by economists – embedded in social choice – is not designed to address institutional complexity. According to social choice theory, society exercises social power when it chooses a particular social state among various alternatives. However, the methodology characterizing this theory is individualistic, abstract, and deductive, and assumptions about agent rationality and the properties of individual preferences eliminate much of the interdependence found in social institutions (see Robert Goodin and Philip Pettit 2000). Amartya Sen (1995) uses this notion of power in his analysis of rationality and social choice.

Questions of agency are implicitly resolved through assumptions made about social choice mechanisms. For example, the assumption may be that a society uses a specific voting mechanism, with each person having a certain number of votes of a certain weight. Agency then becomes tautological, except for a possible discussion of the appropriateness of the voting rules that assign votes and hence agency (see Oliver Williamson 2000: 611). While Sen's discussion in *Development as Freedom* moves beyond this abstract world, his analysis there would benefit from a theoretical grounding that explains the process through which the empowerment of disadvantaged groups occurs, and the social changes involved.[6]

Work on power in recent decades has focused on the role of shared knowledge.[7] Theorists have shown how agency effects changes in institutions, and so in the social choice process itself, through the creation of shared understandings. Feminists such as Patricia Hill Collins (2000) and Nancy Hartsock (1998) have contributed to these theories. As democratization changes embedded institutions, it changes the bases of society: new understandings of social reality emerge, self-definitions are altered, and institutional practices are modified.

Identities, institutions, and shared knowledge

Democratization can be analyzed as a process of change in institutional practices, following a path of innovation and diffusion similar in some ways to that of technological change. Individuals reproduce social institutions over time as they behave in accord with accepted social practices. Change begins when individuals who share a perception that change is necessary or desirable initiate new practices; the process is completed when a new practice becomes the rule. To highlight some key concepts critical to understanding this process, we use the triad framework of V. Spike Peterson.

V. Spike Peterson (2002) posits that identities, social practices/institutions, and meaning/knowledge systems are "co-constitutive dimensions of social reality." The first node of the triad is individual identities. Using a matrix of social domination, so termed by Collins (2000: 288), we can locate each person in different social groups and subgroups that affect his or her identity, including race, gender, class, and other characteristics. One such subgroup, for example, would be $(w, m, c, h, n1, r1 \ldots)$, where w refers to white, m to male, c to capitalist class, h to heterosexual, $n1$ to nation 1, $r1$ to religion 1, etc. It is clear that social practices and rules will affect each subgroup's ability or freedom differently.[8] Acceptable social practices will differ among the groups and subgroups; for instance, some practices acceptable for men may not be acceptable for women. In addition, rules that are the same for all will have impacts that can differ greatly by group: e.g., "last hired, first fired."

Thus, the lived reality of each subgroup will differ, resulting in differing understandings (and epistemologies – see, for example, Hartsock 1998: 240). These differing understandings will impact the behavior of individuals in ways that either perpetuate or change the power relationships between groups. Institutional change that succeeds in adjusting social practices related to gender, race, and similar characteristics will also impact the identities of individuals seen in relation to these groups. The rapidity with which individuals can create and spread a new institution (or institutional practice) depends on their position in the social matrix, and the advantages and disadvantages of the change as perceived by the groups affected.

An individual's values will affect her or his reaction to the possibility of a new, democratizing social practice, such as an end to segregation in housing or the introduction of women's right to vote. Economic values are a consideration, but other values are also involved. Each individual has several interpretive horizons, each with its own value system. Examples include what Jurgen Habermas termed the "life world" (valuing the affection and caring of the home), work (valuing instrumental and purposive action, and success), specific professions such as science or law, religion, and others. Each value system prevails in its own sphere; for instance, Christian businessmen would not consider "turning the other cheek" to business rivals. At times, these value systems come in conflict. For example, a belief in equal opportunity may conflict with a belief in higher company profits. Such cognitive dissonance offers the possibility for individuals to create new behavior patterns and hasten the acceptance of change. What they usually choose, however, is the resolution of individual dilemmas in favor of accepted social rules. This means that the work of innovators in spreading an understanding of the benefits of a proposed new practice can be decisive when they challenge accepted practices. The position of the innovators in terms of their authority and their access to the means of communication has a significant impact on the rate at which the change finds acceptance.

Social institutions and practices, the second node of the triad, are forms of cooperative behavior that result in the reproduction of social relations over time. A society rests on the shared knowledge of its customs, culture, religion, ideology, unspoken rules of behavior, and institutionalized systems of rewards and penalties. This practical knowledge of how a society works brings cohesiveness and identity to that society, enables cooperation, and forms the basis of trust (Mark Haugaard 1997).[9] Cultural, social, and economic capital are embedded in this knowledge, as well as in the other forms of shared knowledge that support institutional arrangements.

In addition to a shared knowledge of social practices, common understandings and values enable communication and provide a sameness of meaning within a culture. Each culture shares some common paradigms (or ordering codes, which Foucault calls epistemes) that frame discussions and debates. During the Renaissance, for example, the common episteme allowed a debate over whether plants were upside-down or right-side-up animals. The veracity of a statement will only merit serious consideration – that is, meet with a felicitous response – if it is found plausible within the culture. Persons will avoid statements and actions that their peers greet with disdain. The exercise of authority depends heavily both on a felicitous response to its commands and suggestions, and on an infelicitous reaction to acts opposing its authority. "It is infelicity and the social failure of certain acts which create the stability necessary to prevent social systems from degenerating into praxiological chaos," notes Haugaard (1997: 168).

Marginal modifications in institutional practices proposed by those in authority can easily meet with the felicitous response required for successful innovation. However, deeply embedded institutional practices, such as the use of a particular language, are difficult to change regardless of who the innovator is. Since every collectivity functions within a complex layering of shared and created institutional practices of varying age, the rate of adoption of new practices can vary greatly among organizations. Oliver Williamson (2000) distinguishes four institutional levels, which characterize institutions by how long they have persisted and by other qualities. At one end are Level 1 institutions (L1), or informal practices and customs that have persisted over hundreds of years. At the other end are Level 4 institutions (L4) with a life span of one to ten years, which include practices such as those guiding the day-to-day allocation of persons by organizations in pursuit of their goals (economic price theory analyzes practices at L4). In general, an individual or an organization can change L1 social customs and norms only marginally, while there is little problem in changing the newer L4 practices of an organization.

Theories of institutionalized power that focus on explanations of its reproduction over time, including the later theories of Foucault, too often leave little room for human agency to change practices that are embedded at L1 and L2 (Jantine Oldersma and Kathy Davis 1991). Individuals must work within common paradigms and follow social rules in order to succeed in their cooperative activities. Resistance entails negative consequences, which most persons seek to avoid.

This brings us to the final member of the triad, knowledge and meaning systems. Change in the knowledge shared by a group provides the link connecting individual agency to change in social practices. Since social systems are dynamic, changes in knowledge and practice are continuous. Haugaard points out that those dominating social power structures actively create and apply knowledge to new situations, continually introducing new practices – which, of course, increases the difficulty of resisting that domination.

This continual need to respond to change has meant that each society has a "regime of truth production," a means of producing social truths whose acceptance cements social practice. As truths, shared knowledge reduces the need for state coercion. Consider how state officials depend on the general knowledge and acceptance of the benefits of vaccination or of the "war on terror," to draw upon a US example.

Social scientists are among those producing knowledge that has the potential of acceptance as social truth. Economics creates certain truths regarding competition, efficiency, and balanced national budgets. Marxists and feminists offer alternative truths about the effects of capitalism or of the gender division of labor on individual well-being. The capability approach is proposing new truths as well; for example, that freedom is part of human well-being and as such is properly a concern of economic policy.

The development of such alternative truths takes place within new discursive formations, which create conditions of "local felicity" for the discussion. In the course of democratization, rival interpretations of truths regarding the group that is contesting its subordinate position will emerge, interpretations that society must evaluate and weigh. This will involve balancing the equity of the processes used to arrive at these interpretations against the likely consequences of adhering to each (Fraser 1989: 182; Sen 1995: 18).[10] The final outcome of a process of democratization will depend on the broad historical factors affecting both resistance to, and acceptance of, the proposed social truths. It is worth noting, as Collins (2000) stresses, that the creators of new truths bear responsibility for the implications of the knowledge and practices they create.

Application to specific power configurations

The above discussion indicates the depth of the problem of democratization. However, it provides only a glimpse of the many collective processes involved. It has not addressed how stable industrialized democracies achieved consonance among their basic institutions, nor the problems that this consonance raises for groups challenging dominant understandings. Specific power configurations, each with its own common understandings and practices, have not been considered. Yet each exercise of power is through specific institutions and collectivities. In some cases, the exercise of power rests primarily on shared values and goals, and in other cases on persuasion, but in general penalties or other negative consequences to dissident behavior play a vital role.

Resistance to the dehumanizing practices (that is, practices with compellingly unjust effects) of a particular form of power will be shaped by that power's specific structure. The differences in the power relations of patriarchy and capitalism, for example, not only mean differing oppressive practices, but also create different modes of resistance. As MacKinnon notes succinctly (1993: 437), "sexuality is to feminism what work is to Marxism: that which is most one's own, yet most taken away." Hence, resistance to power based on gender requires developing liberating theories of sexuality, while a new understanding of work is basic to transforming the workplace.

Finally, those institutions that handle the conflict of interests embedded in struggles to create new knowledge will have a major impact on the outcome of such efforts. If all groups involved accept the institutions that mediate these conflicts, the contest and debate will proceed within accepted norms, although groups may continue to contest any given outcome (Haugaard 1997). Institutional processes that make space available for discourse, that are inclusive of both advantaged and disadvantaged groups, and that are accepted by both can be critical to the avoidance of social disruptions ranging from armed conflict and politically motivated terrorism to crises in healthcare or the environment.

III. IMPLICATIONS FOR THE CAPABILITY APPROACH

During the social choice process, competing visions of appropriate social goals vie for acceptance. The theoretical framework of the capability approach can increase its usefulness to this process by developing a means of evaluating social choice processes as they affect human functionings. This would require drawing on concepts found in studies of true interests and of power. By recognizing and analyzing how individuals participate in reproducing and changing social institutions, the capability approach can enable the economics profession to consider the question of empowerment explicitly in studies that aim at improving the status of different social groups.

One basic task confronting theorists who analyze the exercise of power is the need to offer theoretical insight into the tradeoffs that accompany the shifts in power resulting from democratization.[11] Any improvement in the substantive freedoms of a group through increased democracy is likely to reduce some of the attainable capabilities of many of those losing power. For example, increased equity within corporations could result in increased unemployment benefits and reduced executive pay. Practitioners who evaluate the effect of such changes must be able to make intergroup, if not interpersonal, comparisons.

Those in positions of authority may find that, after democratization, their preferences receive less weight in the social, decision-making process – or that outcomes are less to their advantage. They will likely believe that gains have failed to offset their loss of power *unless* their values change considerably during the process. Such a value change may in fact be necessary for successful democratization. Possible gains from democratization at a national level include more meaningful interpersonal relationships, a reduction in poverty and its associated problems, a more coherent approach to caring for dependents and the environment, and a reduced use of violence in social life (Giddens 1994: 246 – 53).

The democratization process involves changes in practices and shared knowledge that achieve widespread acceptance. Innovators can foster the development of liberating knowledge and practices by building systematically upon positive impulses, such as those for self-organization and caring for others. The development of shared understandings regarding the benefits of expanded human freedom within and across organizations is an intrinsic part of increasing the acceptance of new practices and new voices. Multidisciplinary approaches can provide insight into how to achieve greater inclusiveness in the social choice process. One possibility is the use of inputs from the public and from self-organized groups of the marginalized.

At the micro level, Sabina Alkire (2002) demonstrates how the goal of expanding human freedoms can affect the design and choice of projects. She uses the capability approach to analyze the impact of proposed projects on different categories of human functioning. She groups human functionings into a limited number of categories (e.g., life/health, relationships, knowledge, and self-expression), based on research on human motivation. She then constructs indicators for each category and illustrates this expanded cost – benefit analysis by drawing on actual projects in developing countries. She considers both processes and outcomes in her analysis.

At the national level, Martha Nussbaum (2000: 78 – 80) uses the capability approach to argue that society should make meeting the minimum needs of all a priority, one that she believes should rightfully be embedded in a country's constitution. It can also be argued that society should join its efforts to make meeting minimum needs a priority with efforts to keep inequalities in check by setting maximums, such as on the levels of income and wealth that a small group of persons will be allowed to control without any public discussion. Sen notes, relatedly, that a society should be able to reach agreement in identifying and correcting blatant injustices.

At the macro level, an analysis of the impact of policies on different groups would benefit from the development of instruments that measure capability well-being in the major categories of human functioning. True, human development indices (HDI) now provide measures of the well-being of women as well as of society as a whole in some categories, but an evaluation that is more comprehensive and that disaggregates outcomes by class, nationality, and other characteristics is also needed.

At the international level, democratization is inextricably tied to a shared value system. Common global values – seen, for instance, in the Universal Declaration of Human Rights (UNDP 2000: 14 – 16) – would gain greater currency with a deeper understanding of the meaning of empowerment and democratization. Today's leading problems are poverty (including poverty in post-scarcity societies), environmental degradation, arbitrary power, and the use of violence in social life. These problems, linked to globalization and modernization, require the creation of common values and agendas through worldwide deliberative democracy. The capability approach offers the promise of theoretical grounding for this endeavor.

IV. CONCLUDING REMARKS

The capability approach uses substantive human freedoms as the appropriate evaluative measure of human welfare. Democracy can contribute to identifying, articulating, and advancing social goals that will further those freedoms. Feminists are aware that the viewpoint of the dominant groups, which permeates the common knowledge of how society should function, has obscured the true interests of other groups. Accordingly, women and other marginalized groups recognize the value of democratization, of seeking out the voices of the underrepresented, and of building channels through which they can more effectively enter the social choice process and shape social institutions to advance their welfare.

However, meaningful changes in the distribution of power often meet with strong resistance. History shows that the ultimate success of a disadvantaged group in advancing its true interests depends not only on broad historical trends, but critically on the institutional framework available for resolving conflict and on the group's efforts. Feminist goals, such as an equal ability to participate in political processes or an equal capability to exercise power, are linked to a social transformation that may be as difficult to achieve as that envisioned by Marx in his dictum, "From each according to his ability; to each according to his need." The pursuit of greater equity in the processes and outcomes of society is, however, feasible.

Amartya Sen has opened up the space for discussing these themes through his insistence that substantive freedoms are the proper evaluative measure of human welfare. As feminist economists, we can draw on analyses of power and relevant insights from all disciplines to develop an approach to human empowerment that ties social outcomes to actual institutional arrangements. In this way, we can act as catalysts for the creation of knowledge that effectively advances the goal of human freedom.

ACKNOWLEDGMENTS

The author thanks the four anonymous referees as well as the editors of this volume for their detailed comments and suggested readings, which enabled a transformation of this chapter over the course of the year. She also thanks the Mississippi Center for Policy Research and Planning for its support.

NOTES

[1] Work that is done solely to attain valued functionings (e.g., through gaining income) reduces well-being in the sense that a reduction of such work, all else being equal, would result in an increase in capability well-being. Work, however, will typically be "less valued" rather than "unvalued." This makes a dichotomy between valued and unvalued (or instrumentally valued) work problematic.

[2] Theoretical weakness in regard to the study of intergroup relationships affects the design of indices to measure human development or well-being, and thus limits their usefulness in reducing inequality. For example, Geske Dijkstra and Lucia Hanmer (2000) show how the UNDP gender-related development index (GDI) fails in several respects: as a tool for identifying gender inequality at a given point in time; as a means of identifying the causes of this inequality in order to suggest policies for its reduction; and as a means of monitoring the impact of policies over time. They link this failure in part to the fact that the GDI combines a measurement of gender inequality with measures of absolute well-being. They also note that its focus on inequality at one point in time precludes its use in tracking dynamic relationships among variables and "hence the possible causes of ... gender inequality." The scarcity of suitable statistics hampers other attempts to measure progress in women's status, as in the biennial UNIFEM report; this is also true of other unconventional measures that attempt to include variables reflective of the quality of social arrangements.

[3] The ability to choose among various functionings is valuable in itself; that is, having the choice of doing A or B and preferring to do A is intrinsically different from having no alternative to A and choosing A, even if the end result for the individual's functioning

remains the same. The functioning prospects of the individual are said to be the same in both cases, although the functioning capabilities are not.

4 The "true" capability that concerns an evaluator is not simply what the individual states she wants, the basic needs that she has, or a list of ideal functionings that the evaluator draws up. Rather, the evaluator will need to take into account the individual's preferences and the choices at her command. The evaluator will need to listen to expert opinions and perspectives from different positions regarding what is needed for an individual to live without shame, to meet basic needs, and more generally to achieve equity in society. Valued functionings cannot be completely spelled out in theory for all time. They will change as society changes and as illusions dissipate regarding what is possible for women and for different groups.

5 Although rights entail demands on society, Sen recognizes that rights do not have "complete priority [over needs] irrespective of other consequences" (1999a: 212). He argues for a consequentialist system that incorporates the fulfillment of rights among other goals.

6 Sen brings in the institutional dimension when he notes that "many of the more exacting problems of the contemporary world ... call for value formation through public discussion" (1995: 18) and also that public discourse can improve the informational base on which decisions are made.

7 Steven Lukes (1974) develops the notion that the knowledge and consciousness that inform the decision-making process constitute one of the dimensions of power. Socially structured and culturally patterned behaviors and institutions are inseparably part of the exercise of social power.

8 Members of dominant groups typically benefit from the common (i.e., dominant) values and understandings of society regarding their group. They generally rationalize the advantages associated with belonging to that group, often viewing this dominance as "natural." In contrast, subordinate groups, even though they may also accept the common understandings regarding their group, recognize that because of their membership in that group, they receive less favored treatment in some social situations. That is, they understand that the social acceptability/validity of some aspect of their identity is questionable.

9 Practical knowledge (e.g., society prefers men to women in leadership positions) supports accepted practices, but unconscious knowledge is also at work (e.g., the subsequent discounting or ignoring of someone's opinion simply on account of her race or gender). See Chapter 4 on Giddens in Haugaard (1997).

10 Fraser (1989: 182) notes that society reaches the best interpretations of needs by means of communicative processes based on the ideals of democracy, equality, and fairness. The equal ability of all to participate in political processes is one feminist goal (Fabienne Peter 1999). The problem of equitable treatment of minorities and women remains difficult, however, requiring changes in shared understandings in many areas. Feminist legal theorists stress the potential contribution of the law. Many contend that the objective of the law should be outcome-oriented, aimed at eliminating differences in power and control (see D. Kelly Weisberg 1993: 215). This requires a transformation of the process by which laws are established, as eloquently described by Catharine MacKinnon (1993: 428). Speaking of the changes needed to establish a legal system that does not protect male dominance, she notes: "Male dominance is perhaps the most pervasive and tenacious system of power in history ... because it is metaphysically nearly perfect. Its point of view is the standard for point-of-viewlessness, its particularity the meaning of universality. Its force is exercised as consent, its authority as participation, ... its control as the definition of legitimacy. Feminism claims the voice of women's silence, ... the presence of our absence."

DEVELOPMENT AS EMPOWERMENT

[11] The condition of Pareto optimality, as Sen (1999a: 118) notes, requires for efficiency that "no one's interests could be further enhanced without damaging the interests of others." This condition offers little guidance when considering the effects of democratization. Just as a redistribution of income and wealth, e.g., to the poor or to women, will result in alternative Pareto points, a redistribution of political power will mean a change in attainable efficient outcomes and so involve tradeoffs. Interdependencies of power affect all social institutions and require consideration when the concern is the welfare of individuals. Sen's mathematical elaboration of the capability approach (e.g., Sen 1992) treats functionings as either separable or interrelated. However, one person's functionings are in fact inseparably interconnected to those of others, and the mathematics for consideration of most such connections remains undeveloped.

REFERENCES

Agarwal, Bina. 1997. "Bargaining and Gender Relations." *Feminist Economics* 3(1): 1–51.
Alkire, Sabina. 2002. *Valuing Freedoms: Sen's Capability Approach and Poverty Reduction.* Oxford, UK: Oxford University Press.
Bagchi, Amiya Kumar. 2000. "Freedom and Development as End of Alienation?" *Economic and Political Weekly of India* 35(50): 4408–20.
Collins, Patricia Hill. 2000. *Black Feminist Thought.* 2nd edn. New York: Routledge.
Crocker, David. 1995. "Functioning and Capability," in Martha Nussbaum and Jonathan Glover (eds.) *Women, Culture, and Development,* pp. 153–98. Oxford, UK: Clarendon Press.
Davis, Kathy, Monique Leijenaar, and Jantine Oldersma (eds.). 1991. *The Gender of Power.* London: Sage.
Dijkstra, A. Geske and Lucia Hanmer. 2000. "Measuring Socio-Economic Gender Inequality." *Feminist Economics* 6(2): 41–75.
Ferber, Marianne and Julie Nelson (eds.). 1993. *Beyond Economic Man.* Chicago: University of Chicago Press.
Floro, Maria. 1995. "Women's Well-Being, Poverty and Work Intensity." *Feminist Economics* 1(3): 1–25.
Folbre, Nancy. 1994. *Who Pays for the Kids?* New York: Routledge.
Foucault, Michel. 1989. *The Archaeology of Knowledge.* London: Routledge.
Frank, Robert H. 1992. "Melding Sociology and Economics." *Journal of Economic Literature* 30(1): 147–70.
Fraser, Nancy. 1989. *Unruly Practices.* Minneapolis, MN: University of Minnesota Press.
Fromm, Erich. 1970. *The Crisis of Psychoanalysis.* New York: Holt, Rinehart & Winston.
Gasper, Des. 1997. "Sen's Capability Approach." *Journal of International Development* 9(2): 281–302.
Giddens, Anthony. 1994. *Beyond Left and Right.* Stanford: Stanford University Press.
———and and D. Held (eds.). 1984. *Classes, Power, and Conflict.* Berkeley, CA: University of California Press.
Goodin, Robert E. and Philip Pettit (eds.). 2000. *A Companion to Contemporary Political Philosophy.* Malden, MA: Blackwell.
Habermas, Jurgen. 1984. *The Theory of Communicative Action.* Cambridge, UK: Polity Press.
Hahnel, Robin and M. Albert. 1990. *Quiet Revolution in Welfare Economics.* Princeton, NJ: Princeton University Press.
Hamilton, Lawrence. 1999. "A Theory of True Interests." *Government and Opposition* 34(4): 516–46.

Harding, Sandra. 1995. "Can Feminist Thought Make Economics More Objective?" *Feminist Economics* 1(1): 7–32.

Hartsock, Nancy C.M. 1998. *The Feminist Standpoint Revisited.* Boulder, CO: Westview Press.

Haugaard, Mark. 1997. *The Constitution of Power.* New York: St. Martin's Press.

Hausman, Daniel and M. McPherson. 1993. "Taking Ethics Seriously." *Journal of Economic Literature* 31(2): 671–731.

Held, Virginia. 1984. *Rights and Goods.* New York: Macmillan.

Levin, Jack and William C. Levin. 1982. *Functions of Discrimination and Prejudice.* New York: Harper & Row.

Lewin, Shira. 1996. "Economics and Psychology." *Journal of Economic Literature* 34(3): 1293–323.

Lukes, Steven. 1974. *Power: A Radical View.* London: Macmillan.

MacKinnon, Catharine A. 1993. "Feminism, Marxism, Method, and the State," in D. Kelly Weisberg (ed.) *Feminist Legal Theory Foundations,* pp. 427–53. Philadelphia: Temple University Press.

March, James and Johan Olsen. 1989. *Rediscovering Institutions.* New York: The Free Press.

Margolis, H. 1982. *Selfishness, Altruism, and Rationality: A Theory of Social Choice.* Cambridge, UK: Cambridge University Press.

North, Douglass C. 1991. "Institutions." *Journal of Economic Perspectives* 5(1): 98.

Nussbaum, Martha. 2000. *Women and Human Development.* New York: Cambridge University Press.

——and and Jonathan Glover (eds.). 1995. *Women, Culture, and Development.* Oxford, UK: Clarendon Press.

Okin, Suzanne and M. Justice. 1989. *Gender and the Family.* New York: Basic Books.

Oldersma, Jantine and Kathy Davis. 1991. "Introduction," in Kathy Davis, Monique Leijenaar and Jantine Oldersma (eds.) *The Gender of Power,* pp. 1–20. London: Sage.

Perrow, Charles. 1986. *Complex Organizations.* 3rd edn. New York: Random House.

Peter, Fabienne. 1999. "Social Choice and Concept of Legitimacy." Paper presented at the annual conference of the International Association for Feminist Economics, Ottawa.

Peterson, V. Spike. 2002. "Rewriting (Global) Political Economy." *International Feminist Journal of Politics* 4(1): 1–30.

Pettit, Philip. 2001. Symposium on Amartya Sen's Philosophy. "Capability and Freedom: A Defence of Sen." *Economics and Philosophy* 17(1): 1–20.

Pfeffer, Jeffrey. 1981. *Power in Organizations.* Marshfield, MA: Pitman.

Robeyns, Ingrid. 2000. "An Unworkable Idea or a Promising Alternative? Sen's Capability Approach Re-examined." Discussion Paper 00.30. Center for Economic Studies, University of Leuven.

Rorty, Amelie O. 1992. "Power and Powers," in Thomas Wartenberg (ed.) *Rethinking Power,* pp. 1–13, Albany, NY: State University of New York Press.

Sen, Amartya. 1976. "Poverty: An Ordinal Approach to Measurement." *Econometrica* 45(1): 219–31.

——. 1987. *On Ethics and Economics.* Oxford: Blackwell.

——. 1992. *Inequality Reexamined.* New York: Russell Sage Foundation.

——. 1995. "Rationality and Social Choice." *American Economic Review* 85(1): 1–24.

——. 1999a. *Development as Freedom.* New York: Random House.

——. 1999b. "The Possibility of Social Choice." *American Economic Review* 89(3): 349–78.

Simon, Herbert. 1991. "Organizations and Markets." *Journal of Economic Perspectives* 5(2): 15–44.

Tversky, Amos and D. Kahneman. 1986. "Judgment under Uncertainty," in Hal R. Arkes and Kenneth R. Hammond (eds.) *Judgment and Decision Making*, pp. 44–5. Cambridge, UK: Cambridge University Press.

UN Development Fund for Women. 2000. *Progress of the World's Women 2000*. New York: UNDP.

UN Development Programme. 2000. *Human Development Report 2000*. New York: Oxford University Press.

Wartenberg, Thomas (ed.). 1992. *Rethinking Power*. Albany, NJ: State University of New York Press.

Weisberg, D. Kelly (ed.). 1993. *Feminist Legal Theory Foundations*. Philadelphia: Temple University Press.

Wilk, Richard. 1999. "Quality of Life and the Anthropological Perspective." *Feminist Economics* 5(2): 91–3.

Williamson, Oliver. 2000. "The New Institutional Economics." *Journal of Economic Literature* 38(3): 595–613.

World Bank 2000. *The Quality of Growth*. Oxford, UK: Oxford University Press.

DEVELOPMENT AS FREEDOM – AND AS WHAT ELSE?

Des Gasper and Irene van Staveren

OVERVIEW

To what extent can Amartya Sen's ideas on freedom, especially his conceptualization of development as freedom, enrich feminist economics? Sen's notion of freedom (as the capability to achieve valued ends) has many attractions and provides important opportunities to analyze gender inequalities. At the same time, Sen's recent emphasis on freedom as the dominant value in judging individual well-being and societal development also contains risks, not least for feminist analysis. We characterize the risks as an underelaboration and overextension of the concept of freedom. Drawing on Sen's earlier work and various feminist theorists, we suggest instead a more emphatically pluralist characterization of capability, well-being, and value, highlighting the distinct and substantive aspects of freedom, as well as of values besides freedom, in the lives of women and men. We illustrate this with reference to women's economic role as caregivers.

INTRODUCTION

Amartya Sen's *Development as Freedom* (1999) presents freedom as the central value in development: "Expansion of freedom is viewed, in this approach, both as the primary end and as the principal means of development" (p. xii). He emphasizes what some people call "positive freedom," the capacity to be and do, rather than only "negative freedom," or freedom from interference, adding that sometimes this positive freedom depends more on the government than on markets. This view of freedom as capacity, and not only as absence of active interference, is an important commonality between Sen's work and feminist economics.

Sen's ideas on freedom have significantly influenced feminist development economics. He has addressed, for example, what Diane Elson and Nilufer Cagatay (2000) list as the three gender biases of macroeconomic policy: male breadwinner bias (keeping women financially dependent upon men), commodification bias (ignoring women's unpaid labor), and deflationary bias (cutting public expenditures on basic social services). In each case, he points to the importance of positive freedom for women and men alike: in his analysis of women's poverty at the household level, where he detects the breadwinner ideology as one of the causes of female poverty (Amartya Sen 1984a); in his writings on freedom from hunger, where he probes the results in times of hunger of the commodification of food (Amartya Sen 1989); and in his work on financial conservatism and the treatment of social services expenditure as "non-productive" (Amartya Sen 1998).

Throughout his career, Sen has also recognized values other than desire fulfillment and freedom, such as justice, democracy, and connectedness. In this chapter, we try to assess to what extent Sen's more recent and increasingly strong emphasis on a language of freedom helps feminist economics. First, we will elucidate his conception of positive freedom, embodied in his capability approach and expanded in his book *Development as Freedom*, and determine its value for feminist economics. Second, we will present what we consider to be its shortcomings. As indicated by our title, this chapter primarily addresses *Development as Freedom*, Sen's expansion of his earlier narrower statements of a capability approach. We are aware that the book addresses a wide audience rather than a narrowly scientific one. We will carefully examine some of its key formulations precisely because it has successfully reached such a large readership. Third, we will outline a complementary or broadened approach, building from Sen's own work on a variety of values. This approach more emphatically highlights and examines a plurality of human values and types of capability, as seen, for example, in Martha Nussbaum's "*capabilities* approach." Freedom is perhaps best viewed as a particular family of values that must be embedded within other types of values, including those of caring. We will illustrate the critique and the proposal with reference to the unpaid care economy.

We suggest that Sen's focus on freedom provides an important space for the gender-aware evaluation of female and male well-being. He devised his capability approach, however, to refocus the evaluation of well-being and the quality of life (as compared to conventional welfare economics). His approach is less adequate for other tasks, such as description, understanding, explanation, persuasion, and perhaps pre-scription, concerning well-being from a gender-aware perspective. Such tasks require a broadened picture and an alternative vocabulary. We suggest greater use of the term "capability" and less use of the term "freedom," which has many other associations, and the adoption of a refined vocabulary distinguishing the different types of capability. We also highlight that not all freedoms are good, and that it is necessary to distinguish among types of values and to consider how to variously promote them.

140

I. SEN'S CAPABILITY APPROACH AND "DEVELOPMENT AS FREEDOM"

Negative freedom and positive freedom

Many feminists have struggled for freedom for women, in particular freedom from patriarchy. This includes the freedom of having *more* options, ranging from access to abortion to access to education; the freedom of having *better* choices in their personal lives, such as the options opened by reliable contraceptives or (at work) by women's unions; and freedom from oppression in public as well as private life. Freedom has undoubtedly been, and remains, an important value in the women's movement and in feminist theory and analysis.

Those in mainstream economics typically interpret freedom as "negative freedom," the absence of coercion and interference by others, specifically the absence of government "interference" in the market. This is often the meaning given to "free market": it is a "freedom-from," a freedom from constraints on one's choices in markets, leaving producers and consumers *Free to Choose*, as a book of that title by Milton Friedman and Rose Friedman (1980) terms it. This negative freedom is also accorded instrumental value as a means to promote well-being through individual choice, well-functioning markets, and GDP growth (see, for example, Milton and Rose Friedman's *Capitalism and Freedom*, 1962). In comparison, positive freedom, the ability to attain desired ends, is gauged by real income, albeit for many reasons an imperfect measure.

Gerald MacCallum (1967), among others (e.g., William Connolly 1983), has shown how statements about freedom implicitly use the form "Agent X is free from constraint Y on doing/being/becoming Z, which is an important value." Thus both aspects – constraining factors (Y, seen as "negative") and valuable attainable life-states (Z, seen as "positive") – are present, whether explicitly or not. Arguments that positive freedom is an illegitimate addition to the idea of freedom are thus fallacious. Different conceptions of what are valuable life-states, and differences in the judgment (both explanatory and ethical) of what are constraints, will lead to different assessments of the degree of freedom that a person enjoys. If a woman is free from legal constraints on entering a public activity, but constrained by her commitments to care for old, young, or infirm family members, assessments of her freedom will reflect whether her participation in the public activity is considered important, and whether care is seen solely as a self-fulfilling choice and not also as a burden. The claim that the woman is "free" to participate reflects a focus only on the absence of legal constraints and active prevention, based on a view that there are no other ethically relevant constraints and on a voluntaristic conception of agency. For Sen, this limited interpreta-

141

tion of freedom is problematic: what matters is what this woman is really able to do and be.

Like Sen, feminist economists have criticized the predominant focus in economics on negative freedom (e.g., Julie Nelson 1996; Gillian Hewitson 1999; Graham Dawson and Sue Hatt 2000). They have argued that this implicitly idealizes *Man* as independent, already autonomous, rather than as a social being, someone socialized into the norms and values of a community, cared for by parents, and having personal bonds as well as rights and duties towards society (Marianne Ferber and Julie Nelson 1993). The assumption in mainstream economics that individual utilities are independent and not interdependent is one example of the masculine ideal of independence and autonomy (see, for example, Paula England 1993). Moreover, feminist development economists have argued that more negative freedom does not necessarily reduce women's poverty, increase their relative wages, or improve their share of consumption and decision-making within the household (e.g., Naila Kabeer 1994; Diane Elson 1995). Sometimes more negative freedom even makes things worse for women, rendering justice or other values necessary.

Sen's concern for positive freedom: the capability approach

Amartya Sen (1977, 1987, 1995) has placed his critique of a purely negative conception of freedom first within a wider critique of various components in mainstream economics, including its rationality concept and its utilitarianism, and second within an emergent alternative framework. He stresses freedom in the positive sense of ability to function well in life, in terms of ends that people "have reason to value." His ideas have contributed to the UNDP Human Development Reports, which provide broader measures of welfare and poverty than per capita GDP; these include the Human Development Index (HDI), the Human Poverty Index (HPI), and the Gender-Related Development Index (GDI).

Sen's capability approach includes several features or aspects that need to be distinguished. *Feature 1* is its broadening of the information specified as relevant for the evaluation of well-being and quality of life. Sen argues that more types of information are relevant than those considered by mainstream economics, which emphasizes only people's incomes, assets, and utility satisfaction. Centrally, we should also look at how people actually live and what degree of freedom they have to choose how they live.

Feature 2 is a family of new categories as a particular language for discussing these types of information. "*Functionings*" are components or aspects of how a person lives. A set (a vector or, more formally, n-tuple) of such functionings together make up a person's life. A person's "capability set" is the set of alternative vectors of functionings that she could attain – in other words, the alternative lives open to her, the extent of her positive freedom. For Sen, "capabilities" in the plural refers to the particular attainable functionings.

More specifically (and relevant for Feature 1), Sen argues that in looking at individuals' well-being, we should consider not only what they achieve for themselves ("well-being achievement") – in other words, their actual functionings – but also what they were *free* to achieve. We should assess this freedom in terms of what was open to them, both in terms of their own well-being ("well-being freedom") and of their actual values ("agency freedom"), including their values for other people. His primary category of capability is well-being freedom, which reflects the functionings that a person can herself attain.

Feature 3 concerns which categories and levels have ethical priority. In practice Sen seems often to use the following ranking when comparing spaces in which to measure development and equality: (1) capability, the set of life options a person is able to choose from, placed first because of the priority given to freedom; (2) functionings, or how a person actually lives; (3) utility, meaning feelings of satisfaction or the fact of preference fulfillment – ranked relatively low since preferences might be formed without much reflection or formed in situations of deprivation of information or options; and (4) goods/commodities, possibly placed last as a measure of well-being because people have different requirements. We could read the normative priority given to capability as an evaluative rule that "capabilities are more important than functionings."

If we instead or additionally read the normative priority given to capability as a policy rule to promote capabilities and then "let people make their own mistakes," this takes us to *Feature 4*, namely priority to capability as a policy rule, as distinct from an evaluative rule. For purposes of policy formulation, capability becomes an appropriate measure of how advantaged a person is, rather than a measure of the person's well-being itself, although it would contribute to the person's well-being (in the sense of the value of the person's functionings).

Feature 5 goes further: Sen gives priority within the space of capabilities according to the criterion of what "people have reason to value." The question of how to operationalize this idea in multi-person situations leads us to *Feature 6*, stressed in Sen's more recent work: public procedures for prioritizing and threshold-setting as to which and whose capabilities are put first (e.g., 1999: 148).

The last feature – *Feature 7* – is less central, but periodically emerges in Sen's more applied work: the positing of notions of basic capabilities (basic for survival or dignity) and required minimum attainment levels. While these notions are ones that most people already find reason to value, to explicitly emphasize them helps to guard against cases where a person's reason leads instead to behavior that is damaging to the person herself or to others.

143

Sen's notion of positive freedom is applicable to men and women alike and is potentially sensitive to gender inequalities in social structures (for example, social security systems that depend on families having someone in formal employment), in norms (for example, female seclusion), and in economic institutions (for example, gendered job segregation). Using his capability approach, we can more clearly assess how women's freedom to live the lives that they value is generally less than men's freedom to do so: women have lower levels of education; they suffer reproductive health risks; their behavior in the public domain is often restricted by gender norms; and they suffer from labor market discrimination. These are a few of the many gendered "unfreedoms" that women face. Sen has vividly analyzed women's economic position, notably in writings discussed elsewhere in this Special Issue. His approach provides an orderly disaggregated framework that helps us look far beyond markets and commodities.

The evolution of the capability approach into "Development as Freedom"

Sen's capability approach has grown since the 1980s from a position in welfare economics to a wide-ranging development philosophy presented at length in his 1999 book *Development as Freedom*. The combination of his concerns for positive freedom and for replacing per capita GDP with human development indicators as evaluative measures seems to have led him in the direction of an increasingly unified conception of development as freedom. The term "freedom" now typically replaces "capability" in his work. He highlights freedom as the principal means and end of development (1999: xii) and accords basic political and liberal rights "a general preeminence" (1999: 148). Over time, in assessing well-being and advantage, he has given more priority to capability seen as opportunity (the set of life options one has, what one can attain) and to the procedures of local prioritization within that space (Features 3 and 6 above), and he has de-emphasized a universal specification of basic requirements (Feature 7). At the same time, Feature 7 remains present in some form: his empirical work on India and elsewhere reflects a consistent implicit set of what he considers to be ethically basic capabilities, yet he resists making an explicit list.

The labeling of development as freedom is perhaps in part strategic: *Development as Freedom* evolved from a series of lectures for the World Bank and seeks to influence audiences in mainstream development economics and seats of power (Des Gasper 2000). More than that, Sen's capability approach is centrally about the choice of an evaluative space: it argues that we should measure advantage by the extent of valued opportunities available to individuals. It contains only partial and somewhat implicit views about which opportunities people *should* have.

Sen certainly accepts that there are other values, notably justice in the distribution of resources, but he seems not to treat them fully on a par with freedom. First, he seeks to incorporate many values within his freedom framework by talking about the freedoms to attain the things that one has reason to value. Second, it appears he wishes to leave other values open – free – for specification in each situation. In this respect, none of them appear to be treated on a par with free and reasoned agency as essential features of humanity. Instead his framework seems to be neutral towards, if open to, these other values. Third, because justice in the distribution of advantages depends logically on first clarifying the nature of advantage, he takes his framework of freedom to be the primary framework. He accepts that the capability approach has limits – for example, the limits to a principle of equalizing even basic capabilities, given that women have inherently greater life expectancy – but, as is clear from this example, he sees the limitations as relatively minor qualifications around a valid primary emphasis.

The next section takes a more critical view of how Sen has so far used and extended his concept of positive freedom. A concept put forward to improve the evaluation of well-being – by identifying the dimensions of functionings and (real) opportunity in contrast to felt satisfaction, goods obtained, or other measures of real income – may not suffice for wider purposes. For description, explanation, and prescription there are important additional building blocks, such as the concepts of sympathy and commitment, to be found in other parts of Sen's work and in the work of Nussbaum and others.

II. SEN'S OVEREMPHASIS ON FREEDOM

An underelaborated and overextended notion of freedom

Sen's notion of freedom remains, in some key respects, undercharacterized in *Development as Freedom*. He writes extensively about "unfreedoms" and it becomes clear what the "bads" are when freedom is lacking. But we do not get a clear picture of the content of freedom itself, including the varieties, skills, dispositions, and preconditions involved; it is instead an abstracted umbrella category.

Sen sees freedom as the dominant space for evaluating human well-being, a space spanning many different ends. He uses the word when indicating the relevance of various goods in life, such as knowledge or health (freedom from ignorance, freedom from illness). All the capabilities that human beings could acquire are to be understood as freedoms. This inevitably makes the notion of freedom broad, vague, and potentially confusing. It becomes easy, for example, to confuse the "freedom to

145

survive" with the freedoms that survival brings, as Paul Seabright does.[1] There is also no longer a highlighted distinction between the value of autonomous agency and all the opportunities to achieve other values that may be provided through such agency. Instead Sen elsewhere talks of the 'process aspect' and the 'opportunity aspect' of freedom (e.g., Amartya Sen 2002). Bernard Williams (2001: 7–8) adds:

> This ... idea of liberty as ability or capacity ... has an obvious disadvan-tage: we already have a concept of ability or capacity, and on this show-ing "liberty" or "freedom" turn out boringly just to be other names for it. More importantly, it misses the point of why we want these terms in the first place.

We will come to Williams's point in a minute. For the moment, let us consider whether Sen's generalized language of freedom is the best way of directing attention to various important distinctions. His language needs at the least careful handling in order to avoid misuse. As with any language, the perspective it gives can be corrected by qualifiers and reminders, and Sen himself is well aware of necessary qualifiers. But, as with his use of the terms "entitlement" and "capability," so with his use of the term "freedom": there is potential for confusion since the word is already well-established in everyday language, and he is proposing that it now be understood in a specific and distinct way, diverging from much or most common usage. His concepts of "entitlement" and "capability" provide fruitful distinctions but have been subject to misunderstanding due to the labels themselves (Des Gasper 1993, 2000, 2002). Similarly, in the case of "freedom," we need more differentiation of terms. Having taken the everyday term "capability" to mean not skills but attainable options, Sen has seemingly now downgraded it for communicating to a broader audience and turned to "freedom" as a more evocative term. But that term comes with a lot of other baggage.

In political philosophy, freedom stands out from other values precisely because of its distinctive ethical meaning – as expressed, for example, in the French Revolution maxim "Liberté, Egalité et Fraternité." In a volume on the meanings and normative roles given to freedom in economics, Serge-Christophe Kolm has tried to disentangle the meanings of freedom from other values, emphasizing that freedom is related to individual agency as a combination of will-freedom, namely willful or voluntary acts, and reason-freedom, implying autonomy, as "one's choice of one's principles of choice" (Serge-Christophe Kolm 1998: 22). He argues that in its most common conception, freedom is choice and intentional action. Hence, he recognizes the values of freedom to be related to the self, to autonomy, and to independence, not only as "self-choice, self-determination, self-causa-tion, and self-creation" (Kolm 1998: 28), but also as a condition for "awareness, respect and esteem of oneself, for dignity and for pride" (ibid.). These and related freedom values appear repeatedly in the other contributions to the volume in which Kolm's study appeared (Francois Laslier, Marc Fleurbaey, Nicolas Gravel, and Alain Trannoy 1998) and in a monograph on the value of freedom in political economy by Alan Peacock (1997).

Like Kolm, Williams emphasizes that freedom is about acts, about both doing and the capacity for doing, hence the importance of freedom from coercion and constraints. He goes on to refine this concept of "primitive freedom" (2001: 7). First, he distinguishes five types of coercion and constraints, ranging from force and threats through to the by-products of other arrangements that prove to structurally disadvantage a group of persons (2001: 8–9). For feminist analysis, this is a helpful categorization: gender-based unfreedoms can be found in each of these five categories, ranging from explicit prohibitions for women compared to men, like a prohibition against doing wage work in some regions, to implicit and invisible gender norms, such as those defining certain tasks as masculine and others as feminine.

Second, Williams notes how a "political concept of freedom" emerged historically. It arose to distinguish between, and object to, particular types of constraint, and thus to appeal to a political authority for the removal of such constraints. These are the constraints deemed both obnoxious and humanly imposed (whether intentionally or unintentionally but culpably); plus those not created by humans but culpably not removed by them. He calls the associated political value "liberty." Its justified scope is of course disputed. Many people simply use the term "freedom" for this political value, too.

We thus can see the importance of distinguishing rather than merging concepts within the freedom arena, and of being sensitive to the "complex historical deposit . . . of the idea of freedom" (Williams 2001: 4), its intense historical connotations. Sen is right to emphasize that capability is a language of freedom and a legitimate use of such language, not an illegitimate extension beyond "negative freedom." He seeks to recapture Adam Smith's mantle from the Friedmanites and others in the cause of a humane economics. But in our view, his undifferentiated language of freedom – as if the stream of thought of the Friedmans and kindred spirits has not existed and does not draw on some powerful elements of the historical deposit – is not enough for this.

Given these pre-existing common understandings of freedom, the degree of emphasis on freedom in *Development as Freedom* risks leading some people to ignore contributions to well-being that are not part of one's autonomy and independence, but rather of their opposite. The intense focus on freedom may neglect evaluations of well-being in terms of social relations and personal relationships, which are important sources of women's well-being as well as a result of women's joint efforts to enhance others' well-being. Using a language of freedom in connection with almost every value ("freedom to survive," "freedom from illness," etc.), rather than more strongly emphasizing development as relating to a multitude of distinct human values that demand separate attention, might obscure the substantive contents of specific values. We shall now investigate the importance of highlighting specific values, using examples from Sen's own insightful work on democracy, respect, and friendship, to extend his capability approach.

The importance of other values

The "Development *As* [not *Is*] Freedom" formulation leaves space for asking, "And development as what else?" Sen packages a great deal into his notion of positive freedom. He can bring values other than those related to the independent self under his language of freedom, since he formulates freedom in terms of the ability to affect whatever one has reason to value. When our agenda is not only evaluation, but also explanation and prescription, however, a more differentiated language becomes essential. We will consider here the values of democracy, respect, and friendship.

In his work on poverty and famines (Amartya Sen 1981a), Sen argues that democracy, apart from being valuable in itself, makes a major instrumental contribution, in particular in preventing famines. Democracy is not merely a value which holds that people should choose freely, but a value that sometimes challenges freedoms (defined as willful and reasoned choices). And it is sometimes called upon to discipline freedoms when these allocate food to where the purchasing power is, rather than to where it is most needed. In Sen's language of development as freedom, the need for democracy to discipline freedoms (such as the positive freedom to speculate in basic commodities, especially in times of shortage) might become obscured, even though that is far from Sen's intention or own usage. We need to be clear that while we have good "reasons to value" some freedoms, we also have good reasons to disvalue some other freedoms. The freedom to make a fortune by hoarding grain or (to use or adapt examples from Martha Nussbaum in this volume) the freedom to pollute the environment or to buy political influence are not freedoms that society has good reason to value; yet they are freedoms. Nussbaum's chapter in this volume makes the point forcefully.

Prioritization of poor people's subsistence and survival over affluent people's valued freedoms (as in Feature 7 above) might have to be rooted in a nation's constitution or bill of rights. Otherwise, a language for promoting valued positive freedoms could be used or misused to cloak massive injustice. In hierarchical polities, affluent people's freedoms could be *de facto* prioritized, despite elaborate formal democratic procedures to prevent this (as in Feature 6). Though all priorities supposedly would come

148

from a locally specified process of debate, consultation, and decision, the outcome in practice could be harshly elitist, thanks to the power of wealth, established authority, and differential access. The capabilities and functionings of one gender, for example, might concern public officials more than those of another gender, even when reasoning from a human development perspective (as Thanh-Dam Truong 1997 has argued). For this reason, in her version of the capability approach, Nussbaum sometimes adds a Rawlsian difference principle and stresses a constitutional specification of the rights to basic capabilities. Other responses having the same function are also possible. While none is a cure-all solution, they have an important role to play.

Another value that is different from freedom (defined as personal independence) is respect. Again it has both independent and instrumental significance. Poverty is characterized not only by a lack of money or material resources but equally by a lack of respect from others (Amartya Sen 1984b). Being respected is a significant factor in an individual's success in growing out of poverty, and respect in turn involves and affects the capabilities of self-esteem and confidence. Self-esteem appears frequently as a vital first step for women to improve their well-being – for example, through education or by joining women's NGOs. Interestingly again, an all-encompassing unified language of freedom may not help bring the value of respect to our attention. Women may be free to join a credit program, but without the self-confidence to engage in a business activity, they will not do so. When Sen lists sources of interpersonal variation in well-being in *Development as Freedom*, self-esteem and related learned capacities are conspicuously absent (Sen 1999: 70–1, 88–90; see also Gasper 2000).

Friendship appears as another important value having its own set of skill-capabilities. Sen has shown the instrumental importance of friendship – provided we hold it as an independent value. His example features Donna, who is committed to save the life of her friend Ali, who she knows is likely to become a victim of a planned racist attack (Amartya Sen 1981b). She goes to the police, who dismiss Donna's story as fantasy. Although Ali is entitled to police protection, he does not get it. An alternative for Donna would be to break into the office of someone who happens to have the information where Ali is, but that would violate the law as well as the other person's privacy. In a utilitarian calculation, then, the benefits from the attack to the group of attackers might be greater than the costs to just one person, hence the principle of utility maximization might not help Ali. Sen implicitly suggests in this story that the only value available to Donna that might save her friend Ali is her friendship. Committed as she is to her friend, she is determined to find a way to save him, although it will cost her time and effort and she runs the risk of becoming the next target of the attackers. In Sen's language, this is "commitment," which means that a person follows values whose fulfillment does not raise her own satisfaction. In contrast, "sympathy" means that a person's satisfaction is favorably affected by an increase in another person's well-being.

While the case could still be described using Sen's language of capability as positive freedom, that does not seem the best way. It is not Ali's free agency nor his rights but his close relationship with Donna that will help him eventually to get out of the threatening situation. Friendship is a value that in a particular case contributes more effectively to furthering individual well-being than the value of freedom (as personal independence) is able to do. While Sen acknowledges this in his example of Donna and Ali, he provides no clear place for friendship in his freedom approach.

Achieved functionings, internal freedom, and personhood

The dominant language of freedom might sometimes hinder us from attending to important matters. A conception of human development, as promoted by the UNDP Reports, for example, needs more than one value. Freedom is not enough, even in a version that refers to other values and is supplemented by a justice criterion. Capability is only one relevant space in an evaluation, even for the welfare economics exercise of judging the position of a responsible adult, and it is relevant for adults more than for children. We are not interested only in whether a girl has the potential, the positive freedom, to be healthy, but also in how healthy she is. We are not interested only in whether India has the potential to educate all its girls, but also in whether it actually does so. We are interested both in how far a society enjoys the possibility of fulfilling important values and how far it fulfills them in practice. In the Human Development Index, two of the dimensions – knowledge and longevity – do directly reflect valuable functionings and not only the potential for these. That we must often measure capability via the proxy of functioning has been fortunate, for we need to measure functionings too if we are to evaluate human development adequately.

Sen provides space for other values through his flexible phrase "what we have reason to value." "To value" is in his usage something more considered, more reasoned, than a mere preference, urge, habit, or whimsy, and to underline this he adds the phrase "have reason to." Sebastian Silva Leander (2001) suggests that Sen's capability notion should more clearly distinguish between two types of freedom: having attainable options, which connects with Immanuel Kant's concept of external freedom, and being able to make independent well-reasoned choices, which connects with Kant's concept of internal freedom. Such internal freedom is central in Kant's conceptions of humanity and progress. Sevèrine Deneulin (2003) concludes that Sen's approach says too little about how to assess and promote the capability for freedom itself, other than by mentioning access to good information.

Lawrence Hamilton (1999) argues that Sen holds back from a more substantive theory of values and needs because of excessive faith in a thinly specified version of practical reason.[2] This version presumes that persons are rational and nonvicious, at least if they are provided with information, basic training (thus the theory applies to adults), and opportunities for public debate. These requirements are important but not sufficient for reasonableness. Sen, in any case, assumes and advocates a viable liberal democratic state, where basic rights can be articulated, operationalized, and respected for every group in society. But in a market-oriented, money-dominated world, his capability approach faces some risk of subordination to what comes out of such market- and money-dominated processes, unless it is combined with a richer language for analysis and evaluation. If partnered by richer pictures of personhood, the capability approach might help in identifying and confronting consumerism. In their absence, its emphasis on increasing the range of choice can be distorted into a defense of consumerism.[3]

The "development as freedom" formulation thus needs to be embedded in a broader picture of human values and with more attention to "internal freedom." In the next section, we will trace a move from a relatively thin and unitary picture of persons and values to a more complex and plural picture, drawing in part on Sen's earlier work, to give a more adequately contextualized concept of freedom.

III. A SITUATED AND MORE SUBSTANTIVE NOTION OF FREEDOM

In this section, we consider responses to the underdefinition and overextension of Sen's notion of freedom. As a remedy for freedom's underdefinition, we outline aspects of the thicker notion presented by Martha Nussbaum and others. As a remedy for the concept's overextension, we emphasize the nonhierarchical relationship among a plurality of values that together make up well-being or development. We will illustrate this in the subsequent section, with reference to the values of caring and to women's role in providing unpaid care.

Combating underdefinition with Nussbaum's help

Sen presents a richer picture of persons than that in "rational economic man." He notes the possibility of what he calls sympathy and commitment; and he notes preferences about preferences, as part of reasoning about preference. However, the picture remains predominantly one of choosers who reason, rather than one of more richly scripted actors. The conception of freedom as opportunity is an abstract one about possibilities in a given context, not a substantive one about psychic states, capacities, and propensities.

In defining capability as positive freedom, Sen has built on a usage that is perhaps less common in everyday language. More common is the sense of capability as a skill or an aptitude. We can call this *S-capability* (S for skill) and we call Sen's sense of the word *O-capability* (O for attainable options and opportunities). Nussbaum elaborates the S-capability sense, which she calls "internal capability" (she uses "external capability" for what the person can attain). This skills sense is essential in description and explanation, and thus also for more grounded prescription. An opportunity set is not a picture of personhood or agency. Theorizing capability only as attainable opportunities and not also as skills and traits will limit us in building a more structured picture of personhood and agency. It can lead to underemphasizing key requirements for "free choice" and under-estimating the extent of deprivation. We agree with David Crocker (1995: 182) that "Sen's theory of actual freedom would be more comprehensive and humanly nuanced if he followed Nussbaum and added internal powers to external opportunities and viewed humans not only as capable but as in need of nurture in a context of neediness."

Because Nussbaum gives a richer and a more gender-balanced picture of thought and emotion, and of influences on them, she is stronger than Sen on meanings and action, including on emotional development and making use of freedom. Her approach may have greater potential for helping us understand the requirements of action and for motivating it (Martha Nussbaum 2000, 2001; IDEA 2001).

The broader definition of capabilities, distinguishing between opportunities and skills, makes her approach less abstract than Sen's and closer to the texture of daily life. She proposes ten sets of priority capabilities under the headings: (1) life; (2) bodily health; (3) bodily integrity; (4) senses, imagination, and thought; (5) emotions; (6) practical reason; (7) affiliation, or "Being able to live with and toward others (and) having the social bases of self-respect and non-humiliation ..."; (8) other species, or "Being able to live with concern for, and in relation to, animals, plants and the world of nature"; (9) play; and (10) control over one's environment (Nussbaum 2000: 79–80). This list of capabilities reflects a combination of skills and opportunities. Some concern the internal capabilities of a person, like emotions, which require training and maturing, but afterwards do not depend so much on outside resources – unlike, for example, bodily health. They cannot all be well understood as freedoms in the usual sense. A capability for affiliation is only in part a freedom, as in the ILO Convention specifying workers' right to freedom of association. Affiliation depends also on intimate relationships between people, rather than only on their personal autonomy to engage in relationships with others.

Nussbaum notes, "I am not pushing individuals into the *function*: once the stage is fully set, the choice is up to them" (2000: 88, emphasis added). But this choice is embedded in an individual's social networks, like families and communities, and "the capabilities are an interlocking set; they support one another, and an impediment to one impedes others" (p. 294).

Nussbaum stresses minimum thresholds for individual well-being. Each citizen should enjoy those minimum levels of capability before those people who have the means to do so go on to attain high levels of fuller freedom. In some of her writings, she has even proposed a Rawlsian difference principle: inequalities in capabilities can be tolerated as long as these differences lead to more people attaining the minimum threshold (Martha Nussbaum 1995: 87).

This approach to capabilities moves away from a dominant focus on the language of freedom and towards a greater emphasis on an interlocking set of values, reflected in a diversity of capabilities. For women, Nussbaum notes, this view offers a way out of the dichotomy between exclusive individual freedom, on the one hand, and traditional women's roles, on the other. Nussbaum's approach of using a set of plural capabilities promises that "we are not forced to choose between a deracinated type of individualism, where each person goes off as a loner, indifferent to others, and traditional types of community, which are frequently hierarchical and unfair to women" (Nussbaum 2000: 289).

Nussbaum's approach also enables us to transcend the common dichotomy of masculine and feminine attributions of human agency (reason versus emotion, calculation versus interpretation, or independence versus dependence). She goes beyond such dualities to argue for concrete human capabilities, addressing not only individualistic needs but also social and interpersonal ones. Her approach is more open to highlighting community and family as essential spheres.

True, Nussbaum's capabilities approach has its own limitations. It explicitly acknowledges that it is oriented to the design of political constitutions and policy frameworks rather than to the details of poverty research and administration: it does not indicate how to measure the various capabilities and cannot easily be employed in a quantitative cost-benefit analysis (Martha Nussbaum 1999: 236). And although her list of ten priority capabilities has evolved and improved over many years of debate, and contains considerable room for multiple versions and different local specifications, it will always be contestable (Fabienne Peter 2001). It should be understood not as a universal blueprint, but as an exemplar of an appropriately substantive agenda for the discussion of priorities and basic rights – as a set of criteria for "a decent social minimum in a variety of areas" (Nussbaum 2000: 75). The list can serve as a framework for dialogical investigation. A helpful set of papers on such issues and on her approach's contributions and possible limits is found in IDEA (2001).[4]

Combating overextension: highlighting other values

A variety of authors, such as Michael Walzer (1983) and Elizabeth Anderson (1993), suggest that freedom be seen as just one relevant sphere among others. For these authors, freedom is distinct from, and even incommensurable with, other values. This notion of freedom ensures a recognition of the importance of other values and implies that a more modest weight be given to freedom, here no longer viewed as an overarching or dominant characterization of development. The more clearly defined and the better distinguished it is from other values, the more meaningful becomes the role of freedom as a value operating in economic processes.

Irene van Staveren (2001) has tried to link the idea of a range of distinct values to specific skill-type capabilities phrased in terms of these respective values. She emphasizes three spheres of values in economic life – freedom, justice, and caring. Each encompasses a variety of incommensurable values that are, however, related to one another. Whereas Sen talks of freedoms to attain goods that we find reason to value and of justice in the distribution of those freedoms, a conception that adds caring to these two spheres provides a more substantive characterization of values. This in turn is more helpful for description, explanation, and prescription.

Freedom is seen here as a family of values related to the self and to what one can do, hence to individual agency. Next to these self-related values of freedom lies a sphere of public values of justice, including values of respect and solidarity, as well as a sphere of interpersonal values of caring, which characterizes relationships between people – for example, expressing trust in a community and taking responsibility for family members. To enhance values of freedom, individuals may acquire capabilities related to free choice, autonomy, self-esteem, and most of all, individual agency. But having freedom of choice, for example, will not be particularly helpful for someone who is in mourning because his parents have died. The person's well-being in that situation will benefit more from friends who comfort, as well as from joint participation in a funeral ceremony that is appropriate for the cultural context. Hence, different values require different capabilities. Values of justice, for example, are reflected in capabilities for solidarity and respect for other human beings as well as animals and the natural environment, whereas values of caring emerge in personal relationships expressed by capabilities of trust and trustworthiness, loyalty, and responsibility.

These three spheres are not independent from each other: freedom enables justice and caring, but also constrains them. In turn, the values of justice and caring are related to each other and to freedom. The values should be understood as interdependent, just as Nussbaum argues in relation to her set of priority capabilities: one cannot be well attained without the others. The values can ideally be thought of as continuously balancing each other, at the macro level as well as at the micro level of the individual. Too much of a burden of caring labor will limit women's freedom, for example. But too much freedom, in terms of independence from a household and community, will limit an individual's well-being in times of scarcity or illness: others will not feel responsible for helping someone who has refused to contribute to mutual support networks in the past. An exclusive pursuit of freedom thus diminishes opportunities to receive care when needed.

IV. WOMEN'S ROLE AS CAREGIVERS

Let us consider women's role as unpaid caregivers for the family and community, a role assigned to women worldwide. How far can the issues arising from this be understood within Sen's framework of development as freedom?

In Chapter 8 of *Development as Freedom,* Sen argues for gender policies that focus on women's capability and agency rather than, as is conventional, on women's disadvantaged levels of functionings. For him, a focus on women's agency – their formation, pursuit, and attainment of goals – often implies promoting paid work outside the home for women, giving them independent incomes. "So the freedom to seek and hold outside jobs can contribute to the reduction of women's relative – and absolute – deprivation" (Sen 1999: 194). Paid jobs help women to become financially independent from their husbands and fathers, and to make their own choices in consumer and financial markets. Feminist economists have underpinned this relationship between paid employment and well-being with their critique of the model of the unitary household and with analyses of women's bargaining position. Sen adds that the freedom that goes with paid labor brings important values for women, such as self-esteem, dignity, and autonomy. And he elaborates the effects of greater bargaining power in and outside the household: "Freedom in one area (that of being able to work outside the household) seems to help to foster freedom in others (in enhancing freedom from hunger, illness and relative deprivation)" (1999: 194).

However, women's working lives include a large share of unpaid labor, making up a major part of the care economy (see, for example, Nancy Folbre and Julie Nelson 2000). This unpaid care economy produces goods and services on a vast scale for the benefit of others (households, family members, and communities). Estimates of its monetary value, on the basis of the opportunity costs of women's time, range from 6 percent to 55 percent of GNP as presently calculated (Marga Bruyn-Hundt 1996: 51). The

referring to someone's individual freedom: how can we convince men to do more unpaid caring labor in terms relating to an increase of freedom? As women know from experience, housework and childcare may bring various satisfactions, but they do not bring much freedom. It is the lack of freedom that goes with caring that led Sen to emphasize paid employment in the first place.

Now, Sen's language of development as freedom does not treat freedom as meaning only personal independence. It instead refers to the ability to attain whatever one finds reason to value, which can be stretched to say that caring for the infirm and needy, based on sympathy or acceptance of duty, represents a use of a freedom to further an accepted value of caring for others. But in addition to the danger of misreading this "development-as-freedom" language, given the entrenched other uses of "freedom," this formulation is not helpful for thinking about the content of a value of caring, both how it arises and how it might be promoted. We should highlight the distinct psychological contents of different values and name them appropriately.

An alternative to Sen's unified language of freedom would lie in emphasizing the plurality of development, beyond only freedom. This means highlighting not just values related to the self, values that increase one's independence and autonomy, but also values related to relationships with others, as well as values related to fairness of distribution. The claims of justice themselves may be better grounded and more persuasive (forming a basis for accepted duties and not only claimed rights) through this more substantive attention to personhood and to experiences of care.

V. CONCLUSION

We have analyzed the focus in Sen's capability approach on freedom, presented as the principal means and ends of development.[5] Sen's notion of capability and positive freedom proves to be more useful for gender-aware analysis and the study of women's well-being than the neoclassical ideas of utility and negative freedom. His concern with autonomous agency helps us to analyze women's freedom to live the lives they have reason to value and to identify the constraints to this freedom.

But in comparison to his earlier work, where he analyzed a wide variety of human values next to freedom, Sen's increased emphasis on an umbrella conception of freedom appears less sufficient for the tasks of describing, explaining, motivating, and then developing policy recommendations. This is especially so for the economic roles of women that are tied to different values, such as values of solidarity or connectedness.

We identified two main shortcomings in the treatment of "development as freedom" in his 1999 book. First, we noted an overextension of the emphasis on freedom, to the extent that all capabilities that women and men could acquire are now to be described as freedoms, regardless of their specific content. Some important values, such as those associated with friendship, respect, and care, cannot be adequately understood in terms of individual freedom.

Second, we found its concept of freedom to be underelaborated, since it does not sufficiently distinguish between autonomous agency and the variety of values that may be promoted through such agency, or between capability as a set of opportunities and capabilities as skills and capacities that can be nurtured. We agree with Ingrid Robeyns (2001) that Sen's capability approach in general is deliberately underspecified, and thus risks being coupled with questionable, not least gender-biased, partners. The risk increases if the approach is perceived as a general philosophy of development – unless it is refined and complemented. Sen tries to recapture the language of freedom and the authority of Adam Smith from those, like Milton Friedman, who have tried to claim them exclusively for market libertarian viewpoints. But his highly generalized use of "freedom" may come at the cost of downplaying some necessary distinctions, including those between desirable and undesirable freedoms, and between freedom and other values. Development may be better described as at least comprising freedom *and* justice, and more enlighteningly as involving also the growth and maintenance of the value of caring for others.

To address these shortcomings, we have argued for an alternative language that lays more explicit stress on other values that are as important as freedom (seen as choice and intentional action), values that are also means and ends of development. This requires a recognition of different capabilities as valuable in their own right, not simply as examples of freedom. Freedom – as choice and intentional action – instead should be emphatically embedded within a fuller picture of other values and needs. This suggestion draws on Sen's earlier work in which he shows the contribution of values like democracy, respect, and friendship to well-being and development. These varied values and the corresponding valuable capabilities require more specific and substantive designation, investigation, and support than is available in the generalized language of "development as freedom." Here we endorse aspects of the work of Nancy Folbre, Julie Nelson, and Martha Nussbaum, among others. Without this sort of more substantive theory of personhood, the language of freedom in the capability approach could be co-opted in questionable and gender-biased ways.

We suggest moreover that promotion of individual well-being, in particular the well-being of women, which in so many respects lags behind that of men, benefits from a recognition of minimum required levels – or thresholds, as Nussbaum terms them – for some priority capabilities and functionings. Everyone's attainment of minimum levels for these important aspects would be prioritized over the freedom of those who have already reached higher levels of well-being.

Finally, we propose that such a pluralist understanding of capabilities would help to better acknowledge the contribution of women as caregivers as well as the constraints imposed by this role on women's freedom. On grounds of both personal development and justice, it then becomes possible to argue for some redistribution of caregiving from women to men – which would advance both women's freedom and men's capability of caring.

ACKNOWLEDGMENTS

We have benefited from comments by three anonymous referees and by Jane Humphries, Ingrid Robeyns, Sabina Alkire, and other participants in a workshop in Oxford held on September 11 – 13, 2002, notably Amartya Sen, Martha Nussbaum, and especially Bina Agarwal. The usual disclaimer applies.

NOTES

[1] Paul Seabright (2001: 42) remarks: "... the wish to see freedom as the fundamental value underlying every other even leads Sen at one point to talk about mortality as a denial of 'the freedom to survive.' Well, yes, one can call it that, but is it really illuminating to suggest that what matters about being dead is the lack of freedom that goes with it? Being dead is also bad for the health and has a significant statistical association with dropping out of college, but personally I think it's the deadness that would bother me." Sen in fact refers to the freedom *to survive*, not to the freedom that survival brings, but his wish to bring so much under the label of freedom can cause confusion of this sort. And what of the *right* to survive?

[2] "Practical reason" refers to the reasoning in preparing for and deciding on actions and practices.

[3] In the language of freedom/capability as the range of real opportunities to get valued benefits, the issue of excess freedom hardly seems to arise. Sen does direct us to look at valued positive freedom, the holding of valuable options, but in practice a presumption can easily enter that more freedom ("real" freedom) is always good.

[4] In IDEA (2001), Manabi Majumdar, for example, signals a lack of attention to proactive public action plans to deal with religious fundamentalism; Roberto Gargarella argues

that Nussbaum has not offered sufficient support for her claims that her account of priorities applies to all women; and Xiaorong Li proposes that Nussbaum's capability approach shares some fundamental shortcomings with a human rights approach.

5 Jean Drèze and Amartya Sen have now reduced freedom's status somewhat to "among the principal means as well as the primary ends" of development (2002: 4). Here we have discussed Sen's emphasis in *Development as Freedom*, which has been translated into many languages and achieved remarkable sales.

REFERENCES

Anderson, Elizabeth. 1993. *Value in Ethics and Economics.* Cambridge, MA: Harvard University Press.

Badgett, Lee and Nancy Folbre. 1999. "Assigning Care: Gender Norms and Economic Outcomes." *International Labor Review* 138(3): 311–26.

Bruyn-Hundt, Marga. 1996. *The Economics of Unpaid Work.* Amsterdam: Thesis Publishers.

Connolly, William. 1983. *The Terms of Political Discourse,* 2nd edn. Oxford, UK Martin Robertson.

Crocker, David A. 1995. "Functioning and Capability: The Foundations of Sen's and Nussbaum's Development Ethics," in Martha Nussbaum and Jonathan Glover (eds.) *Women, Culture and Development: A Study of Human Capabilities* pp. 153–198. Oxford, UK: Clarendon Press.

Dawson, Graham and Sue Hatt. 2000. *Market, State and Feminism. The Economics of Feminist Policy.* Cheltenham, UK: Edward Elgar.

Deneulin, Severine. 2003 (Forthcoming). "Beyond Individual Freedom and Agency: The Role of Structures of Living Together in Sen's Capability Approach to Development," in Sabina Alkire, Flavio Comim, and Mozaffar Qizilbash (eds.) *Justice and Poverty: Examining Sen's Capability Approach,* Cambridge, UK: Cambridge University Press.

Drèze, Jean and Amartya Sen. 2002. *India: Development and Participation.* Delhi: Oxford University Press.

Elson, Diane (ed.). 1995. *Male Bias in Economic Development.* Manchester, UK: University of Manchester Press.

—— and Nilufer Cagatay. 2000. "The Social Content of Macro Economic Policies." *World Development* 28(7): 1347–64.

England, Paula. 1993. "The Separative Self: Androcentric Bias in Neoclassical Assumptions," in Marianne Ferber and Julie Nelson (eds.), pp. 37–53. *Beyond Economic Man. Feminist Theory and Economics.* Chicago: University of Chicago Press.

Ferber, Marianne and Julie Nelson (eds.). 1993. *Beyond Economic Man. Feminist Theory and Economics.* Chicago: University of Chicago Press.

Folbre, Nancy and Thomas Weisskopf. 1998. "Did Father Know Best? Families, Markets, and the Supply of Caring Labor," in Avner Ben-Ner and Louis Putterman (eds.) *Economics, Values and Organization,* pp. 171–205. Cambridge, UK: Cambridge University Press.

—— and Julie Nelson. 2000. "For Love or Money–Or Both?" *Journal of Economic Perspectives* 14(4): 123–40.

Friedman, Milton and Rose Friedman. 1962. *Capitalism and Freedom.* Chicago: University of Chicago Press.

—— and Rose Friedman. 1980. *Free to Choose.* New York: Harcourt Brace Jovanovich.

Gasper, Des. 1993. "Entitlements Analysis–Relating Concepts and Contexts." *Development and Change* 24(4): 679–718.

——. 2000. "Development as Freedom: Taking Economics Beyond Commodities– The Cautious Boldness of Amartya Sen." *Journal of International Development* 12(7): 989– 1001.

——. 2002. "Is Sen's Capability Approach an Adequate Basis for a Theory of Human Development?" *Review of Political Economy* 14(4): 435– 61.

Hamilton, Lawrence. 1999. "A Theory of True Interests in the Work of Amartya Sen." *Government and Opposition* 34(4): 516– 46.

Hewitson, Gillian. 1999. *Feminist Economics. Interrogating the Masculinity of Rational Economic Man.* Cheltenham, UK: Edward Elgar.

IDEA. 2001. Symposium on *Women and Human Development* by Martha Nussbaum (2000). International Development Ethics Association. Available at http://www.development-ethics.org (Reports section).

Kabeer, Naila. 1994. *Reversed Realities. Gender Hierarchies in Development Thought.* London: Verso.

Kolm, Serge-Christophe. 1998. "The Values of Freedom," in Jean-Francois Laslier, Marc Fleurbaey, Nicolas Gravel, and Alain Trannoy (eds.) *Freedom in Economics. New Perspectives in Normative Analysis*, pp. 17– 44. London: Routledge.

Laslier, Francois, Marc Fleurbaey, Nicolas Gravel, and Alain Trannoy. 1998. *Freedom in Economics. New Perspectives in Normative Analysis.* London: Routledge.

MacCallum, Gerald. 1967. "Negative and Positive Freedom." *Philosophical Review* 76: 312– 34.

Nelson, Julie. 1993. "Value Free or Valueless? Notes on the Pursuit of Detachment in Economics." *History of Political Economy* 25(1): 121– 45.

——. 1996. *Feminism, Objectivity and Economics.* London: Routledge.

Nussbaum, Martha. 1995. "Human Capabilities, Female Human Beings," in Martha Nussbaum and Jonathan Glover (eds.) *Women, Culture and Development: A Study of Human Capabilities.* pp. 61– 104. Oxford UK: Clarendon Press.

——. 1999. "Women and Equality: The Capabilities Approach." *International Labor Review* 138(3): 227– 45.

——. 2000. *Women and Human Development. The Capabilities Approach.* Cambridge, UK: Cambridge University Press.

——. 2001. *Upheavals of Thought: The Intelligence of Emotions.* Cambridge, UK: Cambridge University Press.

——. 2003. "Capabilities as Fundamental Entitlements: Sen and Social Justice." *Feminist Economics,* this issue.

—— and Jonathan Glover (eds.). 1995. *Women, Culture and Development. A Study of Human Capabilities.* Oxford, UK: Clarendon Press.

Peacock, Alan. 1997. *The Political Economy of Economic Freedom.* Cheltenham, UK: Edward Elgar.

Peter, Fabienne. 2001. "Review of Martha Nussbaum's *Women and Human Development.*" *Feminist Economics* 7(2): 131– 5.

Robeyns, Ingrid. 2001. "Sen's Capability Approach and Feminist Concerns." Paper presented at a conference on Sen's Capability Approach, University of Cambridge, June.

Seabright, Paul. 2001. "The Road Upward." *New York Review of Books,* March 29.

Sen, Amartya. 1977. "Rational Fools: A Critique of the Behavioral Foundations of Economic Theory." *Philosophy and Public Affairs* 6(4): 317– 44.

——. 1981a. *Poverty and Famines: An Essay on Entitlement and Deprivation.* Oxford, UK: Oxford University Press.

——. 1981b. "Rights and Agency." *Philosophy and Public Affairs* 11(2): 3– 39.

——. 1984a. "Family and Food: Sex Bias in Poverty," in Amartya Sen, *Resources, Values and Development*, pp. 346– 68. Cambridge MA: Harvard University Press.

———. 1984b. "Poor, Relatively Speaking," in Amartya Sen, *Resources, Values and Development*, pp. 325–45. Cambridge, MA: Harvard University Press.

———. 1985. *Commodities and Capabilities*. Amsterdam: North-Holland.

———. 1987. *On Ethics and Economics*. Oxford, UK: Blackwell.

———. 1989. "Food and Freedom." *World Development* 17(6): 769–81.

———. 1995. "The Formulation of Rational Choice." *American Economic Review* 84(2): 385–90.

———. 1998. "Human Development and Financial Conservatism." *World Development* 26(4): 733–42.

———. 1999. *Development as Freedom*. New York: Oxford University Press.

———. 2002. *Rationality and Freedom*. Cambridge, MA: Belknap/Harvard University Press.

Silva Leander, Sebastian. 2001. "Sen and Kant on Freedom and Progress." Unpublished paper, Oxford University.

Staveren, Irene van. 2001. *The Values of Economics. An Aristotelian Perspective*. London: Routledge.

Tronto, Joan. 1993. *Moral Boundaries. A Political Argument for an Ethic of Care*. London: Routledge.

Truong, Thanh-Dam, 1997. "Gender and Human Development: A Feminist Perspective." *Gender, Technology and Development* 1(3): 349–70.

UNDP. 1995. *Human Development Report 1995*. Oxford, UK: Oxford University Press.

Walzer, Michael. 1983. *Spheres of Justice*. Oxford, UK: Blackwell.

Williams, Bernard. 2001. "From Freedom to Liberty: The Construction of a Political Value." *Philosophy and Public Affairs* 30(1): 3–26.

GLOBALIZATION AND WOMEN'S PAID WORK: EXPANDING FREEDOM?

Christine M. Koggel

OVERVIEW

In *Development as Freedom*, Amartya Sen takes expanding freedom to be the primary end and the principal means of development. I discuss his emphasis on women's agency as central to development theory and practice and the strategies he advocates for enhancing it. Recent work in feminist economics and postcolonial studies tests Sen's complex account of freedom. Further levels of complexity need to be added when we examine how global forces of power interact with local systems of oppression in ways that often limit women's freedom. This argument rests on an analysis of how globalization affects a domain of freedom that is a central concern for Sen, that of increasing women's freedom to work outside the home as a way of strengthening their agency. Attending to elements missing in Sen's account will enhance freedom in women's lives.

INTRODUCTION

Globalization has reshaped many issues: international relations, population growth, development, human rights, the environment, labor, healthcare, and poverty, among others. It has increased our awareness of the profound ways in which policies and practices in one region can affect the livelihoods of people in other regions, and even in the world as a whole. Recent research in ethics explores the implications of globalization as it affects these and many other areas of inquiry. Some of the products of this philosophical inquiry are the evolution of a language of human rights; attempts to formulate a global ethic; accounts of cross-cultural judgment and interpretation; and research on development ethics. In this context, feminist economics and Third World, postcolonial, and global studies have been vitally important for highlighting the need to be aware of power relations at both the global and local levels when providing accounts of development processes and policies.[1] These theorists argue that many of these processes and policies have had a detrimental impact on women in domains such as the workplace, education, and healthcare, and in terms of their social, political, and economic status and participation. This work is reshaping both the conceptual terrain of these issues and the policies being framed by national and international organizations.

Amartya Sen opens *Development as Freedom* by acknowledging this global context of increasingly close linkages of trade, communication, and ideas across countries and the conditions of "unprecedented opulence" and "remarkable deprivation, destitution, and oppression" that coexist both within countries and across rich and poor countries (Amartya Sen 1999: xi). In fact, Sen provides a rather dismal picture of contemporary life: "persistence of poverty and unfulfilled elementary needs, occurrence of famines and widespread hunger, violation of elementary political freedoms as well as of basic liberties, extensive neglect of the interests and agency of women, and worsening threats to our environment and to the sustainability of our economic and social lives" (Sen 1999: xi). A central goal of development theory and policy is to address these problems that are made all the more stark (and some would say even sustained) by the unprecedented opulence in other parts of the world. Sen's solution is to take the expansion of freedom or the removal of various types of unfreedoms "both as the primary end and as the principal means of development" (Sen 1999: xii). Development, he writes, "consists of the removal of various types of unfreedom that leave people with little choice and little opportunity of exercising their reasoned agency" (Sen 1999: xii). Sen further argues that giving *women* freedom to exercise their agency should be a key goal of development policy:

> The extensive reach of women's agency is one of the more neglected areas of development studies, and most urgently in need of correction. Nothing, arguably, is as important today in the political economy of development as an adequate recognition of political, economic and social participation and leadership of women. This is indeed a crucial aspect of 'development as freedom.'

> (Sen 1999: 203)

Before proceeding, I want to clarify my approach by making two points. First, as shown in the section that follows, Sen provides a complex account of the interconnectedness of various kinds of freedom. He argues that increasing women's freedom to work outside the home is crucial for increasing their freedom in domains such as the home, healthcare, education, reproductive control, and social and political life. Clearly, women's long and continued exclusion from the workforce has limited their freedom, and Sen's work in drawing connections between the freedom to work and other sorts of freedoms is important not only to development theory but to feminist theory more generally. My argument is not that women's workforce participation should not be promoted or that increasing their freedom in this domain does not have a positive impact on their freedom in other domains. Rather I raise questions about whether paid employment necessarily increases women's freedom and agency in all places and, specifically, under conditions of globalization. Second, there has been a longstanding debate about whether paid work necessarily improves the status and material standard of women and the circumstances that make this situation more or less likely. This debate has encompassed related issues such as the family wage and the double shift.[2] In this chapter, I discuss some of these nonliberating aspects, but my focus is on women's paid work in the current context of globalization. If not entirely absent in Sen's account, power and oppression are not sufficiently recognized as factors of inequality in women's lives that are relevant to the kinds of policies required, at both the global and local levels, for increasing women's freedom and agency.

I. WOMEN'S AGENCY AND WELL-BEING

Sen understands freedom to be the end as well as the means of development, in the sense that progress is evaluated in terms of whether freedoms are enhanced and whether enhancing freedom is effective for achieving development:

> [d]evelopment has to be more concerned with enhancing the lives we lead and the freedoms we enjoy. Expanding the freedoms we have rea-son to value not only makes our lives richer and more unfettered, but also allows us to be fuller social persons, exercising our own volitions and interacting with – and influencing – the world in which we live.
>
> (Sen 1999: 14 – 15)

According to Sen, development theorists need to view various kinds of freedom (political, economic, and social) as inextricably interconnected, and they also need to know about the empirical connections that obtain when policies that limit freedom in one domain decrease freedoms in other domains: "[e]conomic unfreedom can breed social unfreedom, just as social or political unfreedom can also foster economic unfreedom" (Sen 1999: 8). Paying attention to kinds and levels of freedom, argues Sen, allows us to be sensitive to the ways in which human diversity and the particularities of social practices and political contexts affect one's ability to satisfy basic needs, perform various human functions, and live lives reflective of human flourishing.

Another vital aspect of Sen's theory of development is that he shifts the focus from people as patients of development to people as agents of development processes and change:

... this freedom-centered understanding of economics and of the process of development is very much an agent-oriented view. With adequate social opportunities, individuals can effectively shape their own destiny and help each other. They need not be seen primarily as passive recipients of the benefits of cunning development programs. There is indeed a strong rationale for recognizing the positive role of free and sustainable agency.

(Sen 1999: 11)

In Chapter 8 of his *Development as Freedom,* Sen distinguishes strategies for promoting women's well-being from strategies that promote women's agency. The former is welfarist in the sense that women are treated as the passive recipients of policies designed to remove inequalities and achieve better conditions for them. An agency approach takes women to be active agents who themselves promote and achieve social and political transformations that can then better the lives of both women and men. Sen acknowledges that the two approaches overlap, since agency strategies have the goal of removing inequalities that affect women's well-being and well-being strategies need to draw on women's agency to effect real changes. However, Sen argues that distinguishing the two is important because treating a person as an agent is fundamentally different from treating him or her as a patient: "[u]nderstanding the agency role is thus central to recognizing people as responsible persons: not only are we well or ill, but also we act or refuse to act, and can choose to act one way rather than another" (Sen 1999: 190).

Sen views the promotion of women's agency as vital not only for improving the economic and social power of women, but for challenging and changing entrenched values and social practices that support gender bias in the distribution of basic goods such as food and healthcare and in the treatment of women and girls within families. He then makes the strong claim that the "changing agency of women is one of the major mediators of economic and social change, and its determination as well as consequences closely relate to many of the central features of the development process" (Sen 1999: 202).

On the face of it, feminists could hardly quarrel with Sen's emphasis on the promotion of women's agency as a way of enhancing their well-being. After all, what better way for well-being to be measured than to have it within women's control as active agents and placed in the context of women's lives? Yet Sen's account of agency involves more than giving women the power to make their own decisions regarding reproduction or childcare, to change the gendered division of labor, and to improve female access to healthcare in their own social and political contexts. He uses empirical studies to substantiate and defend particular policies for increasing women's freedom and agency. He argues that agency in the above-mentioned domains is integrally connected with freedoms in other domains such as the freedom to work outside the home: "freedom in one area (that of being able to work outside the household) seems to help foster freedom in others (enhancing freedom from hunger, illness, and relative deprivation)" (Sen 1999: 194).

Sen notes that in general terms, empirical data show that women's well-being is strongly influenced by "women's ability to earn an independent income, to find employment outside the home, to have ownership rights and to have literacy and be educated participants in decisions inside and outside the family" (Sen 1999: 191).[3] These abilities are aspects of agency in that women are *doing* things and making choices that then give them voice, social standing, independence, and empowerment. In Sen's own words on the case of paid employment:

> ... working outside the home and earning an independent income tend to have a clear impact on enhancing the social standing of a woman in the household and the society. Her contribution to the prosperity of the family is then more visible, and she also has more voice, because of being less dependent on others. Further, outside employment often has useful 'educational' effects, in terms of exposure to the world outside the household, thus making her agency more effective.
>
> (Sen 1999: 192)

My purpose is not to critically analyze the data Sen uses or all of the policies he suggests, but to focus on the connection he makes between promoting women's workforce participation and increasing their agency. For, as soon as we note that doing paid work outside the home is a key policy in his account, we are led to ask: does this necessarily increase women's agency and well-being? What factors might affect the outcome? Among possible factors could be whether women's paid work is located inside or outside the home; whether they have sole responsibility for domestic work in addition to their paid work; whether they work in the formal or informal sector; whether other family members have control over their income; whether the labor market permits high or low earnings; and whether jobs provide safety and leave provisions or control over conditions of work. These factors, which vary from location to location, have an impact on women's agency in local contexts as well as in the global context of multinational corporations. My aim is to examine global factors in more detail to understand how multinational corporations, for example, operate in specific local contexts in ways that sometimes enhance, but often limit, women's freedom and agency. The central question in my analysis thus becomes: is Sen's account sufficiently discerning of the ways in which global forces of power and local systems of oppression operate and interact in ways that limit women's freedom and agency even when they have paid work?

II. WOMEN'S PAID WORK AND THE GLOBAL CONTEXT

Sen's account, as noted, is rooted in empirical analysis, sensitive to the particularities of issues and policies, appreciative of diverse human needs and abilities, and responsive to various social conditions and political contexts. Yet there is reason to worry that there is still something missing, particularly when we examine the issue of women's workforce participation in the context of globalization. A good place to draw out the implications of this examination is with Chandra Mohanty's work. She examines both the local and the global aspects of oppressive conditions in women's lives. Thinking globally means being aware of the ways in which women's work is shaped by the contemporary arena of global corporations, markets, and capitalism. She notes:

> Third-World women workers (defined in this context as both women from the geographical Third World and immigrant and indigenous women of color in the U.S. and Western Europe) occupy a specific social location in the international division of labor which *illuminates* and *explains* crucial features of the capitalist processes of exploitation and domination. These are features of the social world that are usually obfuscated or mystified in discourses about the 'progress' and 'development' (e.g., the creation of jobs for poor, Third-World women as the markers of economic and social advancement) that is assumed to 'naturally' accompany the triumphal rise of global capitalism.
>
> (Chandra Mohanty 1997: 7, her emphasis)

Mohanty's description of discourses about progress and development suggests that providing women with jobs *may* be as inadequate a measure of economic and social advancement as are increases in the GNP or income levels. One of the reasons for this, according to Mohanty, is global capitalism itself and the processes of exploitation and domination generated by it.

Multinational corporate executives and financial institutions are motivated by increasing profits and decreasing costs, not by improving women's workforce participation or their freedom and agency. The drive to decrease costs means that particular women are recruited into specific kinds of jobs, but it does not mean that these women have choices that effectively change their levels of freedom. However, I want to temper the strong connection that Mohanty makes between global capitalism and exploitation by suggesting that women's paid work in a global context has mixed effects. It can provide opportunities for work not otherwise available to women in specific contexts, but it can and often does provide less than ideal work conditions. The complexity of factors relevant to a description of global corporations and their operations in specific locations means that opportunities for and conditions of work can change in both the short and long term. Yet while Mohanty can be said to ignore the positive aspects of global markets and corporations, she does pay attention to the details of women's lives at the local level. Her account, therefore, makes room for a more complex and sophisticated analysis (than she herself provides) of the sorts of global and local factors that can determine the kind of impact that increased workforce participation has on women's freedom and agency.

Mohanty, and the work of feminist economists on which she draws, rejects ahistorical and universal accounts of experiences shared by women, whether Third World women or all women in the workforce, and instead allows commonalities to emerge from detailed descriptions of the lives of working women in specific social contexts. Thus measuring women's increased participation in the workplace does not give us the whole story about the effect on their well-being or agency. For a fuller picture, we need to take account of the many barriers to women's freedom and agency, even when their participation in the workforce is permitted or increased, by examining not only the global context, but also the embeddedness of women's work in localized social practices and political institutions. Recognition of various forces of power at the global level is never far away in the analysis of the local.

Two of Mohanty's studies provide useful leads. In the first, Mohanty uses Maria Mies's work to analyze local systems of oppression affecting the working lives of the lace-makers of Narsapur in Andhra Pradesh, a state in south India. The second considers implications of Mohanty's discussion of electronics workers in the First World context of the Silicon Valley in California (USA) and demonstrates how multinational corporations often make use of gendered and racialized meanings in particular locations in ways that can limit rather than increase women's freedom and agency in the workplace and other domains. Highlighting local factors in the first example and global factors in the second serves to illustrate features of each. However, the descriptions also show that the local and the global cannot but intersect in the contemporary context of globalization.

The account of women's agency that emerges from these descriptions is inherently complex. Local and global factors and their interactions are not static, but are subject to changes in markets, economic conditions, labor demands, and so on. Whether change is possible depends on various factors, including the entrenchment of local gender norms, as illustrated by the example of lace-making in Narsapur. Moreover, even as women experience negative effects on their freedom in the workplace, there can be changes in gender norms and improvements in other spheres of women's lives, as illustrated by the example of electronics workers. A proper assessment of whether women's freedom and agency is improved or diminished needs these complex descriptions of local and global factors and their intersections in particular locations at particular times.

As Maria Mies describes it, understanding the exploitative working conditions of the lace-makers in Narsapur requires understanding the power exercised by social norms in this location. Beliefs about women's proper sphere and the devaluation of their activity in the home, entrenched in this region's cultural practices, are not easily eliminated when women are allowed to "work." For the lace-makers, caste and gender work to transform beliefs about women's unequal status and power in a private sphere into a hierarchical ordering in which women's work in the production of lace is conceptualized as "leisure activity" with little pay, and where the products and proceeds of this industry are controlled by men. Mies demonstrates that the expansion of the lace industry into the global market "led not only to class differentiation within particular communities (Christians, Kapus) but also to the masculinization of all nonproduction jobs, especially of trade, and the total feminization of the production process. ... Men sell women's products and live on the profits from women's work" (Maria Mies 1982: 10). This gendered division of labor coupled with the conceptualization of lace-making as leisure, rather than as work, means that women have no control over their work hours or conditions of work, or even the proceeds of their "leisure" activity. In addition to their labor-intensive work of caring for families and maintaining households, they work six to eight hours a day making lace in confined spaces with poor lighting and little pay. Furthermore, this "leisure activity" is perceived as befitting the women's membership in a caste that promotes women's seclusion in the home as a status symbol. These women are both perceived as and perceive themselves as being of higher status than women who belong to castes of poor peasants or agricultural laborers. These local beliefs about proper gender and caste roles, and women's isolation from one another (because they are home-based), converge to prevent lace-makers from organizing to improve their conditions. They also cause the women themselves to cling to these symbols of higher status, even though women agricultural laborers of lower castes earn "considerably more in the course of a year than the lace workers" (Mies 1982: 15).

At the very least, this description tempers optimism about substantive gains to these women's freedom and agency, in either the private or public sphere, when they are permitted to join the workforce. What makes the case of lace-makers particularly problematic is that no one, not even the workers themselves, perceive them to be in the workforce. The conditions of their work are not only a function of globalized markets in lace, but also of their home-based work that makes them virtually invisible. The number of women dispersed throughout homes in many areas is high, and yet they do not count in labor statistics, where workers are those who earn a living outside the home. It is the men who control the industry and do the visible activities of buying and selling. In this example, the local details matter for an analysis of work and of *this* gendered and caste division of labor in which all the power is in the hands of those who control the markets, the capital, and the returns from the sales.[4] Here women are placed at the lowest and least visible part of the chain of a global industry and market in lace. Counting them as workers in local and international statistics on labor could of course make them visible in terms of numbers, but this in itself cannot change women's oppressive work conditions, for which other strategies would be needed, as discussed in Section III. Indeed, entrenched beliefs about gender and caste shape these women's lives in ways that limit their freedom and agency well beyond factors that could easily be measured in statistical reports on labor. Having "paid work" may do little to promote women's agency if work is inside the home and invisible and if income is appropriated by male heads of households.

The case of women workers in the Silicon Valley in California is different in that these women do perceive themselves to be workers and are also perceived to be so by others. Mohanty (1997) reports that in the 1980s, 80 to 90 percent of the laborer jobs on the shop floor of electronics factories in the Silicon Valley were held by women, half of which again were held by Asian immigrant women. She explains that Third World women's over-representation was the result of their being targeted and recruited into these underpaid jobs. The explanation, she notes:

> lies in the redefinition of work as temporary, supplementary, and un-skilled, in the construction of women as mothers and homemakers, and in the positioning of femininity as contradictory to factory work. In addition, the explanation also lies in the specific definition of Third-World, immigrant women as docile, tolerant, and satisfied with substandard wages.
>
> (Mohanty 1997: 18)

Diane Elson and Ruth Pearson's (1981) early research on women workers in the electronics industry of Southeast Asia throws light on the widespread beliefs within these industries about differences in the innate capacities of men and women and their income needs.

> Women are considered not only to have naturally nimble fingers, but also to be naturally more docile and willing to accept tough work discipline, and naturally more suited to tedious, repetitive, monotonous work. Their lower wages are attributed to their secondary status in the labor market which is seen as a natural consequence of their ability to bear children.
>
> (Diane Elson and Ruth Pearson 1981: 149)

Evidence shows that these widespread beliefs about women play a role at all levels of upper and middle management, human resource departments, immediate supervisors, husbands and relatives, and the women themselves in ways that explain the recruitment of Asian immigrant women into jobs in

California's Silicon Valley as well as the conditions of work that obtain in them. The effect of defining this work as temporary, unskilled, and tedious legitimizes entrapping these women into low-paying jobs, in which work conditions prevent them from engaging in union activity, political struggle, or collective action, activities that could change the exploitation and domination they face. Such systems of oppression that utilize gender and racial stereotypes structure the meaning and conditions of work for these electronic factory workers – and potentially, global perceptions as well.

Elisabeth Fussell's (2000) study of the rise of the female maquiladora labor force in Tijuana, Mexico, shows how multinational corporations operate in Third World countries to keep production costs and wages lower than in First World countries, often because of less rigid labor laws. Fussell points out that since the 1970s, "when global trade began to intensify, new production and labor-control technologies and competition between low-wage production zones combined to make the cost of labor the most variable component of production" (Elisabeth Fussell 2000: 60). To attract multinational corporations and under pressure through NAFTA, the Mexican government implemented policies such as the dismantling of independent labor unions and the lowering of maquiladora wages to the "lowest of developing countries with strong export marketing sectors" (Fussell 2000: 64).

In Tijuana, Mexican women, who are already perceived and perceive themselves as secondary wage earners supplementing men's wages, become ready suppliers of low-wage labor. Fussell defends feminist economists who have argued that there is deterioration rather than improvement in women's opportunities and agency precisely because "maquiladora employers attract a sector of the female labor force with low levels of human capital and a great need for stable employment which willingly accepts the low wages offered by the maquiladoras" (Fussell 2000: 63). The opportunities in this area, in other words, are restricted to a specific segment of women workers – those able to run the smallest risk of losing their jobs. As Fussell points out, "[b]eing 25 or older, having a child younger than 5, and having less than a primary level of education increase women's probability of maquiladora employment" (Fussell 2000: 73). These women are perceived to be and have proved to be docile and accepting of the challenges demanded by tedious assembly processes. They are less likely to risk losing their jobs through labor resistance than those who are more qualified and more likely to demand higher wages and better working conditions. Fussell argues that if there was ever any potential to improve the lives of women in Mexico by providing them with jobs, it has been "lost to the search for low wages and a flexible labor force" (Fussell 2000: 60). One could argue that the maquiladoras hire precisely those most in need of employment, those who would otherwise be worse off. Yet the descriptions of recruitment and work conditions highlight the ways in which corporate interests conspired to "take advantage of women's disadvantages" (Fussell 2000: 75) and "diminished the earnings potential of women employed in the maquiladoras" (Fussell 2000: 76).

In the abstract, maquiladoras provide job opportunities and promote national economic development. They fit the description of places that integrate women into the workforce, a goal that Sen argues is a way of increasing women's freedom and agency. However, a closer examination of how multinational corporations, with a vested interest in maximizing profits and minimizing costs, use entrenched meanings of gender and class casts doubt on the promise of workforce participation as necessarily improving the well-being or agency of these women.[5] In Sen's terms, these women would *seem* to be passive actors rather than active agents seeking to change their work conditions. If we question the motivations of corporate employers who seek to maximize gains by utilizing specific features of labor markets in Third World countries, then we must also question whether these women are truly the recipients of policies designed to remove inequalities and achieve better working conditions. We need to know about these factors at both the local and global levels to make proper assessments of the effects on women's freedom and agency, including factors that can have positive effects.

So far I have concentrated on the negative effects that global markets and multinational corporations can have on women's freedom and agency in particular locations. Global and local factors change, sometimes in ways that can improve women's work conditions. Tighter labor markets, for example, can give workers in some places at some times more bargaining power to negotiate improved wages and better working conditions. As Linda Lim points out, "more and more men are being employed by newly established maquiladoras (export-oriented factories), which are unable to recruit sufficient women due to the export industry boom and resultant tightening labor market in this region" (Linda Lim 1990: 108). More recently, there are reports that many of these factories in the Tijuana belt are closing as multinationals find cheaper labor elsewhere.[6] These are factors that could change the analysis provided in the studies by Fussell and Elson and Pearson. But there is also more serious criticism of these studies.

Lim emphasizes that these studies only focus on the negative impact of these jobs on women's freedom and agency: "feminists who see patriarchy and gender subordination as crucial underpinnings and inevitable consequences of all capitalism refuse to recognize any benefits to women in the Third World from employment in export factories, insisting that such employment intensifies rather than alleviates their gender subordination" (Lim 1990: 116). She adds:

> The predominant stereotype is that First World multinational factories located in the Third World export-processing zones employ mostly

young, single, female rural–urban migrants, who are ruthlessly exploited in harsh factory environments where they suffer long hours, poor working conditions, insecure, unhealthy, and unsafe jobs, and wages so low that they are not even sufficient to cover individual sub-sistence.

(Lim 1990: 111)

Lim does not claim that poor working conditions do not exist in some areas. They were particularly evident when export factories were established. Rather, she makes two points. The first is that changes to labor and market demands can change workforce composition. The second point is about the "tendency to generalize from ... observations in one particular location at one time" (Lim 1990: 113), a tendency that often ignores the ways in which women are changing their lives even as they experience the negative impact of work conditions. Lim defends a dynamic historical approach, one that highlights the importance of being sensitive to changes in local and global factors when reading accounts of women's work. She has us pay attention, for example, to the ways in which *having* employment, where none was available previously, affects "women workers' lives and their position in and relations with their families" (Lim 1990: 114). This dynamic approach endorses an account of women as agents, who, in the process of interacting with and reacting to changing local and global factors, themselves reshape meanings and therefore change the conditions of their own lives.

Pearson has responded to Lim's critique by agreeing that her collaborative work with Elson failed to acknowledge the force of a dynamic approach:

in our desire to pursue the implications for gender positioning of the new geography of women's labour we were ignoring the ways in which that experience continually reformulated specific women's gender identities and the ways in which women were active agents in the inter-action between capital accumulation and traditional forms of gender identities.

(Ruth Pearson 1998: 180)

This concession does not reject descriptions of the negative impact of multinational corporations in places like Tijuana, but it recognizes the importance of avoiding homogenizing, static, and generalized approaches. María Fernández-Kelly demonstrates these principles when she reports her experiences of applying for jobs and working inside maquiladoras. She argues that even as women have limited potential to change the conditions of their work, they are challenging and changing "conventional mores and values regarding femininity" (María Fernández-Kelly 1997: 215) that have prevailed in Mexican society.

III. LESSONS FOR DEVISING POLICY

Generally, enabling women to work outside the home increases their freedom in other domains. Sen's analysis appears to show that there are improvements in domains such as women's access to healthcare, education, and birth control when women are allowed to enter the workplace. But what lessons can be learned from the detailed descriptions of what women's work is actually like? One is that descriptions of women's work in particular contexts complicates Sen's general strategy of advocating work outside the home. If agency enables women to make choices and *do* things that then give them voice, social standing, independence, and empowerment in both the public and private spheres, then care is needed in advocating for women's work participation as a sure way of increasing their freedom and agency. Another lesson is that we must pay attention to the global and the local, as well as to the impact of the global on the local. The weaving together of the analyses by Mohanty, Mies, Fussell, Pearson, Elson, and Lim provides a two-pronged critique of Sen's account. These consist of the local and global, and the critique requires tracing the interconnections between global forces of power and local systems of oppression to achieve a more extensive analysis of women's freedom and agency than that provided by Sen.

Consider, for instance, the local factors of power and oppression and their frequent shaping by global forces. Multinational corporations have relatively easy entry into most countries in the world, and they often shape freedom and agency at the local level. While capital and multinational corporations are highly mobile, labor is much less so. Also, labor is often key in maximizing profits and minimizing costs, which explains why multinational corporations seek to move quickly across borders at the expense of the relative immobility of labor. The maquiladoras in Tijuana illustrate how these features of local labor markets are employed by multinational corporations. They also illustrate how gender, race, and class are understood, defined, and used in specific locations to meet local and global demands for labor. Multinational corporations can determine not only who gets to work and what work they do, but also the social norms and the perceptions regarding workers and work itself. Unlike the lace-makers in South India, maquiladora women in Mexico are perceived to be and perceive themselves to be workers, but they are secondary wage workers with little or no freedom to choose the kind of jobs they want and little or no agency to change their working conditions. This is not to deny some of the benefits. Rather an awareness of the complex features of local and global conditions helps us recognize what spaces women have to negotiate and implement policies that alleviate the negative effects on their freedom and agency. For example, women workers who challenge conventional norms of femininity are also positioned to challenge the double shift of adding work outside the home to caring for children by, for example, pressing for daycare facilities. These changes can in turn positively affect freedoms in other areas such as health and education.

Other examples of women's work point to features of importance at the local level. Apart from conservative social norms, such factors as high unemployment, environmental disasters, persistent poverty, political corruption, civil unrest, and the absence of labor protection laws can all affect the exploitation of workers by local employers. Accounting for these factors would temper Sen's claim that there is a strong or inevitable link between increasing women's workforce participation and increasing their levels of freedom and agency in domains such as the home, reproductive decisions, and the equitable distribution of food, healthcare, and education within families.

Also, global forces of power often interact with local conditions in ways that shape levels of freedom and agency at the local level. Increasing women's freedom through work outside the home can fail as a general policy if pre-existing local conditions are disadvantageous. This is particularly likely where multinational corporations can prevent workers from organizing, challenging, and changing oppressive and exploitative work conditions. It can also fail as a general policy if the interests of multinational corporations, trade agreements such as NAFTA, or the rise and fall of its currency, rather than the interests of its least advantaged citizens, dictate the host government's policy. Again, I do not deny the importance of increasing women's freedom to work. Rather, I emphasize that recognition of the complex, unpredictable effects of these forces on the lives and conditions of women in particular regions is missing in Sen's account.

If transformations are to be truly in terms of increasing women's agency, we need to contextualize them by looking at the particular activities of multinational corporations and their disempowering effects on people in specific contexts. We need to know about the particularities of gender inequalities and injustices and the ways in which race, class, ethnicity, and so on intersect, shape, and sustain relations of power. Such detailed descriptions would reveal that advocating increased workforce participation is not sufficient for a meaningful improvement of women's freedom and agency in all places, and that there may be losses to freedom in some domains even as freedom may be increased in others. Analyses and critiques need to be multi-pronged and conducted at both local and global levels, and policies need to be multifaceted if genuine improvements to women's freedom and agency are to be obtained.

Descriptions of women's work at the local level also highlight the importance of acting locally so that power is transferred to those affected by oppressive norms and practices. Sen supports the idea that control of work needs to be in women's hands. He strongly advocates the promotion of

178

women's agency and provides examples of the successful organizing and managing of businesses and bank loans by women in India (Sen 1999: 200–2). The Self-Employed Women's Association (SEWA), for example, has succeeded in enabling thousands of Indian women to "cut out some middleman activity and to command higher prices for their products in local, regional, and international markets" (Marilyn Carr, Martha Chen, and Jane Tate 2000: 138).[7] But the work of SEWA involves more than this, as Sen notes when he writes that it has been "most effective in bringing about a changed climate of thought, not just more employment for women" (Sen 1999: 116). Further, I would argue that the work of grassroots organizations such as SEWA illuminates how theory and policy need to be multifaceted to be effective. It shows that grassroots organizations themselves need to be vigilant about the ways in which the policies they advocate or put in place can be used, undermined, or reshaped by markets and corporate interests at the global level or even by their own governments.

Governments, for example, might promote women's employment when they need workers (say, as dictated by global markets), but these programs can be quickly withdrawn with shifts in global market conditions or in the local economy. Women's freedom to work can disappear when a multinational corporation decides to move its factories to minimize costs or to avoid government policies detrimental to its profit-maximizing interests. Women's freedom to work can also decline under pressure from religious and cultural groups or through a change in government. Or, women's work can be made invisible or rendered irrelevant in standard accounts of economic participation. These factors and many others need to be taken into account in devising strategies for increasing women's freedom and agency via employment.

At the global level, as suggested earlier, bodies such as the International Labor Organization (ILO) have a role to play in shaping policy regarding work conditions as well as in defining who counts as a worker by revising data-gathering procedures. Sen describes the ILO as the "custodian of workers' rights within the United Nations system" (Sen 2001: 33). He discusses his own work with the ILO and calls on it to implement an approach that is sensitive to diverse needs and context, but at the same time global and universalist:

> A universalist understanding of work and working relations can be linked to a tradition of solidarity and commitment. The need for invoking such a global approach has never been stronger than it is now. The economically globalizing world, with all its opportunities as well as problems, calls for a similarly globalized understanding of the priority of decent work and of its manifold demands on economic, political and social arrangements.
>
> (Sen 2001: 43)

While the role that organizations such as the ILO can play in formulating these policies is clearly important, we need to be clear about what is really needed for a globalized understanding, particularly when it involves women's work. As Lourdes Benería's (1982) research shows, women's "work" is often invisible or not valued because it does not fit the model of commodity production and market exchange that has dominated economic analysis. Economic analysis can, of course, be improved by better data, and Benería claims that some progress has occurred in terms of gathering data that interprets women's work as economic activity rather than leisure or private sphere activities. This includes housework, subsistence agricultural work, and home-based work (Lourdes Benería 1982: 120). But better economic analysis also needs a link with more gender-sensitive policies. The case of lace-makers in India nicely illustrates Benería's point that women's work and their participation in economic activities can be performed without ever leaving the home. As noted earlier, this work is perceived as leisure activity, even though women are carrying the double burden of domestic work and making products for the global market, all in a private sphere where their work is invisible and the returns from it are controlled by men. Features of the global market in lace and their interaction with this local system lead to this work neither increasing women's participation in the public sphere nor enhancing their freedom and agency in the private sphere. But this example also illustrates why simply improving the definitions of work and the collection of data on labor is not enough. Policies will not work if they are too general, rely too heavily on the power and goodwill of international organizations, or are not combined with local strategies for challenging the gendered, racialized, and class divisions of labor.

Carr, Chen, and Tate advocate four interrelated and multidirectional strategies in the case of home-based work: (1) research and statistical studies "to document the number, contribution, and working conditions of home-based workers and to assess the impact of globalization on them"; (2) action programs "to help home-based workers gain access to – and bargain effectively within – labor and product markets (both local and global)"; (3) grassroots organizations "to increase the visibility and voice of home-based workers and other women workers in the informal sector"; and (4) policy dialogues "to promote an enabling work and policy environment for home-based women workers" (Carr, Chen, and Tate 2000: 137). They give substance to their policy proposals by describing the work of several women's organizations, SEWA, HomeNet, and the United Nations Development Fund for Women (UNIFEM), whose work at both local and global levels illustrates their strategy. In 1997 these organizations formed a coalition, Women in Informal Employment: Globalizing and Organizing (WIEGO), "comprised of grassroots organizations, research institutions, and international development agencies concerned with improving the conditions and advancing the status of women in the informal sector" (Carr, Chen, and Tate 2000: 141).

Strategies that make use of the resources of national and international bodies to counteract disempowerment and exploitation experienced by women will be important. Especially in contexts where very large percentages of the female labor force are in the low-paying end of the informal sector, we need grassroots organizing not only for assessing and minimizing the negative impact of multinational corporations and global markets on women's work, but also for putting mechanisms in place to protect earnings at the local level. SEWA, for example, has a system that protects informal sector savings from being appropriated by husbands or other family members. Grassroots organizations can put pressure on national and international organizations to implement or change labor laws that exclude women from being protected from the exploitative working conditions. For such policies to be effective, then, as Sen rightly argues, national and international bodies need to be committed to enhancing well-being and quality of life. But they also need to engage in multifaceted strategies and policies that generate meaningful improvements to women's agency and freedom in particular contexts.

IV. CONCLUSION

Sen rightly argues that allowing people "the freedom to lead lives that they have reason to value" means removing unfreedoms such as malnutrition, premature morbidity, disease, unemployment, and political oppression. Sen urges those interested in alleviating the suffering caused by conditions of poverty, famine, and the destruction and degradation of the environment to attend less to income levels, GDP measures, technological advancements, and industrialization, and more to helping an individual live a healthy, meaningful life. In the face of the objection that Sen's account is too complex and perhaps difficult to embrace as anything other than an ideal,[8] I have defended its complexity and argued for engaging with even greater levels of complexity. Informed discussion of development processes and policies must include accounts of global forces of power and their intersection with and utilization of local systems of oppression. These factors are particularly evident in the area of women's work and have a direct impact on women's freedom and agency in this and other domains. Taking these factors into account expands the discussion of freedom in *Development as Freedom* and identifies further barriers to women's freedom and agency in addition to those that Sen highlights.

There is no single effect of economic globalization on women's participation in the workforce or on their freedom and agency. Sen concentrates on the positive impact of women's increased workforce participation on their freedom and agency. I do not dispute such a

181

potential positive impact, but the potential negative impact must also be recognized. Women's freedom and agency are not always improved when they enter the workforce, and merely increasing women's workforce participation is not an adequate development policy. The dynamic relationship between grassroots activities and national and international policy shows how women's agency can effect positive change, even as women grapple with the negative effects of local and global conditions on their lives.

ACKNOWLEDGMENTS

I am grateful to the anonymous reviewers, to the three editors of this volume, and to the participants of the Oxford Workshop (September 11 – 13, 2002) for their many useful comments and suggestions. Ingrid Robeyns' feedback and support, Jane Humphries' attention to background literature, and Bina Agarwal's detailed comments and input were especially important to this process. I would also like to thank all those who raised challenging questions at conferences where earlier drafts of this chapter were presented, particularly Jay Drydyk, Sue Campbell, Kai Nielsen, Nelleke Bak, Colin Macleod, Sue Sherwin, and David Crocker. Lastly, Andrew Brook's close critical reading and attention to detail can always be counted on and is appreciated.

NOTES

[1] Postcolonial feminist literature is growing rapidly. In this paper, I especially use insights from Jacqui Alexander and Chandra Mohanty (1997) and Uma Narayan and Sandra Harding (eds. 2000). From these collections, papers by Chandra Mohanty (1997), Lorraine Code (2000), Uma Narayan (2000), and Ann Ferguson (2000) have been particularly useful.

[2] Important feminist literature on the topic of women's paid work and its effects on women's status and roles in the private and public spheres includes: Beatrice Leigh Hutchins and Amy Harrison Spencer (1907), Jane Humphries (1977), Elizabeth Roberts (1984), Jane Lewis (1986), and Janet Sayers, Mary Evans, and Nanneke Redclift (1987). In important research on the nonliberating aspects of paid work, S. Charusheela (forthcoming) argues that bargaining models tend to assume the perspective of privileged women and fail to consider work that has not been empowering for women of color, working-class women, ethnic minorities, or Third World women. I am indebted to Jane Humphries for alerting me to this research on paid work.

[3] I am grateful to Bina Agarwal for pointing out that Sen mentions factors such as property ownership in passing and that his main emphasis has been on women's

employment, which is the focus of this paper. See, however, Bina Agarwal (1994) on the significance of control over property in enhancing women's agency and well-being.

[4] In a study of home-based work in domains such as fashion garments, nontraditional agricultural exports, and shea butter, Carr, Chen, and Tate argue that among the most disadvantaged of all workers in a global context are women who produce from their homes. They ask, "[w]hat greater contrast could there be – in terms of market knowledge, mobility, and competitiveness – than that between a large transnational company and a home-based woman producer?" (Marilyn Carr, Martha Chen, and Jane Tate 2000: 125).

[5] In the introduction to a special issue of *Feminist Economics* on globalization and gender, Benería, Floro, Grown, and MacDonald counter the argument that women's greater access to jobs generates gender equity with evidence that suggests that "gender inequality stimulated growth and that growth may exacerbate gender inequality" (Lourdes Benería, Maria Floro, Caren Grown and Martha MacDonald 2000: xi).

[6] The changing composition of the maquiladora workforce is substantiated by Verónica Vázquez García (per. com. 2002), who reports that men from rural areas of Mexico are being recruited. Kai Nielsen (per. com. 2002) has raised the point that lower labor costs in other regions are now resulting in the closing down of maquiladoras in Tijuana.

[7] SEWA, founded in India in 1972, has a membership of over 250,000 women and "has provided a range of services (financial, health, child care, and training) to its members." The work of SEWA is more important for the example it sets than for the number of women it reaches. More recently, SEWA has led an international movement of women workers and negotiated with international trade union federations and the International Labor Organization to recognize informal sector workers (Carr, Chen, and Tate 2000: 139).

[8] See, for example, Paul Seabright (2001).

REFERENCES

Agarwal, Bina. 1994. *A Field of One's Own: Gender and Land Rights in South Asia.* Cambridge, UK: Cambridge University Press.

Alexander, M. Jacqui and Chandra Talpade Mohanty. 1997. "Introduction: Genealogies, Legacies, Movements," in M. Jacqui Alexander and Chandra Talpade Mohanty (eds.) *Feminist Genealogies, Colonial Legacies, Democratic Futures,* pp. xiii–xlii. New York: Routledge.

Benería, Lourdes. 1982. "Accounting for Women's Work," in Lourdes Benería (ed.) *Women and Development: The Sexual Division of Labor in Rural Societies,* pp. 119–47. New York: Praeger.

——. 1999. "Globalization, Gender and the Davos Man." *Feminist Economics* 5(3): 61–83.

——, Maria Floro, Caren Grown, and Martha MacDonald. 2000. "Introduction: Globalization and Gender." *Feminist Economics* 6(3): vii–xviii.

Carr, Marilyn, Martha Alter Chen, and Jane Tate. 2000. "Globalization and Home-Based Workers." *Feminist Economics* 6(3): 123–42.

Charusheela, S. Forthcoming. "Empowering Work? Bargaining Models Reconsidered," in Drucilla Barker and Edith Kuiper (eds.) *Towards a Feminist Philosophy of Economics.* London: Routledge.

Code, Lorraine. 2000. "How to Think Globally: Stretching the Limits of Imagination," in Uma Narayan and Sandra Harding (eds.) *Decentering the Center: Philosophy for a Multicultural, Postcolonial, and Feminist World,* pp. 67–79. Bloomington, IN: Indiana University Press.

Elson, Diane and Ruth Pearson. 1981. "The Subordination of Women and the Internationalisation of Factory Production," in Kate Young, Carol Wolkowitz, and Roslyn McCullagh (eds.) *Of Marriage and the Market: Women's Subordination in International Perspective*, pp. 144–66. London: CSE.

Ferguson, Ann. 2000. "Resisting the Veil of Privilege: Building Bridge Identities as an Ethico-Politics of Global Feminisms," in Uma Narayan and Sandra Harding (eds.) *Decentering the Center: Philosophy for a Multicultural, Postcolonial, and Feminist World*, pp. 189–207. Bloomington, IN: Indiana University Press.

Fernández-Kelly, María Patricia. 1997. "*Maquiladoras*: The View from Inside," in Nalini Vasvanathan, Lynn Duggan, Laurie Nisonoff, and Nan Wiegersma (eds.) *The Women, Gender and Development Reader*, pp. 203–15. London: Zed Books.

Fussell, Elisabeth. 2000. "Making Labor Flexible: The Recomposition of Tijuana's Maquiladora Female Labor Force." *Feminist Economics* 6(3): 59–79.

García, Verónica Vázquez. Personal communication. 12 September 2002.

Harding, Sandra. 2000. "Gender, Development, and Post-Enlightenment Philosophies of Science," in Uma Narayan and Sandra Harding (eds.) *Decentering the Center: Philosophy for a Multicultural, Postcolonial, and Feminist World*, pp. 240–61. Bloomington, IN: Indiana University Press.

Humphries, Jane. 1977. "Class Struggle and the Persistence of the Working-Class Family." *Cambridge Journal of Economics* 1(3): 241–58.

Hutchins, Beatrice Leigh and Amy Harrison Spencer. 1907. *A History of Factory Legislation*. Rev. edn. Westminster, UK: P. S. King & Son.

Lewis, Jane (ed.). 1986. *Labour and Love: Women's Experience of Home and Family, 1850–1940*. Oxford, UK: Blackwell.

Lim, Linda Y. 1990. "Women's Work in Export Factories: The Politics of a Cause," in Irene Tinker (ed.) *Persistent Inequalities: Women and World Development*, pp. 101–19. New York: Oxford University Press.

Mies, Maria. 1982. "The Dynamics of the Sexual Division of Labor and Integration of Rural Women into the World Market," in Lourdes Benería (ed.) *Women and Development: The Sexual Division of Labor in Rural Societies*, pp. 1–28. New York: Praeger.

Mohanty, Chandra Talpade. 1988. "Under Western Eyes: Feminist Scholarship and Colonial Discourses." *Feminist Review* 30(Autumn): 61–88.

———. 1997. "Women Workers and Capitalist Scripts: Ideologies of Domination, Common Interests, and the Politics of Solidarity," in M. Jacqui Alexander and Chandra Talpade Mohanty (eds.) *Feminist Genealogies, Colonial Legacies, Democratic Futures*, pp. 3–29. New York: Routledge.

Nielsen, Kai. Personal communication. 28 September 2002.

Narayan, Uma. 2000. "Essence of Culture and a Sense of History: A Feminist Critique of Cultural Essentialism," in Uma Narayan and Sandra Harding (eds.) *Decentering the Center: Philosophy for a Multicultural, Postcolonial, and Feminist World*, pp. 80–100. Bloomington, IN: Indiana University Press.

Pearson, Ruth. 1998. "'Nimble Fingers' Revisited: Reflections on Women and Third World Industrialization in the Late Twentieth Century," in Cecile Jackson and Ruth Pearson (eds.) *Feminist Visions of Development: Gender Analysis and Policy*, pp. 171–88. London: Routledge.

Roberts, Elizabeth. 1984. *A Woman's Place: An Oral History of Working-Class Women 1890–1940*. Oxford, UK: Blackwell.

Sayers, Janet, Mary Evans, and Nanneke Redclift (eds.). 1987. *Engels Revisited: New Feminist Essays*. London: Tavistock.

Seabright, Paul. 2001. "The Road Upward: *Development as Freedom*." *New York Review of Books* 48(5): (March 29), 41–3.

Sen, Amartya. 1980. "Equality of What?" in S. M. McMurrin (ed.) *Tanner Lectures on Human Values* 1: pp. 195–220. Cambridge, UK: Cambridge University Press.

——. 1990. "Gender and Cooperative Conflicts," in Irene Tinker (ed.) *Persistent Inequalities: Women and World Development*, pp. 123–49. New York: Oxford University Press.

——. 1992. *Inequality Reexamined.* Cambridge, MA: Harvard University Press.

——. 1995. "Gender Inequality and Theories of Justice," in Martha Nussbaum and Jonathan Glover (eds.) *Women, Culture and Development: A Study of Human Capabilities*, pp. 259–73. Oxford, UK: Clarendon Press.

——. 1999. *Development as Freedom.* New York: Anchor Books.

——. 2001. "Work and Rights," in Martha Fetherolf Loutfi (ed.) *Women, Gender and Work: What is Equality and How do We Get There?*, pp. 33–44. Geneva: International Labour Office.

SLAVERY, FREEDOM, AND SEN

Stanley L. Engerman

OVERVIEW

Amartya Sen's *Development as Freedom* argues that the ability to make choices is fundamental to economic development, and that the evaluation of outcomes can provide misleading answers. He uses the example of the high material consumption of US slaves relative to some free whites to illustrate this contrast. This chapter discusses some of the implications of such comparisons and the problem of evaluating what might be regarded as favorable outcomes which come from unfavorable institutions (e.g., slavery). It appears that all good things do not necessarily go together. The past relation of enslavement to the need for subsistence is discussed. Differences in gender roles under slavery and after emancipation are also examined.

INTRODUCTION

Economic historians have long wrestled with the tensions between useful and measurable economic perspectives on changes in welfare associated with development, such as that denoted by *the standard of living*, and a broader, less tangible, approach summarized as *the quality of life*.[1] In *Development as Freedom*, Amartya Sen summarizes his recent thinking on the meaning of development, returning with new insight to this tension in evaluating economic changes.

Sen has long rejected more conventional economic interpretations of the standard of living in terms of *opulence* based solely on material conditions and suggested instead an interpretation in terms of people's *capabilities and functionings*. Functionings are the various things that a person may value doing or being. For example, not being enslaved is a valuable functioning, just as is living a life of normal length (or longer) or being healthy. A person's *capability* refers to the feasible set or sets of functionings that circumstances allow him or her to achieve.[2] As Amartya Sen (1999: 75) says, "capability is thus a kind of freedom: the substantive freedom to achieve alternative functioning combinations (or less formally put, the freedom to achieve various lifestyles)".[3] When the concern is with capabilities that allow a person to achieve a minimum level of well-being (i.e., to escape poverty), Sen discusses *basic capabilities.*

Sen does not discuss *tradeoffs* among these basic capabilities, although he does give one reference as that between the level of living under slavery and freedom in the antebellum US South. Other writers in this tradition follow Sen's lead. Martha Nussbaum, for example, after presenting her list of *Basic Human Functional Capabilities,* says that, "[T]he list is, emphatically, a list of separate components. We cannot satisfy the need for one of them by giving a larger amount of another. All are of central importance and all are distinct in quality."[4] The issue of possible tradeoffs between economic need and political or social freedoms is, however, of critical importance.[5] Sen holds not only that political and economic freedoms are both important but that political freedom is often necessary for satisfying economic needs. He focuses mainly on the complementarity rather than the tradeoffs between freedoms, a relationship that is doubtful not only at low levels of development but also exists at higher levels of income.

The need to deal with tradeoffs among basic rights and the importance of ordering the "good things" cannot be ignored. Culturally and temporally specific standards may mean that we disapprove of choices that have been made, but, nonetheless, they may have seemed necessary to those involved. Slavery, voluntary and otherwise, has been a frequent occurrence in human societies, generally reflecting dire circumstances faced by persons at the lowest income levels. Even in discussing Sen's "goods," tradeoffs exist regarding costs, resources, and expenditure allocations. This chapter shows that for people living at the level of subsistence, important tradeoffs are made between different basic capabilities. The chapter is located empirically in the context of slavery, a context which Sen himself has explored. The literature on slavery shows that, at times, people have been forced to make tradeoffs between basic capabilities. Slavery, therefore, is sometimes the outcome of people having to make choices between different aspects of freedom, such as between the freedom to be liberated and set free and the freedom to survive and be healthy.

Sen's conceptualization of freedom in terms of expanding capabilities has to confront the issue that people, past and present, have had to make tradeoffs between different basic freedoms or capabilities. Examining slavery can give us some insights into the dynamics of those tradeoffs. Finally, and again consistent with Sen's interests, this chapter discusses a gender perspective on the nature of the tradeoffs explored. The freedoms of male and female slaves were violated and curbed in different ways and to different extents, and the nature of new freedoms and the choices that followed emancipation were likewise gendered. This chapter emphasizes the harsh tradeoffs between freedoms that slaves faced and suggests that they are echoed in the bitter choices that continue to confront many disadvantaged peoples today, especially women and children.

I. SLAVERY AND FREEDOM

Slavery has taken many different forms; it has been among the most frequent of human institutions, existing in almost all societies in the past and in most parts of the world. Slaves have experienced different work regimes and differences in physical and material treatment, depending on various economic, political, cultural, and ideological circumstances. Nevertheless, the coercion permitted slaveowners was almost universal with the basic absence of choice allowed to slaves who were always subject to the master's control. Lost liberties were often the outcome of involuntary acts; however, in societies with low and/or highly variable levels of income, people have been willing to sacrifice their liberties and those of their family members in exchange for the ability to survive.

At the lowest levels of income, where slavery becomes a preferred alternative to weakness or death, the conditions of the free were often similarly dire, and moving out of slavery did not mean any material benefits to the newly freed. "Voluntary" slavery has a long and geographically dispersed history, but there is only very limited literature on the topic since societies with voluntary slavery, as all poor societies, seem to have lacked the dynamic and wealth characteristics of some of the large societies based on involuntary slavery (see, e.g., H. J. Nieboer 1910: 428–30, 437–40). Voluntary slavery was the result of an agreement between purchasers and sellers in which both agreed to specific terms. While the existence of severe constraints may mean that the "voluntary" choice reflects an absence of opportunities and might be regarded as nonvoluntary due to the limited choices available, there are similar difficulties in describing arrangements made between legally free people where differences in wealth and opportunities exist.

One important aspect of slavery, a word which seems without any favorable connotations, is that societies reserve the slave status for outsiders, not members of their own society (see, e.g., Orlando Patterson 1982: 7). What societies have considered the definition of the outsider has varied over time; religion, nationality, ethnicity, and race have been utilized. In some cases the outsider characteristic has been socially fabricated, and the discrimination underlying the definition of an enslaveable outsider persists even when slavery has ended. The fact that the modern New World slavery was based on race has meant a continuation of racial beliefs after emancipation, serving to limit the gains from the transition from slavery to freedom. While the pre-existence of slavery is not necessary for racial, religious, or ethnic prejudice, the contemporary role of racism has certainly meant a significant difference for ex-slaves between legal freedom and the achievement of equality.

A frequent source of contention is whether it is possible to compare slave and free societies, or if these statuses are so distinct that any attempts to look at them together can only be misleading. In order to determine how feasible such comparisons might be it is best to focus upon specific questions. To a fundamentalist Marxist, slavery represents a separate mode of production, different from what comes before and after. Forms of institutions and organizations, the nature of decision-making, and the role of technology differ among modes of production, and for some purposes it may be desirable to treat each mode separately. For other questions, however, certain commonalities can make comparisons between modes of production very important. Thus, based on their common humanity, comparing living standards and aspects of the quality of life between slave and free should provide useful information. Descriptions of relative mortality, life expectation, health, consumption, and related aspects of the quality of life may serve to cast light on modes of production based on free or slave labor and may help answer questions as to why individuals might choose to move between these situations.

In explaining his preference for "a freedom-based perspective on development" (Sen 1999: 28) in *Development as Freedom*, Amartya Sen raises the example of the high material standard of living of US slaves to contrast the value of freedom with the judgments made from "an evaluative system that focuses only on culmination outcomes" (Sen 1999: 28, citing Robert Fogel and Stanley Engerman 1974). Freedom implies the ability to make choices, which may include earning less in return for more leisure, less intensity of work, more time with family, more desired geographic location, etc.[6] From this perspective it appears clear that measured income is not to be regarded as an accurate measure of welfare if the achievement of high levels of material consumption is at the cost of actions that can limit individual and family choice. Several questions may be raised about Sen's argument on this point. Freedom is not easy to define, since it may relate to individual rights or to group freedoms. Even what many consider to be freedom (in contrast with slavery) includes a number of legal and social constraints which, while perhaps less limiting than systems based on absolute government fiat, mean that individuals do not have unlimited choice or are always treated equally. The possibility of freedom will vary with the level of living standards and the income of the population (see Nieboer 1910: 292–6). While slavery has never been seen as a desirable condition, the frequency of what can be described as "voluntary" slavery makes it useful to reconsider the conditions under which forms of slavery rather than freedom existed in the past.[7]

II. CHOICES AND FREEDOM

All people make choices from among available opportunities but under constraints, whether imposed by nature, by other people, or by the self. This choice process is examined in the basic economic model of consumer behavior. Individuals do not all choose the same alternative, reflecting differences in tastes, differences in incomes, and differences in the nature of the constraints faced. Changing constraints with unchanged tastes will generally lead to the selection of different alternatives, as will changing tastes with unchanged constraints. The constraints may be natural, as in the Malthusian limit on the capacity of land to provide adequate food, or they may be social, either deriving from the power of certain groups or individuals or else by some apparently agreed upon set of enforced codes, legal or otherwise. The market imposes constraints even though people may be legally free to make choices, as long as prices and incomes limit opportunities (Robert Hale 1952; Robert Steinfeld 2001).[8] The more limiting the constraints and the fewer the alternatives available, the less free we consider individuals, as Sen's discussion of capabilities would suggest. The fewer the constraints and the greater the choices (even if limits and deprivation remain), the more free we generally regard people. Since all people face constraints regarding choices, we cannot describe individuals as entirely autonomous. And freedom does not always protect individuals since it may mean freedom to starve, freedom to be beaten by someone else, or freedom to enter uneven exchange. Freedom to choose, with the ability to exchange and transact, and the capacity to behave in accord with one's chosen values seems preferable to situations devoid of the ability to make choices. Even if freedom is not legally limited, it may be limited based upon restricted alternatives.

In *Development as Freedom* Sen has emphasized the opportunities to choose and to exchange and transact with others as essential aspects of human freedom. The broader the choices that can be made and the less that individuals are coerced and controlled by the state or by other parties, the more freedom exists. The enhancement of choice may reflect either broadened political rights or economic improvement, yielding a larger potential flow of goods and services or of capabilities from which to choose. It has long been argued that freedom is not only a good in itself, but that its occurrence would lead to other benefits, such as greater life expectation, more and better food, and a higher rate of economic growth with benefits for all, than could be achieved by societies with coercion and limited choices. Much of the recent scholarly work on slavery and serfdom has questioned this contention that "all good things come together."[9] This scholarship poses some difficult problems for economic and political theory taken up below.

Most economic examinations of the nature of freedom and its benefits presume that incomes are above subsistence (however defined, whether based on physiological or cultural factors) and therefore no consideration need be given to the problem of survival. Even if incomes were above subsistence, the possibility of nonfreedom providing a higher living standard than freedom could present individuals with difficult choices. Yet in many societies, past and present, some individuals have had very low incomes, either permanently or for shorter periods due to famines or natural disasters. Their incomes were too low for their survival, so that the opportunity to exchange freedom for subsistence, whether for the individuals, their children, or other family members, would be considered essential. In that case they were required to make choices among what could be considered basic capabilities—rights which are generally held to be compatible, not conflicting. It may be that short-term losses in welfare will lead to long-term gains, thus providing some intertemporal, or, for parent—children actions, intergenerational complications concerning the appropriate scheme of investment in human capital. Indeed, to the extent that survival is the major goal, no real choice may exist under these circumstances except, of course, that of life or death.

If survival is seen as a basic desire and people can (despite the prohibitions advocated by Hobbes, Locke, Condorcet, and other philosophers and political theorists) sell themselves or their family members into slavery to ensure survival, the importance of ranking the "good things," and dealing with tradeoffs among basic rights, arises. This problem has been a frequent concern historically.[10]

In the long discussions concerning the relations between persons, three major types have been discussed: master—servant; parent—child; and man—woman.[11] The first two clearly represent dependent relations resting on coercive relationships which are intended to restrict choice, if presumably for the benefit of the coerced. The distinctions drawn between the choices open for men and for women suggest a similar lack of equality and the relative absence of a decision-making capability granted women. The difficulties of defining freedoms within a social group or a family group still remain, as illustrated by recent debates on such issues as the acceptability of the long-term practice of female genital mutilation in some cultures, defining of the rights of children, and the ability of women to redefine the terms of the marriage contract.

Gender, age, and legal status define some of the groups that have confronted limitations on their freedoms. Children are traditionally treated as incapable of making rational choices up to some specified age (the age itself being a major source of disagreement) at which time they become adults able to make their own choices. Women were long regarded as not fully capable of making choices, accounting for their special treatment in legislation. This sometimes meant their being given more favorable treatment than men, although this often meant limitations on their rights to freely choose living and working conditions. Similar types of controls, limiting freedom of action, have been applied to the aged, the mentally disabled, the physically disabled, and convicts and felons among other groups.[12] The most extreme case of constraints on personal freedom is slavery.

III. SLAVERY

Slavery and its relation to freedom have long been difficult issues for political theory as well as political life. Slavery entails the right of ownership in another person, including the ability to buy and sell that individual as well as the power to determine where and how the slave will live and work. Slavery generates numerous questions for defining the meaning of freedom as well as for other important social issues. The attacks on slavery in the nineteenth and twentieth centuries, principally on moral grounds, first arose during the period of the Enlightenment, and the arguments made were premised on the proposition that there were no necessary tradeoffs among various "goods," certainly none between economic gains and individual liberties. An interesting aspect of tradeoffs was suggested by H. J. Nieboer in his classic early twentieth-century study (1910) of worldwide slavery. Among the causes of slavery pointed to was "the condition of women. There is no use for slaves where all disagreeable work can be, and is performed by the weaker sex" (p. 423). Correspondingly Nieboer states that, "Where the women hold a high position, and men are desirous of relieving them of a part of their task, slavery is likely to arise sooner than otherwise would be the case" (p. 423).

Slavery has never been considered a desirable state for one's own people, although it was often regarded as acceptable for others. The basic characteristic of the enslaved in most societies was that the slaves were to be considered "outsiders" to the enslaving society, whereas other groups were considered to be insiders, possible members of society and, therefore nonenslavable. The definition of outsiders could, however, vary over time and place and has been based, in various circumstances, on nationality, ethnicity, religion, or race.

Slaveowners, even when given total power legally, were expected by the society to treat slaves reasonably and possibly to provide them with opportunities to acquire freedom (Eugene Genovese 1974: 3–7, 75–97, 123–33). These policies were not intended to end the system of slavery but rather to define the relations of masters to slaves as individuals and also to legitimate who was to be a slave.[13] An attack on slavery as a system, calling for its abolition and the freeing of all the enslaved, immediately or at some time in the future, awaited ideological and other changes in late eighteenth-century Europe, particularly in Britain and France.

The most-studied slave societies have been those in the Americas between the sixteenth and nineteenth centuries.[14] This slavery began with involuntary capture, usually in warfare, in Africa. Whether the wars that generated slaves changed dramatically in magnitude after European penetration remains debated, since less is known about the demand for slaves within Africa and the Islamic slave trade than about the transatlantic trade. After enslavement the choice of sale or not and with whom to deal was made by the African captors. Pro-slavery advocates argued that enslavement was justified, and led to a beneficial outcome since, in its absence, war captives and criminals would have been killed. This contention, as also the argument by anti-slavery, pro-black advocates that slavery in Africa was not as harsh, socially or physically, as slavery in the New World, helped to maintain slavery and the slave trade in Africa and in other parts of the world into the twentieth century. With the closing of the transatlantic slave trade in the second half of the nineteenth century, continued profitability meant that slavery within Africa persisted until it was ended in the twentieth century by colonial governmental decrees.[15]

Once enslaved in Africa, the captives could be used as slaves by the captors, sold as slaves within Africa, or sold for sale in the Americas. Each of these options was utilized, but once the prospect of a large surplus above subsistence existed for New World purchasers, long-distance transportation became profitable and shipment to the Americas probably became the most frequently used policy over the period when it was legally permitted (Paul Lovejoy 1983).

The transatlantic slave trade was generally male-dominated, in part because of a preference for males in the transatlantic slave trade, in part because of a preference for females in the internal slave trade in Africa. The importance of males in African warfare, leading to more male deaths there, also influenced the sex ratio within Africa and, perhaps, in the slave trade. Females in Africa were more frequently involved in heavy agricultural labor than were free white women in Europe and the Americas, and polygamy was also more prevalent in Africa. Both factors raised the demand for females in Africa and help to explain the higher female than male slave prices within Africa, a pattern quite different from that throughout the Americas.[16] The differential types of use of female slaves from Africa and of white European settlers has been seen as one important factor in the rise of slave agriculture in the Americas (David Eltis 2000: 85–113; see also Edmund Morgan 1975). Over 60 percent of the slaves carried across the Atlantic were generally male, a ratio roughly similar over time and across African ports (David Eltis and Stanley Engerman 1992). It has long been argued that this disproportionate sex ratio, with fewer females, had negative long-term demographic effects in the New World, particularly in lowering the population's birth rate. The sex ratio in the slave trade, however, was relatively more balanced than in many migrations of free populations and considerably more equal than for most movements of indentured servants. Indeed, in the second half of the nineteenth century the British often imposed a minimum requirement on the ratio of female indentured servants or contract laborers compared to males (David Northrup 1995: 74–8).[17]

Whereas we generally regard slavery as a condition based on compulsion and coercion, in many societies in Asia, Africa, and in premodern Europe, slavery was voluntarily entered into. Because of the low levels of income in these societies, sales of children and adults to the wealthy were seen as the only way for individuals to survive. Asian and African societies, as well as medieval Russia, often solved their perceived problems of overpopulation by permitting voluntary slavery for adults as well as children (see, e.g., Frederick Cooper 1977: 122–30). For Western Europe, however, where enslavement of Europeans had been ended, excess births meant abandonment, giving children to the church, or infanticide. Abandonment, at times, was based on a socially accepted pattern involving the expected retrieval of the child by members of the church or by other individuals who would provide permanent arrangements, thus being in effect a transfer of the rights to the child and its labor at a low cost.[18]

Many of the early modern European advocates of liberty, including Samuel Pufendorf and Hugo Grotius, accepted adult and child slavery, but only if this was the best way to maintain alive individuals who were in poverty or disabled or otherwise incapable of earning a living.[19] In sixteenth-century Russia, voluntary slavery was generally entered into in a response to crop failures or crop destruction that caused food shortages and famines.[20] Voluntary slavery declined when incomes rose, as starvation became a more limited threat, and when more successful relief and welfare institutions by the state, the church, or by individuals were devised.[21] It is clear, however, that under certain conditions the loss of freedom could be permanent and was considered acceptable not only to the enslavers, but also the enslaved.[22]

The need (and desire) for survival led to sacrifices of freedom, whether by sales of children by parents, sales of adults by family members, self-sale, or by volunteering to accept enslavement without any payments. In these cases, presumably freedom would have meant being free to starve rather than free to choose. Similarly, late nineteenth-century movements of indentured labor from India to sugar plantations in the West Indies and elsewhere apparently were influenced by the extent of famine and poverty in India (Stanley Engerman 1983).[23]

Although serfdom in Europe was frequently the result of power and coercion, there were conditions under which serfdom could be regarded as voluntary.[24] For those already resident in the area, serfdom could be a preferred option, as a means of acquiring protection and defense in times of political disorder or else as a means of guaranteeing subsistence in low-income societies.

A frequent prediction that allowed for the ending of slavery by a voluntary act of the master class was that given enough time and limited amounts of land, the excess of the value of slave production above necessary subsistence would fall to zero and there would be no surplus to be gained by slaveowners. At such time slaveowners would be indifferent between slave labor and free labor, since neither would yield any surplus. The only economic benefit to owners, no matter which labor form, would then be the rent on the land used with labor, although the amount of rent would be influenced by the magnitude of labor input. The grant of freedom under these conditions would mean that each person would have the same amount of consumption, whether previously slave or free. The incomes of free laborers would be equal to those of the slaves. No material economic gain would accrue to laborers from the freedom under these conditions (Evsey Domar 1970; Moses Finley 1998: 207–17). However correct this theoretical argument, it does not explain the ending of slavery in the New World and might apply only to the long, drawn-out end of slavery in the Roman world.

Individual purchases of themselves by slaves, leading to the granting of their freedom by their owners (manumission), were often based on the amounts that the slave could pay for manumission out of accumulated savings from earnings and gifts. In most societies the more frequent means of manumission was to permit slaves to pay for their own freedom at something close to the slave's market value. Manumission by grant of freedom by the master was much less common. It is striking that in most slave societies, manumission was more frequently of females (often ranging from 60 percent to over 80 percent), whether for social, economic, or, because of the access of the male slaveowners to female slaves, sexual reasons (Ronald Findlay 1975; Frank McGlynn 1989). Manumission was not generally regarded as a threat to an ongoing slave system but functioned more as a safety-valve to maintain the system or as an incentive to slave productivity and good behavior. Most slave societies allowed for manumissions of the enslaved, and their populations included freedmen or free blacks, albeit at times with limited rights compared to other free citizens. The ability to be manumitted generally depended on the actions of specific individuals, slaveowners or slaves, and served both as a reward to individuals and an incentive for them or for other slaves.[25]

IV. SLAVERY, FREEDOM, AND LIVING CONDITIONS

The complexities of contrasting slavery and freedom often arise from the expectation that "all good things go together," and that freedom necessarily entails better living conditions and more rapid economic growth than does slavery. Amartya Sen (1999: 29) notes that while it is possible that slaves did have higher material living standards than did free workers, nevertheless "slaves did run away, and there were excellent reasons for presuming that the interests of the slaves were not well served by the system of slavery." Nevertheless, the low rates of runaways in most slave societies suggest that various means of maintaining the system were used, including force as well as rewards, in the short and long run. The desire to avoid enslavement seems obvious, and the flight of southern US slaves when northern armies moved into the South was not surprising, but under customary conditions in the US South, as in most slave societies, the system of controls and compromises, of power and accumulation, was such that runaways as a share of the total slave population were small in number. Unbalanced powers meant a curtailment of the slaves' ability to leave the plantation and the system. In some societies, although the slaves were freed by law, they had to leave the slaveowner on their own volition. The long periods in which people chose not to leave, and to remain slaves, indicates the complexities of low-income societies.

Runaways in the US and elsewhere were predominantly male, few leaving with women and young children (Gad Heuman 1985; John Hope Franklin and Loren Schweninger 1999: 210–13). The low runaway rate for women no doubt reflected physical and cultural factors, particularly the difficulties of leaving with children or an unwillingness to leave children behind, and not to any difference in women's willingness to accept enslavement.[26] There were some southern petitions to courts by free blacks to be returned to slavery, usually petitions made by older free blacks, and by women with young children, but these were few in number. An interesting case was recorded in Virginia regarding the petition of a woman to be re-enslaved to the master of her slave husband, "from whom the benefits and privileges of freedom, dear and flattering as they are, could not induce her to be separated" (Ulrich Phillips 1918: 446). Such requests existed also in other slave societies. In some cases, such as colonial Africa, legal abolition meant only the ending of the state's willingness to enforce the return of runaways. Since many slaves did not leave their places of residence, *de facto* slavery persisted.

The desire to be re-enslaved or the refusal to accept freedom, while rare in the American South, was generally based on considerations of the benefits and costs of freedom with those of remaining in the slave status. Relevant factors included the desire to remain with family members (since the freed often had to move to another state); the belief that better physical treatment remained possible as a slave, particularly for the elderly or mothers with children; and the feeling that, given the conditions in the South, the position of a free person of color was "more degrading and involves more suffering in this State, than that of a slave who is under the

197

care, protection and ownership of a kind and good master." The freed colored on the other hand, "lives a thousand times harder, and in more destitution, than the slaves of many planters." In addition without the protection of a "trusted white man" the ex-slaves were fearful of kidnapping or violence.[27]

Recent studies of slave societies have shown that slave economies were capable of experiencing rapid economic growth using a production system of gang labor and had an ability to adjust to changes in world demand for export commodities by changing crop patterns and geographic locations to achieve growth (Robert Fogel 1989: 17–113). It has also been shown that some slaves were provided with consumption levels in excess of those of some members of the free populations in the same country and, as was the case for US slaves, most populations elsewhere in the world (Fogel 1989: 132–47). Such higher standards of living may have reflected the master's perceptions of what was needed to secure a greater intensity of work. That skilled slaves were granted higher material compensation while their prices were above those of other slaves indicates that the returns to skilled human capital were divided in some uncertain proportion between slaves and masters. In many cases there was a surplus above subsistence to be fought over, and negotiated divisions between masters and slaves were the outcome. There is a difference, in some important regards, between legal status and economic status. Slaveowners did not always do what they were legally permitted to do (which included rather complete control over the slave's life and body), although at times they exceeded their rights.

This distinction between legal status and economic status, as well as between slave and free, was a central element in several of the debates on slavery in the British colonies in the early nineteenth century. It was claimed by pro-slavery advocates as well as by British workers, whatever their stance on slavery, that employers were able to force workers to endure harsher working conditions, earn less income, and work longer hours than did the West Indian slaves (David Brion Davis 1975: 453–68; Seymour Drescher 1999: 57–86; 399–443). And when it was argued that the British should encourage the use of free laborers in India in the production of sugar replacing the use of slave labor in the West Indies, the benefits of free labor were questioned by pointing to the extremely low agricultural wages in India, compared to the consumption allowed slaves in the West Indies and elsewhere (David Brion Davis 1984: 180–91). It was not argued, of course, that all slaves had high standards of living or that free workers should become slaves in order to benefit from improved living standards, but these cases do indicate that under certain important historical conditions slaves may have been better off materially than some free workers, even though the slaves had more limited freedom of choice.

V. MANUMISSIONS AND EMANCIPATIONS

The process of manumission provided individual slaves with freedom and gave them certain other rights (but not always all those granted citizens), yet without affecting the status of those still enslaved. Newcomers to a nation or newly freed ex-slaves may not be given the full set of rights that belong to the "established" members of society. Those considered, for whatever reasons, to be outsiders may lack key rights and therefore suffer limitations in their freedom. In some cases, freedom can be regarded as a zero-sum game, gains for some coming only at the expense of others, so that measures to increase the freedom of everyone are not possible. While freedom refers to self-ownership by individuals, legal and other constraints may limit the choices open to nominally free individuals.

Slaves were generally given quite limited legal rights relative to the rights that slave ownership gave the masters or that non-slave, non-slaveholders had, and these slave rights were often not enforceable by law and were subject to the master's tolerance. Slaves did not, however, lack all ability to bargain and negotiate terms of living and working, and thus were able to influence their living and working conditions, either within or outside of the legal framework. Their bargaining power, however, was quite limited relative to that of most free workers. Serfs also had limited rights, but there were more limitations on the lords' controls over serfs than of the slaveowners' control over slaves. In most societies, even today, there is a period during which rights of newcomers (immigrants) are limited, particularly those regarding suffrage. Such restrictions can impact on income levels, job opportunities, and the choices available to newcomers in the period before they can become citizens with identical rights to the native born.

In the major slave societies of the New World, freedom for all slaves did not occur until the nineteenth century, taking over one century from the first emancipations in the northern states of the United States. The key dates of the abolition of slavery in the Americas were 1834 for the British colonies; 1848 for the French (besides Haiti) and Danish colonies; 1863 for the Dutch; 1865 for the United States; 1873 for Puerto Rico and 1886 for Cuba, both Spanish colonies; and 1888 for Brazil. Abolishing slavery usually took place twenty-five to fifty years after the ending of the international slave trade. The forms of emancipation differed, some being immediate, some requiring considerable periods of time, some freeing all slaves, some freeing only those born after a certain date, and some requiring a period of continued plantation labor by the slaves. In all cases, except the United States, there was some compensation paid to the slaveowners in cash, bonds, or labor time, and in no case was any form of compensation ever paid to slaves (or, in Europe, where the serfs were freed at roughly the same time, to the serfs).[28]

An understanding of what freedom meant to those enslaved can be seen from observing the patterns of changes in societies after slaves were emancipated. Emancipation usually entailed changes in the institutional structure under which the economy and society operated and also shifts in political and economic power. Legal freedom did not, however, guarantee equality. Central issues such as the need to produce goods, to maintain a family life, and to relate to other members of society existed both under slavery and under freedom, but the changing rules of society with emancipation meant that they could be resolved in rather different ways. The legacy of the past was present but the availability of new opportunities permitted different outcomes even if some things, such as the allocation of land ownership, did not often change (Stanley Engerman 2000).[29]

A general pattern in most New World slave emancipations was the decline of the plantation system.[30] The desire of ex-slaves was to move to smaller agricultural units, whether owned, rented, or labored on resembling in size and structure the farms of those yeomen who had always been free. These, however, were often less productive than were the plantations, so that the end of slavery usually meant a decline in output, and in some cases it took societies several decades to reach the level of per capita output achieved under slavery. The archetypical case here was Haiti, where emancipation, despite some attempts of the new rulers to bring back a sugar plantation system, ultimately meant the development of an economy based on small farms, producing primarily foodstuff for local markets and with a substantial decline in labor productivity. Wherever small farms replaced plantations, the economic benefits of gang labor were lost. Haiti, once possibly the world's richest area, today has a measured level of per capita output possibly below the level at the end of the eighteenth century, and is the one country in the Western Hemisphere to have an income at sub-Saharan levels.[31] Ironically, given the successful end of the plantation system, in the twentieth century Haitian migrants produced sugar on plantations in the Dominican Republic and Cuba.

There were exceptions to this general pattern, reflecting differences in natural and/or political constraints in different areas. On Barbados and Antigua, for example, the population density was so high that ex-slaves had nowhere to go and remained on the plantations at least until their external migration increased in the late nineteenth century. In areas such as Trinidad, Jamaica, and British Guiana, British colonial policy was initially the same since there were large expanses of unsettled land. Although many of the ex-slaves were able to leave the plantations and establish small farms in the interior, not all were able to do so. In those areas where sugar cultivation remained highly productive, such as Trinidad and British Guiana, the plantation system was restored within decades, worked not by ex-slaves, but with a plantation labor force consisting primarily of contract labor, for limited periods, drawn primarily from the Portuguese islands,

India, and China. Even with contract labor, however, Jamaica was unable to successfully compete in the world sugar market.

The decline of the plantation system meant a prolonged decline in measured output as the ex-slaves chose to move to smaller units to produce mainly foodstuffs and not export staples. Presumably if ex-slaves had been willing to remain at work full-time on plantations as perhaps they might have if they were given higher wages and if they had maintained both the same amount of leisure and labor intensity as prior to emancipation, the problem of falling output in these ex-slave societies could have been avoided. Then it would have to be asked what ending slavery had meant for the enslaved. The maintenance of plantation labor had been the goal of planters wishing to maintain profits. It was also the desired policy of many of those in the anti-slavery movement, who wished to demonstrate that ending slavery and shifting to free labor had no significant negative economic or social impacts and would possibly even result in increased production. In this sense, emancipation would be relatively costless or even beneficial to planters and the other free people in society. Emancipation did have significant legal impacts upon ex-slaves, who were now subject to the same laws as whites. What is less clear in most cases is the impact of emancipation on the material conditions of the ex-slaves, although there are indications that in the US South some material conditions initially deteriorated. Clearly, the ex-slaves gained from being free of slavery and of the plantation system, and, where possible, moving to their own small, family-sized, producing units and avoiding the gang labor routines of sugar and cotton production. In avoiding gang labor they made a choice paralleled by that of free whites and free blacks who, centuries earlier at the time of settlement, had chosen to avoid plantation labor as distasteful and to work instead on smaller units. It was the free population's desire to avoid plantation labor that explained the initial demand for slaves in the Americas.

As elsewhere, the ending of slavery in the southern United States meant the decline of the plantation as a producing unit and an expansion of small farms for the ex-slaves who were still primarily producing cotton. There was, however, a decline in productive efficiency compared to the period prior to emancipation. Indicative of the impact of the efficiency decline in the US South was the increased production of cotton on small farms by the white population, previously unable to compete with the more efficient slave plantation. The end of slavery thus increased the production choices of the white population in the South; it also led to greater degrees of occupational divergence between black men and black women than had existed under slavery, as discussed below.

The ending of slavery and the freeing of the labor force had a substantial impact in reducing overall output, particularly the output of plantation export crops, in most societies formerly based on slavery. Where it has been possible to prepare estimates, there have been declines in per capita income of significant magnitudes for several decades. Thus the free labor argument of higher outputs in the aftermath of slavery did not occur quickly, and in several cases it required the importation either of contract labor from India and China or of free European labor from Spain or Italy. What is more difficult to analyze is the effect of emancipation on the consumption level of ex-slaves to determine this aspect of the benefits of emancipation beyond freedom. While the initial changes may not have led to dramatically higher income, freedom permitted the ex-slaves to reap benefits from increased productivity in future years.[32] In the US South the first decades of freedom did see increased mortality for ex-slaves, and there was an overall decline in southern production of foodstuffs. In the West Indies there were declines in food imports, suggesting a lessened availability of foodstuffs there. The estimates of food consumption needed to firmly establish the impact of emancipation upon living standards are still not conclusive, but declines in the initial years would not be implausible given estimates of overall production, and the important fact that redistribution of land ownership did not generally take place, so that some return to landowners continued. Whatever redistribution did occur did not mean that ex-slaves would gain their entire product after the end of slavery.

In most places the gang system no longer existed after slavery, and it is probable that the hours and/or intensity of labor fell with freedom. However, even as freedom broadened the options for mobility and labor choice among ex-slaves, the pattern of the US South, where life expectation declined for several decades, food consumption in rural areas was probably lowered, and dietary diseases became more frequent, suggests significant negative material effects. The relative impact on males and females of the changing life expectation and magnitudes of consumption are not clear, but the nature of living arrangements and provision of consumption goods did change dramatically with the move from plantations and white-owned small units to small farms operated by blacks. Female farm labor was more seasonal after emancipation and took place without a gang system. Presumably the black male was now a stronger family leader, and some have argued that for black females all emancipation meant was a change in who controlled them.[33]

Accompanying emancipation was a southern black striving for education, particularly for children; a desire to purchase and own the farms on which they worked; and a demand for the right to obtain and use the ballot in order to vote for elected officials and to obtain benefits from state and municipal expenditures. The ability to purchase farms and urban dwellings out of accumulated savings after emancipation is one indication of the commitment to labor of ex-slaves, since it is doubtful that they were able to acquire very much low-cost credit in southern postbellum capital markets (Sharon Holt 2000: 52–99). Black women were frequently recorded in the census as unpaid family labor, although some worked as paid field hands, so their major contribution to land purchases was indirect. The racist response due to the decline in the cotton market in the 1890s in the US South did reduce the benefits initially gained with emancipation, including education, landownership, income, and wealth. The behavior and achievements of southern ex-slaves between 1865 and the 1890s suggest what many hoped would be the benefits of freedom. But this phase was ended by the dramatic changes in laws and in education, voting, lynching, transportation segregation, and occupational opportunities.[34]

For freed black females in the United States, the two key occupations were agricultural work and labor, often in white households, as domestic servants. Down to World War II about 90 percent of black women in the labor force were either laborers in agriculture or domestic servants, with the share of domestic servants rising over time, and accounting for over three-fourths of black female employment in 1930 (Claudia Goldin 1990: 74–5). These were low-income occupations, and it was not until after World War I's movement north by blacks, and then World War II, that a broader range of occupational choices became available for black females. Domestic service often required living with whites rather than with blacks and imposed some limitations on marriage and fertility. Prior to emancipation United States slave fertility was unusually high, both for a slave and a free population. After 1880 there was a decline in black fertility, roughly in tandem with the decline in white fertility (Stanley Engerman 1977). There was probably some decline in the percentage of black females married, an increase in the age of first birth, and an increase in the number of black childless women (Engerman 1983). Whether this reflected an increased control of birth and marriage patterns by black females, or as has been argued, an increase in diseases is not clear, but for United States blacks the end of slavery meant declining fertility, whereas in other parts of the Americas there may have initially been some increased fertility after emancipation (see, e.g., George Roberts 1957: 216–72; and Higman 1984: 347–73).

In the US South, as elsewhere where slave emancipation occurred, there were significant changes in family arrangements and gender relations resulting from the shift from plantations of several families to residence on small farms operated by individual families.[35] There were declines in fertility after emancipation, in part because of the increase in the free family's costs of raising children to adulthood with the ending of the plantation's collective childcare arrangement and also the loss of the implicit subsidy to child-raising costs made by plantation owners. In most slave societies females were valued at about 80 to 90 percent that of same-aged males in the same work category, although, until age 15 females were equal in price to males (Manuel Moreno Fraginals, Herbert Klein, and Stanley Engerman 1983). The wage differentials by sex among freed people

203

were often larger than the price and hiring rate differentials had been under slavery. Much of the domestic work, such as food preparation and cleaning, was undertaken during slavery by a limited number of specialized slaves, and a large portion of slave females specialized in field work. After emancipation household work was done in one-family households by women allocating their time among several different functions. Black women now had work patterns that, for whatever reason, resembled those of white females, particularly those of the working class. They spent more time outside the labor force, working in the home, and less in the field than when enslaved, and female wage-earners most frequently worked as domestic servants.

After emancipation in the United States South, ex-slave families frequently followed the pattern of two-parent households (whether co-resident or in separate residence) which had existed under slavery, a pattern which was to change dramatically in the last half of the twentieth century, when the proportion of female-headed households particularly in urban areas increased. Whatever the explanation for this recent rise in the proportion of black female-headed households, it is of interest to note that these current levels did not occur until much later than emancipation.

In recent years there have been some re-interpretations of the role of black women under slavery and afterwards. The labor force participation of slave women in plantation societies was greatly in excess of that of free white women and this high participation may have reflected patterns of agricultural production in Africa (see, e.g., Robertson and Klein 1983). While the basic family pattern that emerged was structurally similar to that of white families – predominantly nuclear households – the nature of slavery and production patterns led to significant differences in actual arrangements in regard to food provision, childcare, and power relations in slave families from those of whites. The relative equality in "earnings" of males and females under slavery suggested a more independent role for slave women than for free women, who were dependent upon the incomes of males. After emancipation there was some carryover of this labor force pattern, with significantly higher labor force participation for black than for white women and a higher proportion of unmarried black women, with or without children. To the extent that there was greater financial independence, black family relations, even with a predominantly nuclear household structure, need not have been identical to that of whites.

The discussion among historians and other scholars of the nature of power relations between males and females in the black family and society has recently re-emerged, regarding both what did happen and what would have been desirable. The black slave female would have been subject to the power of her white master and possibly also by her husband in those slave families with a dominant male role. Ending slavery, which weakened white controls, need not have meant a shift in the power balance vis-à-vis male heads of households (Jacqueline Jones 1985; White 1985). The normative debates relate to the degree to which females should support males in order to improve black living conditions and to what extent females should take advantage of their relative financial independence to exercise power in their own interests, rather than to let themselves be dominated by males. This dilemma is, of course, similar to that confronted by many whites, but the background of lower incomes and the history of discrimination make this problem more acute among blacks.

The study of the link between the black family under slavery and its contemporary circumstance is somewhat puzzling. Abolitionists and proslavery defenders had both believed that the slave family was weak, whether because it consisted of slaves or of Africans (Fogel 1989: 162–86). The post-Moynihan Report arguments about female-headed households and the number of illegitimate births after emancipation drew upon these earlier debates, even though it took almost one century after emancipation before the current rates of female single-headed households began to appear. It is the dramatic change with such a long lag after slavery that makes positing the usual links uncertain. That the recent sharp increases in single-parent households occurred in a time of economic improvement is also puzzling. Works such as Herbert Gutman's (1976) (discussed in Stanley Engerman 1978) point to the existence of a two-parent household under slavery, a point made earlier by the sociologist E. Franklin Frazier before he became influenced by the economic and family difficulties of the 1930s. There were other arguments about the impact of slavery on males and females such as those of W.E. Burghardt Du Bois (1909). Du Bois contended that the so-called "absent father" of the slave family need not have been physically absent, but he was forced to play a much weaker role in the family than did white fathers because of the controls imposed by masters. With the probable psychological costs to female slaves from forced sexual accessiblity by their masters, the two-parent slave household did not function in the same manner as did the free household. In the West Indies the single-parent household was more important in magnitude even at the time of emancipation, and its levels have long exceeded those in the United States, as has the share of illegitimate births (Roberts 1957: 263–306). In neither the United States nor the West Indies did the pattern of black family and gender relations both during and after slavery mirror the patterns in Africa prior to the transatlantic movement.[36] Thus freedom, leading to variations in constraints, did have significant effects, but not all its effects were evaluated positively by contemporaries and by subsequent scholars.[37]

VI. CONCLUSION

This essay has used the systems of slavery and the transition from slavery to legal freedom of the previously enslaved to examine some of the issues raised about capabilities and freedom in Amartya Sen's *Development as Freedom*. The discussion of slavery reminds us that over the past two centuries human capabilities, as described by Sen, have increased in large measure because of the worldwide ending of slavery as a legal institution. While there is a broad range over which the different types of freedoms discussed are complements and mutually supportive, there are conditions, generally at low levels of income, where tradeoffs between such freedoms might become necessary. The existence of voluntary slavery illustrates this. In some cases, freedom meant a lowering of the material well-being, health, and living conditions of ex-slaves. Current-day cases, where women remain in abusive marriages to obtain material consumption for themselves and their children have been argued to demonstrate the operation of an analogous form of tradeoff.

A world which requires tradeoffs is a rather difficult one for individuals, families, and society, and may require extensive state intervention to correct these adverse outcomes. Ensuring increases in the capabilities of those at low levels of income, whether by influencing the market process or outcome by using government funds or power to support activities such as resources to the poor can permit positive social benefits. Legislation ending labor coercion, as well as laws permitting interference within parent–child, husband–wife, and master–servant (labor) relations, might also be regarded as necessary. The need for societies to choose between the rights of individuals and longstanding cultural practices raises a fundamental problem about which disagreements still persist. In *Development as Freedom*, Sen has raised these and other issues of importance for consideration and for resolution. In going beyond the use of income as a primary measure of welfare, Sen has broadened our concerns with social betterment and with the policies necessary to achieve that goal.

ACKNOWLEDGMENTS

I have benefited from comments and suggestions on earlier drafts by Paul Cartledge, Seymour Drescher, David Eltis, Robert Steinfeld, several anonymous referees, and, for continuing encouragement and insights, Jane Humphries.

NOTES

[1] For a survey of the earlier debate on the British standard of living in the Industrial Revolution and some proposed expansions of the concept, see Stanley Engerman (1994).

[2] See, for earlier discussions of these concepts, Amartya Sen (1980, 1993).

[3] Sen (1999, 87–110) points to certain important deprivations of individual capacities related to, but not conceptually the same as, low incomes, premature mortality, undernourishment, persistent morbidity, widespread illiteracy, and missing women. All but the last have been considered to be major problems by more conventional measures of welfare, and presumably similar issues of desired lifetime vs. desired healthy lifetime (not just a recent problem as seen in the Greek myth of the difficulties of Tithonus, promised by the gods an eternal life but not an eternal youth); of choices of consumption patterns that yield utility to individuals but at costs in terms of health and life expectation; of group vs. individual decision-making; and of allocations of resources within the family remain to be analyzed under any of the welfare criteria noted.

[4] Martha Nussbaum (1995: 85). Why this "listing limits the trade-offs it will be reasonable to make, and thus limits the applicability of quantitative cost–benefit analysis" is not clear (pp. 85–6).

[5] The relationship between political freedom and economic growth has been frequently discussed. Is political freedom a necessary prerequisite for economic development, or, alternatively, does economic growth lead to political freedom? Henry Sumner Maine (1885: 112) poses the problem of whether with an extended franchise of working-class voters would have permitted the introduction of labor-saving innovations in England. There are more general problems of majority rule that he points to, which can lead to loss of minority rights and the refusal to provide rights, including that of immigration, to noncitizens.

Another type of tradeoff was described by Orson Welles in the classic movie, *The Third Man* (1949). Justifying his illegal activities in post-World War II Vienna, he points out that the bloodshed, murder, etc., of the Italian states under the Borgias led to Michelangelo, da Vinci, and the Renaissance, while all the Swiss had to show for 500 years of democracy was the cuckoo clock. Welles claims that this elicited a letter from a Swiss official claiming that, contrary to general opinion, the Swiss have never produced cuckoo clocks. See Frank Brady (1990: 450–1).

[6] The dilemma was, of course, well-known, and goes back a very long time. The Greek atomist Democritus wrote, apparently some time in the middle of the fifth century BC, "poverty in a democracy is preferable to so-called prosperity among dictators to the same extent as freedom is to slavery." On the gender issue, Democritus claimed (as have many others in later years), that "some men rule cities but are slaves to women." See Paul Cartledge (1998: 35, 38).

[7] For John Locke, and other moral philosophers, individual freedoms did not include the right to sell oneself into slavery (1963: 324–9, 402–3). The prohibition on self-enslavement was often considered similar to the restrictions on suicide. Individuals did not have the freedom to choose either course of action which presumably would end their freedom. For a discussion of the debate on the enslavement of English workers, presumably in their own interests, see Michael Rozbicki (2001).

[8] For a comparison of labor coercion under slavery and freedom, see O. Nigel Bolland (2002).

[9] See, e.g., Sen (1999: Ch. 6), and numerous recent World Bank publications. Sen does point to some "dissonances" in outcome, but more frequently argues that there is a

"remarkable empirical connection that links freedoms of different kinds with one another" (Sen 1999: 11).

[10] See, e.g., Hugo Grotius (1925: 231–59) and Samuel Pufendorf (1934: 936–7).

[11] See, for this breakdown, Grotius (1925: 231–59), Pufendorf (1934: 839–946), and William Blackstone (1979: 410–54).

[12] Debates, similar for all these groups, relate to the questions whether appropriate policies to offset inequality are affirmative action programs, cash grants, or provision of more education, and also concerning the tradeoff between short-run and long-run benefits.

[13] According to Barbara Bush (1990: 28–30) there were few differences in the slave laws in the Caribbean regarding men and women, at least until late eighteenth-century concerns with amelioration and childbearing.

[14] New World slavery differed from ancient slavery and modern slavery elsewhere, being more productive in large-scale agriculture and very commercial in its trading arrangements. In Brazil and the US South slaves account for about 30 percent of the population (as they had also in ancient Greece and Rome), while in the British, French, and Dutch West Indies the slave share was 90 percent. In most other slave societies, slaves accounted for a smaller share of the population, worked on smaller units, and were less frequently involved in agricultural production. In these societies the relative unimportance of the legal and economic impact of slavery has meant less attention given to that institution.

[15] For the ending of slavery in Africa, see the studies in Suzanne Miers and Richard Roberts (1988).

[16] See Claire Robertson and Martin Klein (1983) for a survey of the literature and citations to relevant sources on women and slavery in Africa.

[17] The ratio was generally 30 or 40 females per 100 males.

[18] There are few usable data that I have seen concerning the sex of children abandoned or killed in slave societies. Based on a frequent historical pattern it would be expected that more females than males would be killed or abandoned (Susan Scrimshaw 1983; John Boswell 1984).

[19] Novak describes the nineteenth-century American jurist, Thomas Rutherford, as arguing "like Grotius and Pufendorf." "Rutherford contended that an extreme want of food or clothing justified theft," since, according to Rutherford, "necessity sets property aside" (William Novak 1996: 72).

[20] The sex breakdown of voluntary enslavement in Russia, according to Hellie, was about two-thirds male, with infanticide, predominantly of females, serving to generate a more equal sex ratio (Richard Hellie 1982: 442–59).

[21] Another acceptable form of aid to the poor was suggested in 1572 by Thomas Wilson (1925: 258, 288), in *A Discourse Upon Usury*, with the provision of money to those suffering "famine in time of extreme death," "to relieve the poor and afflicted in every town and parish that be not able to help themselves." The ability of individuals and of the state to provide financial help, long-term or short-term, with little expectation of direct returns would make enslavement unnecessary as a solution to the survival problem, and this became the dominant solution once national income increased.

[22] Alternatively, geographic movement often took place in response to income declines leading to external migrations. The Irish movement to the United States and Canada as a result of the Irish Famine was not the only migration to the United States that was influenced by European economic conditions, and many similar famine-related movements have taken place in Asia and Africa.

[23] Indentured labor represented a payment in terms of labor time for the costs of transportation to a new nation, during which time the indentured laborer could be

brought and sold and had few rights in regard to labor conditions. Servants complained that the limited time period meant that they were treated worse than were slaves, who had a longer period to labor for owners. The two major streams of modern indentured labor migration were those from the British Isles to the British colonies in the first three-quarters of the eighteenth century, and that from India, China, and elsewhere primarily to the Caribbean, Fiji, and Australia, between 1850 and 1917. See David Galenson (1981) and Northrup (1995). On the conditions leading to acceptance of indenture, see the wistful comments of the Trinidad Government Emigration Agent in Calcutta: "Recruiting conditions and prospects at present are abnormally bad in almost every district. The recent good harvest had done away with the chief inducement of laboring classes to emigrate and recruits are almost unobtainable" (CO 295/430, letter of March 10, 1904). The minutes of December 22, 1904, noted that: "It is unfortunate that the Emigration Agencies must view with alarm a good harvest in India." For an earlier comment on this pattern, see G. A. Grierson (1883).

24 See, e.g., Douglass North and Robert Thomas (1973: 19–32). Serfdom differed from slavery in that laborers could not be sold apart from the land on which they lived and worked. Slaves were not tied to the land. In general, slavery was more frequent where long-distance movement of labor was required, and was of peoples regarded as outsiders. Serfdom occurred where the population was already in site, and movement to new areas was not necessary. Unlike modern slavery, where ethnicity of the enslaved and enslavers differed, in most cases of serfdom the ethnicities of landlords and serfs were the same.

25 Aristotle (1962: 335–9), for example, pointed to the value of manumission as an incentive and means of control, while for Jamaica, Michael Craton (1978: 222) points to the use of manumission as an incentive for labor productivity. Charles Price, the owner of Worthy Park, personally manumitted each year that slave who had distinguished himself "by hard work and fidelity." While the frequency of manumissions was often limited in the New World, those nations with low rates of manumissions (the United States and the British West Indies) ended slavery before those countries with higher rates of manumission (Cuba and Brazil).

26 In most New World slave societies, as in much of the world today, slave men apparently had a different tradeoff between individual freedom and maintenance of the family than did women. Men have apparently been more willing to leave families and children behind than have women.

27 See Ulrich Phillips (1909, II: 161–4; 1918: 446–7); Kenneth Stampp (1956: 92–3); Genovese (1974: 399–401); Deborah White (1985: 117–8); and Patterson (1982: 297).

28 See Stanley Engerman (1995), which also includes dates for the former Spanish colonies in South America and Central America.

29 The one area with a dramatic change in land ownership patterns was Haiti, where the slaves freed themselves in a revolt and drove out their former owners.

30 Exceptions, in the British Caribbean, were Barbados and Antigua, where land shortages meant the workers had limited opportunities, and Trinidad and British Guiana, which attracted indentured laborers to work on their plantations. Later Cuba attracted immigrants to help maintain the plantation system.

31 Haiti's difficulties were due, in part, to external interferences, such as the lack of desire on the part of most countries to trade with it, and a need to pay an indemnity to France in exchange for the opening of trade, but it was politically and economically unstable.

32 Food for slaves could be obtained either by master purchase and provision or by the slaves growing their own food on master-provided plots of land. For a discussion of food provisioning in the British West Indies, see B. W. Higman (1984: 204–18). Under the system of master provision by purchase of foodstuffs females could spend

more time in field labor and presumably learn less about small-scale production of foodstuffs, due to the shift from food production to staple production.

[33] For a discussion of the role of slave women in the antebellum South, see White (1985). On the changing role of women with emancipation in the British West Indies, see Bridget Brereton (1999).

[34] Lynchings, as a form of social control, were almost exclusively limited to males. Stewart Tolnay and E. M. Beck (1995: 269) estimate that only 3 percent of all lynchings of freed blacks were of females.

[35] The precise effects on fertility of the antebellum pattern of some slave couples living on different farms, or with separate residences on fertility were, however, unclear. Under slavery, particularly in Virginia, there were cross-unit marriages with visiting, etc. Yet the areas in which these occurred seem to have been regions of high fertility.

[36] The effect of planter policy on fertility is difficult to resolve. There were apparently more pro-natalist measures in the British West Indies than in the United States, possibly because they were thought more necessary there, given the lower fertility. Second, the decisions of women in one-parent vs. two-parent households may lead to differences in fertility, whether in slavery or in freedom.

[37] Thus it is debated whether the prevalence of the mother-headed household reflects a desired outcome or rather is the outcome of various forms of social problems.

REFERENCES

Aristotle. 1962. *Oeconomica.* Cambridge, MA: Harvard University Press (written *c.* 320 BC).

Blackstone, William. 1979. *Commentaries on the Law of England. Vol. I: Of the Rights of Persons.* Chicago: University of Chicago Press (first published 1765).

Bolland, O. Nigel. 2002. "The Hundredth Year of Our Emancipation: The Dialectics of Resistance in Slavery and Freedom," in Verene A. Shepherd (ed.) *Working Slavery, Pricing Freedom: Perceptions from the Caribbean, Africa, and the African Diaspora,* pp. 320–39. Oxford, UK: James Curry.

Boswell, John Eastburn. 1984. "*Expositio* and *Oblatio*: The Abandonment of Children and the Ancient and Medieval Family." *American Historical Review* 89(1): 10–33.

Brady, Frank. 1990. *Citizen Welles: A Biography of Orson Welles.* New York: Scribner's.

Brereton, Bridget. 1999. "Family Strategies, Gender and the Shift to Wage Labour in the British Caribbean," in Bridget Brereton and Kevin A. Yelvington (eds.) *The Colonial Caribbean in Transition: Essays on Postemancipation Social and Cultural History,* pp. 77–107. Gainesville, FL: University Press of Florida.

Bush, Barbara. 1990. *Slave Women in Caribbean Society, 1650–1838.* Bloomington, IN: Indiana University Press.

Cartledge, Paul. 1998. *Democritus.* London: Phoenix.

Cooper, Frederick. 1977. *Plantation Slavery on the East Coast of Africa.* New Haven, CT: Yale University Press.

Craton, Michael. 1978. *Searching for the Invisible Man: Slaves and Plantation Life in Jamaica.* Cambridge, MA: Harvard University Press.

Davis, David Brion. 1975. *The Problem of Slavery in the Age of Revolution, 1770–1823.* Ithaca, NY: Cornell University Press.

——. 1984. *Slavery and Human Progress.* New York: Oxford University Press.

Domar, Evsey D. 1970. "The Causes of Slavery or Serfdom: A Hypothesis." *Journal of Economic History* 30(1): 18–32.

Drescher, Seymour. 1999. *From Slavery to Freedom: Comparative Studies in the Rise and Fall of Atlantic Slavery.* New York: New York University Press.

Du Bois, W. E. Burghardt. 1909. *The Negro American Family*. Atlanta, GA: Atlanta University Publications Series.

Eltis, David. 2000. *The Rise of African Slavery in the Americas*. Cambridge, UK: Cambridge University Press.

——and Stanley, L. Engerman. 1992. "Was the Slave Trade Dominated by Men?" *Journal of Interdisciplinary History* 23(2): 237–57.

Engerman, Stanley L. 1977. "Black Fertility and Family Structure in the US, 1880–1940." *Journal of Family History* 2(2): 117–38.

——. 1978. "Studying the Black Family." *Journal of Family History* 3(1): 78–101.

——. 1983. "Contract Labor, Sugar, and Technology in the Nineteenth Century." *Journal of Economic History* 43(3): 635–59.

——. 1994. "Reflections on 'The Standard of Living' Debate: New Arguments and New Evidence," in John A. James and Mark Thomas (ed.) *Capitalism in Context: Essays on Economic Development and Cultural Changes in Honor of R. M. Hartwell*, pp. 50–79. Chicago: University of Chicago Press.

——. 1995. "Emancipations in Comparative Perspective: A Long and Wide View," in Gert Oostindie (ed.) *Fifty Years Later: Antislavery, Capitalism and Modernity in the Dutch Orbit*, pp. 223–41. Leiden: KITLV Press.

——. 2000. "Comparative Approaches to the Ending of Slavery," in Howard Temperly (ed.) *After Slavery: Emancipation and its Discontents*, pp. 281–300. London: Frank Cass.

Findlay, Ronald. 1975. "Slavery, Incentives, and Manumission: A Theoretical Model." *Journal of Political Economy* 83(5): 923–33.

Finley, Moses I. 1998. *Ancient Slavery and Modern Ideology* (expanded edition). Princeton, NJ: Markus Wiener (first published 1980).

Fogel, Robert William. 1989. *Without Consent or Contract: The Rise and Fall of American Slavery*. New York: W. W. Norton.

——and Stanley, L. Engerman. 1974. *Time on the Cross: The Economics of American Negro Slavery*. Boston, MA: Little, Brown.

Franklin, John Hopeand Loren Schweninger. 1999. *Runaway Slaves: Rebels on the Plantation*. New York: Oxford University Press.

Galenson, David. 1981. *White Servitude in Colonial America: An Economic Analysis*. Cambridge, UK: Cambridge University Press.

Genovese, Eugene D. 1974. *Roll, Jordan Roll: The World the Slaves Made*. New York: Pantheon.

Goldin, Claudia. 1990. *Understanding the Gender Gap: An Economic History of American Women*. New York: Oxford University Press.

Grierson, G. A. 1883. *Report on Colonial Emigration from the Bengal Presidency*. Calcutta.

Grotius, Hugo. 1925. *The Law of War and Peace*. Oxford, UK: Clarendon Press (first published 1646).

Gutman, Herbert G. 1976. *The Black Family in Slavery and Freedom, 1750–1925*. New York: Pantheon.

Hale, Robert. 1952. *Freedom through Law: Public Control of Private Governing Power*. New York: Columbia University Press.

Hellie, Richard. 1982. *Slavery in Russia, 1450–1725*. Chicago: University of Chicago Press.

Heuman, Gad (ed.). 1985. "Out of the House of Bondage: Runaways, Resistance and Marronage in Africa and the New World." *Slavery and Abolition* 6(4).

Higman, B. W. 1984. *Slave Populations of the British Caribbean, 1807–1834*. Baltimore, MD: Johns Hopkins University Press.

Holt, Sharon Ann. 2000. *Making Freedom Pay: North Carolina Freedpeople Working for Themselves, 1865–1900*. Athens, GA: University of Georgia Press.

Jones, Jacqueline. 1985. *Labor of Love, Labor of Sorrow: Black Women, Work, and the Family from Slavery to the Present*. New York: Basic Books.

Locke, John. 1963. *Two Treatises of Government*. New York: Mentor Books (first published 1690).

Lovejoy, Paul E. 1983 *Transformations in Slavery: A History of Slavery in Africa*. Cambridge, UK: Cambridge University Press.

Maine, Henry Sumner. 1885. *Popular Government*. London: John Murray.

McGlynn, Frank (ed.). 1989. *Perspectives on Manumission: Slavery and Abolition* 10(4).

Miers, Suzanne and Richard Roberts (eds.). 1988. *The End of Slavery in Africa*. Madison, WI: University of Wisconsin Press.

Moreno Fraginals, Manuel, Herbert S. Klein, and Stanley L. Engerman. 1983. "The Level and Structure of Slave Prices on Cuban Plantations in the Mid-Nineteenth Century: Some Comparative Perspectives." *American Historical Review* 88(5): 1201–18.

Morgan, Edmund S. 1975. *American Slavery, American Freedom: The Ordeal of Colonial Virginia*. New York: W. W. Norton.

Nieboer, H. J. 1910. *Slavery as an Industrial System: Ethnological Researches*. 2nd revd. edn. The Hague: Nijhoff.

North, Douglass C. and Robert Paul Thomas. 1973. *The Rise of the Western World: A New Economic History*. Cambridge, UK: Cambridge University Press.

Northrup, David. 1995. *Indentured Labor in the Age of Imperialism, 1834–1922*. Cambridge, UK: Cambridge University Press.

Novak, William. 1996. *The People's Welfare: Law and Regulation in Nineteenth-Century America*. Chapel Hill, NC: University of North Carolina Press.

Nussbaum, Martha C. 1995. "Human Capabilities, Female Human Beings," in Martha C. Nussbaum and Jonathan Glover (eds.) *Women, Culture, and Development: A Study of Human Capabilities*, pp. 61–104. Oxford, UK: Clarendon Press.

Patterson, Orlando. 1982. *Slavery and Social Death: A Comparative Study*. Cambridge, MA: Harvard University Press.

Phillips, Ulrich Bonnell. 1909. *Plantation and Frontier, Documents, 1640–1863*. Cleveland, OH: A. H. Clark.

——. 1918. *American Negro Slavery: A Survey of the Supply, Employment, and Control of Negro Labor as Determined by the Plantation Regime*. New York: D. Appleton.

Pufendorf, Samuel. 1934. *On the Law of Nature and Nations*. Oxford, UK: Clarendon Press (first published 1688).

Roberts, George W. 1957. *The Population of Jamaica*. Cambridge, UK: Cambridge University Press.

Robertson, Claire C. and Martin A. Klein (eds.). 1983. *Women and Slavery in Africa*. Madison, WI: University of Wisconsin Press.

Rozbicki, Michael J. 2001. "To Save Them from Themselves: Proposals to Enslave the British Poor, 1698–1775." *Slavery and Abolition* 22(3): 29–50.

Scrimshaw, Susan C. M. 1983. "Infanticide as Deliberate Fertility Regulation," in Rodolfo A. Bulatao and Ronald D. Lee (eds.) *Determinants of Fertility in Developing Countries. Vol. 2: Fertility Regulation and Institutional Influences*, pp. 245–66. New York: Academic Press.

Sen, Amartya. 1980. "Equality of What?" in Sterling M. McMurrin (ed.) *The Tanner Lectures on Human Values*, pp. 195–220. Cambridge, UK: Cambridge University Press.

——. 1993. "Capability and Well-Being," in Martha Nussbaum and Amartya Sen (eds.) *The Quality of Life*, pp. 30–53. Oxford, UK: Clarendon Press.

——. 1999. *Development as Freedom*. New York: Alfred A. Knopf.

Stampp, Kenneth M. 1956. *The Peculiar Institution: Slavery in the Ante-Bellum South*. New York: Knopf.

Steinfeld, Robert J. 2001. *Coercion, Contract, and Free Labor in the Nineteenth Century*. Cambridge, UK: Cambridge University Press.

Tolnay, Stewart E. and E. M. Beck. 1995. *A Festival of Violence: An Analysis of Southern Lynchings, 1882–1930*. Urbana, IL: University of Illinois Press.

White, Deborah Gray. 1985. *Ar'n't I a Woman: Female Slaves in the Plantation South.* New York: W. W. Norton.

Wilson, Thomas. 1925. *A Discourse Upon Usury.* New York: Harcourt Brace & Co. (first published 1572).

DOES CONTRACEPTION BENEFIT WOMEN? STRUCTURE, AGENCY, AND WELL-BEING IN RURAL MEXICO

Austreberta Nazar Beutelspacher, Emma Zapata Martelo, and Verónica Vázquez García

OVERVIEW

The authors of this chapter examine Amartya Sen's contributions to the concept of human well-being from a gender perspective and argue that this concept is particularly useful for explaining women's decisions on contraceptive use. The study draws on data collected in six rural communities of Chiapas, Mexico. It emphasizes the ways in which public discourse articulates the apparent benefits of having small families; the context of the household and community in which rural women make reproductive decisions; and the impact of family planning programs on women's sense of subjective well-being. In particular, it questions the assumption that reduced fertility through contraception necessarily enhances women's well-being and points to the importance that women attach to being a party to reproductive decisions. The authors also explore the links between women's assessment of these decisions and of paid work, and their actual education levels and real possibilities of employment.

INTRODUCTION

Women's sexual and reproductive rights were central issues at the 1994 World Conference on Population and Development held in Cairo. Women's groups succeeded in placing the issue of population growth within the context of sustainable development, highlighting the importance of women's empowerment and of an improvement in their living conditions for attaining such development (Lori Ashford 1995). Similarly, at the 1995 World Conference on Women, held in Beijing, feminists stressed the "explicit recognition and reaffirmation of the right of all women to control all aspects of their health, particularly regarding their own fertility" (Carmen Martínez and María José Montero 1997: 27), as well as the need to integrate gender analysis into all policies, programs, and projects.[1]

From a gender perspective, population policies need to be defined within a framework of individual freedoms and social justice. Feminists emphasize the importance of women's rights both as a means for development and as a goal of development.[2] These views resonate with some of the assertions by Amartya Sen (1985, 1996, 2000), particularly those regarding agency and well-being. Our goal in this paper is to apply Sen's concept of well-being to analyze population policies from a gender perspective. We focus on the impact of such policies on rural women in the Mexican state of Chiapas.

Sen's concept of well-being is useful especially in two ways. First, it helps us understand the context in which rural women make decisions about their own fertility, as well as the elements intervening in such decisions, such as women's educational levels, their assessment of paid work, and their real possibilities of employment. Second, it allows us to problematize the apparent benefits that population policies (operating through family planning programs) offer to rural women.

For our analysis, we draw on data gathered in six rural communities in Chiapas, and in particular on our interviews with 300 women in the 30–49 age group. We examine (a) whether there is a significant relationship between women's educational levels and their assessment of paid work; and (b) how women assess paid work, and whether having such work influences the number of children they have and their participation in the decision to use contraception.

As detailed in the chapter, our analysis shows that there need be no straightforward relationship between the adoption of contraceptive methods promoted by a state, and an increase in women's well-being as defined by Sen. Rather, a number of factors can affect women's contraceptive choices, such as their educational levels, how they assess paid work, and their actual employment prospects. In turn, these factors can increase the possibility of contraception improving women's well-being. However, in the absence of certain enabling factors, contraception may be imposed on women and render them less (rather than more) satisfied with their lives.

In the discussion below we first outline Sen's concept of well-being and its usefulness for analyzing population policies from a gender perspective. Subsequently, we draw on this concept to analyze the context in which rural women in Chiapas make decisions regarding their own fertility, and to problematize the apparent benefits of family planning programs for women. We highlight the factors that shape women's decisions around contraception in rural Chiapas, and conclude by stressing the importance of considering women's agency and well-being when designing population policies.

I. WELL-BEING, GENDER, AND PUBLIC POLICY

Sen (1985, 1996) suggests that well-being is a combination of doings and beings, that is, functionings that may range from being well-nourished and healthy to having self-respect, human dignity, and the ability to participate in community life. He assigns paramount importance to the freedom to choose between alternative functionings, which he terms as the "capability to function" (Amartya Sen 1988), that is, the freedom a person has for leading the life s/he values and achieving valuable functionings. Sen further stresses that we must pay attention to both the achievement of well-being (achieved functionings) and well-being freedom.

Capabilities express the real opportunities available to people for achieving well-being. According to Sen (1985), in evaluating people's well-being it is important to consider individual assessments of both the functionings achieved and the set of opportunities available to them for achieving well-being. Sen thus pays considerable attention to context. The articulation of these elements constitutes the key for analysis in real-life situations. However, to evaluate women's well-being two issues must be considered. First, as Martha Nussbaum and Amartya Sen (1996) point out, applying the concept of well-being to women's lives raises the dilemma of cultural differences. On what bases can we compare different groups of women? Second, the concept of well-being rests on an information-pluralistic structure. Below, we address each issue and offer some ways of dealing with them.

Sen typically does not explicitly deal with gender issues in his concept of well-being. However, by considering agency and freedom as central elements thereof, he makes space for examining the subjective and normative dimensions of gender inequality. Moreover, Sen's concept leaves room to discuss an issue that is crucial from a gender perspective: women's right to pursue alternatives and gain access to opportunities for enhancing personal well-being. As we know, a primary demand of the women's movement has been for women to have the freedom to make decisions about their own lives (Claudia García-Moreno and Amparo Claro 1994). Thus, a gender perspective on well-being will allow us to understand women's assessments (mediated by identities, norms, and institutions) and their implications for women's well-being, by considering the different ways in which gender differences construct social reality (Joan Scott 1996).

Amartya Sen (1990) argues that for women, self-interest and agency are socially molded by notions of obligation and legitimacy, which affect their behavior and the choices they make. In this respect, Sen acknowledges that agency itself is not enough to achieve well-being, since it is mediated by what society considers "good" and as such is based on moral judgments. In fact, he recognizes that agency is broader than well-being, since not all choices are aimed at achieving valuable functionings for oneself (Sen 1996). Furthermore, agency and well-being are two separate aspects that may or may not have the same relationship with personal well-being and, therefore, need to be assessed in independent or complementary terms (Sen 1985). Thus, when analyzing women's reproductive choices, we need to consider not only the choices themselves, but also the underlying values that lead to a certain choice, and whether that choice translates into well-being for women.

As Sen (1985) and Julia Annas (1996) point out, women's perceptions of themselves, and of what they want to be or do, are largely constituted by the circumstances and options they see before them. Hence, in societies in which women have fewer options than men, women might be prone to settle for less. In other words, people's well-being cannot be based only on their perception of needs and their satisfaction, but on what they can actually be and do in life, that is, on their capabilities. We acknowledge the importance of taking into account individual assessments underlying the choices made, not as an evaluative criterion of well-being, but for clarifying the role played by gender identities and norms in determining women's well-being.

To sum up, the key elements in women's well-being derive from both subjective and objective dimensions. These elements are: individual assessments mediated by gender identities and norms that give legitimacy to what is chosen, and the possibility of choosing functionings that enhance personal well-being (where gender conflict may arise). In this sense, the context in which women make decisions is fundamental to understanding their well-being cross-culturally.

Sen (1988) highlights the central role of the state in promoting human well-being through policies such as distributing food, and providing education and medical care among certain groups of people. Public policies are established in order to modify the circumstances, assessments, or activities of certain groups for the sake of the "common good," namely, the promotion of certain personal functionings that the state considers important for the collectivity.

Analyzing state policy is one way of dealing with the plural views outlined above. The state's actions provide a basis for assessing people's well-being by looking at the apparent benefits offered by certain policies and programs. For instance, we are particularly interested in the functionings that are affected by a specific program, namely that aimed at reducing family size. These functionings are implicitly or explicitly contained in the discourse and practice of the programs, and they enable us to disclose their scope and limitations for promoting human well-being.

From this perspective, the critical issue is not the acceptance or rejection of the program by a certain group of people, or its overall impact (for example on aggregate fertility rates), but rather how the program is viewed by its potential beneficiaries. Do these programs really translate into women's personal well-being? Women's agency, as reflected in the autonomy women have to make decisions regarding contraception, for instance, can affect the personal well-being outcomes of the programs. We need to identify the individual and social elements that enable people to benefit from a particular program.

Interpersonal evaluations can be conducted within the same context, or by comparing different contexts. In examining Mexico's family planning program in rural Chiapas, we undertake three levels of analysis. First, we take into account the structure of well-being options available to people, particularly the options relevant to the functionings promoted by a certain program. Second, we examine individual assessments and life expectations by looking at the options people have and those that they consider possible, as well as their perceptions of the program's likely impact on the achievement of their life objectives. Third, we assess achieved functionings, namely, achievements measured in terms of the personal well-being that people derive from accepting the program, the circumstances in which they accept it (whether or not through the exercise of agency), and the apparent benefits of such a program.

We will now analyze Mexico's family planning program in rural Chiapas. Our purpose is to examine the validity of the presumed positive relationship between contraception use and women's well-being, and the factors that intervene in women's contraceptive choices, such as their educational levels, their assessment of paid work, and their job prospects.

II. FAMILY PLANNING IN MEXICO AND WOMEN'S OPTIONS IN RURAL CHIAPAS

Family planning in Mexico is a legal right that has been coupled with an extended institutional coverage of health services and dissemination campaigns.[3] The use of contraceptives was first promoted by the State in the 1970s with the slogan "a small family lives better," using the argument that it would improve living standards. The 1980s, however, were dominated by the slogan "have few children to give them more," when the country was in economic crisis, public expenditure was being cut, and unemployment was rising. The Cairo Conference of 1994 influenced the Mexican government to restructure its family planning program by including some safeguards for women's autonomy and reproductive rights. The slogan during the 1990s was "family planning ... it's a matter of choice," which emphasized individual life projects and decision-making (Consejo Nacional de Población 1998).

According to the Mexican government, family planning, by promoting the spacing of pregnancies and limiting the number of children, offers all women the option of improved well-being. Moreover, by participating in

219

such a program, women can access other aspects of well-being, regardless of the socio-economic and cultural contexts within which they make decisions. Women can be healthier and wealthier; they can live longer and enjoy better sex since they need not worry about unwanted pregnancies; and they can work outside their homes and have better educated children (Secretaría de Salud 1996).

In recent years, the official discourse has been accompanied by an intensification of family planning programs among the rural and marginal urban populations of Mexico, viewed as a strategy to "fight poverty" (Secretaría de Hacienda y Crédito Público 1995). Since the mid-1990s, the state of Chiapas has been especially targeted by such programs. In the early 1990s, Chiapas had the highest poverty levels and fertility rates in Mexico (Consejo Nacional de Población 1993; Miguel Cervera 1994), as well as the lowest contraception rates (Yolanda Palma and Jesús Suárez 1994). The implementation of family planning programs increased the state's contraception prevalence rate for all women in the age group 15–49 from 49.9 percent in 1992 to 53.5 percent in 1997. The most commonly used method was the surgical sterilization of women, and Chiapas with 55.7 percent sterilized women, presently ranks first in all Mexico in the percentage of sterilized women among contraceptive users (Consejo Nacional de Población 2000).

A recent study conducted by Benito Salvatierra (2000) in Chiapas shows that the sharpest decline in fertility took place among rural *mestizo* populations (from 4.4 children per woman to 2.8 between 1976 and 1996), followed by marginal urban populations (4.7 to 3.7), native rural populations (4.6 to 3.8), and middle urban settlements (2.2 to 2.0).[4] Salvatierra attributes the decline to an increase in the use of contraceptives: in 1996, 72.6 percent of the women aged 15–49 years in rural mestizo communities used contraceptives, compared to 46.8 percent in 1976. These figures illustrate the intensity of the family planning programs implemented in Chiapas, and can be seen as an indicator of program success. However, we believe it is important to assess to what extent limiting the number of children has actually contributed to women's well-being in Chiapas.

For our analysis, we drew on data gathered in six rural communities of Chiapas, located along the border between Chiapas and Guatemala, each community having less that 2,500 *mestizo* inhabitants. We focused on the female population aged 30–49 years, since Salvatierra's study had shown that 85 to 90 percent of the women who limited their number of children, did so when they were between 30 and 34 years of age. The estimated sample size for the six communities was 288 and we interviewed a total of 300 women.[5] Using a structured questionnaire and some open-ended questions, we asked these 300 women about their pregnancy histories, their use of contraceptives, and their opinions of traditional gender roles and life expectations. We also conducted participant observation in the six communities. Fictitious names are used throughout the paper to keep the respondents' personal information confidential.

Below, we first discuss the characteristics of the six Chiapas communities and then analyze the relationship between contraception use and women's well-being. We examine the structure of well-being options available to women, particularly those that provide educational or employment alternatives to women's traditional roles of wives and mothers. We also examine women's assessment of such options, followed by an analysis of the apparent improvement in women's personal well-being resulting from their acceptance of the family planning program (as an agency achievement or otherwise). In our analysis, we explore two hypotheses: one, that women's views of paid work are conditioned by their educational levels; and two, that women's views of paid work, and whether or not they have such work, influences the number of children they have and the decision-making process around contraception methods. A novel feature of our approach is that it puts the assessment of paid work, and whether or not women do such work, on center stage, as aspects that can critically impinge on demographic decision-making.

Community characteristics and women's categories

We have used two criteria to classify the six communities under study: the dominant production system and the sexual division of labor. Both define the options available to women in each community in terms of education and work opportunities. We found that the activities that women performed were largely determined by the specific production structure and associated life options in their communities, as well as by gender identities and norms. Tables 1 and 2 outline some of the characteristics of the communities and of women's activities within them.

 Agriculture is the main economic activity in all six communities, but the land ownership patterns and prospects for paid employment differ. In Piedra Labrada and Emiliano Zapata, production is mostly for self-consumption. In these communities, 75.1 percent of the families own land (they are *ejidatarios* and sons of *ejidatarios*),[6] the amounts ranging from 2 to 30 hectares, with an average of 13.5 hectares per family. Much of this is low productivity, unirrigated land, located in mountainous terrain. Farming is done mainly through family labor with little use of wage labor. However, there is a sexual division of labor, whereby men do most of the agricultural work and women most of the domestic work. Occasionally women participate in agriculture alongside their husbands and/or children. Only 1.7 percent of the women are employed as seasonal agriculture workers for some four weeks or less during the year, while 49.2 percent are exclusively home based. Almost all women rear animals (pigs) and poultry in their

Table 1 Production systems and the sexual division of labor in the six communities under study

Production system	Community	Region/municipality	Main productive activity	Number of households (total/with land)	Average hectares per landowning household	Number of inhabitants
Subsistence production with male and female unpaid labor	PIEDRA LABRADA	Border (Chicomuselo/Bella Vista)	Cultivation of corn, beans, and coffee (2,850 hectares of mountain rain-fed agriculture, all cultivated area)	214/171 (79.9%)	16.7	1,088
	EMILIANO ZAPATA	Mountain (Bella Vista)	Cultivation of corn, beans, and coffee (2,050 hectares of mountain rain-fed agriculture, all cultivated area)	269/192 (71.4%)	10.7	1,225
Subtotal			4,900 cultivated hectares	75.2%	13.5	2,313
Subsistence production of corn; market production of other products, with the remunerated participation of women	CONQUISTA CAMPESINA	Soconusco (Tapachula)	Cultivation of corn; fishing as a secondary activity (2,050 hectares of mangrove swamp, ocean and rain-fed agriculture/231 cultivated hectares)	66/66 (100.0%)	3.5	381

(continued overleaf)

Table 1 (continued)

Production system	Community	Region/municipality	Main productive activity	Number of households (total/with land)	Average hectares per landowning household	Number of inhabitants
	20 DE NOVIEMBRE	Soconusco (Suchiate)	Cultivation of corn, beans, sesame seeds, soy beans, nuts, cotton, banana, and mango (588 hectares of rain-fed agriculture/288 cultivated hectares)	124/116 (93.5%)	2.5	748
Subtotal			519 cultivated hectares	95.8%	2.8	1,129
Production for the market with the remunerated participation of women	JOAQUÍN MIGUEL GUTIÉRREZ	Soconusco (Tapachula)	Cultivation of soy beans, sorghum, sesame seeds, and corn (795 hectares of irrigated agriculture, all cultivated area)	109/60 (55.5%)	13.3	438
	CONGREGACIÓN REFORMA	Soconusco (Tapachula)	Cultivation of soy beans, sorghum, banana, cotton, and nuts (917 hectares of irrigated agriculture, all cultivated area)	211/92 (43.6%)	10.0	874
Subtotal			1,712 cultivated hectares	47.5%	11.3	1,312

Source: Own fieldwork, Chiapas (1998).

223

Table 2 Women's educational and employment opportunities by community location

Community/sample size (n = 300)	Educational level		Occupation (Women from 30 to 49 years of age)				Employment opportunities for women	Maximum level of formal education offered at the community
	Women: 30 to 49 years, without schooling % (n)	Daughters: 13 to 19 years, without schooling[a] % (n/N)	Housewives % (n)	Self-employed % (n)	Agricultural laborers % (n)	Other remunerated workers[c] % (n)		
PIEDRA LABRADA (n=60)	8.3 (5)	4.8 (4/83)	40.0 (24)	46.7 (28)	3.3 (2)	10.0 (6)	Negligible	Telesecondary[b]
EMILIANO ZAPATA (n=60)	5.0 (3)	1.6 (2/122)	58.3 (35)	31.7 (19)	0.0 (0)	10.0 (6)	Negligible	Telesecondary
Subtotal (n=120)	6.7 (8)	2.9 (6/205)	49.2 (59)	39.2 (47)	1.7 (2)	10.0 (12)	Negligible	Telesecondary
CONQUISTA CAMPESINA (n=22)	59.1 (13)	13.5 (7/52)	72.7 (16)	13.6 (3)	4.5 (1)	9.2 (2)	Yes (Outside the community-banana planatations)	Primary school
20 DE NOVIEMBRE (n=45)	42.2 (19)	9.1 (5/55)	68.9 (31)	11.1 (5)	17.7 (8)	2.3 (1)	Yes (Outside the community-banana plantations)	Telesecondary
Subtotal (n=67)	47.8 (32)	11.2 (12/107)	70.1 (47)	11.9 (8)	13.4 (9)	4.6 (3)	Yes (Outside the community)	Telesecondary
JOAQUÍN MIGUEL GTZ. (n=44)	23.2 (10)	9.0 (6/67)	43.2 (19)	27.3 (12)	6.8 (3)	22.7 (10)	Yes (inside the community)	Telesecondary
CONGREGACIÓN REFORMA (n=69)	31.8 (22)	2.6 (3/114)	40.6 (28)	26.0 (18)	23.2 (16)	10.2 (7)	Yes (inside the community)	High school
Subtotal (n=113)	28.3 (32)	5.0 (9/181)	41.6 (47)	26.5 (30)	16.8 (19)	15.1 (17)	Yes (inside the community)	High school

Notes (a) This refers to illiterate women who did not attend school.
(b) The first three years of high school offered through television programs.
(c) This includes women working as midwives, seamstresses, artisans, housemaids, store employees, and professional workers.
Source Own fieldwork, Chiapas (1998).

backyards. Of the rest, 39.2 percent have other forms of self-employment, such as preparing and selling food, running retail outlets for groceries, and selling clothes, cosmetics, and home products. Most undertake such self-employment at home, and some few outside it. It is notable that many women prefer informal commercial activities because they are compatible with childcare and household chores and also generate an income. Finally, 10 percent of the women in these communities have paid jobs such as those of midwives or seamstresses, working from the home, and a few (8) work as housemaids in the nearby city of Frontera Comalapa, to which they commute daily.

In contrast, the communities of Joaquín Miguel Gutiérrez and Congregación Reforma produce for the market. In these two communities taken together, only 47.5 percent of the families own land, with an average of 11.3 hectares per family. These are the best lands of the region. The farmers have irrigation, use machinery (tractors and threshers), and hire labor from within the community. Women agricultural laborers represent 16.8 percent of the total sample in these two communities and come from the landless families. Women of land-owning households rarely participate in agricultural work. Some 41.6 percent work exclusively at home; another 26.5 percent are self-employed in small commercial ventures within and outside their homes; and 15.1 percent do paid work as housemaids, teachers in public schools, nurses, and other professionals.

In between are the communities of Conquista Campesina and 20 de Noviembre which produce for self-consumption but also have opportunities for women to secure paid employment in nearby farms. In these two communities families own an average of 2.8 hectares each. In Conquista Campesina, all households own some land, but much of it is rainfed land of poor quality, close to the ocean, where only corn is grown for self-consumption. The average farm size is 3.5 hectares per family. In 20 de Noviembre, 93.5 percent of the households own land, and although they, too, depend only on rainfall, their land is more fertile than that in Conquista Campesina. In 20 de Noviembre, 70.1 percent of the women work at home and rear backyard animals. They also occasionally undertake agricultural work on the family farms, along with their husbands and sons. In this community, 13.4 percent of the women work as agricultural day laborers, while 11.9 percent have small commercial ventures within or outside their homes, and only 4.6 percent have paid jobs as housemaids or artisans.

According to Sen (1985), the evaluation of women's well-being must take into account the activities that women perform or may be able to perform. Thus our analysis includes both women's own assessment of potentially valuable functionings, such as paid work outside the home, and whether they actually perform such work. Moreover, Sen gives particular importance to the "visibility" of women's work in enhancing their agency. Paid employment outside the home is visible in both physical and monetary terms. We have thus placed particular emphasis on women's paid work outside the home.

For our analysis, we have divided women of the six Chiapas communities into four categories, using a modified version of the schema provided by Joan Manuel Batista-Foguet, Joseph María Blanch, and Maité Artés (1994). In accordance with this schema, we identify the four categories of women, constituted from a combination of the activities they undertake and their perceptions of these activities.[7] Category 1 includes the "willingly home based": these women do not perform paid work and also assess such work negatively (that is, they would not like to do it). They are engaged either exclusively in domestic work or at best in some form of self-employment along with domestic work. In Category 2 are the "unwillingly home based," namely, women who again do not perform paid work (because of their husbands' opposition or the lack of local opportunities), but who consider such work desirable. Category 3 consists of the "unwillingly employed" – women who perform paid work but assess it negatively; that is, as undesirable. In other words, these women participate in activities other than only housework and childcare, but do so unwillingly. Finally, Category 4 consists of the "willingly employed." These women perform paid work and also assess such work positively.

We use cross-tabulations and the chi-square statistic to examine interrelationships between these four classifications of women and their distribution according to other variables such as women's assessment of paid work outside the home, the communities in which they live, their educational levels, their use of contraception, and so on. The chi-square statistic tests whether an observed joint frequency distribution could have occurred by chance. It involves the comparison of observed frequencies with those that would be expected if there were no relationship between the variables. We have used three types of chi-square tests: the standard chi-square (χ^2); the log-likelihood chi-square (χ^2_{LR}), which helps deal with the problem of small sample size and small frequencies in individual cells (Jerrold H. Zar 1984); and the Mantel Haenszel chi-square (χ^2_{LR}), which helps compare two variables, one of which is ordinal (e.g., schooling levels) (Steve Selvin 1996).

Options for paid work and education

Most of the women we interviewed think that paid work outside the home conflicts with their traditional roles as mothers and wives. This translates into a negative assessment of such work. As seen from Table 3, only 24.8 percent of the women interviewed consider paid employment to be a valuable activity. Of these, only 6.6 percent are actually employed.[8]

As expected, in the communities that offer job opportunities for women, more women evaluate female employment positively (44.7 percent) than in other communities (12.3 percent). Because of the existence of opportunities for paid work women perceive such work as possible and valuable; and the work enhances their possibilities for achieving agency and well-being. Table 4 shows that there are important differences in the distribution of the women across the categories within each community. Of the 14 (out of 214) women in the willingly employed category, 12 (that is, 85.7 percent) are found in the two communities (Joaquín Miguel Gutiérrez and Congregación Reforma) in which paid employment is available for women within the community, while of the 140 women in the

Table 3 Classification of women by their assessment of paid work and actual employment status

		ACTIVITY (Objective)		
		No paid work outside the home	*Paid work outside the home*	
ASSESSMENT (subjects: norms and identities)	Assessment of paid work negative	Willingly homebased 140 (65.4%)	Unwillingly employed 21 (9.8%)	161 (75.2%)
	Assessment of paid work positive	Unwillingly homebased 39 (18.2%)	Willingly employed 14 (6.6%)	53 (24.8%)
		179 (83.6%)	35 (16.4%)	214* (100.0%)

$$\chi^2 = 5.21; \text{ d.f.} = 1; \ p = 0.022$$

Notes: The answers of 86 women could not be classified in any of the four boxes. The proportion of women with unclassified assessments is not different among women who have paid employment (29.0%) and those who do not (28.4%). Accordingly, there were no differences in the proportion of women who have paid employment outside their homes among the women with classified assessments (45.8%) and those whose assessments could not be classified (46.5%). We will thus base our discussion on the 214 women whose answers could be classified without the risk of bias.

Table 4 Women's fourfold classification by their community location

Communities	Willingly employed	Unwillingly employed	Unwillingly homebased	Willingly homebased	Total
Piedra Labrada and Emiliano Zapata (*n*=85)	1.2 (1)	2.3 (2)	9.4 (8)	87.1 (74)	100.0
Conquista Campesina and 20 de Noviembre (*n*=53)	1.9 (1)	13.2 (7)	13.2 (7)	71.7 (38)	100.0
Joaquín Miguel Gutiérrez and Congregación Reforma (*n*=76)	15.8 (12)	15.8 (12)	31.6 (24)	36.8 (28)	100.0
Total (*n*=214)	6.6 (14)	9.8 (21)	18.2 (39)	65.4 (140)	100.0

Notes: Figures in parentheses give the absolute numbers; $\chi^2_{LR} = 53.496$; df = 6, $p = 0.000$.

227

category of "willingly home based" 112 (or 80 percent) are from the four communities (Piedra Labrada, Emiliano Zapata, Conquista Campesina, and 20 de Noviembre).

It is also notable, and perhaps not surprising, that the communities with the highest percentage of landless families (Joaquín Miguel Gutiérrez and Congregación Reforma) are those where we also find the smallest percentage of the "willingly home based" and the largest percentage of the "willingly employed." Clearly, both demand and supply factors are at work here. On the one hand, women of the landless families are economically compelled to find wage employment, and on the other hand there is a greater local demand for wage labor in these communities. The chi-square results also show a significant relationship between localities and women's fourfold classification ($\chi^2 = 53.496$; df $= 6$; $p = 0.000$).

Regarding the effect of education, as Figure 1 shows, the women with more years of schooling are more prone to consider paid work outside the home as a valuable activity. In terms of the positive assessment of paid work, the percentages range from 14.6 among the uneducated women to 66.7 among those who have completed secondary studies or higher. In other words, the higher the women's educational levels the more likely are they to assess paid work outside the home positively ($\chi^2_{MH} = 20.329$; df $= 1$; $p = 0.000$). This is particularly true among women with nine or more years of schooling.

However, as Table 5 shows, only 9.8 percent of women have studied for nine years or more, and only 2 percent have professional degrees (there are two teachers, two nurses, and two biochemists); 17.8 percent have completed primary school (six years of schooling); 50.0 percent have had one to five years of schooling; and 22.4 percent are illiterate. Women

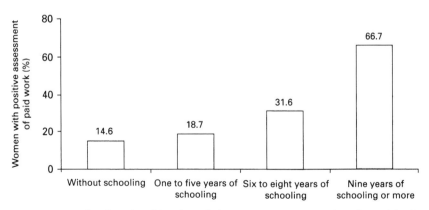

Figure 1 Women's educational levels and their assessment of paid work outside the home ($n = 214$) *Note:* $\chi^2_{MH} = 20.329$; df $= 1$; $p = 0.000$.

withdraw from school for various reasons: a lack of support from their parents (59.5 percent), a dearth of economic resources (35.5 percent), and the remoteness of schools (5 percent).

Table 5 also shows a strong relationship between the level of education, paid employment, and assessment of paid work ($\chi^2_{LR} = 33.974$; df $= 9$; $p = 0.000$). The willingly employed group has the highest proportion of women with nine or more years of schooling, while the willingly home-based group has the lowest proportion of women with this educational level. It is notable that in the unwillingly home-based group, 17.9 percent of the women have nine or more years of schooling, which could explain their positive assessment of paid work, even if they do not perform it. In rural Chiapas, women's schooling and local job opportunities play an important

Table 5 Women's educational levels by their fourfold classification

Women's schooling levels	Willingly employed % (n)	Unwillingly employed % (n)	Unwillingly homebased % (n)	Willingly homebased % (n)
More than nine years of schooling (21) = 9.8%	50.0 (7)	9.5 (2)	17.9 (7)	3.6 (5)
Six to eight years of schooling (38) = 17.8%)	21.4 (3)	14.3 (3)	23.1 (9)	16.4 (23)
One to five years of schooling (107) = 50.0%	21.4 (3)	33.3 (7)	43.6 (17)	57.1 (80)
Without schooling (48) = 22.4%	7.1 (1)	42.9 (9)	15.4 (6)	22.9 (32)
Total (n = 214) = 100.0%	100.0 (14)	100.0 (21)	100.0 (39)	100.0 (140)

Notes: Figures in parentheses give the absolute numbers; $\chi^2_{LR} = 33.974$; df $= 9$, $p = 0.000$.

Table 6 Women's marital status by their fourfold classification

Women's marital status	Willingly employed % (n)	Unwillingly employed % (n)	Unwillingly homebased % (n)	Willingly homebased % (n)
Married or consensual union (n = 185) = 86.5%	78.6 (11)	66.7 (14)	74.4 (29)	93.6 (131)
Unmarried (n = 3) = 1.4%	14.3 (2)	0.0 (0)	2.6 (1)	0.0 (0)
Separated, divorced or widowed (n = 26) = 12.1%	7.1 (1)	33.3 (7)	23.0 (9)	6.4 (9)
Total (n = 214) = 100.0%	100.0 (14)	100.0 (21)	100.0 (39)	100.0 (140)

Notes: Figures in parentheses give the absolute numbers; $\chi^2_{LR} = 26.28$; df $= 6$, $p = 0.000$.

role in their assessment of paid work outside the home. Despite dominant gender norms that center women's life expectations on marriage and maternity, women's formal education (mainly when they have been at school for nine years or more) positively affects their assessment of paid work outside the home, as well as their prospects for employment.

In addition, as seen from Table 6, the category to which women belong is related to their marital status ($\chi^2_{LR}=26.28$; df = 6; $p=0.000$). Among the 140 women in the category of willingly home based nearly 93.6 percent are married, while among the 21 women in the unwillingly employed category only 66.7 percent are married. The percentages for married women in the categories of unwillingly home based and the willingly employed are 74.4 and 78.6 respectively.

As can be seen, the fourfold classification of women shows important links between women's educational levels, employment situations, and marital status. These patterns influence women's contraceptive choices, as well as the possibility that contraception use really leads to an improvement in women's personal well-being.

III. AGENCY, CONTRACEPTIVE CHOICE, AND WOMEN'S WELL-BEING

In the six communities we studied, the rate of contraceptive adoption among women is very high. As Table 7 indicates, some 85 percent out of 214 women have adopted contraception, with the percentage varying from 75.6 to 95.0 across the different locations. The most prevalent method is surgical sterilization, used by 61.7 percent of the women, with the range

Table 7 Women's use of contraceptives by their fourfold classification

	Contraceptive use (%)			
Categories of women	Salpingectomy	Other methods (hormones, IUD, rhythm, withdrawal, condom)	Never users	Total
Willingly employed ($n=14$)	50.0 (7)	28.6 (4)	21.4 (3)	100.0
Unwillingly employed ($n=21$)	66.7 (14)	19.0 (4)	14.3 (3)	100.0
Unwillingly homebased ($n=39$)	59.0 (23)	17.9 (7)	23.1 (9)	100.0
Willingly homebased ($n=140$)	62.9 (88)	25.0 (35)	12.1 (17)	100.0
Total ($n=214$)	61.7 (132)	23.3 (50)	15.0 (32)	100.0

Notes: Figures in parentheses give the absolute numbers; $\chi^2_{LR}=4.12$; df = 6, $p=0.659$.

being 40.0 to 81.2 across the locations. The percentage of women using other contraceptive methods was 23.3 percent ($n = 50$), ranging between 5.8 and 43.3 percent. Approximately seven out of ten women who had undergone salpingectomies had previously used another contraceptive method. These figures confirm our earlier point that rural Chiapas has been subjected to a particularly intensive family planning program.

However, as Table 7 also shows, there are no significant differences in the overall use of contraception or in the type of contraceptive method used among the four categories of women ($\chi^2_{LR} = 4.12$; df = 6; $p = 0.659$). At the same time, despite this commonality, we do find important differences in the number of children borne by women in the four different categories ($\chi^2_{LR} = 16.4$; df = 6; $p = 0.012$) (Table 8). Women in the willingly employed category have significantly fewer children than women in the other categories. Of these, 35.7 percent have only one to two children. In the unwillingly home-based category we again find a notable percentage (20.5) of women with only one or two children. This is probably because some women have higher levels of schooling than others in the sample, and consider paid work outside the home to be a valuable activity, even if they do not perform it.

Our analysis demonstrates that women who positively assess paid work outside the home and actually perform such work (the willingly employed category), generally have fewer children than those who greatly value their roles as mothers and wives (the willingly home-based category). This is true even to women who must work outside their homes without wanting to do so (the unwillingly employed). However, limiting the number of children does not necessarily translate into broader opportunities for paid work outside the home or improved personal well-being for the women. Rather,

Table 8 Number of children by women's fourfold classification

Categories of women	Mean (SE)	Number of children			
		1 to 2 % (n)	3 to 4 % (n)	5 or more % (n)	Total % (n)
Willingly employed ($n = 14$)	3.28 (0.47)	35.7 (5)	42.9 (6)	21.4 (3)	100.0
Unwillingly employed ($n = 21$)	4.81 (0.45)	14.3 (3)	33.3 (7)	52.4 (11)	100.0
Unwillingly homebased ($n = 39$)	3.77 (0.28)	20.5 (8)	51.3 (20)	28.2 (11)	100.0
Willingly homebased ($n = 140$)	5.04 (0.19)	8.6 (12)	37.9 (53)	53.6 (75)	100.0
Total ($n = 214$)	4.67 (0.13)	13.1 (28)	40.2 (86)	46.7 (100)	100.0

Notes: Figures in parentheses give the abolute numbers; $\chi^2_{LR} = 16.4$; df = 6, $p = 0.012$.

women's socio-economic situations and life conditions translate into different life expectations and prospects for paid work, which in turn shape their reproductive options.

Choosing a contraceptive option is central to women's well-being. On the one hand, there can be conflict in the decision-making process between women's personal interests and those of the household, as well as in the distribution of benefits derived from such decisions. As Sen (1990) notes, this distribution can be influenced by gender differences in the evaluation of women's contribution to the household's well-being. On the other hand, we also have to contend with the state's interest in reducing fertility rates, a goal which may be achieved by using coercive methods among the most deprived countries and most populated sectors (Christine Korsgaard 1996; Amartya Sen 1995). Sen (1995) strongly criticizes the use of coercion to reduce fertility rates. He argues that such coercion reflects a lack of social freedom, which is a major loss in itself. Moreover, coercive mechanisms may have an insignificant impact on fertility rates, since the most effective method for reducing fertility is to promote women's access to formal education and employment, thereby increasing their well-being and agency.

The family planning program in Chiapas has succeeded in achieving its goal of lowering fertility rates by either convincing or forcing women and their husbands to accept methods such as salpingectomy. Of the 186 women who have undergone salpingectomy in the total sample, we could classify only 132 in terms of our four categories of women, so in Table 9 we discuss the results only for those 132 women. We found that 64.4 percent participated in the decision. Of these, 41.7 percent said they had made the decision jointly with their husbands and 22.7 percent said they had made it

Table 9 Salpingectomy decisions by women's fourfold classification

Categories of women[a]	Who made the salpingectomy decision? (%)			
	Other people	Women	Women and their husbands	Total
Willingly employed (n=7)	14.3 (1)	28.6 (2)	57.1 (4)	100.0
Unwillingly employed (n=14)	14.3 (2)	28.6 (4)	57.1 (8)	100.0
Unwillingly homebased (n=23)	30.4 (7)	34.8 (8)	34.8 (8)	100.0
Willingly homebased (n=88)	42.0 (37)	18.2 (16)	39.8 (35)	100.0
Total (n=132)	35.6 (47)	22.7 (30)	41.7 (55)	100.0

Notes: (a) Of the 186 surgically sterilized women, 54 could not be classified in any one of the four categories.
Figures in parentheses give the abolute numbers; $\chi^2_{LR}=8.474$; df=6, $p=0.205$.

on their own; 35.6 percent had no say in the decision. We also found that although all the four categories contain some women who were denied autonomy in decision-making, among the employed women (whether willingly or unwillingly employed), the percentage of decisions made by other people was lower than among the home-based women (again whether willingly or unwillingly home based). However, overall, the relationship between the category to which women belonged and who made the decision regarding salpingectomy was not found to be significant ($\chi^2_{LR} = 8.474$; df $= 6$; $p = 0.205$).

Women said they had undergone a salpingectomy for either economic reasons (70.2 percent) or health-related reasons (29.8 percent), and there were no significant differences in these percentages among the four categories of women. Rodolfo Tuirán (1990) argues that women's post-surgery discontent can be attributed not only to the cumbersome bureaucratic procedures followed by health institutions, but also to the attitudes of women's husbands, who either impose or forbid surgery. In a nation-wide study, Juan Guillermo Figueroa (1989) found that 26 percent of the women who had been sterilized did not have any prior information about other contraceptive methods and the irrevocable aspect of the surgery. Forty percent of the women were never asked to sign a consent form permitting the procedure, and those who were asked did not read it. Most of the women of rural Chiapas whom we studied were similarly unaware of the exact nature of the procedure.

The 47 women (35.6 percent of the cases) who were not involved in the decision believed that their husbands and/or the medical personnel had ignored their feelings: "In the clinic, we were forced. The female doctor told me to have the operation because I already had too many children. He [her husband] consented, but I did not want to" (Lilia, 36 years old, six children born alive, six surviving). "I did not want to, but when my husband was told that he had just had a baby-boy, he gave his consent ..." (Margarita, 38 years old, three children born alive, three surviving). "My husband had already signed. I did not want to. Forty days after the birth of my son, he left me for another woman" (Guillermina, 35 years old, three children born alive, two surviving). "My husband forced me because of the [economic] situation. Sometimes we are doing well and sometimes we are not doing so well" (Antonia, 41 years old, eight children born alive, six surviving). "He made the decision because he comes from a family of fourteen or sixteen children and has worked a lot to support them. He did not want the same to happen to him again" (Martha, 35 years old, three children born alive, three surviving).

Seventy-nine percent of these 47 women were in the willingly home-based category, and 14.9 percent in the unwillingly home-based category. There were hardly any between the two categories of employed women. Not surprisingly, of these 47 women who did not participate in the contraceptive decision (and who gave classified answers), 68.1 percent felt frustrated because they could not fulfill their desire to have more children after sterilization. This was in contrast to 35.3 percent of the 85 women who did participate in the decision. In fact, 80.6 percent of all women who expressed their desire to have more children after the operation saw children as an important source of affection: "Children are very cute. We are sorry [for having had the salpingectomy] because our children are leaving us and we are left here alone" (Esperanza, 35 years old, five children born, four living). "My children are going to leave me soon, so if I had one who was 7 or 8 years old, he [or she] would stay with me a little longer" (Debustina, 49 years old, four children born, four living).

Eighty-seven percent of women in the willingly employed and unwillingly employed categories decided on their own to have a surgical sterilization. However, the impact on women's sense of well-being was different for each group. The willingly employed did feel that the operation has given them the opportunity to undertake new activities, and reduced their risks and concerns about unwanted pregnancies. Similarly, by deciding to have a salpingectomy, women in the unwillingly employed category demonstrated their agency, thanks to the family planning programs in their communities.

However, most of these women decided to undergo surgical sterilization in order to stem a further deterioration in their economic situations. Thus the operation was not a means for improving their personal well-being, as claimed by the family planning program, because women have few alternatives for following a different life trajectory: "I made the decision because the money is not enough ... and then men drink and that makes it even more difficult" (Eustalina, 46 years old, four children born alive, four surviving). "I decided it because my husband was an alcoholic. He hardly got involved" (Alma Delia 35 years old, four children born alive, three surviving). "Five children are a sufficient source of suffering, since their father is not with us. Sometimes there is poverty and ... without a husband ..." (María del Socorro, 40 years old, five children born alive, five surviving).

Did the operation bring women any additional benefits in terms of reducing their work burden and increasing their opportunities for undertaking new activities outside the home? Did it enable them to have a more enjoyable sex life, as the family planning discourse promised? Only 7 percent of the 186 women who had been sterilized, most of whom belonged to the willingly employed group, said that surgical sterilization had reduced their domestic chores, given them more freedom to carry out activities outside the home, and/or had enhanced their sex lives: "[I feel] well. Because I am not worried about having any more babies, I can go on with the older ones" (Carolina, 32 years old, five children born, four living); "[I feel] happy and safe about not having to get pregnant" (Amanda, 43 years old, five children born, five living); "I can take care of my children ... I have time to go to church (Mercedes, 41 years old, ten children born, seven living).

These comments indicate increased personal well-being from women's viewpoint, but the numbers of such women were very small.

IV. CONCLUSIONS

Amartya Sen's work provides a number of concepts for understanding the complexity of factors underlying contraceptive choice and its implications on women's personal well-being. His nonutilitarian approach to well-being points to the intrinsic value women place on personal well-being and on the underlying freedoms that support the notion that women as human beings should be able to make their own choices for promoting their personal well-being. This becomes a compelling guideline for reorienting programs that claim to increase the well-being of the population in general, and of women in particular.

In our chapter, we applied Sen's concept of well-being to the family planning program operating in rural Mexico. We did not evaluate the program's achievements in terms of contraceptive acceptance or the decrease in fertility. Rather, we assessed the actual possibilities that women had of making choices and gaining access to valuable functionings.

We find Sen's distinction between agency and well-being essential in evaluating women's well-being, since it enables us to compare the options offered by various policies and programs, with achieved functionings, in different cultural contexts. From a gender perspective, these elements allow us to evaluate women's well-being in both its subjective and objective forms. These elements are both individual (mediated by gender identity) and socio-economic (such as educational background, marital status, and employment opportunities).

Our results show that although family planning programs in the *mestizo* rural settlements of Chiapas have led to extensive use of contraception and a significant reduction in fertility, the assumption that this would necessarily improve the well-being of all women is incorrect. The availability of the family planning program is a positive option for some women, especially those in the willingly employed and unwillingly employed categories, who recorded the highest percentages of participation in contraceptive decisions, and the smallest (albeit still high) percentages of cases in which the decisions were made by other people. In both instances, surgical sterilization was an agency achievement. However, personal well-being varied greatly between women of different socio-economic backgrounds. While for some the operation led to a reduction of domestic chores, satisfactory paid work, and greater sexual enjoyment, for others it was a survival strategy to prevent a further deterioration in their quality of life. Overall, the program's benefits were reaped only by a small number of women, since several factors intervened in women's contraception decisions.

The largest percentage of contraceptive decisions made by other people occurred among women in the willingly home-based category, namely women who accept and perform traditional gender roles. This category of women constitutes the largest percentage of women in these six communities (65.4), and is the main target of family planning programs, since 93.6 percent among them have partners, and 53.6 percent have five or more children. Yet it is in this group of women that the impact of surgical sterilization is assessed to be the most negative, since the decision was often imposed by their husbands and/or by health personnel and because of the loneliness these women feel in the absence of young children living with them.

Our analysis demonstrates that there is no straightforward positive relationship between the adoption of contraceptive methods promoted by state family planning programs, and an increase in women's well-being as defined by Sen. Several factors intervene in women's contraceptive choices, such as their educational levels, their assessment of paid work and their actual chances of getting such work. The combination of these factors enhances the possibility of contraceptive use increasing women's well-being. In this sense, an examination of the life options that rural communities offer to women is a key element in understanding women's well-being. Our analysis shows that local opportunities for education and paid work outside the home translate into stronger possibilities of women achieving well-being. Women with higher educational levels are likely to assess paid work outside their homes in a positive way. And this positive assessment plus their actually having such work are likely to increase their power to decide whether or not to use contraception, which method to use, and the number of children to have.

This chapter also shows the importance of promoting women's reproductive rights in public health institutions. In rural Chiapas, a fair number of women do not participate in the decisions that directly concern their bodies and health. Therefore, in agreement with Sen, we can say that regardless of what is locally considered a "good life," for facilitating women's agency achievements and for enhancing their positive freedoms, the state should offer the means to achieve these goals (such as education, health, land, well-paid jobs, and so on). Without such efforts, even with a major decline in fertility, it will be difficult to claim that the quality of women's lives has really improved.

ACKNOWLEDGMENTS

We thank Dr. Benito Salvatierra Izaba for his intellectual and technical support in the statistical analysis of the data presented in this chapter. We also greatly appreciate the suggestions made by the three anonymous reviewers and the editors of this book. We are particularly grateful to Bina Agarwal for her detailed comments on successive drafts that added considerable analytical strength to the chapter, and her extensive editorial input to ensure clarity and flow. We also thank Jane Humphries for her useful suggestions on aspects of the statistical analysis. Finally, we appreciate the opportunity to interact with Amartya Sen and other participants of the Oxford workshop.

NOTES

[1] See also The Beijing Declaration and the Platform for Action on Women and Health (1995).

[2] See, Claudia García-Moreno and Amparo Claro (1994); Gita Sen (1994); and Naila Kabeer (1998).

[3] Article 4 of the Mexican Constitution reads: "Men and women are equal vis-à-vis the law. ... Everybody is entitled to decide freely, responsibly and in an informed manner on the number and spacing of their children" (*Constitución Política de los Estados Unidos Mexicanos* 1995). By law, all women who are 18 years old and older must have access to contraceptive methods, regardless of their marital status. The National Human Rights Commission establishes that the contraceptive decision depends on women and that "women's lack of power to convince their partners" must be taken into account when analyzing the exercise of reproductive rights in Mexico (Laura Salinas 2001: 230, our translation).

[4] The word *mestizo* originally referred to those with mixed Indian and Spanish blood. Today *mestizos* are characterized as people who do not speak any native language and do not identify themselves as Indians. The family planning program in Chiapas makes no distinction between Indian and non-Indian populations.

[5] We designed a stratified sample. Each stratum consists of two communities with similar production systems and sexual division of labor, totaling three strata (see Table 1). For estimating the sample size the following parameters were taken into account: a 95 percent ($z=1.96$) level of confidence; a 10 percent ($d=0.1$) sampling error; and an unknown prevalence or variance ($p=0.5$). The estimators were replaced in the following formula: (William Cochran 1985: 106–7). The result was $n=96$ for each strata, giving a total *minimal* sample size of 288. In each community, data were collected from women in the 30–49 age group. In total, 300 women were interviewed.

6 After the Mexican revolution of 1910, large private holdings were expropriated and *ejidos* were created. An *ejido* is a group of individual parcels of land which are collectively managed. *Ejido* land was expected to be used for subsistence purpose. Until 1991 this land could not be sold because it was granted by the State. With the Agrarian Counter Reform, *ejido* land can now be sold and used for private investment.

7 The evaluation of women's attitudes to socially prescribed gender roles, and to paid work outside the home, is based on answers classified only into two: "positive" and "negative" (Batista-Foguet, Blanch, and Artés 1994). In this study, answers which could not clearly be classified as positive or negative were excluded from the analysis. However, as detailed in the note to Table 3, this does not lead to a bias in the sample.

8 Women in the self-employed category had the same negative assessment of paid employment outside the home ($n=71$; 71.8 percent) as did women dedicated exclusively to their homes ($n=128$; 69.5 percent) ($\chi^2=2.81$; df = 1; $p=0.094$).

REFERENCES

Annas, Julia. 1996. "Las Mujeres y la Calidad de Vida: ¿Dos Normas o Una?," in Martha C. Nussbaum and Amartya Sen (eds.) *La Calidad de Vida*, pp. 363–85 Trans. Roberto Reyes Mazzoni. México: Fondo de Cultura Económica, (Original title: *The Quality of Life*. Oxford: Clarendon Press, 1993.)

Ashford, Lori. 1995. "Nuevas Perspectivas sobre población: lecciones aprendidas en El Cairo." *Boletín de Población*. Washington, DC: Population Reference Bureau (50), (Original title: "New Perspectives on Population: Lessons from Cairo." *Population Bulletin* 50(1): 2–46, 1995.)

Batista-Foguet, Joan Manuel, Joseph María Blanch, and Maité Artés. 1994. "Actitudes y Calidad de Vida: La medida de la calidad de vida percibida por la mujer," in Mariano Alvaro Page (ed.) *Propuesta de un sistema de indicadores sociales de igualdad entre los géneros*, pp. 335–52. Madrid: Ministerio de Asuntos Sociales, Instituto de la Mujer.

Cervera, Flores Miguel. 1994. "La fecundidad en 1993. Descenso de más de 50% en 20 años." *Carta demográfica sobre México*: 7–8.

Cochran, William G. 1985. Técnicas de muestreo. Trans. Andres Sestier Bouclier. México: Compañía Editorial Continental, SA de CV, (Original title: Sampling Techniques. Boston, MA: Trans-Editions, Inc./John Wiley & Sons, Inc., 1977.)

Consejo Nacional de Población 1993. *Indicadores Socioeconómicos e Indices de Marginación Municipal 1990*. México.

———. 1998. *La situación demográfica de México*. México.

———. 2000. *Cuadernos de Salud Reproductiva. Chiapas*. México.

Constitución Política de los Estados Unidos Mexicanos. Ley sobre el Escudo, la Bandera y el Himno Nacional (actualizadas). 1995. México: Ediciones y Sistemas Especiales, SA de CV.

Figueroa, Juan Guillermo. 1989. "Características de la aceptación de métodos quirúrgicos," in Dirección General de Planificación Familiar (ed.), *Encuesta Nacional Sobre Fecundidad y Salud, 1987: memoria de la reunión celebrada el 30 de septiembre de 1988*, pp. 151–92. México: Dirección General de Planificación Familiar, Secretaría de Salud.

García-Moreno, Claudia and Amparo Claro. 1994. "Challenges from the Women's Health Movement: Women's Rights versus Population Control," in Gita Sen, Adrianne Germain, and Lincoln C. Chen (eds.) *Population Policies Reconsidered: Health, Empowerment, and Rights*, pp. 47–72. Harvard School of Public Health, and Cambridge, MA: Harvard University Press.

Kabeer, Naila. 1998. Realidades Trastocadas. Trans. Isabel Vericat. México: Paidós/ PUEG-UNAM, (Original title: *Reversed Realities: Gender Hierarchies in Development Thought*. London: Verso, 1994.)

Korsgaard, Christine M. 1996. Comentario a "Igualdad de qué?" y a "Capacidad y Bienestar," in Martha C. Nussbaum and Amartya Sen (eds.) *La Calidad de Vida*, pp. 363–85 Trans. Roberto Reyes Mazzoni. México: Fondo de Cultura Económica, (Original title: *The Quality of Life*. Oxford: Clarendon Press, 1993.)

Martínez, Fernández Carmen and María José Montero Corominas. 1997. *¿Qué ha supuesto la Conferencia de Beijing para las Mujeres? Aproximación de los acuerdos adoptados en la IV Conferencia Mundial de Naciones Unidas sobre las Mujeres. Beijing (China), 4–15 de septiembre de 1995*. Madrid: Gabinete de Relaciones Internacionales, Instituto de la Mujer.

Nussbaum, Martha C. and Amartya Sen. 1996. "Introduction," in Martha C. Nussbaum and Amartya Sen (eds.) *La Calidad de Vida*, pp. 15–23 Trans. Roberto Reyes Mazzoni. México: Fondo de Cultura Económica, (Original title: *The Quality of Life*. Oxford: Clarendon Press, 1993.)

Palma, Cabrera Yolanda and Jesús Suárez Morales. 1994. "Diferencias regionales en la práctica anticonceptiva." *Carta demográfica sobre México*: 39–40.

Salinas, Berinstáin Laura. 2001. "La salud reproductiva como problema de derechos humanos," in Juan Guillermo Figueroa and Claudio Stern (eds.) *Encuentros y desencuentros en la salud reproductiva. Políticas publicas, marcos normativos y actores sociales*, pp. 223–32. México: El Colegio de México.

Salvatierra, Izaba Benito. 2000. "Población y Desarrollo Rural. El Caso del Soconusco, Chiapas," *Tesis de Doctorado*. México: Colegio de Postgraduados.

Scott, Joan W. 1996. "El Género: una categoría útil para el análisis histórico," in Marta Lamas (ed.) *El Género: la construcción cultural de la diferencia sexual*, pp. 265–302 Trans. Eugenio and Marta Portela. México: Programa Universitario de Estudios de Género, Universidad Nacional Autónoma de México.

Secretaría de Hacienda y Crédito Público 1995. *Plan Nacional de Desarrollo 1995–2000*. México.

Secretaría de Salud, Servicios Estatales de Salud en Chiapas 1996. *Programa Estatal de Salud Reproductiva 1996*. México.

Selvin, Steve. 1996. Statistical Analysis of Epidemiologic Data, 2nd edn. Oxford: Clarendon Press.

Sen, Amartya. 1985. "Well-Being, Agency and Freedom. The Dewey Lectures 1984." *Journal of Philosophy* 82(4): 169–221.

——. 1988. "Freedom of Choice. Concept and Content." *European Economic Review* 32: 269–94.

——. 1990. "Cooperation, Inequality, and the Family," in Geoffrey McNicoll and Cain Mead (eds.) *Rural Development and Population: Institutions and Policy*, pp. 61–76. New York: The Population Council and Oxford University Press.

——. 1995. "Population Policy: Authoritarianism versus Cooperation," *International Lecture Series on Population Issues*. New Delhi, India: The John D. and Catherine T. MacArthur Foundation.

——. 1996. "Capacidad y Bienestar," in Martha C. Nussbaum and Amartya Sen (eds.) *La Calidad de Vida*, pp. 54–83 Trans. Roberto Reyes Mazzoni. México: Fondo de Cultura Económica, (Original title: *The Quality of Life*. Oxford: Clarendon Press, 1993.)

——. 2000. *Desarrollo y Libertad*. Trans. Esther Rabasco and Luis Toharia. México: Planeta, (Original title: *Development as Freedom*. Alfred A. Knopf, Inc./Random House, Inc., 1999.)

Sen, Gita. 1994. "Development, Population, and the Environment: A Search for Balance," in Gita Sen, Adrianne Germain, and Lincoln C. Chen (eds.) *Population Policies Reconsidered. Health, Empowerment, and Rights*, pp. 63–73. Harvard School of Public Health, and Cambridge, MA: Harvard University Press.

"The Beijing Declaration and the Platform for Action on Women and Health." 1995. *Population and Development Review.* 21(4): 907–13.

Tuirán, Gutiérrez Rodolfo. 1990. "Esterilización anticonceptiva en México: satisfacción e insatisfacción entre las mujeres que optaron por este método," *ponencia presentada en la IV Reunión Nacional sobre la Investigación Demográfica en México.* México: Sociedad Mexicana de Demografía.

Zar, Jerrold H. 1984. *Biostatistical Analysis.* 2nd edn. England Cliffs, NJ: Prentice-Hall.

SEN, ETHICS, AND DEMOCRACY

Elizabeth Anderson

OVERVIEW

Amartya Sen's ethical theorizing helps feminists resolve the tensions between the claims of women's particular perspectives and moral objectivity. His concept of "positional objectivity" highlights the epistemological significance of value judgments made from particular social positions, while holding that certain values may become widely shared. He shows how acknowledging positionality is consistent with affirming the universal value of democracy. This chapter builds on Sen's work by proposing an analysis of democracy as a set of institutions that aims to intelligently utilize positional information for shared ends. This epistemological analysis of democracy offers a way to understand the rationale for reserving political offices for women. From a political point of view, gendered positions are better thought of as an epistemological resource than as a ground of identity politics – that is, of parochial identification and solidarity.

INTRODUCTION

People evaluate things from multiple points of view. Sometimes they evaluate something from their individual point of view, considering how it bears on their personal interests, projects, or welfare. At other times, they evaluate it from various wider points of view – for example, they consider how it bears on the interests, projects, or welfare of their family, firm, ethnic group, country, or humanity as a whole. Following through on the spatial metaphor embodied in talk of "points of view," let us say that an evaluative perspective is "local" or "parochial" if it is taken up by one or a few people, "more global" if it is shared by larger groups, and "global" (without qualification) or "universal" if it is or could be shared by everyone. One of the tasks of moral philosophy is to theorize the relations among these evaluative perspectives.

There are two broad types of strategy for coming to terms with the multiplicity of evaluative differences due to variations in perspective. One strategy, adopted most commonly by nonfeminist philosophers, regards local evaluative perspectives as sources of bias, error, or intolerable conflict. It strives to *reduce* evaluative perspectives to a small number – typically only to the individual (self-interested) and moral (universal) points of view (Thomas Nagel 1978; Richard Brandt 1979; Henry Sidgwick 1981). It then tries to *subsume* one under the other, either by deriving the moral point of view from the self-interested bargaining of individuals (David Gauthier 1986), or by arguing that the moral point of view has authority over the individual point of view (Immanuel Kant 1981). The moral point of view is often achieved by *abstracting* from individual differences – for example, deriving it from people's choices behind a "veil of ignorance" in which individuals don't know their differences from others (John Rawls 1971).

The second strategy, adopted more commonly by feminist philosophers, regards the plurality of evaluative perspectives in a more epistemological vein. It sees such variations not simply as sources of error and bias to be eliminated or transcended through abstraction, but as *information resources* for *constructing* more global points of view through their critical interaction (Sandra Harding 1993; Helen Longino 1993). It focuses on the *irreducibly* numerous, intersecting ways people's social positions – of wider scope than the individual, but narrower than all of humanity (as of gender, race, ethnicity, class, and so forth) – affect their points of view.[1] Instead of seeking one point of view that has authority over all the rest, it views the authority of different points of view in pragmatic terms. The solutions to different problems require different evaluative information, which is accessible only from certain perspectives. To solve some problems, we must think "locally." To solve others, we must construct more global perspectives from which different sorts of evaluative information are accessible. The more global perspectives represent contingent achievements for particular purposes.

The pragmatic – epistemological strategy for dealing with the multiplicity of evaluative perspectives generates several questions. (1) Is there any sense in which local evaluative positions can claim to be objective? (2) What reasons do we have for constructing more global perspectives? (3) What are the information requirements for solving the problems that we see from a more global perspective? (4) How do institutions differ with respect to their ability to marshal the perspectival information needed to solve our problems? (5) How can institutions dedicated to solving more global problems take advantage of the information resources of local points of view?

Amartya Sen's ethical thought helps us answer these questions. He shows us how to apply the concept of objectivity to value judgments made from local positions. At the same time, he recognizes that we often seek more global points of view to work out solutions to problems we share. His ethical thought helps us analyze the information requirements for solving such problems, and the epistemic capacities of institutions we might use to solve them. These concerns underlie Sen's capability approach to measuring development, and his discussion of the relative merits of authoritarian states, democratic states, and markets for dealing with the problem of famine. Democracy plays a central role in Sen's ethics. His arguments for the universal value of democracy fit into a conception of democracy as a way of constructing a more global point of view out of more local points of view. I shall show how his work on the epistemological value of social identities helps us understand the point of policies for increasing the participation of women in representative assemblies, in ways complimentary to feminist approaches, and thereby helps advance feminist ethics.

I. POSITIONAL (LOCAL) AND TRANS-POSITIONAL (GLOBAL) OBJECTIVITY

Let us begin our exploration of evaluative perspectives with a consideration of the vexed question of whether any such perspectives can be "objective." "Objectivity" is usually linked to universality: a judgment is said to be objective if and only if *everyone* would accept that judgment, regardless of their location, if they reasoned consistently from the available evidence and arguments. The core idea is that of interpersonal invariance of judgment. Amartya Sen (1993b: 126) has argued that the concept of objectivity as interpersonal invariance can be extended by relativizing it to a position. A judgment about an object is *positionally objective* if anyone *in that position* would accept the same judgment. Observation statements provide the clearest illustration of a positionally objective judgment. "The Sun and Moon appear to be of the same size," is interpersonally invariant for observers standing on Earth, but not for observers in most other positions in space. Many parameters besides spatial location can affect a person's judgment of an object, including the person's background beliefs and attitudes, cognitive limitations, personal relations to the object, and so forth. One could say of any judgment that it is positionally objective if anyone standing in the same position (affected by the same parameters) would make the same judgment. This would not make the judgment true, but at best warranted relative to the perhaps limited or defective parameters defining that position.

The concept of positional objectivity is particularly useful as applied to value judgments, because value judgments are essentially "perspectival" in ways that other judgments are not. Call a judgment "perspectival" if it essentially asserts a relation to someone's point of view, as constituted by her mental states of perceiving, feeling, and willing. The contents of some judgments, such as "2 + 2 = 4," or "electrons have negative charge" are *not* perspectival, for they do not essentially involve any mental states. By contrast, value judgments essentially lay a normative claim on people's mental states, directing them to feel, desire, or deliberate in certain ways with respect to the valued object. Value claims, then, are perspectival in that they essentially assert a relation between the valued object and an agent's will or emotion.

Because different people often stand in different positions relative to the same objects, it often makes sense for them to value these objects in different ways. It makes sense for the Brazilian football team and its fans to wish for and be elated at Brazil's victory over the German team, even while the same event reasonably disappoints the German team and its fans. "Brazil's victory over Germany is a disappointment" is a positionally objective judgment for anyone affiliated with the German team, but not for those affiliated with the Brazilian team. Many emotions and attitudes, such as loyalty, pride, love, and enmity, are characteristically local in this way: their warranting conditions are relative to social positions that cannot be occupied by everyone, since the positions are defined against contrasting social locations (member vs. nonmember, partner vs. rival, friend vs. stranger or enemy, and so forth).

Such cases of positionally objective but interpersonally varying valuations are not troubling, because there is good reason for people to occupy the different positions from which it makes sense for them to value the same things in different ways. Some positions, however, ought not to be occupied at all (except perhaps notionally, as an exercise in understanding). Given the racist beliefs of the Nazis, contempt for Jews made sense. But the cognitive position of the Nazis was not one that could bear critical scrutiny, shaped as it was by lies, distortions, and pseudo-science. That their position could not bear critical scrutiny is a universally objective judgment, one that even the Nazis would have had to accept had they viewed the evidence and arguments impartially.[2]

Appreciating the perspectival character of value does not presuppose that each agent's position is singular or fixed. An individual often stands in multiple relations to the same object, and so may have mixed feelings about it. As a patriotic citizen, a woman may support her nation's war effort, including the draft that takes her son, even though as a loving mother, she dreads her son's being drafted. People often have reason to change their position. Some such reasons are cognitive, as when people discover that their valuation is warranted only relative to a factually erroneous position. Others are motivational. Let us focus on motives people may have for seeking a shared, trans-positional, more global evaluative position. I would like to distinguish four such motives: ascriptive identification, sympathy, practical identification, and respect.

Ascriptive identification with others, seeing them as extensions of oneself – as tied by relations of birth, such as of kinship, ethnicity, race, and caste, or related in some other socially ascribed way, as sharing a common language, culture, or religion – can be a powerful source of shared positioning. Identification on the basis of such ascriptive identities may motivate loyalty, solidarity, and attachments to the in-group members which take the form of feeling group members' joy, pain, pride, and indignation as one's own.

Sympathy is a motive for taking up the perspective of others that is distinct from and of wider scope than identification (Amartya Sen 2000b). It can lead people to evaluate the world through the eyes of others whom we do not identify as extensions of ourselves. Martha Nussbaum (1999: 29) describes the predicament of Metha Bai, a young Indian widow who hates the caste system because, in forbidding her from working outside the home, it threatens her and her children's survival. Sympathy for Metha Bai can lead Nussbaum's comfortably situated academic readers to share Bai's hatred of the caste system, although we do not imagine that her pain is our own, or that we share a common socially ascribed position that makes us vulnerable to the same threats. As Max Scheler (1954: 14) has stressed, the truly sympathetic person is vividly aware that the pain that arouses her concern is *someone else's pain*, not a pain felt by the sympathizer herself, and that the concern so aroused is *for another person*, not for an extended "me" or for "us." Sympathy is distinct from the egoism of an extended self.

Practical identification occurs when people see themselves as members of the same collective agency – as participants in a common cooperative enterprise such as a firm or interest group, in a shared practice such as a hobby, sport, or artistic endeavor, or as committed to living and hence reasoning together about what to do, as in a democracy. Practical identification need not rely on prior ascriptive identification. People of many different ascriptive identities of race, gender, ethnicity, religion, and the like may join forces in common projects. Indeed, perhaps the defining feature of globalization is its transcendence of ascriptive identities, especially national and ethnic identities, as a ground of cooperation. While global markets are a major social context for forging trans-ascriptive practical identities, science, art, athletics, and nongovernmental organiza-tions also play major roles. The key point is that to engage in effective cooperation (as opposed to coerced coordination, as in a slave labor system), people must construct a shared point of view from which reasons are assessed.

Respect involves recognizing and valuing others by acting only for reasons that they can reasonably accept as a permissible basis for anyone similarly situated to act. It is to commit oneself to act only on principles that can be reasonably shared by those one respects. In Kantian and neo-Kantian versions of respect, this attitude is owed to all rational agents (Immanuel Kant 1981). Respect differs from sympathy. When one acts out of sympathy for another, the aim of one's action is the other's good. When one acts out of respect, the other's good places a constraint on what one may do in pursuit of one's own aims, but one's own ultimate aims need not be devoted to the other's good.

While not exhaustive, these four motives cover most of the grounds people have for *sharing* reasons and evaluations, for coming to occupy a common position from which to evaluate actions or the world, and thereby for expanding the scope of interpersonal invariance – the degree of objectivity – of a value judgment. They differ, however, in their potential for forming the basis of a fully universal or global evaluative position comprehending all of humanity. Ascriptive identification has no such potential. Ascriptive identities are necessarily parochial, since they are defined through contrast with outgroups. By contrast, it is not unreasonable to hope for and even demand universal respect and sympathy for others. Certain cooperative organizations, such as international human rights movements, which are bound by practical identification motivated by respect and sympathy for humans generally, may be effective vehicles for cultivating and institutionalizing respect and sympathy on a global scale.

Yet even universal value judgments do not escape the perspectival character of value judgments. In the realm of values, there is no "view from nowhere." Universal value judgments reflect instead the "view from everywhere" – a position capacious enough that all can reasonably occupy it, and perhaps can reasonably be expected to occupy. Without denying this, I shall henceforth reserve the unqualified term "positional" for local or parochial perspectives.

II. INFORMATION ANALYSIS OF EVALUATIVE PERSPECTIVES: CAPABILITY ASSESSMENTS

The expansion of motives of sympathy and respect to include people across the world has given many people a shared interest in promoting development worldwide. To the extent that we share this interest, the destitution, suffering, and oppression of individuals in far-flung parts of the globe is a problem not simply for those individuals but for us. It is something we must take responsibility for through our collective efforts, as channeled through various organizations that aim to advance development. To coordinate our efforts toward this common aim requires that we adopt a more global perspective from which to evaluate development. Which perspective should we choose?

Every evaluative perspective is sensitive to certain kinds of information about what it evaluates, and insensitive to others. For example, measures of development in terms of income alone are sensitive to people's access to marketed goods, but insensitive to other goods, such as freedom of association and the right to vote in democratic elections, that are not commodities. The choice of what perspective we should choose, then, is partly justified by consideration of what information we ought to be sensitive to. This epistemic judgment is, in turn, grounded in the constitutive aim of our cooperative efforts – in this case, of development. The precise specification of this aim depends on the background motives of sympathy and respect that prompt us to adopt it in the first place. That is, we need assessments of development that are sensitive to the normative demands of sympathy and respect for all.

This pragmatic – epistemological approach to evaluation underwrites Sen's so-called "capability" perspective on human development (Amartya Sen 1985, 1993a), which constitutes his most important and distinctive contribution to the foundations of welfare economics. Sen defines "capabilities" as freedoms to achieve valuable "functionings." "Functionings" are states of the person that constitute or advance her well-being or agency, such as health, adequate nourishment, literacy, and participation in community life. He champions capabilities as superior to other standards of development, such as subjective utility and income, partly on the ground that the "information bases" of the latter exclude important dimensions of development that are captured by capabilities (Amartya Sen 1999b: 56 – 76). For example, as noted above, income measures fail to consider the role of non-commodity values, such as rights, liberties, and social recognition, in people's well-being. They are also correlated to a surprisingly poor degree with other important goods, such as longevity (Sen 1999b: 21 – 3).

Subjective utilities, the standard measure of welfare in economic theory, suffer from additional information defects. Contemporary economists measure utility in terms of individual preference satisfaction. Utility measures are deeply positional, immediately tied to the individual agent's parochial and idiosyncratic view of the world. They are so positional that they do not permit interpersonal utility comparisons. This makes them ill-suited to inform practical projects grounded in sympathy for others, because sympathy directs our helping efforts to more urgent cases – those more disadvantaged, or more in need, within a given domain of concern. To identify those cases, we need welfare assessments that support interpersonal comparisons.

Utility measures also fail to deal effectively with the ways people adapt their preferences to circumstances of deprivation and oppression. If individuals, due to poverty or lack of freedom, have no hope of achieving some valuable functioning, or would be punished if they tried to achieve it, they may give up the desire to achieve that functioning so as to avoid frustration and suffering. Or they may never form such a desire if they are deprived of knowledge of that functioning or how to achieve it. From the perspective of utility, where there is no desire, there is no unsatisfied desire. So utility measures fail to register deprivations as such, to the extent that the poor and downcast have adapted to them.

In fact, all welfare measures that rely on the subjective valuing of individuals fall prey to the problem of adaptation to deprivation. Sen illustrates this point with the case of subjective reports of health. Men are far more likely than women to complain of poor health in India, even though women have higher rates of morbidity (Sen 1993b: 135). This is partly due to the fact that Indian women have lower rates of literacy and overall education than men. They therefore have lower access to the information needed to enable them to recognize their bodily states as *symptoms* – that is, as signs of poor health potentially correctable by medical treatment. It may also be partly due to the fact that many women accept gender inequality as a "normal" or inevitable condition of life, so do not expect or demand more than they have. They have adjusted both their feelings and their preferences to their lower expectations.

Recognition of these causes of a positional assessment give us, *and the women themselves*, reason to seek a position beyond their immediate local one from which to assess their well-being. The first cause shows how their position is conditioned by medical ignorance. This gives everyone a reason to seek a better informed perspective. The second cause shows how their position is caused by an ignorance of possibilities of gender equality, which again gives them, and us, a reason to seek a more informed perspective.

These reflections give us reason not only to move beyond the positional health assessments of individuals themselves, which are relative to their varying levels of knowledge and adaptation to deprivation, but to construct a trans-positionally invariant or global point of view from which to assess people's health. For the background interest that motivates the quest for interpersonal health comparisons is a shared project in advancing human well-being, motivated by sympathy for others. Because this is a collective project, it requires a shared standard of assessment to be advanced. To the extent that it is a fully global project, it requires a universal standard. Sen's capability approach, in taking objectively assessed health status as a valuable functioning for everyone, meets this requirement of universality.

This account limits the authority of the capability perspective to particular shared purposes and motivations. It does not deny that, for other purposes, subjective utilities can be very important. To the extent that individuals are acting simply on their own account and within the constraints of morality, they have good reason to act on their local valuations (at least when these are not based on factual errors or ignorance). Moreover, respect for others gives us reason to ensure that individuals have the freedom to act on their local valuations.

III. INFORMATIONAL ANALYSIS OF INSTITUTIONS: THE CASE OF FAMINE

The same informational analysis that helps us choose the appropriate evaluative perspective from which to guide our actions for different purposes can also be used to help us choose the best institutions through which to pursue our purposes. As we have seen, practical problems can be partially specified in terms of the information needed to identify, evaluate, and solve them. Because they are identified pragmatically, in terms of what needs or ought to be done, their information basis involves value judgments. We can therefore ask how positional or local are the value judgments that form the information basis of the solutions to the problems at issue, and how effectively different institutions are able to utilize information from those positions. The answer to this question will go far in determining which institutions ought to be charged with the task of solving the problem in question, and how they ought to be designed to utilize the necessary information.

Sen takes this epistemic approach to evaluating institutions in his famous comparisons of the performance of markets, authoritarian states, and democratic states with respect to the problem of preventing famines. In his classic study of famine, Sen (1981) argued that aggregate declines in food availability are not the fundamental cause of famine. Rather, famine is caused by a severe decline in the *entitlements* of a subset of the population in a region – that is, a decline in their command over income or other legal means by which they can acquire food. His analysis points to a defect in the information basis of markets, relative to the problem of famine. The force of preference information ("demand") in a market setting is conveyed by the money backing it up. Thus, the needs and wants of the poor register faintly in markets. Because famines are caused by a shortfall in entitlements, those suffering the shortfall lack the means to signal their needs in an open food market. Free markets, all by themselves, lack sensitivity to the information needed to prevent famine, and so cannot be counted on to do so.

Sen also faults the performance of authoritarian states with respect to famine prevention on epistemic grounds. He cites the contrasting experiences of democratic India and communist China in preventing famine. India's last famine took place in 1944, when India was still under British imperial rule. The institution of democracy ended famine there, despite the persistence of great poverty and periodic shocks leaving segments of the population without the means to buy food. It did so because public pressure facilitated by the publicity offered by a free press induced the state to adopt policies enabling the dispossessed to make up the shortfall in food entitlements (Sen 1999b: 180–1). By contrast, China suffered a devastating famine in 1959–60, despite Mao's desire to achieve food security for Chinese peasants. Communist party officials assigned to agriculture faced overwhelming incentives to exaggerate performance to their superiors. Neither the press nor the public were free to report on starvation in remote districts. So the Chinese state, lacking free speech and transparency to the public, didn't even know what it was doing. Without the feedback needed to determine whether its policies were working, it pressed on dogmatically with its agricultural plans, with disastrous results (Sen 1999b: 181–2).

The key difference between democratic India and communist China was not in their ends. Both wanted to ensure food security for their populations. It lay in their ability to learn from their mistakes, to adjust policies in light of information about how they were doing. A regime based on hierarchy, secrecy, unquestioning obedience, and punishment for bearers of bad news has an institutional structure that embodies dogmatism and self-ignorance. A democratic regime based on participation, transparency, freedom of speech, and accountability has an institutional structure that enables learning and adjustment of action in light of this information.

Sen admits that his instrumental argument does not show that existing democracies are fully responsive to policy failures (Sen 1999b: 154–6). While they have prevented famine, many have done far less well in preventing malnourishment, poverty, and other chronic capability deprivations. Here too, an informational analysis of the difficulties democracies face in responding to these problems is illuminating. Sen observes that the causes and consequences of these problems are harder to understand and more difficult to politicize. Adaptive preferences and feelings also play a significant role in this failure. Dramatic change for the worse arouses public complaint and demands for public action, because it violates expectations. But continuous deprivation is something to which people inure themselves. Only a vivid awareness of the feasibility of alternatives inspires dissatisfaction with "normal" states of chronic deprivation. The poor state of public education in many democracies, which leaves so many people illiterate or ill-informed, contributes to their lack of awareness of alternatives and hence quiescence on these issues. For these reasons, and others to be discussed at the end of this chapter, many democratic states receive weak signals about these chronic unmet needs.

The case of famine shows that there are some problems whose recognition and solution require shifting from a highly positional or local point of view to a more global point of view. Democracy is a way to construct such a shared point of view. The more global point of view does not eliminate the need to get access to widely dispersed, local information. A state-run famine relief program needs to know who needs relief. But the local information required must be cast in a form deemed relevant from the more global perspective. The people entitled to relief are not simply those who are dissatisfied with their access to food – this would indulge spoiled gourmands, and neglect those so starved to exhaustion that they no longer desire and hope – but those who, from the more global capability perspective, lack adequate nutrition. This is why the public and the press need to aim to speak from what they take to be a shared position, one they put forth as a worthy location from which citizens should speak. Democratic discussion is a means through which we forge such a position.

IV. DEMOCRACY AS A UNIVERSAL VALUE

Sen's epistemic argument for the crucial role of democratic states in preventing famines reflects a broader understanding of democracy as an institutional embodiment of collective reasoning and experimentation over how we should live together. This conception of democracy as a collective engagement in practical reason – that is, reasoning about what to do – lies at the heart of Sen's arguments for the universal value of democracy. Reason, as this term is used here, is no metaphysical abstraction. We reason whenever we subject our views to critical scrutiny in light of evidence and arguments that may come from any source. Discussion with others, the gathering and sharing of evidence and arguments about what is good and what works, lies at the heart of reason. When reason works, we say we have learned something. Practical learning is a process that moves us from less to more adequate evaluative perspectives.

Sen's arguments for the universal value of democracy can be cast in terms of such rational learning processes. Sen argues that democracy (1) embodies, (2) promotes, and (3) is the object (conclusion) of processes of practical reason or learning. Since such processes move us to what we judge to be more adequate evaluative perspectives, we all have reason to embrace them. Democracy is therefore a universal value. Consider each of these arguments.

Democracy as an embodiment of collective practical reason

Democratic theory is largely divided between two conceptions of democracy: aggregative and deliberative. According to the more familiar aggregative conceptions, democracy is majority rule. This conception stresses voting as the core institution of democracy, and represents voting as a mechanism for aggregating given individual preferences. Arguments for this conception of democracy try to show that the aggregation mechanism of majority rule is more likely to maximally satisfy people's preferences than alternative aggregation rules. This conception of democracy fits with the welfarist tradition of economics, elaborated in social choice theory, to which Sen made significant contributions earlier in his career (Amartya Sen 1970). However, Sen has rejected the idea that social institutions are to be evaluated solely according to their contributions to human welfare. Other values, such as freedom and respect for rights, matter too (Sen 1999b: 62). Sen's work has come to stress a more deliberative conception of democracy.

According to deliberative conceptions, democracy is government by discussion among equals (John Dewey 1927; Jürgen Habermas 1996; Iris

251

Young 2000). This conception stresses the universal accessibility of a state's permanent residents to equal citizenship, freedom of speech, assembly, and the press, and mechanisms for holding public officials accountable for their actions (including not just periodic elections, but the right to petition, transparency of public dealings, and the rule of law) as the core institutions of democracy. These institutions enable collective deliberation, feedback mechanisms informing democratic bodies about the performance of their policies as judged by the public, and opportunities for changing these policies in light of that feedback. This view departs from the welfarist view of democracy as a static mechanism for aggregating given individual preferences into a social decision. Instead, it regards democracy as a dynamic institution for collectively experimenting with different public policies that enables citizens to learn what joint goals make sense for them and how best to achieve them. Learning from experience, trying out different policies to see what works, and acting in accordance with discussions and deliberations about how to live together, are all paradigmatic exercises of practical reason. Democracy, then, is the institutional embodiment of practical reason for a collective agency composed of equal citizens.

Amartya Sen's (1999a) instrumental defense of the universal value of democracy fits into this picture. On this defense, democracy is instrumentally valuable for the ways it promotes government responsiveness to the people's needs. We have seen, in the case of famines above, that such promotion requires that states be capable of learning from their mistakes. Democratic states are superior to authoritarian states in this regard, because they embody an experimentalist rather than a dogmatic structure. Sen's arguments about famine thus vindicate the experimentalist defense of democracy, put forward most vigorously by John Dewey (1927).

Democracy as promoting practical reason

Sen also defends democracy–a practice not confined to official state action, but including public discussions among ordinary citizens in civil society–for its constructive role in helping citizens learn about better values or ways of life. "The practice of democracy gives citizens an opportunity to learn from one another" (Sen 1999a: 10). Democratic discussion plays a transformative role insofar as citizens need to work out, through discussion, a common framework of reasons through which to discuss state policies. "Even the idea of 'needs' ... requires public discussion and exchange of information, views, and analyses. In this sense, democracy has *constructive importance*" (Sen 1999a: 10). Public discussion can also change people's perceptions of what is feasible, especially by expanding possibilities for collective action. It can therefore play a role in changing individuals' preferences that have been adapted to deprivation and a sense of resignation or inevitability (Sen 1999a: 11). For example, if a democratic state, responding to public demands for gender justice, starts promoting women's access to health services, this can have a transformative effect on individual women's desires. Once women no longer perceive women's lesser access to healthcare as "normal," they may no longer adapt their desires to this condition.

Democracy as the conclusion of practical reason

Suppose two people disagree about the value of something. Suppose also that neither side's advocacy is rooted in internal inconsistency or error, relative to their background beliefs. Then both people are making a *positionally objective* judgment – a judgment that is warranted *relative* to their position. If each side stands fast, the disagreement will persist. But suppose there is a path from one position to the other that is reasonably described as a process of *learning*: of grasping an alternative previously unimagined, discovering its feasibility, trying it out and finding it more satisfactory than what one did before, recognizing that certain bad outcomes were caused by the alternative one had originally endorsed, or that certain good outcomes are caused by the new alternative, that disaster will not befall those who choose the new (notwithstanding earlier fears), and so forth. If there is such a path, this gives us reason to believe that the position at its end point provides a superior evaluative perspective to the other, which in turn gives us a reason to move to that position. If all learning paths ultimately lead to this position, that would vindicate its claim to universal value.

Sen claims something like this dynamic on behalf of democracy. The decisive feature of the twentieth century has been the spread of democracy (Sen 1999a: 3). This by itself is not vindicating, since it could have spread for reasons other than learning of its superiority to alternatives. What is vindicating is the fact that once people have enjoyed democracy they don't want to go back. Even in the poorest countries, attempts to repress democratic civil rights are met with outrage and, if it has not been made too dangerous, protests (Sen 1999b: 151–2). Of course, democracies have been crushed through force. But this is no argument for the rational superiority of authoritarianism, since force is not a learning process. And the twentieth century has witnessed reversals, of which Weimar Germany is perhaps the most notorious. But no informed person doubts that the Germans made a serious mistake in choosing Nazism over democracy. That the spread of democracy, and people's support for it, are arguably the result of learning is powerful evidence of its universal superiority to the other types of regime tried thus far.

The more complex challenge that Sen has to meet concerns cases of democratic failure in which (unlike in the case of Weimar Germany) both the masses and the elite appear willing to give democracy a serious try.

When military takeovers of democratically elected regimes are welcomed by substantial numbers of their inhabitants, as has happened in states such as Turkey and Pakistan, this calls Sen's unidirectional narrative into question. To meet the challenge posed by such potential counter-examples, Sen needs to argue that the failures in question are due either to factors beyond the control of any type of regime, but misattributed to democracy, or to a failure to fully implement democracy. The latter possibility – that some failures of democratic regimes could be due to their not being democratic enough – deserves further exploration, as attempted below.

V. IMPROVING DEMOCRACY: ENHANCING THE REPRESENTATION OF WOMEN

Many democracies have failed to correct chronic capability deprivations in substantial subsets of their populations. I have argued that the informational approach to analyzing institutions helps us understand why this is so. To count as *fully* democratic, state policies must be constructed from the critical interactions of the local perspectives of citizens from *all* social positions. If citizens in certain social positions – for example, women, the poor, lower castes – chronically suffer from significant capability deprivations, this is evidence that their perspectives have not been heard or taken seriously in the deliberations that shape public policies. Capability deprivations may, of course, *cause* such failures as well, through adaptation of preferences to deprivation, a lack of freedom and resources to participate in public discussion, and status demotion, whereby the privileged take deprivation as a sign that the disadvantaged are not worth listening to. To correct these problems, steps need to be taken to ensure that members of disadvantaged groups are heard. In a context of global gender inequality, this supports the call by many feminists to adopt policies to increase the representation of women in democratic offices, especially legislative bodies.

Several countries have heeded this call. Political parties in the Nordic countries, the Netherlands, and Germany have adopted this idea. In Norway, for example, the Labor Party requires that 40 percent of its candidates in local and national elections be women (Anne Phillips 1993: 98). Such policies have dramatically increased the representation of women in the Nordic countries, which boast representative assemblies that are one-third or more female (Anne Phillips 1995: 59). Other countries have institutionalized gender quotas through national legislation. Argentina requires political parties to place women in 30 percent of the electable positions on their party lists for its national deputies (Mark Jones 1996). France has adopted a law requiring 50 percent of party lists for local political offices to be female (Suzanne Daley 2001). In India, 33 percent of local government seats are reserved for women. This has brought 1 million

Indian women into local government (Margaret Alva 2001). This is an important step forward, although of course, as discussed in Elizabeth Anderson (1995), simply ensuring the presence of subordinated group members in representative assemblies does not ensure that their views will be taken seriously.[3]

Arguments over the proper composition of representative bodies reproduce in political form the two approaches – subsumption/abstraction, and pragmatic-epistemic – to dealing with positional differences that were introduced at the beginning of this chapter. According to the first strategy, positional differences are causes of bias and intolerable conflict that can be avoided only by adopting a global point of view that *abstracts* from these differences. Abstraction requires the state to *not* recognize certain positional information among citizens, such as their religion, race, ethnicity, and gender. The state should be "color-blind," "gender-blind," and so forth: it should ignore the social composition of the formulators and beneficiaries of state policies, so long as they are produced by procedures that do not explicitly discriminate between citizens on the basis of their social locations. This is supposed to ensure equal and impartial treatment of citizens.

Against this, critics argue that in practice, given the structural inequalities that disadvantage women, a policy of gender-blindness is biased in favor of the interests and perspectives of men. Without policies to increase women's representation, politics-as-usual will effectively preclude women from getting access to political offices. This will mean that their voices are not heard in legislative deliberations, and that their interests and perspectives will be ignored. Parallel arguments have been advanced by proponents of group-specific representation for ethnic and religious minorities. However, two distinct perspectives underwrite such arguments. Calls for the specific representation of ethnic and religious minorities usually reflect a politics of identity, based on ascriptive identification. Feminist calls for increasing the representation of women primarily reflect the pragmatic-epistemological perspective that has been the focus of this paper. Amartya Sen's ethics help us distinguish and evaluate the two perspectives.

Consider first the perspective of identity politics. On this view, most modern states are composed of separate ethnic or religious groups whose members have a primary stake in preserving their relatively parochial ascriptive identities. These identities are held together by common practices and parochial affiliations, which generate claims on the central government for a devolution of power to ethnic – religious groups, to enable self-determination in matters affecting their group identities (Will Kymlicka 1995; Bhikhu Parekh 1998). The resulting forms of government include both full-blown "consociational" democracy and the more limited communal self-government. In the former, separate religious, ethnic, or linguistic communities enjoy proportional group representation in legislative bodies, proportional division of public funds, and a veto power over policies particularly affecting their groups (as in the case of Belgium's pre-1993 constitution, dividing power between Flemish- and French-speaking communities at the national level: Arend Lijphart 1977). The more limited forms are observed today in Israel and India, where distinct systems of family law are administered by the different religious bodies. Identity politics resists the project of constructing more global, cosmopolitan, trans-group perspectives.

Sen has much to say against ethno-religious identity politics, drawing on his experience of the partition of India and Pakistan, which was achieved at the cost of mass displacement and bloodshed. Sen lays the blame for this on the promulgation by partitionists of a faulty conception of ethno-religious identity as singular, exclusive, and given. Singularity ignored the fact that individuals occupy multiple positions, not just as Hindus or Muslims but as members of cross-cutting associations such as neighborhoods, schools, and firms. Exclusivity fetishized difference through definition-by-contrast, whereby one defines one's own identity in terms of putative contrasts with an outgroup. This process ignored the commonalities of groups and perversely denied the possibility of practical identification in collective agencies, despite long histories of peaceful cooperation between Hindus and Muslims in India. Givenness ignored the fact that separatists *chose* to adopt an exclusionist identity and assign it supreme authority. The divisive politics of pre-partition India did not passively reflect but rather caused "the massive identity shift" by which Amartya Sen (1998: 20) argues:

> ... people's identities as Indians, as Asians, or as members of the human race seemed to give way – quite suddenly – to sectarian identification with Hindu, Muslim, or Sikh communities. The broadly Indian of January was rapidly and unquestioningly transformed into the narrowly Hindu or finely Muslim of March. The carnage that followed had much to do with unreasoned herd behavior by which people, as it were, 'discovered' their new divisive and belligerent identities, and failed to subject the process to critical examination.

This was a failure of "reasoned humanity" (Amartya Sen 2000a: 37). By this, I think he means not simply that the identities adopted licensed cruelty to others, but that they precluded identification as, and with, humanity as such, as well as with other practical identities that included both Hindus and Muslims. Thus, Sen's fundamental objection to identity politics is not that it necessarily leads to violence – although this is a lamentably common outcome – but that it imposes arbitrary obstacles to expanding the scope of cooperation through practical identification.

Identity politics, as Sen understands it, is premised on skepticism about the possibility and desirability of constructing trans-group practical identities and evaluative perspectives. The skepticism may be justified under certain conditions – for example, when subordinated groups have no realistic hope of being justly treated in a governing association including their dominators. In such cases, the best feasible solution may be separation, or else consociational democracy, as a last-ditch attempt to avoid the violence and turmoil that separation would bring about. Sen worries, however, that resigning to separate, mistrustful identities can be a self-fulfilling prophecy, entrenching suboptimal parochial self-understandings.

By contrast, the pragmatic-epistemological approach to the variety of evaluative perspectives recognizes that we can have compelling reasons, based on sympathy, respect, and more cosmopolitan practical identities, to govern our assessments and actions for certain purposes on more global perspectives. Concern for the representation of disadvantaged groups in more cosmopolitan decision-making bodies arises not from a desire to reinforce parochial group identities as ends in themselves, but from a desire to construct a more global perspective that can validly claim to pay due regard to the interests and perspectives of all.

The key idea of the pragmatic-epistemological approach is that more global, more objective perspectives arise through the critical interaction of positional differences (Longino 1993; Harding 1993). Legitimate deliberation in democratic institutions therefore requires the effective participation of those whose perspectives reflect positional differences. On this approach, calls to enhance the presence of women and members of other disadvantaged groups in representative bodies are meant to improve the quality of democratic deliberation (Phillips 1995; Jane Mansbridge 1999; Melissa Williams 1999; Young 2000).

This argument for increasing the representation of disadvantaged groups contrasts with both identity politics and the subsumption/abstraction strategy for dealing with positional differences. Against identity politics, feminist deliberative democracy presupposes the possibility and necessity of cross-group sympathy: enhanced representation of disadvantaged groups won't improve collective deliberation unless "we listen sympathetically to another's claim that our practices treat them unjustly" (Williams 1999: 67). Against the subsumption/abstraction strategy, feminist deliberative democracy rejects the thought that representatives do or ought to participate in deliberation only as undifferentiated citizens, as if their social identities, as defined by structural inequalities, did not matter to what they say (Iris Young 1990: 116 – 121; Williams 1999: 67). It is also skeptical of the tendency of deliberative democrats following the abstraction strategy, such as Habermas (1996), to sharply separate "ideal" deliberation – in which arguments should be assessed and accepted apart from considerations of interest – and appeals to particular interests. Where certain groups are unjustly disfavored, they need to be able to complain that the system specifically works against *their* interests.

257

Feminist advocates of the pragmatic-epistemic strategy for justifying increased representation of disadvantaged groups have been sensitive to the objection that such policies might inflame a divisive politics of identity. In particular, they have acknowledged the dangers of promoting a false group essentialism that purports to define groups in terms of common traits (Phillips 1995: 166; Mansbridge 1999: 637–9). The groups whose representation they think needs to be enhanced are defined rather by the disadvantages produced by their external social relations (Melissa Williams 1998: 15–18). Some argue that group essentialism and identity-freezing can best be avoided by policies that enhance the presence of disadvantaged groups in representative bodies through indirect or less formal means (Mansbridge 1999: 652–3; Young 2000: 149–52).

It remains a delicate matter to explain how representatives from disadvantaged groups should conceive of their role. Should they see themselves as specifically representing the disadvantaged groups to which they belong? The diffidence of some feminists on this score reflects difficulties with the idea of group representation. Anne Phillips (1993; 1995: 54–5), who has considered this problem most deeply, argues that female representatives cannot be said to represent women as a group unless they are accountable to women as a group. Such accountability would be possible only if women were organized as a distinctive electoral body, such that women alone would vote for female representatives. Iris Young (1990: 43, 183–91) at one time advocated such a model of group representation, in conjunction with a conception of social groups that mixed desires for ingroup affiliation (based on ascriptive identification) with a more structural account of group differences.[4]

Such a model, in focusing citizens' minds on their own ascriptive group identities, fails to consider how this form of identification affects the way others identify themselves. If women representatives are publicly understood as speaking by and for women as a group, how is the public supposed to understand what male representatives are doing? If women specifically represent women, then it would seem to leave male representatives the job of specifically representing men. One could reply that this is what male politicians have been doing all along, implicitly – which is why women are needed in office in the first place. This reply fails to consider the ominous implications of converting a regrettable fact into a norm. It is one thing to critically observe that male representatives have a sorry record of neglecting women's interests. It is quite another to insist that, lacking ascriptive identification with women, they *cannot* represent women. For if ascriptive identification is the basis of competent representation, then male politicians can *only* represent men, and it must be their job to do so. The implications of imposing this self-understanding on men can only be to *excuse* them for their neglect of women's interests, and to pitch men's and women's interests in competition with each other. This cannot be good for women.

To avoid this, one could argue that while it is all right for oppressed groups to act especially on behalf of their group, it is not all right for dominant groups to act especially on behalf of their groups. They must consider only the general interest of society, without favoring one group over another. This proposal, however, reproduces the sexist association of men with the universal and women with the particular on the basis of which men have traditionally claimed superiority. And it raises the question: if men already have access to a universal perspective, inclusive of women's interests, why do we need special representation for women's local perspective? A politics based on the solidarities of ascriptive identification with women leaves men with no good place to stand, from a feminist perspective.

Sen's reflections on positionality, universality, and democracy offer a different way to understand the point of reserving political offices for women, in terms of the pragmatic-epistemological strategy. Consider two cases of the differences women have made to politics, which have been made possible by the reservation of office. Indian observers have remarked that women representatives have focused local government energies on the previously neglected areas of safe drinking water and sanitation, in contrast to the traditional focus of men on building roads and municipal buildings (Vasantha Surya 1999; Staff Reporter, *The Hindu* 2000; Alva 2001). As one observer explains, "the kitchen and the latrine continue to occupy the old, old space, they are where women and the lowest class of dalits have to function," so it is no surprise that "most men just do not share or care" about the inadequate facilities in these spaces, and that women were needed to mobilize improvements in these areas (Surya 1999). In Norway, feminist politicians have set their sights on a more ambitious agenda of transforming men's identities. Feminism is not just about raising the consciousness of women, but of recruiting men into the movement for gender equality, in part by expanding their opportunities to share in childrearing. Women politicians have led successful efforts to reserve four weeks of a family's paid parental leave for the father, an action that increased men's use of parental leave to a stunning 70 percent by 1995 (Murray Lundberg 2001). Norwegian feminists have also ended the default practice of awarding child custody to the mother in cases of divorce, so as to give divorced men a chance to continue involved relationships with their children.

On the pragmatic-epistemological model, deliberative democracy is a means of mobilizing local positional knowledge for shared ends. The improvements witnessed in India due to the inclusion of women in local politics reflect this mobilization. Inclusion enables democracy to utilize the local knowledge that women are more likely to have in virtue of the gendered division of labor. The Indian women bring their knowledge to local government in the expectation that they can persuade men to share

259

their concerns. Their quest is not for validation of their parochial positionality *as particular*, but to offer up their perspective as universal, as properly shared by all. The Norwegian feminists agree. As mothers, most have experienced the joys of childrearing. But instead of celebrating the perspectives this activity generates as specifically feminine, and supposing that these perspectives are women's special preserve, they want, in the name of gender equality, to expand access to these joys and these perspectives to men. This is represented as a gain for people generally. When men come to see themselves as responsible for rearing children, it is easier for all to see that rearing children is a human function, not just a female function. What begins as highly positional knowledge can become more global, as more people find compelling reasons to share that position.

The same lesson applies even to cases in which the knowledge that women bring to deliberation includes the ways women are unjustly disadvantaged by their group position, and thereby have conflicts of interest with those who benefit from their disadvantage. It is tempting to represent such cases as ones in which women are specifically representing *women*, rather than acting on behalf of the "common good" of all citizens. But even here, this knowledge is deployed in the name of the common good of justice. It appeals to others' desire to be just, although it is typically accompanied by appeal to others' desires to avoid the costs of social conflict (Williams 1999: 69–70).

Thus, the fundamental political significance of positionality – of parochial social identity – is epistemological, and not a matter of parochial solidarity. Sen (2000b: 29) urges us to accept the same lesson:

> In sympathizing with others, there are two quite different uses of identity: an "epistemic" use, in trying to know what others feel and what they see by placing oneself in the position of others, and an "ethical" use, in counting them as if they were the same as oneself. The epistemic use of identity is inescapably important, since our knowledge of other people's minds has to be derivative, in one way or another, on our placing ourselves in the position of others. But the ethical use of identity may be far from obligatory. To respond to the interests of others, we can see ourselves as "impartial spectators," as Smith described the role; but this demand of impartial concern is not the same thing as promoting the interests of others on the ground that they are, in some sense, extensions of oneself. As people capable of abstraction and reasoning, we should be able to respond humanely to the predicaments of others who are different and are seen to be different.

To put the point another way, the fundamental point of seeking a gender-integrated representative body is not so that women can represent women's interests, and men men's interests. It is that only through a representative body of men and women working together can we have a democracy able to adequately serve the interests of *all* its people.

In conclusion, the epistemological themes in Sen's explorations of variations in people's ethical judgments are complimentary to feminist work. Where traditional approaches to objectivity presume that variations in judgments fundamentally reflect error and bias, Sen, like feminists, has construed such variations as potential resources for constructing more objective points of view. In both Sen's work and in much feminist work, democracy provides the key to transforming differences from biases into resources.

ACKNOWLEDGMENTS

I would like to thank Bina Agarwal, Ingrid Robeyns, and the anonymous referees for extensive and helpful comments.

NOTES

[1] Elizabeth Anderson (2002) surveys the different ways feminist theorists deal with the influences of social position on people's points of view.

[2] I defend these claims, and explore further the connections between the normative validity of perspectives and their factual presuppositions, in Elizabeth Anderson (1998).

[3] For example, subordinates may have difficulty getting access to the floor, speaking without interruption, and obtaining a respectful and accurate hearing. The same stigmatizing representations of subordinates' supposed group characteristics that are used to justify their subordination may also lead hearers to systematically distort or discount what members of subordinated groups say (as when women expressing their grievances are dismissed as hysterical). Internalized norms of deference to dominant groups may also make it difficult for representatives of subordinate groups to find their own voices. I discuss these problems and some approaches to dealing with them in Elizabeth Anderson (1995).

[4] She has since withdrawn the suggestion, without, however, fully divesting herself from the ingroup affiliation model (Young 2000: 149–52, 216–17).

REFERENCES

Alva, Margaret. 2001. "India: Democracy Starts at the Grassroots, and Trickles Up," in WEDO PRIMER 50/50 CAMPAIGN. Women's Environment & Development Organization, March. On-line. Available http://www.wedo.org/5050/india.htm (June 2002).

Anderson, Elizabeth. 1995. "The Democratic University: The Role of Justice in the Production of Knowledge." *Social Philosophy and Policy* 12: 186–219.

——. 1998. "Pragmatism, Science, and Moral Inquiry," in Richard Fox and Robert Westbrook (eds.) *In Face of the Facts*, pp. 10–39. Cambridge, UK: Cambridge University Press.

——. 2002. "Feminist Epistemology and Philosophy of Science," in Edward Zalta (ed.) *Stanford Encyclopedia of Philosophy*. On-line. Available http://plato.stanford.edu/entries/feminism-epistemology/ (June 2002).

Brandt, Richard. 1979. *A Theory of the Good and the Right*. Oxford, UK: Clarendon Press.

Daley, Suzanne. 2001. "French Twist: Parity, Thy Name is Woman." *New York Times*, February 11.

Dewey, John. 1927. *The Public and Its Problems*. New York: H. Holt.

Gauthier, David. 1986. *Morals by Agreement*. Oxford: Clarendon Press.

Habermas, Jürgen. 1996. *Between Facts and Norms*. Cambridge, MA: MIT Press.

Harding, Sandra. 1993. "Rethinking Standpoint Epistemology: 'What is Strong Objectivity'?" in Linda Alcoff and Elizabeth Potter (eds.) *Feminist Epistemologies*. Totowa, NJ: Routledge.

Jones, Mark P. 1996. "Increasing Women's Representation via Gender Quotas: The Argentine Ley de Cupos." *Women and Politics* 16: 75–98.

Kant, Immanuel. 1981 [1785]. *Grounding for the Metaphysics of Morals*. Trans. James Ellington. Indianapolis: Hackett.

Kymlicka, Will (ed.). 1995. *Rights of Minority Cultures*. Oxford, UK: Oxford University Press.

Lijphart, Arend. 1977. *Democracy in Plural Societies*. New Haven, CT: Yale University Press.

Longino, Helen. 1993. "Essential Tensions – Phase Two: Feminist, Philosophical, and Social Studies of Science," in Louise Antony and Charlotte Witt (eds.) *A Mind of One's Own*. Boulder, CO: Westview Press.

Lundberg, Murray. 2001. "The Position of Women in Norway," in *Arctic/Northern Culture*. On-line. Available http://arcticculture.about.com/library/weekly/aa053101a.htm (July 2001).

Mansbridge, Jane. 1999. "Should Blacks Represent Blacks and Women Represent Women? A Contingent 'Yes'." *Journal of Politics* 61: 628–57.

Nagel, Thomas. 1978. *The Possibility of Altruism*. Oxford, UK: Oxford University Press.

Nussbaum, Martha. 1999. *Sex and Social Justice*. New York: Oxford University Press.

Parekh, Bhikhu. 1998. "Cultural Diversity and Liberal Democracy," in Gurpreet Mahajan (ed.) *Democracy, Difference, and Social Justice*. Delhi: Oxford University Press.

Phillips, Anne. 1993. "Democracy and Difference," in *Democracy and Difference*. University Park, PA: Pennsylvania State University Press.

——. 1995. *The Politics of Presence*. Oxford, UK: Clarendon Press.

Rawls, John. 1971. *A Theory of Justice*. Cambridge, MA: Harvard University Press.

Scheler, Max. 1954. *The Nature of Sympathy*. Trans. Peter Heath. New Haven, CT: Yale University Press.

Sen, Amartya. 1970. *Collective Choice and Social Welfare*. San Francisco: Holden-Day.

——. 1981. *Poverty and Famines: An Essay on Entitlement and Deprivation*. Oxford, UK: Clarendon Press.

——. 1985. *Commodities and Capabilities*. Amsterdam: North-Holland.

——. 1993a. "Capability and Well-Being,." in Martha Nussbaum and Amartya Sen (eds.) *The Quality of Life*, pp. 30–53. Oxford, UK: Clarendon Press.

——. 1993b. "Positional Objectivity." *Philosophy and Public Affairs* 22: 126–45.

——. 1998. *Reason Before Identity*. The Romanes Lecture for 1998. Oxford, UK: Oxford University Press.

——. 1999a. "Democracy as a Universal Value." *Journal of Democracy* 10: 3–17.

——. 1999b. *Development as Freedom.* New York: A. A. Knopf.

——. 2000a. "East and West: The Reach of Reason." *New York Review of Books,* July 20.

——. 2000b. "Other People." *The New Republic,* December 18.

Sidgwick, Henry. 1981 [1907]. *The Methods of Ethics.* 7th edn. Indianapolis: Hackett.

Staff Reporter 2000. "Grass-Roots Democracy at Its Best." *The Hindu,* June 2.

Surya, Vasantha. 1999. "Recognizing Their Worth." *The Hindu,* April 18.

Williams, Melissa. 1998. *Voice, Trust, and Memory.* Princeton, NJ: Princeton University Press.

——. 1999. "Impartial Justice and Political Perspectives," in Patrick Hanafin and Melissa Williams (eds.) *Identity, Rights, and Constitutional Transformation.* Brookfield, VT: Ashgate.

Young, Iris Marion. 1990. *Justice and the Politics of Difference.* Princeton, NJ: Princeton University Press.

——. 2000. *Inclusion and Democracy.* Oxford, UK: Oxford University Press.

"MISSING WOMEN": REVISITING THE DEBATE

Stephan Klasen and Claudia Wink

OVERVIEW

In a series of papers in the late 1980s, Amartya Sen claimed that about 100 million women were "missing," referring to the number of females who had died as a result of unequal access to resources in parts of the developing world. A subsequent debate has refined these estimates using different demographic techniques. In this chapter, we review this debate, provide an update on the number of "missing women," and investigate the determinants of current trends in gender bias in mortality. We find that the number of "missing women" has increased in absolute terms, but fallen as a share of the number of women alive. There have been improvements for women's relative survival in most of South Asia and the Middle East, but deteriorations in China. Improving female education and employment opportunities has helped to reduce gender bias, while the increasing recourse to sex-selective abortions has worsened it.

INTRODUCTION

Apart from his well-known work on famines and hunger (Amartya Sen 1984; Jean Drèze and Amartya Sen 1989), Amartya Sen's work on gender bias in mortality is surely among his most important contributions to the field of development economics. First, he has contributed to the emerging literature on gender bias in the allocation of resources, nutrition, and health outcomes in South Asia (e.g., Pranab Bardhan 1974; Stan D'Souza and Lincoln Chen 1980; Lincoln Chen, Emdadul Huq, and Stan D'Souza 1981; Mark Rosenzweig and Paul Schultz 1982; Monica Das Gupta 1987) with important theoretical and empirical papers (e.g., Amartya Sen 1990a; Amartya Sen and Sunil Sengupta 1983; Jocelyn Kynch and Amartya Sen 1983). Second, he has analyzed the abnormally high sex ratios (number of males divided by the number of females) in South Asia, particularly India. While Pravin Visaria (1961) had already raised this issue in the Indian context and had linked it to gender bias in mortality, Sen focused on the worsening of the sex ratio in India from the beginning of the twentieth century and the sharp regional differences within the country (e.g., Amartya Sen 1982; Kynch and Sen 1983; Jean Drèze and Amartya Sen 1995).

Based on the insights of the literature on gender bias in mortality and the unusually high sex ratios in parts of the developing world (particularly in South Asia, China, the Middle East, and North Africa), a critical third contribution was to develop the concept of "missing women." This is a way to assess the cumulative impact of gender bias in mortality by estimating the additional number of females of all ages who would be alive if there had been equal treatment of the sexes among the cohorts that are alive today. Those additional numbers of women he referred to as "missing" because they had died as a result of unequal treatment in the allocation of survival-related goods. By showing that the number of "missing women" was close to 100 million in the regions suffering from excess female mortality (Amartya Sen 1989, 1990b), he demonstrated that gender bias in mortality is far from a minor issue, but ranks among the worst human catastrophes of the twentieth century.[1] For example, the number of "missing women" in the early 1990s is larger than the combined casualties of all famines in the twentieth century. It also exceeds the combined death toll of both world wars and the casualties of major epidemics such as the 1918–20 global influenza epidemic or the currently ongoing AIDS pandemic. Only continuous excessive morbidity and mortality caused by poverty, endemic deprivation, and poor public services in many developing countries has claimed more victims.[2] Both gender bias in mortality and the mortality caused by endemic deprivation share the feature that they occur largely unnoticed and do not generate the moral outrage and flurry of activity and intervention that the more "sensational" catastrophes such as famines, floods, earthquakes, wars, and refugee crises typically create.[3] Sen's concept of "missing women" helped to generate the publicity, concern, and policy discussions that this issue deserves.

While this contribution and the important impact it had in putting gender issues in the forefront of development policy discussions is universally recognized, his particular way of calculating the number of "missing women" (reviewed in Section I) soon attracted the interest of researchers who proposed refined methodologies for computing the female deficit caused by gender bias in mortality (Ansley Coale 1991; Stephan Klasen 1994). These alternative methodologies affected the estimates (see below) although they did not call into question the huge human toll that gender bias in mortality is exacting. They also yielded additional insights into the magnitude and regional distribution of the phenomenon. However, all the published estimates of "missing women" were based on demographic information from the 1980s and early 1990s. Since then, there has been considerable speculation about current trends of gender bias in mortality, with some observers suggesting a falling intensity and others predicting the opposite (e.g., Klasen 1994; Monica Das Gupta and P. N. Mari Bhat 1997; Drèze and Sen 1995; Peter Mayer 1999; Elizabeth Croll 2000). By now nearly all countries with considerable excess female mortality have conducted new censuses that allow us to see whether there has indeed been a worsening or an improvement. By analyzing those returns and other available information on mortality differentials, we can better understand the current trends and the most important factors driving them.

I. "MISSING WOMEN": CONCEPT AND MEASUREMENT ISSUES

There are principally two ways to examine the impact of gender bias in mortality. One is to compare actual age and sex-specific mortality rates with "expected" rates that we would obtain, given equal treatment of both sexes. If actual female mortality rates exceed expected rates, one may speak of "excess female mortality." Most microanalysis of gender bias in mortality have used these data to determine the extent of gender bias (e.g., D'Souza and Chen 1980; Jane Humphries 1991; Mamta Murthi, Anne-Catherine Guio, and Jean Drèze 1995; Stephan Klasen 1998).[4] The advantage of this approach is that it allows a more careful investigation of the age structure of gender bias in mortality, and thus helps to determine its proximate causes.

There are, however, two shortcomings of this approach. First, the data needed for such a detailed investigation are either not available or not reliable in many developing countries where gender bias in mortality is a serious issue. In particular, while there may be reliable data from small samples or surveys, reliable national age- and sex-specific mortality rates are not available for most countries, as these require a complete and reliable vital registration system. Second, such an analysis only yields a flow measure of gender bias in mortality, that is, how many females die in excess per year. It may, however, be of interest to have a stock measure that examines the total impact of past and present gender bias on the generations currently alive.

The second method, which was developed by Sen, is to compare the actual population sex ratio (the number of males divided by the number of females in the most recent census)[5] with an "expected" population sex ratio that we would obtain given equal treatment of the sexes in the distribution of survival-related goods. If the actual ratio exceeds the expected, the additional females that would have to be alive in order to equate the actual with the expected sex ratios, would then be the number of "missing women" at that point in time.[6]

This measure does not share the shortcomings of an analysis based on mortality rates. It is based only on the population sex ratio which is likely to be the most reliable demographic figure in developing countries, as it "only" requires an accurate census count but no accurate monitoring of vital statistics.[7] Also, as a stock measure it allows an estimate of the cumulative impact of gender bias in mortality. Finally, as a measure that compares actual with expected sex ratios, it would include female victims of sex-selective abortions among the "missing women," which would not be included in an assessment of sex-specific mortality rates.

Clearly, however, this is a very aggregative statistic that does not allow a precise analysis of the mechanisms of gender bias in mortality. It can also be subject to biases, including sex-selective under-enumeration and sex-biased international migration (see Section III). Thus both methods complement each other and both are needed to arrive at a complete analysis of the magnitude of the phenomenon, as well as the details of its occurrence. As the focus of this chapter is on "missing women," we will largely concentrate on the sex ratio statistic and will only draw on mortality data as supporting evidence where appropriate.

The critical question in the calculation of the number of "missing women" is the expected sex ratio in the absence of discrimination. Since no society in the world, past or present, has been entirely gender-neutral in the allocation of resources, opportunities, and behavioral patterns, it is quite difficult to speculate on what the sex ratio would be in the absence of gender discrimination. For example, the high female excess in European countries is not a sign of discrimination against males in the allocation of resources, but is, in part, related to male behavioral patterns, mainly smoking, drinking, dangerous driving, and a higher incidence of violence against oneself and others, that reduce their life expectancy considerably vis-à-vis females (Ingrid Waldron 1993). Moreover, as will be clear below, the expected sex ratio in a society depends on the demographic make-up of that society, including its age structure and its overall mortality conditions.[8]

As a rough estimate, to provide "some idea of the enormity of the problem" (Amartya Sen 1992), Sen simply used the sex ratio then prevailing in Sub-Saharan Africa, where females outnumbered males by about 2 percent, as the expected sex ratio.[9] Given the similarity of circumstances between the developing region of Sub-Saharan Africa and the developing regions of South and East Asia and the Middle East, this appears a logical choice. It turns out, however, that the demographic conditions in Sub-Saharan Africa are quite different from those in Asia and the Middle East in three ways. First, fertility is much higher, which leads to a very different age structure with implications for the population sex ratio (see below). Second, mortality is also higher, which again has a differential impact on the expected mortality experience of males and females. And third, African populations have a slightly but significantly lower sex ratio at birth than other populations, which partly explains their comparatively low population sex ratio.[10]

For these reasons, Ansley Coale pointed out that the "expected sex ratio" of a population is not a constant but depends on four factors. First, the sex ratio at birth suggests a slight male excess in all populations. Viewed in isolation, this would suggest an expected population sex ratio slightly favoring males. The sex ratio at birth referred to here is that which would be obtained by biology alone, excluding the effects of interventions such as sex-selective abortions or more sophisticated sex-selection techniques. By using this expected sex ratio at birth rather than the actual ratio, which may be influenced by external interventions, female victims of sex-selective abortions and other sex-specific pre-birth manipulations will, in our calculation, also be counted as "missing."[11] Second, the sex ratio depends on the expected sex-specific mortality rates that would exist in a nondiscriminating society. Coale (1991) suggested that the Regional Model Life Tables should be used as the benchmark for nondiscriminating societies. These Model Life Tables are made up of some 240 Life Tables from all parts of the world (but with a predominance from Europe) dating largely from the mid-nineteenth century until the mid-twentieth century (Ansley Coale, Paul Demeny, and Barbara Vaughan 1983). They are aggregated into four regional groupings ("West," "East," "North," and "South") based on observed differences in the patterns of mortality, especially the relationship between childhood and adult mortality rates, and then calculated for different mortality levels (see Coale, Demeny, and Vaughan 1983 for details).[12]

All four sets of Model Life Tables show a considerable female survival advantage in infancy and in older age groups (particularly above age 50). In between, women enjoy a survival advantage only in moderate to low mortality environments. In high mortality environments (with female life expectancy below 40), girls suffer from higher mortality than boys, particularly in the tables "West" and "South," while adult women additionally suffer from slightly higher mortality than men of the same age in the "East" and "South" tables.[13] In the "North" tables, based on the mortality experience of Scandinavian countries, this female disadvantage is generally the smallest. Whether this female disadvantage is a true reflection of biological differences in mortality or a sign of gender bias in mortality in the populations that form the basis of these Model Life Tables will be considered below (see also Klasen 1994). But using any of the Model Life Tables would imply that over the lifecycle, men will suffer overall from higher mortality rates than females, particularly in infancy and old age, which accords well with the biological literature on the subject (see Ingrid Waldron 1983, 1993, 1998). As a result, we would expect that the male excess at birth erodes as people age. In high mortality environments, parity between males and females of a cohort is expected to be achieved by ages 10–15, while in low mortality environments it is achieved only after age 50.

This combination of a male excess among the young and a female excess among the old (and the middle-aged, depending on the overall mortality environment), clearly implies that the age structure of the population, which is largely driven by past and present fertility patterns, will have an impact on the expected sex ratio. The population growth rate and the resulting age structure is therefore the third factor that influences the expected sex ratio of a population. Countries experiencing high population growth, and thus have a large share of young people, have a higher expected sex ratio than populations with low fertility and thus a larger share of the elderly.

Lastly, the expected sex ratio might be influenced by international migration, if such migration is unbalanced in its gender make-up. Given the paucity of reliable data on migrant flows and their sex composition, this effect was not considered by Sen (1989), Coale (1991), or Klasen (1994). The most important migrant flows that could potentially affect sex ratios are from South Asia to the Middle East and North Africa, particularly to the oil-rich Arab States and, to a smaller degree, from Egypt and the occupied territories of Palestine to the oil-rich Arab States. These flows have been considerable, particularly in the 1970s, with a predominance of male migrants. This contributed to increasing sex ratios in the receiving countries, particularly Saudi Arabia, Kuwait, UAE, Oman, Qatar, and Libya. But the male excess in these migrant flows, as a share of the populations of the countries of origin (particularly India, Bangladesh, Egypt, and Pakistan) is quite small, given their huge populations.[14] Also, these flows have generally stagnated or become smaller in recent years, partly as a result of falling oil prices in the 1980s and 1990s, and partly in the aftermath of the Gulf War of 1990–1991. Ignoring these flows would therefore only very slightly underestimate the number of "missing women" in South Asia and Egypt since the actual sex ratio, due to male-dominated migration, is artificially smaller and thus reduces the implied number of "missing women." Conversely, it may increase the implied number of "missing women" in West Asia, the most important receiving region. For the global estimate of "missing women," where the number of "missing women" from the sending region is added to the number from the receiving region, these effects largely cancel each other.[15]

Coale (1991) then made the following assumptions to arrive at his estimate of "missing women." First, he assumed a sex ratio at birth of 1.059, which he derived as an average from the sex ratios at birth in rich countries. Second, he assumed that the populations with gender bias in mortality could be considered quasi-stable,[16] meaning that they have a roughly constant age structure of the population. This assumption allowed him to use the Model Life Tables for an estimate of "missing women" as they are generated for stable or quasi-stable populations. Third, he assumed that the "expected" mortality pattern in the absence of discrimination would conform to the Model Life Tables "West." They are based on 132 Model Life Tables detailing the mortality experience of Western European, and some Asian, Australasian, and South African (white) populations, mostly from the late nineteenth to the mid-twentieth century. Fourth, he chose the Model Life Tables that corresponded to the mortality and population growth patterns these countries experienced in the early 1970s, to approximate the average mortality and fertility levels of the cohorts alive at the time of the census. Lastly, he ignored international migration, as did all other studies.

Based on these assumptions, Table 1 shows how Coale arrived at some 60 million "missing women" in the populations most affected by gender bias in mortality.[17] While this estimate was considerably smaller than Sen's, it supported the massive human toll of gender bias in mortality.

In a paper published in 1994, Klasen adopted Coale's general approach but questioned two of the assumptions. First, he argued that the use of the Model Life Tables "West" led to an underestimation of gender bias in mortality, particularly in high mortality environments, as the countries that formed the basis for those Model Life Tables had themselves experienced episodes of excess female mortality, particularly in the nineteenth century. He noted that the Model Life Tables "West" assumed that girls between 1 and 20 have higher mortality rates than boys in high mortality environments, which was contrary to the biological evidence and likely to be related to actual episodes of gender bias in mortality in the nineteenth century (e.g., Klasen 1998, 1999; Humphries 1991; K. McNay, Jane Humphries, and Stephan Klasen 1998). He then tried to correct these Model Life Tables for this gender bias in mortality. This increased the number of "missing women" by some 5 million, particularly in the high mortality countries of Bangladesh, Nepal, and India. When using the Model Life Tables "East," which did not show such pronounced excess female mortality among girls and showed a larger survival advantage for adult women, the number of "missing women" increased by a further 4 million, thus totaling 69.3 million.

Klasen's second criticism of Coale's method was the assumption of a constant sex ratio at birth in all countries. Based on long time series of sex ratios at birth, Klasen showed that there had been a secular upward trend in the sex ratio at birth in rich countries. The biological literature on the subject also suggested that improved overall health conditions should raise the sex ratio at birth since male fetuses disproportionately suffer from spontaneous abortions and stillbirths.[18] Whenever better health and nutrition lower the rates of such spontaneous abortions and miscarriages and reduce the incidence of stillbirths, the sex ratio at birth increases. He then used available evidence on sex ratios at birth from around the world

Table 1 "Missing women": estimates by Sen, Coale, and Klasen in the early 1990s

Country	Year	Number of women (millions)	Actual sex ratio	Sen's estimate based on the actual sex ratio in Sub-Saharan Africa			Coale's estimate based on Model Life Tables "West" and constant sex ratio at birth			Klasen's estimate based on Model Life Tables "East" and variable sex ratio at birth		
				Expected sex ratio	Missing women (m)	% missing	Expected sex ratio	Missing women (m)	% missing	Expected sex ratio	Missing women (m)	% missing
China	1990	548.7	1.066	0.977	49.98	9.11	1.010	30.42	5.54	0.993	40.14	7.32
India	1991	406.3	1.077	0.977	41.59	10.24	1.020	22.76	5.59	0.990	35.87	8.83
Pakistan	1981	40.0	1.105	0.977	5.24	13.10	1.025	3.12	7.80	1.002	4.09	10.23
Bangladesh	1981	42.2	1.064	0.977	3.76	8.90	1.025	1.61	3.80	0.969	4.13	9.78
Nepal	1981	7.3	1.050	0.977	0.55	7.47	1.025	0.18	2.44	0.980	0.52	7.13
West Asia	1985	55.0	1.060	0.977	4.67	8.50	1.030	1.60	2.91	1.005	3.01	5.47
Egypt	1986	23.5	1.047	0.977	1.68	7.16	1.020	0.62	2.65	0.996	1.20	5.12
Total		1,123.0			107.47	9.57		60.26	5.37		88.96	7.92

Source: Klasen (1994). The percent missing is arrived at by dividing the number of "missing women" by the actual number of women alive. These numbers are as they appeared in Klasen (1994) and do not take into account the impact of revised census counts and other adjustments mentioned in Section II.

and found that they are indeed closely correlated with life expectancy. Based on this regression (which is reproduced in Column 1 of Table 2), he then estimated that the expected sex ratio at birth in high mortality countries should be considerably below the 1.059 suggested by Coale. Lower male excess at birth would then reduce the expected population sex ratio and thus increase the resulting number of "missing women." As shown in the bottom panel of Table 1, using the Model Life Tables "East" and the revised assumptions about the sex ratio at birth, increased the number of "missing women" to about 89 million, which was slightly closer to Sen's 107 million than to Coale's 60 million. Clearly, the assumptions underlying the calculations make a large difference and there is considerable empirical support for the general approach by Coale with the two amended assumptions by Klasen.

While all three estimates concur that the cumulative impact of gender bias in mortality has claimed a very large number of female victims, there are important differences in the three estimates. First, the methodology differs greatly. Sen's approach, in particular, may be appropriate for a rough calculation, but it would not be suitable for a careful assessment of differences across space and time, as it assumes a standard that is not adjusted to suit local demographic conditions. Coale and Klasen's methods are more similar but Klasen's assumption of a variable sex ratio at birth significantly influences the distribution of the phenomenon across region and time. As Table 1 shows, Coale's figures suggest that the share of "missing women" in China is nearly as high as that in India, and much worse than in Bangladesh, while the problem is rather negligible in Nepal, Egypt, and West Asia. Klasen's method, in contrast, shows that the share of "missing women" is considerably worse in India than in China, is much worse in Bangladesh than in China, and is significant in all the countries studied. Moreover, it much more clearly identifies South Asia (the countries Nepal, Bangladesh, Pakistan, and India) as the region with the worst problem. This is less apparent in Coale's figures.

All of these calculations and discussions were based on demographic information from the 1980s and early 1990s. With new census information available, it is critical to know how gender bias in mortality, including its regional distribution, has changed over time.

II. UPDATING THE NUMBER OF "MISSING WOMEN"

Before providing an update on the number of "missing women," three points are noteworthy. First, the actual sex ratios for Egypt, China, and India in Coale (1991) and Klasen (1994) were based on preliminary census figures. The final census figures led to some changes in the numbers. Most notably there was a downward revision of the sex ratio in China from 1.066 to 1.060 which thereby reduced the number of "missing women" by some

3.5 million (regardless of the assumption used to generate the expected sex ratio). In contrast, revisions to the figures from India and Egypt increased the number of "missing women" by 0.8 and 0.05 million, respectively.[19] Finally, we use a slightly revised assumption about the sex ratio at birth based on a more expanded analysis (see below). All in all, the baseline to compare current figures is some 87 million "missing women" (or 7.7 percent of women) for the 1980s and early 1990s, instead of the 89 million reported in Table 1. Similarly, some of the new census data (from China, India, Pakistan, Nepal, and Bangladesh) are based on preliminary census returns and might also be adjusted later.[20]

Second, Coale (1991) and Klasen (1994) missed out on a few countries with possibly considerable excess female mortality. In particular, Iran, Afghanistan, Taiwan, South Korea, Algeria, and Tunisia were not included in the assessment despite having high sex ratios or showing other evidence of female disadvantage. They have now been included to generate a more complete assessment of the total number of "missing women" in the world.[21] Sri Lanka has also been added, as it used to have high sex ratios which have, however, fallen considerably recently. Finally, despite having comparatively low sex ratios, Sub-Saharan Africa might also suffer from excess female mortality, which is masked by the unusually low sex ratios at birth prevailing in African populations and populations of African descent (see Stephan Klasen 1994, 1996a, 1996b). Thus, one should also include this region in the list of candidates, particularly since the population sex ratios have been increasing considerably in recent years (Klasen 1996a, 1996b).[22] We not only include them in the current assessment but also estimate a baseline of "missing women" in the 1980s and early 1990s. Including these additional countries, the baseline is about 95 million for that time period, or 6.5 percent of all women in the countries affected (see Stephan Klasen and Claudia Wink 2002 for details).

Third, we now have more data on sex ratios at birth from a larger list of countries and these can be used to re-estimate the relationship between life expectancy and the sex ratio at birth. This is done in Table 2. The data are based on sex ratios at birth reported in the Demographic Yearbooks of the last twenty years. Countries included in the sample must have complete birth registration, at least 5,000 births per year, no evidence of sex-selective abortions, and, in the first two columns, must not contain a significant proportion of African populations referring to populations from Sub-Saharan Africa or descendants from there. The regressions in columns 3 and 4 are then done for countries where Africans form the vast majority as well as for African-Americans in the USA, at different points in time. The regression in column 5 then combines all the data and just uses a dummy variable for African populations.

In column 1, the regression from Klasen (1994) is reproduced which was based on 62 observations. It showed a significant positive relationship

Table 2 Life expectancy and the sex ratio at birth

Sample	(1) Non-African	(2) Non-African	(3) African	(4) Just African-Americans	(5) All combined
Constant	0.997 (0.023)***	0.991 (0.015)***	0.888 (0.041)***	0.982 (0.014)***	0.957 (0.015)***
Life Expectancy	0.00079 (0.0002)***	0.00087 (0.0002)***	0.00216 (0.0006)**	0.00070 (0.0002)*	0.00134 (0.0002)***
African Population (dummy)					−0.0157 (0.0038)***
Adj. R-Squared	0.188	0.071	0.254	0.458	0.326
N	62	212	31	11	243
Predicted sex ratios at birth based on regression:					
China	1.0500	1.0492			1.0481
India	1.0404	1.0388			1.0307
Pakistan	1.0436	1.0423			1.0361
Bangladesh	1.0412	1.0396			1.0320
West Asia	1.0428	1.0414			1.0347
Egypt	1.0452	1.0423			1.0387
Sub-Saharan Africa			0.9946	1.0165	1.0070

Notes: Standard errors shown in parentheses. *** Refers to 99.9%; ** to 99%; and * to 95% significance levels. Sources: United Nations (1984, 1987, 1993, 1999), US Department of Health and Human Services (1991). African refers to populations of Sub-Saharan Africa, the Caribbean, and African-Americans.

275

between the two variables and suggested that 10 years of greater longevity are associated with a 0.8 percentage point higher sex ratio at birth. Column 2 is based on that same set of observations, augmented by another 150 data points from more recent years. The results are nearly identical, suggesting a rather robust relationship.

Column 3 shows the regressions for countries with African populations (from Sub-Saharan Africa, the Caribbean, and African-Americans in the US). Here we see not only the expected lower overall sex ratio but also a more significant influence of life expectancy on the sex ratio at birth. One should caution, however, that these relationships are estimated using fewer and possibly data of worse quality. If we restrict the sample to African-Americans in the US at 11 points in time (from the 1940 to 1988), the impact of longevity is smaller and more similar to the other regions, but the difference in the level of the sex ratio at birth prevails.

The fifth regression pools the data from the non-African and African populations. Life expectancy continues to exert a significant influence on the sex ratio at birth with the coefficient being about halfway between the non-African and the African regressions. Also, the dummy for African populations again shows the lower sex ratio at birth of some 1.6 percentage points, even if one controls for the influence of life expectancy.[23]

The table also shows predictions for the sex ratio at birth in selected countries with missing females based on the regressions.[24] They are all below the rate of 1.059 assumed by Coale and we will see below that these seemingly small differences have a large impact on the estimate of "missing women." These predictions also do not appear unreasonable for the countries in question. Actual sex ratios at birth in Sri Lanka and the Indian state of Kerala, where we suspect little current gender bias in mortality, have oscillated around 1.04–1.05 in the past decade, just as one would predict from the regressions above (Registrar General 2001; United Nations 1993, 2000). In Pakistan, China, India as a whole, and South Korea they are reported to be much larger. This is likely to be due to selective under-reporting and the increasing recourse to sex-selective abortions (see below). The differences between the regression from Klasen (1994) and our new expanded regression are very small, while the combined regression and the two African regressions show some more significant differences.

Based on the predicted sex ratios at birth from regressions 2 and 4 and the Model Life Tables "East," we calculate a baseline estimate of the number of missing females in the world, based on the most recent census information and population estimates for all regions with presumed excess female mortality.[25] Beginning with the global calculations, we present two figures. The first is just for the regions and countries considered in Coale (1991) and Klasen (1994) (called "Total comparable"), while the second includes the additional countries as discussed above.[26] The first figure shows an increase in the number of "missing women" from 87 million to 93 million. Thus, the cumulative impact of gender bias in mortality is exacting an increasing absolute toll on women world-wide. While this points to an *absolute* worsening, it suggests a slight *relative* improvement. The population in the countries suffering from excess female mortality increased by some 21 percent while the number of "missing women" increased by "only" about 7 percent. Thus gender bias in mortality has not increased in proportion to the population suggesting that, as a share of the female population, females now have slightly less unequal survival chances vis-à-vis males. This can also be seen in the share of "missing women" in the various countries considered. Compared to Table 1, this share has decreased in most regions, although the extent of the drop differs greatly between regions. The "total comparable" share of "missing women" has declined from 7.7 to 6.8 percent.

The largest drop, in percentage terms, occurred in Nepal, where results from the 2001 census suggest that the problem of "missing women" has all but disappeared. In fact, this drop had occurred already in the 1991 census and has held steady since. This sudden drop of the sex ratio is not very plausible, as will be shown below, so this result should be treated with some caution. The drop, in percentage terms, is also considerable in Bangladesh, Pakistan, and West Asia where the share of "missing women" (compared to the revised baseline) dropped by 3-5 percentage points. The fall is more modest in India and Egypt where it dropped by some 1-2 percentage points. In China, the share of "missing women" has actually increased by 0.4 percentage points to 6.7 percent (and the absolute number of missing females has increased to nearly 41 million), compared to the revised baseline where, after the census adjustments, the share was 6.3 percent and the absolute number of women stood at 35 million. As a result of improvements elsewhere, over 80 percent of the increase in the absolute number of "missing women" in the world is due to the increase in "missing women" in China. Owing to reductions in the share of "missing women" in Pakistan and Bangladesh, India now has the dubious distinction of having the largest share of "missing women" among the comparable set of countries, followed closely by Pakistan.

When we consider the additional countries, the total number of "missing women" increases to some 101 million, or 5.7 percent of the female population in the countries affected. The largest relative problem appears in Afghanistan which has the highest share of "missing women" anywhere in the world. These figures are, however, the least reliable in the table, and are based on United Nations estimates. The last census took place in 1979, and since then wars, refugee flows, and regime changes are likely to have affected sex ratios. Also, policies by the recently deposed Taliban regime that sharply limit women's access to education, healthcare, and employment are likely to have worsened the mortality situation for women and girls considerably, so that even these estimates might understate the true

277

state of affairs for women there. Taiwan also appears to have a considerable problem of gender bias in mortality, although the estimate suggests that it has improved over the past ten years. There are small shares of "missing women" in South Korea, Sri Lanka, Tunisia, Algeria, Sub-Saharan Africa, and Iran.[27] In Sub-Saharan Africa, the figures are highly sensitive to the assumptions about the sex ratio at birth and should therefore be treated with some caution (see below and also Klasen 1994, 1996a, 1996b). In this expanded set of countries, the trend points to a falling share of "missing women," with the exception of South Korea where the problem appears to have worsened slightly from a previously negligible share of "missing women."

When examining the factors underlying this overall relative improvement, one can distinguish between changes in the expected sex ratio and changes in the actual sex ratio. With the exception of South Korea, the expected sex ratio has increased in all other countries included. This is mainly due to the increase in the expected sex ratio at birth, as a result of improved longevity. The higher longevity has a second effect on the expected sex ratio. In populations that are growing and thus have a large share of young people, expanded longevity actually increases the expected sex ratio since males, due to their greater vulnerability in infancy and childhood, benefit relatively more from an equiproportionate mortality decline, so that the male excess at birth persists to higher ages. Conversely, falling population growth rates in some (though not all) regions would have reduced the expected sex ratio as the populations would age and females would dominate more. Since the expected sex ratios increased everywhere except in South Korea, the first two effects dominate the third.

What, however, happened to the actual sex ratio? With the exception of China, South Korea, and Sub-Saharan Africa where it increased slightly, it has fallen in all other regions. The decrease varies considerably. The largest decrease (which appears implausible and suggests past or present enumeration problems) was in Nepal, but there were also substantial reductions in Pakistan, Bangladesh, Taiwan, Sri Lanka, and West Asia. In Egypt, Syria, Turkey, Afghanistan, Algeria, Tunisia, and India the decrease was slight.[28] In countries that were not included in Coale (1991) and Klasen (1994), most have also experienced a decrease in their sex ratio. It is particularly noteworthy that the sex ratio in Sri Lanka dropped from 1.04 in 1981 to an estimated 1.00 in 1991. This is all the more impressive since Sri Lanka had a sex ratio of about 1.15 in 1951, much worse than India's at the same time, after which it fell consistently (Klasen 1999).

If gender bias in mortality had remained constant in relative terms, we would have expected rising actual sex ratios in all regions except South Korea.[29] Combined with population growth, this would have led to drastically rising numbers of "missing women." In reality, the actual sex

278

ratios dropped in most regions and these two factors combined are responsible for the more favorable relative picture, although existing population growth ensured that the *absolute* number of "missing women" increased in China, India, Pakistan, South Korea, Afghanistan, Egypt, and Sub-Saharan Africa.

Table 4 presents a sensitivity analysis on the number of "missing women," using five alternative calculations. They are designed to present not only other plausible alternative estimates, but also the impact of the various factors associated with the calculation of the expected sex ratio. Column 1 reproduces the figures from Table 3, our preferred estimates. Columns 2 and 3 only change the Model Life Tables to "West" and "North." As can be seen, the choice of Model Life Tables has a moderate impact on the estimated number of "missing women." Using the "West" tables and the comparable total (world total), the number of "missing women" is some 9 (12.5) million lower, while the "North" tables show a number of some 7 (8) million fewer "missing women," which gives some reassurance that particular mortality assumptions in the "East" tables are not largely driving the results. The various estimates also largely concur on the regional distribution of the problem and temporal trends. They all imply that while the absolute number of "missing women" has increased in the past decade, the share of "missing women" has declined.[30]

There are, however, slight shifts in relative emphasis. While the "West" tables generate lower numbers of "missing women" for all countries than the "East" tables, they do so particularly in high mortality environments (e.g., Sub-Saharan Africa) implying that females are expected to do relatively worse than males in these environments, while in low mortality environments, women are expected to do much better than males. The converse is the case in the "North" tables. Here females are not expected to do worse in high mortality environments, and as a result the number of "missing women" in South Asia and Sub-Saharan Africa is only slightly smaller than in the "East" tables. At the same time, in the "North" tables women's survival advantage is not presumed to increase so much as countries move from high to low mortality environments. As a result, the numbers and shares of "missing women" in low mortality environments such as China, Taiwan, or South Korea is the lowest in the "North" tables. Although they presume a larger overall natural female survival advantage than the other two, the "East" tables are thus in-between the "West" assumption of a drastically rising female survival advantage and the "North" assumption of only a very small increase in the female survival advantage, as countries move from high to low mortality populations.

Column 4 shows the number of "missing women" if we used the expected sex ratio at birth for non-African populations from Klasen (1994), reproduced in column 1 in Table 2 and column 3 in Table 2 for Sub-

Table 3 Number of "missing women," latest estimate (based on Model Life Tables "East" and adjusted sex ratio at birth)

	Year	Actual number of women	Actual sex ratio	Expected sex ratio at birth	Expected sex ratio	Expected number of women	Missing women	% missing
China	**2000**	**612.3**	**1.067**	**1.050**	**1.001**	**653.2**	**40.9**	**6.7**
Taiwan	1999	10.8	1.049	1.052	1.002	11.3	0.5	4.7
South Korea	1995	22.2	1.008	1.047	1.000	22.4	0.2	0.7
India	**2001**	**495.7**	**1.072**	**1.039**	**0.993**	**534.8**	**39.1**	**7.9**
Pakistan	**1998**	**62.7**	**1.081**	**1.042**	**1.003**	**67.6**	**4.9**	**7.8**
Bangladesh	**2001**	**63.4**	**1.038**	**1.040**	**0.996**	**66.1**	**2.7**	**4.2**
Nepal	**2001**	**11.6**	**0.997**	**1.037**	**0.992**	**11.7**	**0.1**	**0.5**
Sri Lanka	1991	8.6	1.005	1.052	1.006	8.6	0.0	0.0
West Asia	**2000**	**92.0**	**1.043**	**1.042**	**1.002**	**95.8**	**3.8**	**4.2**
of which:								
Turkey	1990	27.9	1.027	1.047	1.003	28.5	0.7	2.4
Syria	1994	6.7	1.047	1.048	1.016	6.9	0.2	3.1
Afghanistan	2000	11.1	1.054	1.024	0.964	12.1	1.0	9.3
Iran	1996	29.5	1.033	1.039	0.996	30.6	1.1	3.7
Egypt	**1996**	**29.0**	**1.048**	**1.044**	**1.003**	**30.3**	**1.3**	**4.5**
Algeria	1998	14.5	1.018	1.043	1.005	14.7	0.2	1.2
Tunisia	1994	4.3	1.021	1.043	1.000	4.4	0.1	2.1
Sub-Saharan Africa	2000	307.0	0.987	1.017	0.970	312.5	5.5	1.8
Total (Comparable)		**1,366.7**					**92.8**	**6.8**
Total (World)		1,774.8					101.3	5.7

Notes: Total (Comparable) includes China, India, Pakistan, Bangladesh, Nepal, West Asia, and Egypt and shown in bold. Total (World) additionally includes Taiwan, South Korea, Iran, Algeria, Tunisia, and Afghanistan. Turkey and Syria are subsumed in West Asia and are therefore not added separately. The expected sex ratio at birth is based on regressions 2 and 4 in Table 2. Actual and expected sex ratios refer to the number of males per females in the entire population; the expected sex ratio at birth refers to the number of males per female at birth.

Sources: Registrar General (2001), United Nations (1999, 2000), State Statistical Bureau (2001), Statistical Bureau of Taiwan (2001), Mustak Hossain (2001), and Sanjaya Dhakal (2001).

Table 4 Number of "missing women" using alternative assumptions

	(1) Preferred estimate		(2) West and adj. sex ratio at birth		(3) North and adj. sex ratio at birth		(4) East old adj. sex ratio at birth		(5) Coale: West fixed sex ratio at birth		(6) Sen: new sex ratio for Sub-Sah. Africa	
	No.	%	No.	%	No.	%	No.	%	No.	%	No.	%
China	40.9	6.7	37.8	6.2	36.0	5.9	40.5	6.6	32.3	5.3	49.9	8.2
Taiwan	0.5	4.7	0.4	3.9	0.4	3.7	0.5	4.7	0.3	3.2	0.7	6.3
South Korea	0.2	0.7	0.0	0.1	0.0	0.1	0.1	0.6	−0.2	−1.0	0.5	2.1
India	39.1	7.9	34.8	7.0	37.8	7.6	38.3	7.7	24.6	5.0	42.6	8.6
Pakistan	4.9	7.8	4.5	7.2	4.7	7.5	4.8	7.6	3.4	5.5	6.0	9.6
Bangladesh	2.7	4.2	2.2	3.5	2.5	4.0	2.6	4.1	1.0	1.6	3.3	5.2
Nepal	0.1	0.5	−0.0	−0.3	0.0	0.3	0.0	0.3	−0.3	−2.4	0.1	1.0
Sri Lanka	0.0	0.0	−0.1	−0.7	−0.1	−0.9	−0.0	−0.1	−0.1	−1.4	0.2	1.9
West Asia	3.8	4.2	3.3	3.6	3.6	3.9	3.8	4.1	1.8	2.0	5.3	5.7
of which:												
Turkey	0.7	2.4	0.5	1.9	0.6	2.0	0.6	2.3	0.2	0.7	1.1	4.0
Syria	0.2	3.1	0.2	2.7	0.2	2.7	0.2	3.0	0.1	1.6	0.4	6.1
Afghanistan	1.0	9.3	0.9	8.0	1.0	9.1	1.0	9.0	0.5	4.4	0.7	6.8
Iran	1.1	3.7	0.8	2.9	1.0	3.4	1.0	3.5	0.3	0.9	1.4	4.7
Egypt	1.3	4.5	1.1	3.9	1.2	4.1	1.3	4.3	0.7	2.4	1.8	6.2
Algeria	0.2	1.2	0.1	0.7	0.1	1.0	0.2	1.1	−0.1	−0.8	0.5	3.1
Tunisia	0.1	2.1	0.1	1.6	0.1	1.7	0.1	2.0	0.0	0.0	0.2	3.5
Sub-Saharan Africa	5.5	1.8	1.6	0.5	3.9	1.3	12.3	4.0	−3.6	−1.2	0.0	0.0
Total (Comparable)	92.8	6.8	83.7	6.1	85.8	6.3	91.3	6.7	63.6	4.7	108.9	8.0
Total (World)	101.3	5.7	87.6	4.9	92.3	5.2	106.5	6.0	60.6	3.4	113.0	6.4

Notes: The preferred estimate is taken from Table 3. In panel 2 (3), the only change is to switch from Model Life Tables "East" to "West" ("North"). In panel 4, we are back to using the "East" tables but use regressions 1 and 3 in Table 2 for the sex ratio at birth. In panel 5, Coale's method is reproduced, i.e. using the "West" tables and a sex ratio at birth of 1.059 is assumed for all countries except Sub-Saharan Africa where a sex ratio of 1.034 is assumed for Sub-Saharan Africa. In panel 6, we apply Sen's approach of using the population sex ratio of Sub-Saharan as the benchmark, but apply the current population sex ratio for that region.

281

Saharan Africa. This leads to little change in the comparable figure. The only significant change is the much larger number of missing females in Sub-Saharan Africa.

Column 5 shows the impact if we used the "West" tables and chose (inappropriately, as we have argued above) a constant sex ratio at birth of 1.059 as done in Coale (1991). The number of "missing women" would drop by some 40 million, and 30 million on a comparable basis to Coale (1991).[31] But Coale's method would also suggest a rising absolute and a falling relative number of "missing women."

Column 6 shows the impact of Sen's assumption by using Sub-Saharan Africa's current sex ratio as the benchmark. Since the sex ratio in Sub-Saharan Africa has been increasing, this benchmark no longer yields numbers that are much greater than the preferred estimates presented here. It suggests that there are some 113 million "missing women" (and 109 on a comparable basis), and the increase in this number over the past ten years is the smallest (in absolute and relative terms) when this assumption is used.

While the different estimates differ in terms of the total numbers of "missing women" and partly also in their regional distribution, they are similar in terms of a rising absolute number and a falling relative number of "missing women." This is reassuring given the differences in assumptions underlying the calculations.[32]

III. ANALYZING TRENDS IN GENDER BIAS IN MORTALITY

From the tables in the last section, we can generate the following stylized facts regarding trends in gender bias in mortality. While in absolute terms, the number of "missing women" has increased, in relative terms it is falling in most places. Sharp reductions, in relative terms, occurred in North Africa, and parts of South Asia, most notably Nepal, Bangladesh, and Pakistan (from very high levels) as well as West Asia. In Sri Lanka, gender bias in mortality disappeared entirely. Moderate reductions took place in India, Tunisia, Turkey, Syria, Iran, Afghanistan, and Egypt, while slight increases in the share of "missing women" occurred in South Korea and Sub-Saharan Africa. Lastly, China has experienced a significant increase in gender bias which is largely responsible for the world-wide increase in the absolute number of "missing women." What factors are driving these uneven developments?

Before discussing this it is important to briefly review the most important findings on both the mechanisms and the causal factors associated with excess female mortality. Most studies have shown that the most important process driving excess female mortality is unequal access to healthcare which leads to higher mortality of young girls (e.g., Chen, Huq, and D'Souza 1981; Alaka Basu 1992; Harold Alderman and Paul Gertler 1997;

Ian Timaeus, Katie Harris, and Francesca Fairbairn 1998; Klasen 1999; Croll 2000; Gautam Hazarika 2000). In contrast, differences in access to nutrition appear to be a smaller factor, if present at all (e.g., Chen, Huq, D'Souza 1981; Sen and Sengupta 1983; Basu 1992; Kenneth Hill and Dawn Upchurch 1995; Elizabeth Somerfelt and Fred Arnold 1998; Hazarika 2000). This comparative neglect of female children, which is generally worse in rural areas, appears to be particularly severe for later-born girls and among them even worse for girls with elder sisters (Das Gupta 1987; Pradib Muhuri and Samuel Preston 1991; Drèze and Sen 1995; Klasen 1999).

In addition, sex-selective abortions seem to have played an increasing role in some countries experiencing "missing women," most notably China, South Korea, and recently also India (Judith Banister and Ansley Coale 1994; Chai Bin Park and Nam-Hoon Cho 1995; Croll 2000; Registrar General 2001). The most important evidence of this is the rising observed sex ratios at birth which appears to be due largely to sex-selective abortions rather than the under-registration of female infants (Croll 2000; Banister and Coale 1994; Chu Junhong 2001; Registrar General 2001). While excess deaths due to unequal access to resources and sex-selective abortions have the same result, namely missing women, it is not clear whether the two processes should be seen as ethically equivalent. On the one hand, one may argue that female deaths due to sex-specific neglect are equivalent to abortions of female fetuses as they both terminate female life prematurely and are an outgrowth of discriminatory and demeaning attitudes towards women. In fact, one may argue that sex-selective abortions are more problematic as it leads to death (or prevention of female life) with certainty, while female neglect only increases the chance of female mortality. Moreover, sex-selective abortions are associated with late-term abortions which pose other health hazards to women. On the other hand, one may argue that sex-selective abortions are a somewhat lesser evil, as one should distinguish between pre-birth and post-birth interventions, with the latter usually judged worse than the former. This may be particularly the case if greater recourse to sex-selective abortions leads to a reduction of female neglect of those girls that end up being born, which some claim to be the case empirically (Daniel Goodkind 1996). Also, in the case of sex-selective abortions, interventions to combat the practice, such as (largely unen-forced) bans on pre-natal sex determination in India and China, would have to balance the rights of a fetus with those of a woman. It is not possible to resolve this issue here, which is treated more fully elsewhere.[33] But it is important to note that the evaluation of "missing women" might depend on the process by which they went "missing" in the first place.

While these appear to be the most important processes generating gender bias in mortality, there is now an increasing literature on the most important underlying causes of this neglect of female children. Cross-sectional evidence suggests that high sex ratios and high relative female mortality are associated with low female employment opportunities (e.g., Mark Rosenzweig and Paul Schultz 1982; Sen 1990a; Mamta Murthi, Anne-Catherine Guio, and Jean Drèze 1995; Stephan Klasen 2001), and higher female education appears to lower excess female mortality, although the effects of this appear to be nonlinear (Das Gupta 1987; Drèze and Sen 1995; Murthi, Guio, and Drèze 1995; World Bank 2001). There also are a number of customs and cultural practices that appear to hurt females in some regions. Among them are virilocal marriage patterns, ancestor worship undertaken by sons, high dowry payments for brides, and the emulation by the lower strata of practices prevalent among the upper strata of society (e.g., Tim Dyson and Mick Moore 1983; Drèze and Sen 1995; Croll 2000).

Also, it appears that scarcity of economic resources is a necessary but not sufficient condition for gender bias in mortality. Although the differential treatment of girls emerges when households are forced to ration scarce resources allocated to nutrition and healthcare, in many countries the poorest sections of the population experience less gender bias in mortality than slightly richer groups (e.g., Drèze and Sen 1995; Murthi, Guio, and Drèze 1995; Klasen 1999, 2001). This is presumably related to greater female economic independence and fewer cultural strictures among the poorest sections of the population.[34]

Lastly, state policy can critically influence gender bias in mortality. To the extent that the state provides free access to nutrition and healthcare, the need to ration scarce household resources is lessened. This can especially help disadvantaged girls. Similarly, state activism in the field of female education and employment can improve the situation of girls. Conversely, strict family planning policies, such as the one-child policy in China, can heighten discriminatory practices as couples try to ensure that their registered and surviving child is a boy.[35]

Based on these factors influencing the survival patterns of girls, a tentative interpretation of current trends in the different regions can be attempted.

(a) North Africa and West Asia

In North Africa and West Asia, the relative improvement in female survival is not only apparent in the sex ratios but can also be deduced from mortality statistics. In all countries, female life expectancy surpassed male life expectancy in the last two decades and female advantage is growing (Dominique Tabutin 1991; Carolyn Makinson 1994; Carla Obermeyer and Rosario Cárdenas 1997). The most important factors accounting for this relative improvement appear to be improved female education and employment opportunities, and generally rising prosperity in these middle-income countries, which lessens the need to ration scarce health and nutrition resources to the disadvantage of little girls.

(b) Sub-Saharan Africa

Here there is great uncertainty about levels and trends in gender bias in mortality as shown in Table 4. The estimates range from significant gender bias against females to a slight bias favoring females, although the latter is based on the problematic assumption of a fixed sex ratio at birth. But it is clear that gender bias in mortality is smaller than in South, East, and West Asia. This is also consistent with available mortality data as well as with the much stronger economic roles and labor force participation of women, particularly in rural areas, and with prevailing marriage practices. These mortality data, however, point to a worsening situation for females in the last twenty years (Klasen 1996a, 1996b).

(c) East Asia

In East Asia, we see a decrease in gender bias in mortality in Taiwan, a deterioration from low levels of gender bias in South Korea, and high and increasing levels of gender bias in China. In the former two countries, rapidly rising prosperity has reduced the need to ration scarce resources and has sharply improved female education and employment opportunities (World Bank 2001). At the same time, there continues to be considerable discrimination against female infants which by now appears to have shifted largely to sex-selective abortions. In South Korea, the sex ratio at birth has increased to above 1.1 in the early 1990s which points to a considerable incidence of sex-selective abortions (Park and Cho 1995). But due to very low overall fertility rates, the demographic impact of this phenomenon is smaller than elsewhere (Park and Cho 1995; Ulla Larson, Woojin Chung, and Monica Das Gupta 1998; Croll 2000), while the survival advantage of females in older age groups now has a considerably larger demographic impact. Similarly, Taiwan has unusually high sex ratios at birth. This appears to be linked to sex-selective abortions (Croll 2000).

China is the country that has experienced a rising overall sex ratio and a worsening of the share of "missing women." A disaggregation by age group shows that most of the worsening has taken place in the first few years. The sex ratio among the 0–4-year-olds rose from 1.07 to 1.10 between 1982 and 1990 and is believed to have increased further after that (State Statistical Bureau 1997).[36] A smaller rise took place among the 5–9 age group while the sex ratio remained constant among the 10–19 group. Conversely, the sex ratio has fallen considerably among all age groups between 20 and 65 (State Statistical Bureau 1997).

This worsening in the overall sex ratio in China comes despite considerable improvements in the first few decades of communist rule where the expansion of free public health services and public provision of nutrition greatly reduced the previously existing discrimination against female children (see Drèze and Sen 1989, 1995; Klasen 1999). The most important reasons for the deterioration in recent years appear to be twofold. First, the significant changes in the organization of public services in connection with the economic reforms that began in the late 1970s. This involved the dissolution of the communes that had previously provided free healthcare and food. Now the provision of these goods is largely back in the hands of households, which has enabled discriminatory practices to re-emerge (Judith Banister 1987; Drèze and Sen 1995; Klasen 1993, 1999). Second, the one-child policy has sharply increased the incentive of parents to discriminate against female children as they want to ensure that the officially registered child is a boy. This policy has led parents to adopt several strategies, including the abandonment of girl children, illegal adoptions, the hiding of girls, the refusal to get the one-child certificate in the case of a first-born girl, and an increasing incidence of sex-selective abortions (e.g., Banister 1987; Sten Johannson and Ola Nygren 1991; Banister and Coale 1994; Klasen 1999; Junhong 2001). The rising sex ratio at birth is testimony to these strategies, although it is unclear to what extent the different strategies mentioned are responsible for this rise in the sex ratio at birth from 1.08 in the 1982 census, to 1.17 in the 2000 census and the correspondingly high sex ratios among the young (Croll 2000; Junhong 2001; Shanghai Star 2002). Clearly, however, the one-child policy is one of the most important underlying causes for the continued rise of "missing women" in China. Conversely, falling sex ratios among all adult age groups suggest that improving overall health conditions, incomes, female education, and employment opportunities have extended female life spans beyond the childhood years. Largely due to the pressures inherent in the one-child policy, the former effect clearly overshadows the latter and leads to the lamentable worsening of the sex ratio in China.

(d) South Asia

In South Asia, we saw dramatic progress in Nepal and Sri Lanka, substantial progress in Bangladesh and Pakistan, and moderate progress in India. Beginning with Nepal, recent censuses showed dramatic variations in the sex ratio over time. In 1961 it was alleged to be 0.91, rising to 1.05 in 1981, falling to 0.99 in 1991, and stabilizing at around 1.00 in 2001. While some of these oscillations are due to male-dominated migration to and from India, they also raise some serious questions about the validity of these estimates. In particular, the massive increase in the sex ratio in 1981 and the subsequent drop in 1991 appears highly implausible. One way to see this is to examine the ratio of 20–24-year-old women in 1991 to 10–14-year-old girls in 1981, which we call the survival rate. In the impossible case of no mortality between 1981 and 1991 of the cohort aged 10–14 in 1981 the survival rate would be 1. In fact, it is 1.09, indicating that there are 9 percent more 20–24-year-old females in 1991 than there were 10–14-year-old girls in 1981; and for 25–29-year-old women in 1991 to 15–19-year-old women in 1981 it is an even more implausible 1.15 (Central Bureau of Statistics 1995).[37] This points to an improved enumeration of females in 1991, compared to 1981. Examining the sex ratio by age group does not allow a full resolution of the issue. The "missing women" in 1981 were mainly concentrated in the 10–19 age group as well as in the age groups above 45, and it is precisely in these age groups where there are the largest improvements in 1991. Both could be due to under-enumeration of females in 1981 (as shown in the survival rates for the 10–19 age group) and also partly due to some improvement of female survival moving slowly upwards along the age cohorts. At the same time, the sex ratios are particularly low in the age groups 20–45. This is likely to be related to male out-migration and could thus understate the extent of existing gender bias in mortality (as these "missing men" reduce the sex ratio and thus the estimate of "missing women" who died as a result of gender bias in mortality).

Existing analyses of mortality trends continue to point to higher mortality of girls between 1 and 4 years, although the extent of excess female mortality is smaller than elsewhere in South Asia (Ajit Pradhan, Ram Hari Aryal, Gokarna Regmi, Bharat Ban, and Pavalavalli Govindasamy 1997). Given the paucity of data, at present it is difficult to tell to what extent there has indeed been an improvement, but it appears clear that some of the allegedly "missing women" in 1981 had not been enumerated then (rather than having died) and have been enumerated in subsequent censuses. Conversely, significant male out-migration underestimates the extent of gender bias in mortality. Overall, Nepal's record of gender bias in mortality points to considerable and continued gender bias in mortality, although its record is somewhat better than that of its southern and northern neighbors.

In Pakistan, there has been a considerable reduction in the sex ratio between 1981 and 1998, which followed an earlier reduction between the 1972 and the 1981 censuses. But these improvements came from extremely high initial levels. In 1972, the population sex ratio stood at 1.14, and dropped to a very high 1.10 in 1981 (Government of Pakistan 1995). Part of the improvement is likely to be related to improved enumeration of females, particularly between 1972 and 1981, but also to some extent between 1981 and 1998.[38] At the same time, there appears to have been a real improvement as well, mostly related to improved female education and employment opportunities as well as growing urban populations where sex ratios have fallen particularly fast. But clearly, female disadvantage prevails, as illustrated by higher female than male post-neonatal and child mortality rates and discrimination against females in access to medical care (Alderman and Gertler 1997; Claudia Wink 2000).

In Bangladesh, there have been steady reductions in the sex ratio since 1951 when it stood at 1.10, with a small setback between 1961 and 1974 (Bangladesh Bureau of Statistics 1999). Bangladesh's age–sex structure is unusual in the sense that the male excess is larger in older than younger age groups, and is surprisingly small among the young. This points to a combination of continued discrimination in survival chances for females throughout the lifecycle (and not just in infancy and childhood), combined with very high overall mortality (in the earlier census) that, as discussed above, ensured that the male excess at birth eroded quickly due to high overall mortality and higher proportional male susceptibility. The improvements in the overall sex ratio are largely due to reductions among the age groups older than 10. While some of this might also be related to improved enumeration of females in later censuses,[39] there also appear to have been real improvements that can be seen in mortality statistics, particularly in older age groups (Bangladesh Bureau of Statistics 1999; Wink 2000). Rapidly rising female education (from a very low level), reductions in maternal mortality, and growing female employment opportunities are likely causes for these improvements.

Sri Lanka is a country that has experienced a dramatic turnaround in gender bias in mortality. The sex ratio declined from 1.15 in 1951 more or less continuously to an estimated 1.00 in 1991. While the early high sex ratio was partly driven by male-based immigration and estate labor, data on mortality differentials bear out the change from high excess female mortality to its complete disappearance over the past forty years (Patrick Peebles 1982; T. Nadarajah 1983; Department of Census and Statistics 1988; Christopher Langford and Pamela Storey 1993).[40] Critical to the success in Sri Lanka were the free provision of food and healthcare, which obviated the need for households to ration these vital resources differentially and ensured adequate access for girls. Investments in female education and employment added to this positive trend (see Drèze and Sen 1995; Klasen 1999).

Lastly, we turn to India. While some authors had predicted an improvement in the sex ratio basing their assessment on improvements in female relative mortality rates (Drèze and Sen 1995; Wink 2000), others had predicted a deterioration (Das Gupta and Mari Bhat 1997; Mayer 1999). In particular, it was argued that fertility decline would lead to an intensification of gender bias, since parents would attempt to ensure that they had at least one male child. The method of achieving this would partly be a rise in infanticide but mostly greater recourse to sex-selective abortions (Das Gupta and Mari Bhat 1997; Alaka Basu 1999; S. Sudha and S. Irudaya Rajan 1999). Moreover, it was argued that gender bias was worsening and would continue to worsen particularly in South India, where the marriage and female employment patterns that led to large bias in northern India were increasingly emulated (Basu 1999; S. Irudaya Rajan, S. Sudha, and P. Mohanachandran 2000).

As shown above, we observe a slight reduction in the sex ratio in the 2001 census after a deterioration in 1991. In fact, the 2001 results are similar to the 1981 results, and there are reasons to believe that some of the oscillations in those three censuses are also due to better female enumeration in 2001 and deficits in enumeration of females in 1991 (Dyson 2001).[41]

In fact, several opposing trends seem to be operating here. On the one hand, there is evidence of clear improvements in female survival, particularly in the older age groups. The relative mortality of females above age 30 has steadily declined over the past decades (Drèze and Sen 1995; Wink 2000), leading to considerable reduction in the sex ratio of the population age 7 and above from 1.083 in 1991 to 1.070 in 2001.[42] Conversely, the sex ratio among 0–6-year-olds has steadily increased (between 1991 and 2001 it increased from 1.058 to 1.079), pointing to the increasing disadvantage faced by young girls or to increasing use of sex-selective abortions. While mortality statistics do not generally indicate either a worsening or an improvement in female relative survival in these young age groups (Wink 2000), the latest census results point particularly to the latter phenomenon over the past twenty years. This is consistent with the rise in the sex ratio at birth (Registrar General 2001; Jean Drèze and Mamta Murthi 2001).[43]

One way to examine trends in India more closely is to explore the determinants of the large regional variation in the sex ratio in recent censuses. This is done in Table 5 where we use the insights from the theoretical discussions about the determinants of gender bias reviewed above. In particular, we expect women's education and employment to strengthen their economic independence and thus reduce gender bias in mortality and sex ratios. In addition, we test for the influence of fertility in order to examine whether fertility reduction leads to an intensification of gender bias, and also control for urbanization, infant mortality, and population density, which have all been found to play a role in the literature. Third, we include regional dummy variables to control for large differences in marriage practices that are likely to influence relative mortality. Lastly, we include time dummies to investigate recent trends.

We present three regressions here. The first is a more complete model predicting the sex ratio of India's sixteen largest states. For this model we only have data for 1971 to 1991. The second model is more restricted in the choice of variables but allows us to include 2001 in the analysis. The third model is the most parsimonious but allows us to additionally include 1961 in the assessment. A number of interesting results emerge. First, female labor force participation (female main workers as a share of the total female population) and female literacy (share of women age 7 and above

Table 5 Determinants of the state-specific sex ratios in India, 1961–2001

Time period	(1) 1971–91	(2) 1971–2001	(3) 1961–2001
Constant	117.42	111.99	115.43
	(7.69)***	(2.36)***	(2.14)***
Female Labour Force Participation	− 0.21	− 0.19	
	(0.06)***	(0.06)***	
Female Literacy	− 0.17	− 0.16	− 0.20
	(0.10)*	(0.03)***	(0.04)***
Male Literacy	− 0.06		
	(0.10)		
Total Fertility Rate	0.20		
	(0.96)		
Infant Mortality Rate	− 0.03		
	(0.02)*		
Urbanization Rate	0.26	0.31	
	(0.07)***	(0.05)***	
Population Density	0.007	0.005	0.014
	(0.004)**	(0.002)**	(0.003)***
South Dummy	− 6.81	− 7.99	− 8.14
	(1.30)***	(1.11)***	(1.07)***
East Dummy	− 5.57	− 4.90	− 7.24
	(1.42)***	(0.93)***	(1.18)***
West Dummy	− 2.66	− 4.35	− 0.65
	(1.60)*	(1.34)***	(1.30)
1961 dummy			− 5.26
			(2.01)***
1971 dummy	− 3.15	− 2.83	− 4.03
	(1.57)**	(1.43)**	(1.83)**
1981 dummy	− 3.12	− 3.25	− 4.11
	(1.11)***	(1.20)***	(1.65)***
1991 dummy		− 0.86	− 1.40
		(0.89)	(1.40)
Adj. *R*-Squared	0.872	0.822	0.606
N	43	60	75

Notes: Standard errors in parentheses. *** Refers to 99%; ** to 95%; and * to 90% significance levels. The states included are grouped into four regions: North consisting of Haryana, Himachal Pradesh, Punjab, Madhya Pradesh, Rajasthan, and Uttar Pradesh; East consisting of Bihar, Orissa, and West Bengal; South consisting of Andhra Pradesh, Karnataka, Kerala, and Tamil Nadu; and West consisting of Gujarat and Maharashtra. In 2001, data for new additional states that were carved out of the existing states of Uttar Pradesh, Bihar, and Madhya Pradesh, are reported. We add the figures for these new states (Jharkhand, Chhatisgarh, and Uttaranchal) to the figures for the remaining (but now smaller) states of UP, MP, and Bihar to make them comparable with the previous state figures.

who are literate) have the expected large effect on reducing sex ratios. This is the case in all three regressions and thus appears to hold strongly across space and time in India. It is important to point out that the two effects, while of similar magnitude, play a different role in explaining trends in gender bias in mortality. While female labor force participation has increased very slowly across time and thus did not greatly influence the development of the sex ratio over time, female literacy has increased very

sharply and thus would have, *ceteris paribus*, led to a considerable reduction
in sex ratios. Second, reduced fertility does not appear to influence the sex
ratio as was feared by some authors (e.g., Das Gupta and Mari Bhat 1997).
Third, both population density and urbanization are associated with higher
sex ratios, which suggests that the univariate finding of improved relative
mortality in urban areas is driven by greater female education and
employment in urban areas rather than urbanization per se. In recent
years, urbanization could also be an indicator of the availability of sex-
selective abortions. Fourth, there remain sizable regional variations
captured by the dummy variables, suggesting that the South and the East
are much less affected than the North, with the West taking an intermediate
position.[44] They are likely to be related to cultural practices (particularly
relating to marriage arrangements) as well as state policies that differ
dramatically across regions in India (e.g., Dyson and Moore 1983; Bina
Agarwal 1994; Drèze and Sen 1995). Lastly, there appears to be a time trend
suggesting worsening sex ratios. This is partly a result of a rising expected
sex ratio due to improved longevity (and its impact on the sex ratio at birth
and mortality patterns) as discussed above, and partly a result of a general
intensification of gender bias for a given level of female literacy,
employment, and urbanization. More recently this may be captured by
the effect of the spread of sex-selective abortions. Earlier, this may capture
the effects of "sanskritization," or the effect of the increasing emulation of
marriage and location patterns (especially dowries) across social classes and
regions that are disadvantageous to females (Basu 1999). The aggregate
evidence could thus be interpreted as suggesting that improving female
education and labor force participation in recent years has helped reduce
the sex ratio, while improved methods of discrimination (such as sex-
selective abortions) and the spread of marriage practices unfavorable to
women have worsened matters, which shows up in the worsening time
trend. Since the sex ratio fell slightly in the last ten years, it appears that the
former trends have been slightly more important than the latter ones. The
existence of the latter ones have, however, militated against more dramatic
improvements in gender bias in mortality as have been observed in other
parts of South Asia, and now make India the country with the highest share
of "missing women" in the region. Thus we are presented with mixed
evidence on the development of gender bias in India. The future path of
gender bias in mortality will depend on the strength of these two opposing
forces and their regional trajectories.

IV. CONCLUSION

Amartya Sen set off an important debate when he raised the issue of
"missing women" as a way to estimate and illustrate the cumulative impact
of female survival disadvantage in parts of the developing world. In this

chapter we have presented a short review of that debate as well as discussed current trends in gender bias in mortality. We find that the number of "missing women" has increased in absolute terms to over 100 million, based on our preferred methodology. At the same time, there appears to have been a relative improvement in the share of "missing women," suggesting that the phenomenon has stabilized at a high level. Regional analyses point to a definite improvement for women in North Africa and West Asia, some improvements in South Asia which, however, appear overstated and are partly related to better enumeration of females, and a deterioration in China that is related largely to its strict family planning policies. Larger improvements in Bangladesh and Pakistan ensure that India (where improvements have been small and subject to opposing factors and regional variations), now has the largest share of missing females in South Asia. The deterioration in China leads to a considerable increase in the absolute number of "missing women," which accounts for most of the global increase in "missing women." Improving female education and employment continue to be important avenues for lowering the sex ratio. This is an important area of state intervention, as are ways to directly deliver adequate nutrition and healthcare for girls. The latter has been shown to be remarkably successful in Sri Lanka and pre-reform China. Lastly, the increasing ability to discriminate against girls, particularly through sex-selective abortions, necessitates greater effort to combat the underlying causes of gender bias in mortality. Despite slight improvements in recent years, much greater efforts are needed to combat this most egregious form of gender discrimination in the future.

ACKNOWLEDGMENTS

We would like to thank Amartya Sen for having inspired us to work on this issue over the past several years and for helpful comments and discussion. We also want to thank Katarina Smutna and Andreas Beivers for excellent research assistance, the journal's three anonymous referees, the editors of this volume, and the participants of workshops at the Center for Population and Development Studies (Harvard University), at Oxford University, and at the University of Munich, for helpful comments and discussions.

NOTES

[1] The first academic reference to "missing women" was in Amartya Sen (1986) which only focused on India, China, Bangladesh, and Pakistan, and came up with a figure of about 75 million based on the census returns from the early 1980s. Sen (1989, 1990b) also included other regions, notably the Middle East and North Africa.

[2] Also here Sen made a number of important contributions, most notably in Drèze and Sen (1989, 1995). As with gender bias in mortality, he made some illustrative calculations to show the magnitude of the problem. By comparing China with India, he showed that the higher mortality caused by endemic deprivation and poor public services in India was claiming 4 million additional deaths per year, compared to China's much better record in this regard (Drèze and Sen 1989).

[3] This is not to criticize the concern and support that is extended in the case of these catastrophes, which surely helps to mitigate their impact. Instead, we want to support Sen in arguing that the silent killer of women and girls ought to provoke similar responses.

[4] There are difficult methodological issues to resolve, in particular regarding the "expected" mortality rates of women relative to men in the hypothetical case of "equal treatment." See Stephan Klasen (1998, 1999) for a discussion.

[5] In contrast to Coale and Klasen, Sen, in line with practice in India, always used the female – male ratio, the inverse of the sex ratio. To avoid confusion, we consistently use the sex ratio, i.e., the number of males divided by females, and have modified Sen's data accordingly.

[6] By holding the number of men constant in that hypothetical calculation, the implicit assumption (as also in the other method) is that the number of women could be increased without correspondingly reducing the number of males. Since the distribution of survival-related goods is, at least in part, a zero-sum game, it is not clear whether one could increase the number of females without at least somewhat reducing the number of males.

[7] As we show below, even censuses contain biases and (often sex-specific) under-registration. Apart from being the only national statistic available, they also tend to be more reliable, since vital registration data often have selective under-registration of births and/or deaths.

[8] In particular, since women have a large survival advantage in older age groups, the aging societies of the industrialized world are increasingly female-dominated. Another factor responsible for the high female excess in European countries is the legacy of World War II, which decimated male cohorts disproportionately.

[9] In some publications, Sen also used the sex ratio (males/females) prevailing in rich countries of 0.95 as an alternative benchmark (see, e.g., Sen 1990a). This benchmark is more problematic than Sub-Saharan Africa for four reasons (see also Coale 1991). First, as noted above, the low sex ratio in Europe is partly the result of World War II, which heavily decimated male cohorts. Second, and of increasing importance, is the large share of elderly among European populations compared to those of developing countries. Since women predominate among the elderly, a large share of the elderly reduces the sex ratio beyond the levels one would expect in the young societies of developing countries. Third, the behavioral patterns that lead to high mortality among males (compared to females) are particularly prevalent in rich countries where all population groups have widespread access to products which can cause death, such as automobiles, cigarettes, and alcohol. Fourth, the mortality resulting from these behavioral patterns constitutes a larger share of overall mortality in these otherwise low-

mortality populations, thus leading to particularly depressed sex ratios favoring females.

[10] This is not only apparent from data on sex ratios at birth in Africa, but also from Africans in the US and the Caribbean, and has been well-documented (e.g., Michael Teitelbaum 1970; Michael Teitelbaum and Nathan Mantel 1971; John W. Khoury, J. D. Erickson, and L. M. James 1983; Anoushe Chanazarian 1986; William James 1986). For a more detailed discussion, see Klasen (1994). While it is likely that sex ratios at birth in other regions of the world differ slightly, and that, due to its high genetic diversity, the sex ratio at birth also likely differs within Africa, these differences have not been found to be large enough to be detected with any certainty in available demographic data. The precise biological reasons for these slight differences in the sex ratio are unclear; interestingly, they appear to be inversely related to twinning rates. For details, refer to James (1986) and Chanazarian (1986).

[11] This is explicitly the case in the calculations of Coale and Klasen, and implicitly so in Sen's benchmark, since sex-selective abortions in Sub-Saharan Africa are likely to be extremely rare. See Section III for a discussion of these issues.

[12] There is another set of Model Life Tables, the regional Model Life Tables produced by the United Nations (1982) which are based on the actual mortality experience of different regions of the developing world. They are, however, entirely unsuitable for this type of analysis since gender inequality in mortality is their built-in feature. For example, the South Asian tables would suggest that girls and women would "normally" die at higher rates than boys and men, so that comparing actual mortality in South Asia with these tables would not reveal a problem of excess female mortality at all. This is not consistent with the biomedical evidence of the large survival advantages of females in infancy and old age and the slight advantage in most groups in-between.

[13] In contrast, the female survival advantage in infancy and older ages is larger in the "East" tables, which consequently generates the highest number of implied "missing women" below.

[14] For example, Kuwait, an important destination for migrants in the 1970s and early 1980s, had a sex ratio of 1.32, clearly above what one would expect. Among natives, the sex ratio was 0.99 while among the foreign-born population it was a staggering 1.61, showing the male bias in immigration. But the excess of males among the foreign-born population, which mostly originated from Egypt, Bangladesh, India, and Palestine, was a mere 0.3 million, thus hardly affecting the sex ratios in the countries of origin with a combined population of some 900 million at the time (United Nations 1991).

[15] Thus the estimate of "missing women" in the world and most countries affected by it is not very sensitive to international migration. In contrast, a more significant portion of the generally small changes in the number of "missing women" over time in a particular country can be affected by changes in sex-specific international migration and will therefore be considered when we discuss trends in individual countries.

[16] Stable populations are those that have constant fertility and constant mortality rates and thus generate a stable age distribution. Quasi-stable populations are populations that have roughly constant fertility and constantly falling mortality and will also generate a stable age distribution. Coale assumed that the developing countries with missing women were quasi-stable. To adjust for the fact that most countries not only have falling mortality but also falling fertility levels, he did not take the fertility levels at the time of the census but rather the levels prevailing some twenty years earlier. This generates roughly average fertility levels for the cohorts alive at the time of the census. See below and Stephan Klasen and Claudia Wink (2002) for a discussion of this assumption.

[17] The expected sex ratio is calculated in the following manner. First, based on life expectancy some fifteen years earlier, the level of the life table is chosen from the "West" tables in Coale, Demeny, and Vaughan (1983). Then according to population growth some fifteen years earlier, the stable population structure is chosen for that level based on the same source. Finally, the indicator population size per births for males is multiplied by the sex ratio at birth (here assumed to be 1.059), and then divided by the population size per births for females. The population size per births is also found in the Model Life Tables. The procedure is explained with an example in Coale, Demeny, and Vaughan (1983). See also Klasen and Wink (2002) for further details.

[18] There is a large literature documenting that the sex ratio *in utero* is considerably higher than at birth, and that the sex ratio of miscarriages, spontaneous abortions, and stillbirths is much larger than the sex ratio at birth. As a result, improving health conditions that reduce the incidence of miscarriages and stillbirths will increase the sex ratio at birth, which is consistent with the secular trends in the sex ratio at birth. For a detailed discussion see Klasen (1994) and Chanazarian (1986).

[19] Moreover, Coale (1991), and, by implication, Klasen (1994) erroneously reported the sex ratio in West Asia in 1990, in the quoted source, to be 1.060 instead of the correct 1.073 (United Nations 1991). This increased the number of "missing women" there by about 0.7 million. Lastly, the life expectancy assumptions underlying the choice of life tables and the appropriate sex ratio at birth in Bangladesh in Klasen (1994) were too low. This led to an overestimation of the number of missing women in Bangladesh by some 0.5 million. This does not, however, invalidate the differences between Coale and Klasen in the relative assessment of gender bias in mortality in Bangladesh, especially vis-à-vis China.

[20] For example, the census figures for Bangladesh in 1991 have been adjusted several times, with implications for the sex ratio. While the preliminary count of the 1991 census found 105 million people and a sex ratio of 1.063, after two sets of adjustments, the population was fixed at 111 million and a sex ratio of 1.059 (see People's Perspectives 1993).

[21] We also show figures for Syria and Turkey, although they are already included in the regional estimate for "missing women" in West Asia.

[22] Population estimates for the region as a whole are included, since censuses from individual countries are less reliable than elsewhere and migration within Africa is quite significant.

[23] If we restrict the pooled regression just to observations from African-Americans from the US (not shown here), the African population dummy is even larger (− 0.019) and as significant, and the impact of life expectancy on the sex ratio at birth similar to regressions 1, 2, or 4.

[24] These predictions are based on life expectancy in the early to mid-1980s to ensure that they roughly capture the average sex ratio at birth for the cohorts alive today. This is in keeping with Coale's (1991) suggestion.

[25] Note that using regression 5 would have yielded much larger estimates of "missing women," since the predicted sex ratios at birth are considerably lower and thus the expected sex ratios would be lower as well, leading to more "missing women." See also the sensitivity analysis below.

[26] Klasen and Wink (2002) provide a baseline estimate of "missing women" for these additional countries for the 1980s and early 1990s.

[27] The estimate for Iran might understate the true impact of gender bias in mortality since the Iran – Iraq war claimed the lives of more than a million men, and this artificially reduced the sex ratio and might therefore hide a considerable problem of gender bias in mortality.

[28] The decrease in India might be due partly to a more accurate count of females in 2001, compared to 1991 (Tim Dyson 2001), in which case the high sex ratio in 1991 and the resulting number of missing females was somewhat overestimated. In any case, we no longer see a worsening of the sex ratio in India.

[29] In South Korea, the only country where we would have expected to see a decline in the sex ratio, we find an increase and thus the emergence of "missing women."

[30] This last point cannot be read from the table, since no calculations are presented using these assumptions and the earlier data, but these can be found in Klasen and Wink (2002).

[31] Note that the difference between this assumption and the preferred estimate proposed here is slightly smaller in relative terms than it was in Klasen (1994), where the preferred estimate increased the number of missing women by some 50 percent. This is because the assumption of a constant sex ratio would, by definition, exclude the increase in the expected sex ratio at birth that is partly driving the somewhat smaller relative female disadvantage.

[32] Apart from these assumptions, one may also question whether the assumption of a quasi-stable population, inherent in all estimates except Sen's, is still appropriate in some of the countries. Clearly, the age structure in China, as well as in India, South Korea, Taiwan, and most North African countries, is changing rapidly as low fertility rates generate an increasingly aged population. Ignoring this effect would potentially underestimate the number of "missing women," since the falling birth rates hit particularly the young cohorts which are more male-dominated. This would reduce the true expected sex ratio of a population and thus increase the number of "missing women." Since we have used the demographic conditions (especially population growth) from 1980–85 rather than the current ones, we have tried to minimize this bias. Using simulations, we show that the bias introduced is very small (less than 0.002 change in the expected sex ratio) and would therefore not greatly affect the results. For details, see Klasen and Wink (2002).

[33] See, for example, Stephan Klasen (2003, and the literature cited therein), Dolly Arora (1996), and Daniel Goodkind (1999). These questions might evolve further since new technologies, such as sperm sorting, are becoming increasingly available, which will also generate "missing women" but might raise different ethical questions. For a discussion, see Klasen (2003).

[34] For example, in India, discrimination against girls is most marked in the lower middle classes who try to emulate supposed behavioral patterns of upper socio-cultural strata. These behavior patterns (such as not allowing one's wife and daughter to work, the willingness to pay large dowries which place a huge burden on raising a daughter, etc.) harm girls and women. Among the poorest these practices are less frequent. For a discussion, see Drèze and Sen (1995) and Das Gupta (1987).

[35] See Klasen (1999) for a more detailed development of these arguments.

[36] In the 1996 1 percent sample survey, the sex ratio is believed to have increased to 1.2 (State Statistical Bureau 1997). As the age breakdown of the 2000 census is not yet available, it is difficult to verify this massive increase, which may partly be due to sampling and under-enumeration issues.

[37] Since the age breakdown is not yet available for the 2001 census, it is not possible to calculate survival rates for 1991 to 2001.

[38] In particular, the survival rates for females between 1972 and 1981 are larger than one in the (1972) age group 0–4, 15–19, 20–24, and 40–44, and suspiciously close to 1 in neighboring age groups, suggesting that the improvement in 1981 was partly based on better enumeration. Between 1981 and 1998, there are also survival rates above 1 in some isolated age groups, but there is less of a gender differential. They could also

be due to age heaping, as there are correspondingly low survival rates in neighboring age brackets.

[39] Conversely, an analysis of survival rates between 1981 and 1991 indicates rates above one mainly for males in the middle age groups. This may be an indication of males returning from international migration, which would thereby even underestimate the reduction in the number of "missing women."

[40] Male life expectancy exceeded female life expectancy until 1962, after which there was a reversal. Women already enjoyed a three-year advantage in 1971 (Peebles 1982). The DHS also demonstrates that excess female mortality between the ages of 1 and 5 disappeared in the late 1970s (Department of Census and Statistics 1988).

[41] There appeared to have been a particular problem of under-enumeration of females in Bihar in 1991. The 2001 data confirm this as they show a 2 percentage point reduction in the sex ratio (Das Gupta and Mari Bhat 1997).

[42] This is partly due to reductions in maternal mortality (both reduced risks of dying at each birth and reduced fertility levels, which lower the exposure of women to possible maternal mortality). But the improvement extends beyond the child-bearing years and is larger than one would expect from a decline in maternal mortality alone. For a discussion, see Wink (2000).

[43] The time trend in the reported sex ratio at birth from the Sample Registration System is, however, not consistent with a steady and continuous increase in sex-selective abortions. While the sex ratio at birth has risen sharply since the late 1980s to levels as high as 1.13 in 1994, it has fallen back to levels of about 1.09 between 1994 and 1998 (Registrar General 2001). If these data were correct, perhaps the phenomenon has already peaked, but these trends could also largely be driven by measurement problems. Other data, particularly from the Family Health Surveys, suggest an overall worsening of the sex ratio at birth between 1992–93 and 1998–99 from about 1.051 to 1.069. North India has much higher sex ratios, suggesting that sex-selective abortions may be playing an increasing role there (IIPS 1995, 2000).

[44] These regional classifications are based on census definitions. Bina Agarwal (1994) has suggested a five-way classification, including Northeast as a separate category. We have no observations from the (relatively small-sized) states that she groups in this category. She also suggests the inclusion of Madhya Pradesh with "West (and Central) India" rather than with North India. We tried this classification and found that then the North stands out more (and the West correspondingly less) in terms of having unusually high sex ratios. The other results are not seriously affected, but the fit of the regression is slightly enhanced. We also looked at correlation coefficients among the independent variables and found them all to be below 0.5, so we do not believe multicollinearity is a serious problem.

REFERENCES

Agarwal, Bina. 1994. *A Field Of One's Own: Gender and Land Rights in South Asia.* Cambridge, UK: Cambridge University Press.

Alderman, Harold and Paul J. Gertler. 1997. "Family Resources and Gender Differences in Human Capital Investments: The Demand for Children's Medical Care in Pakistan," in Lawrence Haddad, John Hoddinott, and Harold Alderman (eds.) *Intrahousehold Resource Allocation in Developing Countries: Models, Methods, and Policy.* Baltimore, MD: Johns Hopkins University Press.

Arora, Dolly. 1996. "The Victimizing Discourse: Sex Determination Technologies and Policy." *Economic and Political Weekly* 31(7): 420–4.

Bangladesh Bureau of Statistics 1999. *Statistical Yearbook of Bangladesh.* Dhaka: BBS.

Banister, Judith. 1987. *China's Changing Population.* New York: Oxford University Press.

—— and Ansley J. Coale. 1994. "Five Decades of Missing Females in China." *Demography* 31(3): 459–79.

Bardhan, Pranab. 1974. "On Life and Death Questions.." *Economic and Political Weekly* 9: 1283–304.

Basu, Alaka Malwade. 1992. *Culture, the Status of Women, and Demographic Behavior.* Oxford, UK: Oxford University Press.

——. 1999. "Fertility Decline and Increasing Gender Imbalance in India, Including a Possible South Indian Turnaround." *Development and Change* 30: 237–63.

Central Bureau of Statistics 1995, 1999. *Statistical Yearbook of Nepal 1995, 1999.* Kathmandu: Ramshah Path.

Chanazarian, Anoushe. 1986. "Determinants of the Sex Ratio at Birth." PhD dissertation. Princeton University, NJ.

Chen, Lincoln, Emdadul Huq, and Stan D'Souza. 1981. "Sex Bias in the Family Allocation of Food and Health Care in Rural Bangladesh." *Population and Development Review* 7(1): 55–70.

Coale, Ansley. 1991. "Excess Female Mortality and the Balance of the Sexes." *Population and Development Review* 17(3): 517–23.

——, Paul Demeny, and Barbara Vaughan. 1983. *Regional Model Life Tables and Stable Populations.* Princeton, NJ: Princeton University Press.

Croll, Elizabeth. 2000. *Endangered Daughters.* London: Routledge.

Das, Gupta Monica. 1987. "Selective Discrimination against Females in Rural Punjab, India." *Population and Development Review* 13(1): 77–100.

—— and P. N. Mari Bhat. 1997. "Fertility Decline and Increased Manifestation of Sex Bias in India." *Population Studies* 51(3): 307–15.

Department of Census and Statistics 1988. *Sri Lanka Demographic and Health Survey 1987.* Colombo: Ministry of Plan Implementation.

Dhakal, Sanjaya. 2001. "More But Not Merrier." *Spotlight* 20, August 17–23.

Drèze, Jean and Amartya Sen. 1989. *Hunger and Public Action.* Oxford, UK: Clarendon Press.

—— and Amartya Sen. 1995. *India Economic Development and Social Opportunity.* Oxford, UK: Clarendon Press.

—— and Mamta, Murthi. 2001. "Fertility, Education, and Development: Evidence from India." *Population and Development Review* 27: 33–63.

D'Souza, Stan and Lincoln C. Chen. 1980. "Sex Differences in Mortality in Rural Bangladesh." *Population and Development Review* 6: 257–70.

Dyson, Tim. 2001. "The Preliminary Demography of the 2001 Census in India." *Population and Development Review* 27: 341–56.

—— and Mick Moore. 1983. "On Kinship Structure, Female Autonomy, and Demographic Behavior in India." *Population and Development Review* 9(1): 35–57.

Goodkind, Daniel. 1996. "On Substituting Sex Preference Strategies in East Asia: Does Prenatal Sex Selection Reduce Postnatal Discrimination?" *Population and Development Review* 22: 111–25.

——. 1999. "Should Prenatal Sex Selection be Restricted? Ethical Questions and their Implications for Research and Policy." *Population Studies* 53: 49–61.

Government of Pakistan "Pakistan Statistical Yearbook. 1995. Karachi: Federal Bureau of Statistics.

Hill, Kenneth and Dawn, Upchurch. 1995. "Gender differences in child health: Evidence from the Demographic and Health Surveys." *Population and Development Review* 21: 127–151.

Hossain, Mustak. 1991. "Fourth Population Census 'Riddled with Inconsistencies'." *Daily Star,* September 3.

Humphries, Jane. 1991. "Bread and a Pennyworth of Treacle." *Cambridge Journal of Economics* 15: 451–73.

IIPS (International Institute for Population Science) 1995. *National Family Health Survey (NFHS) 1992–93.* Mumbai: IIPS.

———. 2000. *National Family Health Survey (NFHS-2) 1998–99.* Mumbai: IIPS.

Irudaya, Rajan S., S. Sudha, and P. Mohanachandran. 2000. "Fertility Decline and Worsening Gender Bias in India: Is Kerala No Longer an Exception?" *Development and Change* 31: 1085–92.

James, William H. 1986. "The Sex Ratio of Black Births." *Annals of Human Biology* 11: 39–44.

Johansson, Sten and Ola Nygren. 1991. "The Missing Girls of China–A New Demographic Account." *Population and Development Review* 17(1): 35–51.

Junhong, Chu. 2001. "Prenatal Sex Determination and Sex-Selective Abortion in Rural Central China." *Population and Development Review* 27: 259–82.

Khoury, John W., J. D. Erickson, and L. M. James. 1983. "Paternal Effects on the Human Sex Ratio at Birth: Evidence from Interracial Cases." *American Journal of Human Genetics* 36: 1103–8.

Klasen, Stephan. 1993. "Human Development and Women's Lives in a Restructured Eastern Bloc: Lessons from the Developing World," In Alfred Schipke and Alan Taylor (eds.) The Economics of Transformation: Theory and Practise in the New Market Economies. New York: Springer.

———. 1994. "Missing Women Reconsidered." *World Development* 22(7): 1061–71.

———. 1996a. "Nutrition, Health, and Mortality in Sub Saharan Africa: Is There a Gender Bias?." *Journal of Development Studies* 32: 913–33.

———. 1996b. "Rejoinder." *Journal of Development Studies* 32: 944–8.

———. 1998. "Marriage, Bargaining, and Intrahousehold Resource Allocation." *Journal of Economic History* 58: 432–67.

———. 1999. "Gender Inequality in Mortality in Comparative Perspective." Mimeographed, University of Munich.

———. 2001. "Warum fehlen 100 Millionen Frauen auf der Welt?." in O. Fabel and R. Nischik (eds.) *Femina Oeconomia: Frauen in der Ökonomie.* München: Rainer Hampp.

———. 2003. "Sex Selection." *Encyclopedia of Population.* (forthcoming).

——— and Claudia Wink. 2002. "A Turning Point in Gender Bias in Mortality? An Update on the Number of Missing Women." *Population and Development Review* 28(2): 285–312.

Kynch, Jocelyn and Amartya Sen. 1983. "Indian Women: Well-Being and Survival." *Cambridge Journal of Economics* 7: 363–80.

Langford, Christopher and Pamela Storey. 1993. "Sex Differentials in Mortality Early in the 20th Century–Sri Lanka and India Compared." *Population and Development Review* 19(2): 263–82.

Larson, Ulla, Woojin Chung, and Monicas Das Gupta. 1998. "Fertility and Son Preference in Korea." *Population Studies* 52: 317–25.

Makinson, Carolyn. 1994. "Discrimination against the Female Child." *International Journal of Gynecology & Obstetrics* 46: 119–25.

Mayer, Peter. 1999. "India's Falling Sex Ratio." *Population and Development Review* 25(2): 323–43.

McNay, K., Jane Humphries, and Stephan Klasen. 1998. "Death and Gender in Victorian England and Wales: Comparisons with Contemporary Developing Countries." DAE Working Paper No. 9801. Department of Applied Economics, Cambridge University.

Muhuri, Pradib K. and Samuel H. Preston. 1991. "Effects of Family Composition on Mortality Differentials by Sex Among Children in Matlab, Bangladesh." *Population and Development Review* 17(3): 415–34.

299

Murthi, Mamta, Anne-Catherine Guio, and Jean Drèze. 1995. "Mortality, Fertility, and Gender Bias in India: A District-Level Analysis." *Population and Development Review* 21(4): 745–82.

Nadarajah, T. 1983. "The Transition from Higher Female to Higher Male Mortality in Sri Lanka." *Population and Development Review* 9(2): 317–25.

Obermeyer, Carla M. and Rosario Cárdenas. 1997. "Son Preference and Differential Treatment in Morocco and Tunisia." *Studies in Family Planning* 28(3): 235–44.

Park, Chai Bin and Nam-Hoon Cho. 1995. "Consequences of Son Preference in a Low-Fertility Society: Imbalance of the Sex Ratio at Birth." *Population and Development Review* 21(1): 59–84.

Peebles, Patrick. 1982. *Sri Lanka: A Handbook of Historical Statistics.* Boston, MA: G. K. Hall.

People's Perspective 1993. "Population Clock and Census '91 in Bangladesh: Ticking Falsehood & Manipulating Numbers," *The People's Perspectives* No. 4–5, November–December, 1993.

Pradhan, Ajit, Ram Hari Aryal, Gokarna Regmi, Bharat Ban, and Pavalavalli Govindasamy. 1997. *Nepal Family Health Survey 1996.* Kathmandu: Ministry of Health, Nepal.

Registrar General 2001. *Provisional Population Totals. Census of India Series 1, Paper 1 of 2001.* New Delhi: Ministry of Home Affairs.

Rosenzweig, Mark P. and Paul T. Schultz. 1982. "Market Opportunities, Genetic Endowments, and Intra-Family Resource Distribution." *American Economic Review* 72(4): 803–15.

Sen, Amartya. 1982. "Food Battles: Conflicts in the Access to Food." 12th Coromandel Lecture delivered on December 13, in New Delhi. New Delhi: Coromadel Fertilisers Limited.

——. 1984. *Poverty and Famines.* Oxford, UK: Oxford University Press.

——. 1986. "Africa and India: What Do We Have to Learn from Each Other?." *Proceedings of the Eighth World Congress of the International Economic Association.* London: Macmillan.

——. 1989. "Women's Survival as a Development Problem." *Bulletin of the American Academy of Arts and Sciences* 43(2): 14–29.

——. 1990a. "Gender and Cooperative Conflict." in Irene Tinker (ed.) *Persistent Inequalities – Women and World Development,* pp. 123–49. New York: Oxford University Press.

——. 1990b. "More than 100 Million Women are Missing." *The New York Review of Books,* December 20.

——. 1992. "Missing Women." *British Medical Journal* 304: 586–7.

—— and Sunil Sengupta. 1983. "Malnutrition or Rural Children and the Sex Bias." *Economic and Political Weekly* 18: 855–64.

Shanghai Star 2002. "China's Missing Girls." *Shanghai Star,* October 24.

Somerfelt, Elizabeth and Fred Arnold. 1998. "Sex Differentials in the Nutritional Status of Young Children," in United Nations (ed.). *Too Young to Die – Genes or Gender?* New York: United Nations.

State Statistical Bureau. 1997. *China Population Yearbook 1997.* Beijing: State Statistical Bureau.

State Statistical Bureau. 2001. *Communique on Major Figures of the 2000 Population Census.* Beijing: National Bureau of Statistics.

State Statistical Bureau of Taiwan. 2001. *Population Estimates of Taiwan.* Taipeh: State Statistical Bureau.

Sudha, S. and S. Irudaya Rajan. 1999. "Female Demographic Disadvantage in India 1981–91: Sex Selective Abortions and Female Infanticide." *Development and Change* 30(3): 585–618.

Tabutin, Dominique. 1991. "La Surmortalité Féminine en Afrique du Nord de 1965 à Nos Jours – Aspects Descriptifs." *Population* 4: 833–54.

Teitelbaum, Michael S. 1970. "Factors Affecting the Sex Ratio in Large Populations." *Journal of Biosocial Sciences,* Supplement 2: 61–71.

—— and Nathan Mantel. 1971. "Socio-Economic Factors and the Sex Ratio at Birth." *Journal of Biosocial Sciences* 3: 23–41.

Timaeus, Ian, Katie Harris, and Francesca Fairbairn. 1998. "Can Use of Health Care Explain Sex Differentials in Mortality in the Developing World?" in United Nations (ed.). *Too Young to Die – Genes or Gender?* New York: United Nations.

United Nations 1982. *Unabridged Model Life Tables Corresponding to the New United Nations Model Life Tables for Developing Countries.* New York: United Nations.

US Department of Health and Human Services 1991. *Vital Statistics of the United States.* Washington, DC: Government Printing Office.

——. Various years. *Demographic Yearbook.* New York: United Nations.

Visaria, Pravin. 1961. *The Sex Ratio of the Population of India. Monograph 10, Census of India 1961.* New Delhi: Office of the Registrar General.

Waldron, Ingrid. 1983. "The Role of Genetic and Biological Factors in Sex Differences in Mortality." in Alan D. Lopez and Lado T. Ruzicka (eds.) *Sex Differentials in Mortality,* pp. 141–64. Canberra: Australian National University Press.

——. 1993. "Recent Trends in Sex Mortality Ratios for Adults in Developed Countries." *Social Science Medicine* 36: 451–62.

——. 1998. "Sex Differences in Infant and Early Childhood Mortality." in United Nations (ed.). *Too Young to Die – Genes or Gender?* pp 64–83. New York: United Nations.

Wink, Claudia. 2000. "Weibliche Übersterblichkeit in Entwicklungsländern." MA dissertation, University of Munich.

World Bank 2001. *Engendering Development.* Washington, DC: The World Bank.

THE HUMAN DEVELOPMENT PARADIGM: OPERATIONALIZING SEN'S IDEAS ON CAPABILITIES

Sakiko Fukuda-Parr

OVERVIEW

Amartya Sen's ideas constitute the core principles of a development approach that has evolved in the Human Development Reports. This approach is a "paradigm" based on the concept of well-being that can help define public policy, but does not embody a set of prescriptions. The current movement from an age of development planning to an age of globalization has meant an increasing attention to agency aspects of development. While earlier Human Development Reports emphasized measures such as the provision of public services, recent ones have focused more on people's political empowerment. This chapter reflects on Sen's work in light of this shift in emphasis. Gender analysis has been central to the development of the new agency-driven paradigm, and gender equity is a core concern. A gender perspective has also helped highlight important aspects of this paradigm, such as the role of collective agency in promoting development.

INTRODUCTION

The recognition of equal rights for women along with men, and the determination to combat discrimination on the basis of gender are achievements equal in importance to the abolition of slavery, the elimination of colonialism and the establishment of equal rights for racial and ethnic minorities.

(United Nations Development Programme 1995)

The Human Development Reports (HDRs), published annually for UNDP since 1990, have used Amartya Sen's capability approach as a conceptual framework in their analyses of contemporary development challenges. Over time these reports have developed a distinct development paradigm – the human development approach – that now informs policy choices in many areas, such as poverty reduction, sustainable development, gender inequalities, governance, and globalization. What, then, are the policy implications of Sen's work on capabilities, development, freedom, and human rights?

Sen's ideas provide the core principles of a development approach whose flexible framework allows policy-makers to analyze diverse challenges that poor people and poor countries face, rather than imposing a rigid orthodoxy with a set of policy prescriptions. This chapter identifies the key elements of Sen's paradigm as they have been applied to diverse policy questions. It shows how the emphasis has evolved over the years from the provision of public services to political empowerment and how gender issues have been central to this paradigm shift. Not only is gender equity a core concern, but also gender analysis has shaped some important aspects of this paradigm, such as the role of collective agency in promoting development.

In the discussion below, I will first outline the central features of the human development approach and how it differs from other paradigms such as the basic needs and human rights approaches, including their attitude towards gender. Then I will highlight some of the gender dimensions more specifically.

I. SEN AND THE HUMAN DEVELOPMENT REPORTS

The first Human Development Report launched by Mahbub ul Haq in 1990 had an explicit purpose: "to shift the focus of development economics from national income accounting to people centered policies" (Mahbub ul Haq 1995). The report is not just *any* report that the UNDP might commission on a given development theme, nor is it a status report for monitoring development. It has a much broader ambition, namely setting out a comprehensive approach to development, including an agenda of policy priorities, tools of analysis and measurement, and a coherent conceptual framework. As Richard Jolly (2003) notes:

> [The] Human Development (HD) approach embodies a robust paradigm, which may be contrasted with the neoliberal (NL) paradigm of the Washington consensus. There are points of overlap, but also important points of difference in objectives, assumptions, constraints and in the main areas for policy and in the indicators for assessing results.

To launch the HDRs, Haq brought together a group of fellow development economists and friends, among them Paul Streeten and Frances Stewart, who had worked with him on the basic needs approach; Gus Ranis and Keith Griffin, his collaborators in Pakistan; and others, such as Sudhir Anand and Meghnad Desai, who had creative expertise in quantitative methods. Dozens more who shared his vision also contributed (Haq 1995). But it was Sen's work on capabilities and functionings that provided the strong conceptual

foundation for the new paradigm. His approach defined human development as the process of enlarging a person's "functionings and capabilities to
function, the range of things that a person could do and be in her life,"
expressed in the HDRs as expanding "choices" (Amartya Sen 1989).[1]

Sen would continue to influence the evolution of the human development approach, refining and broadening the basic concepts and
measurement tools as new areas of policy challenges were tackled, from
sustainable development (*United Nations Development Programme* 1994) to
gender equality (*United Nations Development Programme* 1995), poverty
(*United Nations Development Programme* 1997), consumption and sustainable
development (*United Nations Development Programme* 1998), human rights
(*United Nations Development Programme* 2000), and democracy (*United Nations
Development Programme* 2002). In turn, the HDRs have paralleled Sen's own
work on freedom, participation, and agency, incorporating more explicit
references to human rights and freedoms. With Anand, Sen also played a
critical role in developing the measurement tools of human development,
starting with the Human Development Index (HDI) and going on to cover
issues such as gender equality–the Gender-Related Development Index
(GDI) and the Gender Empowerment Measure (GEM) were developed in
1995–and the measurement of poverty in human lives rather than incomes
through the Human Poverty Index (HPI), published in the 1997 HDR.

Thus, while Sen helped develop the initial conceptual framework and
measurement tools used in the HDRs, the reports carried Sen's work even
further as they explored the policy implications of this development
approach in areas that are of major contemporary significance.[2]

II. THE HUMAN DEVELOPMENT APPROACH: KEY ELEMENTS

Sen's theory of development as an expansion of capabilities is the starting
point for the human development approach: the idea that the purpose of
development is to improve human lives by expanding the range of things
that a person can be and do, such as to be healthy and well nourished, to be
knowledgeable, and to participate in community life. Seen from this
viewpoint, development is about removing the obstacles to what a person
can do in life, obstacles such as illiteracy, ill health, lack of access to
resources, or lack of civil and political freedoms.

It is important to emphasize that the human development approach
contains two central theses about people and development, and to
distinguish between them. They are what Sen calls the "evaluative aspect"
and the "agency aspect" (Amartya Sen 2002). The first is concerned with
evaluating improvements in human lives as an explicit development
objective and using human achievements as key indicators of progress.
This contrasts with paradigms that focus on economic performance. The

second is concerned with what human beings can do to achieve such improvements, particularly through policy and political changes. The human development approach is commonly associated with the evaluative aspect. The agency aspect is less widely appreciated.

To understand these key elements of the human development approach and their relevance for development policy and strategy, it helps to compare it with other approaches that have influenced public policy debates, such as the dominant neoliberal paradigm and a predecessor to the human development approach, the basic needs approach.[3]

Explicit philosophical foundations and conceptual roots

As Martha Nussbaum (2000) points out, all public policy formulation unavoidably reflects normative positions and so should be subjected to critical philosophical reasoning. An important feature of the human development approach is that it has an explicit basis in philosophical reasoning. Sen has written extensively about the conceptual roots of capabilities in the longstanding intellectual traditions of philosophy, political economy, and economics, dating back to Aristotle and including the works of Adam Smith and Immanuel Kant, among others. Both Sen's own work (e.g., Sen 1989) and the HDRs (*United Nations Development Programme* 1990, 1996) trace these connections.

Not only do the philosophical underpinnings of neoliberalism and the basic needs approach differ from those of the HDA, but they are also less explicit. Although all three approaches are ultimately concerned with human well-being, they give this concept different meanings. Neoliberalism defines well-being as utility maximization. Sen sets out the limitations of this approach (Amartya Sen and Bernard Williams 1982), among which the most significant is the neglect of rights, freedoms, and human agency. The basic needs approach places people at the center of development, but the emphasis on specifying "basic needs" in terms of supplying services and commodities points to a commodities basis rather than a capabilities basis in defining human well-being. Although many of the proponents of the basic needs approach, such as Streeten, emphasized people's participation and political constraints, the absence of a strong and explicit philosophical foundation left the approach open to translation into policy that focused mainly on meeting people's material needs, or "count, cost, and deliver," rather than on the human rights, freedoms, and agency emphasized in the human development approach.

Evaluative aspects

The human development approach is unique in its emphasis on assessing development by how well it expands the capabilities of all people. Thus,

THE HUMAN DEVELOPMENT PARADIGM

economic growth is only a means and not an end in itself. Furthermore, the concern with the well-being of *all* people emphasizes equity as a major policy objective, requiring monitoring not only through national averages, but also via measures of deprivation and distribution.

The establishment of measurement tools for evaluating human achievements was central to introducing human development as an alternative paradigm and to gaining the attention of policy-makers. Haq was convinced that a simple combined measure of human development was essential for convincing the public, academics, and policy-makers that they should evaluate development by advances in human well-being and not only by advances in the economy. Although Sen initially opposed this idea, he went on to help Haq develop the Human Development Index (HDI), a composite index of achievements in human development. Sen was concerned by the difficulties of capturing the full complexity of human capabilities in a single index. But he was persuaded by Haq's insistence that only a single number could shift the attention of policy-makers from material output to human well-being as a real measure of progress (*United Nations Development Programme* 1999).

The HDI had a significant policy impact when first formulated and continues to command policy attention. HDI estimates of countries, as well as the "disaggregated HDIs" for different regions or ethnic groups within countries, had the intended effect of focusing greater attention on basic human capabilities, especially those included in the HDI (the capability to survive and be healthy, to be knowledgeable, and to enjoy a decent standard of living). The HDI ranking of countries provoked policy-makers to examine how each country fared in this regard and to ask why some countries and regions, such as Costa Rica, Sri Lanka, or the state of Kerala in India, managed to achieve much higher levels of "human development" in comparison to countries with similar income levels. The comparison of a country's HDI rank with its GDP per capita rank became, in this regard, more critical than the HDI itself as a measure of a country's human development.

Two decisions made in devising the HDI were particularly important: one concerned the choice of capabilities to be included, and the other had to do with the focus on national averages rather than disparities.

One of the most difficult tasks in applying the capabilities approach to development policy is deciding which capabilities are most important.[4] The range of human capabilities is infinite and the value that individuals assign to each one can vary from person to person. Even if some capabilities deserve greater public attention than others, the relative importance of capabilities can vary with social context – from one community or country to another, and from one point of time to another. Thus "the task of specification must relate to the underlying motivation of the exercise as well as dealing with the social values involved" (Sen 1989).

307

HDRs have used two criteria in deciding which capabilities are most important: first, they must be *universally valued* by people across the world; and second, they must be *basic*, meaning their lack would foreclose many other capabilities. But the human development approach has deliberately remained open-ended in the choice of capabilities, letting them vary over time and place. This approach contrasts with that of the basic needs approach, which listed the important human needs without an explicit explanation justifying the selection and without providing a rationale for who should be making the list. It also contrasts with other work using the capability approach, such as Nussbaum's efforts to finalize a list of essential capabilities (Nussbaum 2000).[5] But the HDRs have argued that the capabilities given priority within public policy will change over time and from one community to another. As an exercise in the global evaluation of development, the HDRs had to focus simply on those capabilities that are universally valued and "basic" (i.e., capabilities on which many choices in life depended), reflected in the three HDI capabilities: to be knowledgeable, to survive, and to enjoy a decent standard of living.

A second significant question that arose in devising the HDI was whether it should reflect equity. Conceptualized as a measure of average achievements, HDI does not take into account the distribution of achievements, which leaves out equity, an essential outcome by which to evaluate progress. Gender disparities were a central feature of the concern with equity, along with other disparities such as those of class, ethnicity, or rural/urban residence. Some argued that to combine a distribution measure with an average achievement measure would be like adding apples and oranges. Moreover, there are many forms of disparities, predicated on gender, ethnicity, race, and so on, and the importance and relevance of particular forms of disparities can differ from one country to another.

Given these difficulties, HDI remains a measure of average achievement and its strength lies in its simplicity: a simple measure is more understandable to the policy-maker and the public, sending a clear message about what makes the measure go up or down (Sakiko Fukuda-Parr, Kate Raworth, and A. K. Shiva Kumar 2003). But from the beginning, attempts were also made to develop supplementary measures that adjust the HDI by gender disparity, showing that even if two countries have the same average achievement in terms of HDI, this average may hide differences with respect to gender disparity. To make this point initially, HDRs disaggregated HDIs for women and men. Later, an index of human development that incorporated gender disparity was developed. The Gender-Related Development Index (GDI) adjusts the HDI for gender disparity and penalizes countries accordingly (*United Nations Development Programme* 1995 and subsequent issues). The 1995 HDR, which marked the Fourth World Conference on Women in Beijing, concluded that "human development is endangered unless it is engendered."

Unfortunately, the human development approach has often been misconstrued as being narrowly limited to the three capabilities included in the HDI, or even more narrowly to their indicators (literacy and schooling, life expectancy, and adjusted income). This, in turn, has led many to conclude that the human development approach has little to offer that is different from the basic needs approach or the concept of human resource development.

But the intent of the human development approach was never to limit itself to the narrow definitions of the HDI. The concept of human development is much more complex and broader than its measure; it is about people being able to live in freedom and dignity, and being able to exercise choices to pursue a full and creative life. Development priorities are therefore about removing restrictions. Illiteracy, ill health, and a lack of command over resources restrict choices, but so do many other conditions such as social and political oppression that restrict one's participation in the life of a community, or the exercise of autonomy in making decisions about one's own life. Ironically, the very success of the HDI has contributed to this narrow interpretation of the human development approach, and the absence of indicators for freedom in the HDI and in the HDR statistical tables contributes to a widespread misperception of human development as equivalent to social development combined with equitable economic growth. The human development concept has been trapped inside its reduced measure (Sakiko Fukuda-Parr 2003).

Over the years, however, other human capabilities have received greater attention, especially those linked to freedom from social and political oppression. Gender issues have played a central role in highlighting these issues. The 1995 HDR on gender thus went far beyond education, health, and income outcomes to emphasize the importance of women's equal participation in political and professional life, their autonomy in decision-making, and the unequal sharing of unpaid work with men. The GEM was developed as a measure of "gender empowerment," and more recent HDRs have explored the role of human rights and human rights instruments (*United Nations Development Programme* 2000) and the role of democratic political institutions (*United Nations Development Programme* 2002) in human development. These reports have asserted that enjoying political and civil freedoms and participating in community decision-making processes are as important as being literate and enjoying good health. Even the definition of human development has changed subtly, with a stronger and unambiguous emphasis on civil and political freedoms. In 1990 the HDR stated:

> Human development is a process of enlarging people's choices. The most critical of these wide-ranging choices are to live a long and healthy life, to be educated and to have access to resources needed for a decent

309

standard of living. *Additional choices* include political freedom, guaranteed human rights and personal self-respect [my emphasis].[6]

In 2001 it stated:

The most basic capabilities for human development are to lead long and healthy lives, to be knowledgeable, to have access to the resources needed for a decent standard of living *and to be able to participate in the life of the community.*

And in emphasizing the freedom to choose, the 1995 HDR specifically recognized the injustice of gender inequality:

Human development is a process of enlarging the choices of all people, not just for one part of society. Such a process becomes unjust and discriminatory if most women are excluded from its benefits.

(*United Nations Development Programme* 1995)

The policy implication of this evolution in the prioritizing of capabilities is a corresponding shift in focus from social and economic policies to political institutions and processes. Political reforms have become important aspects of the human development policy agenda. This contrasts with the neoliberal and basic needs approaches. The neoliberal approach emphasizes institutional efficiency – either in the market or in the provision of public services. These concerns dominate the current debates on "good" governance, while the human development approach is concerned with governance for social justice, a governance that enlarges the participation, power, and influence of the people, especially those who are disadvantaged, such as women, ethnic minorities, and the poor. From this viewpoint, a measure that reflects disparities, such as the GDI or the disaggregated HDIs developed in national human development reports that show huge differences in human development by region or ethnic group, is particularly powerful.

Agency aspects

The opening lines of the very first 1990 HDR stated: "People are the real wealth of a nation" (*United Nations Development Programme* 1990). People are not simply beneficiaries of economic and social progress in a society, but are active agents of change. The human development approach shares with other approaches the idea that investing in people's education and health is a powerful means to achieve overall economic and social progress in societies. But it goes much further in at least two ways: first in its concern with the role of human agency for changing policy, social commitment, and norms that require collective action, and second in its concern with human rights.

310

Human beings can be agents of change through both individual action and collective action. Individual action shapes development through activities such as the upbringing of children. Collective action is an important force that can pressure changes in policies and bring about political change. Strategies for human development initially emphasized investing in education and health, and promoting equitable economic growth – the three dimensions of the HDI. These mobilize the individual agency of people and strengthen their productive capacity for their own private interest. But to these must be added a third pillar – expanding participation through democratic institutions within stronger democratic governance. Indeed, collective action, especially in the form of social movements, has been the essential motor behind progress in achieving major policy shifts necessary for human development, such as the recognition of gender equality, the need to protect the environment, or the promotion and protection of a comprehensive set of human rights.

The concept of human capital or human resource development is typically about individual agency for material production. For example, a healthy worker is more productive than an ill worker, an educated mother is more likely to have healthy children, and so on. But the idea of agency in human development is also about demanding rights in decision-making. This can be individual in form: for example, the ownership of personal assets would empower women to demand their rights within the household. But it is also about collective agency in the public sphere and in a political process. People aiming to influence public decisions, whether for access to schooling, for the right to vote, or for decent working conditions, can rarely be effective on their own. A good deal of evidence shows that effectiveness requires a process of forming associations, making alliances, and generating public debates. Democratic governance through political institutions that expand the power and voice of people, and ensure the accountability of decision-makers, is an important condition for promoting human development.

In this context, examining development through the lens of gender has been especially important in bringing out the importance of collective agency in the human development approach. The 1995 HDR (p. 1) proclaimed: "One of the defining movements of the 20th century has been the relentless struggle for gender equality, led mostly by women, but supported by growing numbers of men. ... Moving toward gender equality is not a technocratic goal – it is a political process" (*United Nations Development Programme* 1995). In subsequently devising measures for the gender dimensions of human development, the HDR 1995 developed both an evaluative measure (GDI), which assesses achievement in human development with gender equity, and an agency measure (GEM). The GEM measures the extent to which women have influence in decision-making, in politics, in professional life, and in organizations. The GEM has been used

311

widely in advocating women's empowerment, for example, in debates over reserving seats in parliament for women.

The recognition and promotion of human rights, and the legal frameworks that guarantee these rights, are important in the human development approach, not only for their intrinsic value, but also for their instrumental value in promoting agency, both individual and collective. A human right is a claim on society that carries obligations for others to promote, protect, and respect that right (*United Nations Development Programme* 2000). These obligations require the accountability of the "duty bearers," enforceable by law. This provides a powerful basis for public policy that can facilitate human agency. The legal guarantee of a freedom of speech and association is critical for people to bring issues up for public debate, whether they are demands for priority attention to health facilities or for holding corrupt officials to account.

A comparison of approaches

The differences between the human development approach, the neoliberal alternative, and the human development approach's precursor, the basic needs approach, are summarized in Table 1.

III. POLICIES FOR HUMAN DEVELOPMENT: A FIVE-POINT AGENDA

The ideals of human development have great appeal to many policy-makers and practitioners, such as parliamentarians, ministers, government officials, and the staff of donor agencies or NGOs. Having bought into the values, they invariably ask, "So what do we do? What policy priorities do we follow?"

The human development approach is not a recipe of policy prescriptions with a set of "destinations" and a list of ingredients on how to get there. It claims to be instead a "robust paradigm" that can be used over time and across countries as development challenges and priorities shift. Nonetheless, in the context of the current challenges that face most countries today, five elements of a general human development agenda can be proposed. They constitute what might be called a "New York consensus," as these points are reflected in many UN agreements:

1 Priority to "social development" with the goals of expanding education and health opportunities.
2 Economic growth that generates resources for human development in its many dimensions.
3 Political and social reforms for democratic governance that secures human rights so that people can live in freedom and dignity, with greater collective agency, participation, and autonomy.

Table 1 The human development approach, the neoliberal alternative, and the basic needs antecedent: comparing key features

	Human development	Neoliberalism	Basic needs
Philosophical underpinnings			
Normative assumptions	Explicit	Implicit	Not fully specified
Concept of well-being	Functionings and capabilities	Utility	Meeting basic needs
Evaluative aspect			
Leading criterion for evaluating development progress	Human capabilities, equality of outcomes, fairness and justice in institutional arrangements	Economic well-being, economic growth, efficiency	Poverty reduction in terms of income, access to basic social services
Measurement tools favored	Human outcomes, deprivational and distributional measures	Economic activity and condition, averages and aggregate measures	Access to material means, derivational measures
Agency aspect			
People in development as ends and/or means	Ends: beneficiaries; means: agents	Means: human resources for economic activity	Ends: beneficiaries
Mobilizing agency	Individual action and collective action	Individual action	Concern with political will and political base
"Development strategy"			
Key operational goals	Expanding people's choices (social, economic, political)	Economic growth	Expanding basic social services
Distribution of benefits and costs	Emphasis on equality and on the human rights of all individuals	Concern with poverty	Concern with poverty
Links between development and human rights and freedoms	Human rights and freedoms have intrinsic value and are development objectives. Current research on their instrumental role through links to economic and social progress	No explicit connection. Current search for a link between political and civil freedoms and economic growth	No explicit connection

313

4 Equity in the above three elements with a concern for all individuals, with special attention to the downtrodden and the poor whose interests are often neglected in public policy, as well as the removal of discrimination against women.

5 Policy and institutional reforms at the global level that create an economic environment more conducive for poor countries to access global markets, technology, and information.

This five-point agenda contains a mix of old and new priorities. Social development continues to be important, given that illiteracy is still high, and basic health and survival is far from guaranteed in most developing countries. Economic growth also continues to receive attention, since low growth in developing countries is a major obstacle to human development: over sixty countries ended the decade of 1990–2000 poorer than at its beginning. At the same time, the human development approach has seen a notable evolution. In the early 1990s, the HDRs emphasized public expenditure allocations in health and education; today priorities in those areas are on service quality, efficiency, and equity of delivery (for which governance reforms are often a precondition), as well as on the level of resources–in education, today's competitive global markets require higher levels than basic primary schooling. Institutional reforms that enable the poor to monitor the use of local development funds also are playing a significant role in ensuring the equitable and efficient delivery of basic services. Most importantly, the HDRs have placed an increasing focus on social and political institutions that would "empower" the poor and disadvantaged groups (such as women) so that they have more voice in public policy-making and can fight for their interests. Gender equity in particular (as outlined in the next section) has received prominent attention in this "New York consensus." Finally, it is increasingly apparent that the global environment matters, raising such issues as access to global markets, dealing with the spread of global diseases, the creation of global public goods, and so on. It is imperative that global policies and institutions cease favoring only the rich countries. A critical question now is whether global institutions be restructured or created to function on democratic principles mandating the inclusion and participation of all countries and all people.

The changes in the human development approach over time highlight its openness to accommodating new concerns and taking up new policy challenges. Evolving significantly over the last decade, a period that has seen dramatic changes in the world as globalization has sped forward, the HDRs have reflected these changing circumstances. They have shifted emphases in the policy priorities of the human development agenda from public investments to incentives, from economic measures to democratic politics, from education and health to political and civil liberties, and from economic and social policies to participatory political institutions. They also recognize that people's capabilities to undertake collective action in today's era of rapid globalization will play an increasingly important role in shaping the course of development.

It is not surprising that in 1990 advocacy for human development focused on shifts in planning priorities and on state action: what the state could do to expand capabilities in education and health constituted an important pillar of a human development strategy, for both the intrinsic and the instrumental values of education and health. Today, economic liberalization and political democratization are dominant influences in most countries, which shifts priorities for human development. Capabilities to participate in social action have now become more important. In the same way that economic entrepreneurship drives markets, social entrepreneurship is expected to drive policy debates on issues that matter for people's well-being. A consensus is emerging on the importance of collective action by actors other than the state, notably people and civil society groups, for promoting development.

The political shifts of the 1980s and 1990s have also built greater consensus about the intrinsic value of political freedoms and all human rights, in principle, if not in practice.[7] In 1990, the legacy of the Cold War still divided the world on the importance of political freedom and public participation. In today's context of economic and political liberalization, and growing global interdependence, political freedom, public participation, and collective agency have gained greater universal acceptance as important human goals.

IV. GENDER EQUITY AND THE HUMAN DEVELOPMENT APPROACH

Gender equity has been a prominent aspect of equity concerns in public policy. The gender dimension has led to widespread advocacy and focused attention on equity in other than economic areas, such as education and political participation. The women's movement and studies by feminist scholars have contributed to this expansion of the notion of equity.

The human development approach offers a capability-based approach to gender equity in development that is a departure from traditions focused on income and growth. The analytical framework for gender equity that it provides encompasses the following aspects:

- the philosophical foundation of equality of capabilities and freedoms, focusing on individuals as the objective of gender in development;
- the evaluative aspect of capability expansion;

- the agency aspect of capability expansion;
- measurement tools of the above.

This framework contrasts with the gender equity agenda seen from a growth-oriented development perspective. Compare, for example, the different measures of gender equity. Other approaches measure women's "poverty" by the income gaps between female-headed and male-headed households. Women's "poverty" in the human development approach goes beyond the lack of income to deprivation in capabilities, such as lack of education, health, and the channels to participate in economic life and in decision-making (Sakiko Fukuda-Parr 1999). GDI accordingly provides an evaluative measure of development that includes gender equity, while GEM measures gender equity in women's agency. The human development approach also provides an alternative framework to those that justify improving women's health and education as "human resource development," instrumental to the well-being of others and to economic growth. The capability-based framework for gender equity argues for parity rather than equity.

Overall, the human development approach provides a more gender-sensitive agenda to public policy than its alternatives. First, gender equity is a central concern of the approach, which emphasizes the importance of expanding the capabilities and functionings of all individuals. The fact that discrimination continues to be widespread is a priority concern. Second, the human development approach is sensitive to aspects of discrimination that are particularly important in women's lives, but are unrelated to incomes and economic growth, such as lack of autonomy in decisions about their lives and the ability to influence decision-making within the family, community, and nation. Third, the human development approach has the scope to delve into complex issues, such as the unequal sharing of unpaid work, that constrain women's life choices.

Gender analysis and the issues that feminists have raised have kept the approach vibrant, contributing particularly to the development of its agency aspects. Gender concerns have given the approach the power and flexibility to encompass aspects of inequality that would otherwise go unremarked. Its sensitivity to gender in turn has made it sensitive to a range of potential inequities and unfreedoms that can affect all people. The fact that progress in equal rights for women has come about largely through the efforts of women has highlighted the essential role of collective agency in human progress. Moreover, given the constraints on women's agency in almost all societies by political institutions such as male-dominated political parties, social institutions such as the family, and social norms such as women's responsibilities for care work, these issues and their underlying causes clearly must be tackled head on.

V. CONCLUSION

Over the last decade, the human development approach has evolved in directions that pay more attention to the agency aspects of human development – to political freedoms and institutions as well as political processes. Advocating equal rights for women has been and will continue to be an important factor underlying this evolution.

Many challenges remain in refining the conceptual underpinnings of the human development approach, developing better measurement tools, and above all making the approach useful for policy purposes. They include, for example, more conceptual clarity about the role of groups and about environmental sustainability, better measures of human development that take account of political freedoms, and better measures of gender equality, especially in the area of empowerment. Over the last decade, the human development approach has evolved as a result of a rich academic debate. The hope is this will continue into the next decade.

ACKNOWLEDGMENTS

This chapter is a personal contribution and is not intended to present UNDP's policy position. It reflects my experience in conceptualizing and writing the annual HDRs as director of Human Development Reports 1995 to present. For many useful comments, I thank Paul Streeten, Moez Doraid, Saraswathi Menon, David Stewart, Paul Segal, Sabina Alkire, contributors to the NHDR network on-line review, the anonymous reviewers of the journal, and the three editors of this volume (especially Bina Agarwal, who provided detailed comments and editorial inputs). I also appreciate the responses to my chapter during the September 2002 All-Souls workshop at Oxford on the theme of this volume.

NOTES

[1] It is unclear why the term "choices" replaced "capabilities" in the HDRs. This replacement can cause confusion, since "choice" is a common term that means different things to different people.

[2] Amartya Sen and Sudhir Anand provided the background papers for many (though not all) of the conceptual chapters and measurement tools of the HDRs: in 1990 on human development, concept and measurement (HDI) (Sen and Anand 1990); in 1994 on sustainability and environment (Sen and Anand 1994a, 1994b); in 1995 on measuring gender equality and human development (Sen and Anand 1995); in 1996 on

defining human poverty and the human poverty measure (Sen and Anand 1997); in 1998 on consumption and human development (Sen and Anand 1998); and in 2000 on human rights and human development (Sen and Anand 2000). In 2002 (the HDR on democracy), while Sen did not provide a written text, his writings on democracy, freedom, and development provided the conceptual framework for the report, and his careful reading and comments on draft texts had a decisive influence. Sen's role in the HDR, however, should not be misinterpreted: the reports should not be attributed to Sen, although he has made decisive contributions.

[3] Richard Jolly (2003) develops the contrasts between neoliberalism and the human development approach.

[4] The capabilities approach to development and its application in terms of human development leaves open the final definition of valuable ends to social and individual values. According to Sen (1989), "there are many ambiguities in the conceptual framework of the capability approach," and these ambiguities are in fact part of the concept (see Sen 1989 for elaboration).

[5] There is a rich debate in the literature on whether or not to explicitly identify a list of the most important capabilities. See, for example, Nussbaum (2000) and Martha Nussbaum and Amartya Sen (1993).

[6] It is unclear whether "additional choices" meant these were less important than the three others listed. By 2001 the HDR had removed this ambiguity.

[7] In the third wave of democracy of the 1980s and 1990s, some eighty countries took significant steps towards democratization. Progress has been uneven, however, and some countries have reverted back to less democratic governance. Human rights continue to be deplorable in many countries. Nonetheless, now more than ever before there is a greater overall recognition of the principles of democracy, human rights, and freedoms. This is reflected, for example, in the dramatic rise in the ratification of major human rights instruments, in the number of countries undertaking democratic reforms, and in the emphasis on democracy and human rights in the Millennium Declaration of the United Nations adopted in September 2000 (*United Nations Development Programme* 2002).

REFERENCES

Fukuda-Parr, Sakiko. 1999. "What does Feminization of Poverty Mean? It Isn't Just Lack of Income." *Feminist Economics* 5(2).
———. 2003. "Rescuing Human Development Concept from the Human Development Index," in Sakiko Fukuda-Parr and A. K. Shiva Kumar (eds.). *Readings in Human Development: Concepts, Measures and Policies for a Development Paradigm.* New Delhi: Oxford University Press.
———, Kate Raworth, and AK Shiva Kumar. 2003. "Human Development Index as a Policy Tool: The Potential for Stimulating Public Action," in Sakiko Fukuda-Parr and A. K. Shiva Kumar (eds.) *Readings in Human Development: Concepts, Measures and Policies for a Development Paradigm.* New Delhi, Oxford University Press.
Haq, Mahbub ul. 1995. *Reflections on Human Development.* New York: Oxford University Press.
Jolly, Richard. 2003. "Human Development and Neoliberalism, Paradigms Compared," in Sakiko Fukuda-Parr and A. K. Shiva Kumar (eds.) *Readings in Human Development: Concepts, Measures and Policies for a Development Paradigm.* New Delhi: Oxford University Press.
Nussbaum, Martha. 2000. *Women and Human Development, the Capabilities Approach.* Cambridge, UK: Cambridge University Press.
——— and Amartya Sen, (eds). 1993. *Quality of Life.* Oxford, UK: Oxford University Press.

Sen, Amartya. 1989. "Development as Capabilities Expansion." *Journal of Development Planning* 19: 41–58.

——. 2002. *"Foreword,"* in Sakiko Fukuda-Parr and A.K. Shiva Kumar (eds.) *Human Development, Essential Readings.* New Delhi: Oxford University Press.

—— and Sudhir Anand. 1990. "The Concept of Human Development." *Background Paper for the Human Development Report 1990.* New York: Human Development Report Office.

—— and Sudhir Anand. 1994a. "Sustainable Human Development: Concepts and Priorities." *Background Paper for the Human Development Report 1994.* New York: Human Development Report Office.

—— and Sudhir Anand. 1994b. "Human Development Index: Methodology and Measurement." *United Nations Development Programme Occasional Paper 12.* New York: Human Development Report Office.

—— and Sudhir Anand. 1995. "Gender Inequality in Human Development: Theories and Measurement," *Background Paper for the Human Development Report 1995.* New York: Human Development Report Office.

—— and Sudhir Anand. 1997. "Concepts of Human Development and Poverty: A Multidimensional Perspective." in *Human Development Papers 1997: Poverty and Human Development,* pp. 1–19. New York: United Nations Development Programme.

—— and Sudhir Anand. 1998. "Consumption and Human Development: Concepts and Issues." *Background Paper for the Human Development Report 1998.* New York: Human Development Report Office.

—— and Sudhir Anand. 2000. "The Income Component of the Human Development Index." *Journal of Human Development* 1(1): 83–106.

—— and Bernard Williams. 1982. *Utilitarianism and Beyond.* Cambridge, UK: Cambridge University Press.

United Nations Development Programme. 1990. *Human Development Report 1990.* New York: Oxford University Press.

——. 1994. *Human Development Report 1994.* New York: Oxford University Press.

——. 1995. *Human Development Report 1995.* New York: Oxford University Press.

——. 1996. *Human Development Report 1996.* New York: Oxford University Press.

——. 1997. *Human Development Report 1997.* New York: Oxford University Press.

——. 1998. *Human Development Report 1998.* New York: Oxford University Press.

——. 1999. *Human Development Report 1999.* New York: Oxford University Press.

——. 2000. *Human Development Report 2000; Human Rights and Human Development.* New York: Oxford University Press.

——. 2001. *Human Development Report 2001; Making New Technologies Work for Human Development.* New York: Oxford University Press.

——. 2002. *Human Development Report 2002; Deepening Democracy in a Fragmented World.* New York: Oxford University Press.

CONTINUING THE CONVERSATION

Amartya Sen talks with
Bina Agarwal, Jane Humphries,
and Ingrid Robeyns

BA, JH, IR: What factors first led you to examine gender concerns intellectually? For instance, you have often said that your experience during the Great Bengal famine shaped your interest in and work on famine. Have any such social or personal experiences shaped your work on gender?

AS: My interest in inequality, which goes back to my school days, was initially quite fixed on class divisions. My involvement with gender inequality grew more slowly. There was much greater concentration on class in standard politics (including standard student politics), and when in the early 1950s I was studying at Presidency College in Calcutta, it was taken for granted that class divisions were incomparably more important than other social divisions. Indeed, when later on, in the late 1960s, I started working on gender inequality (I was then teaching at Delhi University), many of my close friends still saw this as quite an "unsound" broadening of interest, involving a "dilution" of one's "focus on class."

But, in addition to that political issue of priority, it is also true that class-based inequalities are, in many ways, much more transparent, which no one – even a child – can miss, without closing one's eyes altogether. Even my sense of agony and outrage at the Great Bengal famine of 1943, to which you refer (and which did strongly shake even my 9-year-old mind), was also linked to the class pattern of mortality. Aside from the anger and outrage at the fact that millions could actually die of hunger and hunger-related diseases, I was amazed by the extraordinary recognition that no one I knew personally, through family connections or social ones, had any serious economic problem during the famine, while unknown millions, men, women, and children, roamed the country in search of food and fell and perished. The class character of famines in particular and of economic deprivation in general was impossible to escape.

There was, of course, evidence of inequality between men and women as well. But its severe and brutal manifestations (on which I researched much later – from the late 1960s to the 1990s) were well hidden from immediate observation. And the less extreme expressions were con-founded by a prevailing attitudinal fog. For example, in comparison with the firm aspirations of the boys in my class, the girls, even very talented ones, seemed far less ambitious, with much less expectation. But this had the outward appearance of a difference in their respective "preferences": "Who are you to tell people what they should do with their lives?" My troubling thoughts about the widely held implicit belief that men's preferences were more focused and their interests, as a result, demanded more attention than women's, seemed to be superficially answered by the fact this was an assumption that women typically made themselves – not just men. I was really struck by the fact that the female students seemed as convinced as the boys that there was no real issue of gender inequality, at least in their lives.

I guess those discussions, confusing and frustrating as they were at that time, later helped me to understand, in retrospect, how gender inequality survives and flourishes, working in a valuational mist that engulfs all and which works by making allies out of the victims. Many years later when I started working on gender inequality, those baffling memories proved very useful for my understanding of the nature and mechanism of gender inequality, and got me particularly interested in studying the role of values and "positional" observations as part of the process that sustains gender disparities. But, of course, I had not seen all this at all clearly in my student days.

Indeed, later on, when I got involved in gathering new empirical data on gender inequality, the attitudinal fog made regular appearances. For example, in the spring of 1983, I studied (with the help of wonderfully enthusiastic associates) the health status and weight of every child below 5 in two substantial Indian villages, and found that girls, born as healthy as the boys, gradually fell behind, mainly as a result of differential healthcare. But even though the physical evidence for it was quite conclusive, I was still being reassured by the parents that boys and girls received much the same attention, except that the boys' "needs" were quite different from those of girls. Also, when the admission data from Indian hospitals that I was able to collect and use (with the help of a great collaborator, Jocelyn Kynch) gave clear evidence that girls had to be a lot more ill for them to be taken to a hospital, compared with boys, the family's own beliefs and theories seemed to perceive little discrimination in treatment, only a sharper recognition of the seriousness of the ailments of the boys. So my early encounters, when I was a student, with the role of tilted attitudes and positional observations and slanted habits of thought did prove, in retrospect, highly educational for me (even though I did not know in my student days what a good education I was receiving through the frustrating conversations).

To turn to a different type of influence, I should also add one tremendously tragic personal experience, much later in life, that helped me to understand better one particular aspect of gender inequality. In 1985, with the sudden death of my wife, Eva Colorni (who was a strong

CONTINUING THE CONVERSATION

influence on my work on gender), I had to raise, as a single parent, two children (respectively 10 and 8 years old when Eva died), through their childhood and teenage years. I did, of course, have excellent help from my friends, but I also acquired a much clearer understanding of some of the problems that working mothers face in pursuing a career while looking after children. This "learning by doing" directly enriched my understanding of gender relations, and especially influenced my conceptual formulation of the interconnections between household obligations, outside work, and the division of benefits and chores of family life.

BA, JH, IR: Your work has been inspirational to feminist scholars on many fronts. Indeed many of us claim you as a feminist economist. Have some feminist writings also influenced you? Also, has a gender perspective contributed to any of your theoretical formulations?

AS: I am very interested in the works of contemporary feminist economists, and I have enormously benefited from the richness of contributions in this growing field (this journal itself, under the proficient editorship of Diana Strassmann, has done a tremendous job in facilitating this remarkable development). But a long time ago, my interest in feminist ideas was particularly stimulated by Mary Wollstonecraft's *A Vindication of the Rights of Women*. It is, of course, a truly visionary book, and it made me think about subjects I had tended to neglect in my earlier years. I was, however, also interested in the question as to how such a great book could be altogether ignored by philosophers such as Jeremy Bentham, who would have gained so much from reading her. This applies not only to the issue of women's deprivations, but also to such general matters as the understanding of how to think about "rights" in general, especially for any deprived group, women or any other underprivileged group.

Indeed, in the same year in which Wollstonecraft's *Vindication* was published, that is in 1792, Jeremy Bentham was busy writing his *Anarchical Fallacies: Being an Examination of the Declaration of Rights Issued during the French Revolution*. Bentham chastised the French revolutionaries for "abusing" the concept of rights, by seeing them as social demands, rather than as legal commands: "from real laws come real rights," he said, "but from *imaginary* laws" can come only "*imaginary* rights." This made Bentham jump to the conclusion that what the French revolutionaries were talking about was "simple nonsense" and perhaps even "rhetorical nonsense, nonsense upon stilts." That bit of legalism, combined with Bentham's inability to get anything out of his ethical hat other than the rabbit of utility, led him to overlook the great reach and expanse of political and moral thinking that the idea of the rights of the underprivileged could constructively stimulate. The full title, incidentally, of Wollstonecraft's book is *A Vindication of the Rights of Women: with Strictures on Political and Moral*

Subjects, and it is the inescapable need for political and moral reasoning that is often missed, even today, when one theorist or another chastises the very notion of "human rights" as being imaginary nonsense.

Mary Wollstonecraft was also ahead of the "human rights" thinkers who, while differing from Bentham's legalism, saw human rights to be, as it were, "legal rights in waiting," that is, as ethical claims that must be legalized for them to be effective. Wollstonecraft's analysis of the variety of processes through which subjugation and deprivation come about pointed to the constructive role that "recognition" can play (even without formal legalization). This provides a kind of theoretical backdrop to the nonlegal but influential "Universal Declaration of Human Rights," adopted in 1948 (more than *150* years after Wollstonecraft's book). It also provides a prescient understanding of the need for activism (well reflected in modern feminist movements – campaigning for rights of women and also of underprivileged men), employing a variety of means, such as political agitation, public debates, and monitoring of iniquities and abuses. Since the deprivations of different groups have much in common, Wollstone-craft's gender perspective opened the way to the understanding of other kinds of denials and rejections. That, by the way, is one reason why the relevance of feminist economics extends far beyond the specific domain of gender relations (important as that domain is).

I can similarly describe the impact that other feminist writings, new and old, have had on my thinking. Even Simone de Beauvoir's *The Second Sex,* though focused on rather different issues, gave me some ideas that proved useful in my being able to understand how it comes about that many deprived women readily accept the fog of pro-inequality apologia as a true description of reality. Incidentally, Marx's concept of "false consciousness," with which de Beauvoir was very familiar, applies much more readily to spurious perceptions regarding gender inequality than to class inequality, in which Marx himself was most interested. Similarly, Ester Boserup's *Women's Role in Economic Development* gave me several insights, especially about the linkage between women's economic activities and the deals that women get.

I do see myself, in part, as a feminist economist, in addition to having other descriptions to which I respond. This is partly because of my direct involvement with gender-related issues, but also because of my conviction that the perspective of gender inequality gives us real insight into asymmetries and deprivations of other kinds as well. Inequality (in which I am comprehensively interested) may not be an undifferentiated whole, but nor is it a mechanical mixture of disparate components that do not interact with one another, nor in any way resemble each other.

You ask about the impact of feminist ideas on my "theoretical formulations." There is quite an embarrassment of riches here. My understanding of inequality and deprivation in various fields was directly influenced by what I learned about the nature, causation, and mechanism of gender inequality. For example, my skepticism about relying on utility or on unscrutinized preferences for moral assessment, or for political evaluation, or for social choice, has been strongly influenced by what I have learned from studies of gender inequalities, particularly about the role that adaptive preferences and attitudes play in socially sustaining these inequalities. This certainly has had a substantial impact on the formulations I have used in moral and political philosophy, and in social choice theory, and also on my understanding of the process of economic development and social change.

BA, JH, IR: Many argue that although you have written extensively on gender inequality, you do not directly address the question of power within gender relations. Do you agree?

AS: I do not think I can agree with that. I cannot even understand how it could be possible to discuss gender inequality extensively (as it is suggested, I have done), without going into the question of power within gender relations, since power is so central. In fact, the importance of power is part and parcel of my understanding, both directly and indirectly, of gender inequality.

First, if one is assessing gender inequality not in the mental or psychological scale of utilities, but primarily in terms of the real "capabilities" that women and men respectively have (which is how I formulate the problem), the powers they respectively have – to do or be what they value – are constitutively important. This can vary from such elementary powers as not being subjected to physical abuse or violent assault and the freedom to lead unsubjugated lives (where power can enter in a very crude form) to having the opportunity to develop one's talents and to achieve self-respect and the respect of others (where power can take more sophisticated forms). So power is directly involved in the "assessment" of gender inequality.

Second, on the "causal" side, one type of power asymmetry leads to, or helps to facilitate, power asymmetries of other types. Power has a central role in what I call "cooperative conflict" which is central to my understanding of gender inequality within the family and ultimately in the society at large. Women and men have both *congruent* and *conflicting* interests affecting family living. Because of the extensive areas of congruence of interest, decision-making in the family tends to take the form of the pursuit of cooperation, with some agreed solution, usually *implicit,* of the conflicting aspects. Each of the parties has much to lose if cooperation were to break down, and yet there are various alternative "cooperative solutions," each of which is better for both the parties than no cooperation at all, but which respectively give different, possibly *extremely* different, relative gains to the two parties. In the emergence of some cooperative solution among the many that are available, the powers of the two parties play a crucial part: for example, the more powerful party can obtain more favorable divisions of the family's overall benefits and chores.

There are, thus, far-reaching causal impacts of the presence and use of powers of different kinds, from physical powers (even the asymmetry in brute physical strength) to institutionally mediated powers (such as the social powers arising from traditional roles inside and outside the household). I would have some difficulty in grasping how someone can read, say, my "Gender and Cooperative Conflict" (in the Irene Tinker collection: *Persistent Inequalities*, 1990) or the chapter on "Women's Agency and Social Change" in *Development as Freedom* (1999), and still think that I am not interested in the role of power in gender relations. Perhaps the point is not about whether the *concept* of power is being used, but about the frequency with which the *word* "power" occurs in my writing (as opposed to the ones I tend more often to use, such as "empowerment" or "capability" or "freedom" or "agency" or "threat" or "vulnerability").

BA, JH, IR: In your frequent references to Kerala's success with gender-related development indicators, you mainly highlight state policy. But don't you think Kerala's largely matrilineal tradition, which gave most women notable property rights and made daughters more sought after than sons, is also a critical and interrelated factor?

AS: I entirely agree that the presence of a matrilineal tradition of property ownership and inheritance in Kerala has made a major difference. In fact, I have discussed this connection in *Development as Freedom* (pp. 220 – 1), and also in my joint books with Jean Drèze, *Hunger and Public Action* (1989: 224 – 5) and *India: Economic Development and Social Opportunity* (1995: 142 – 3). Perhaps I should emphasize it more, compared with other favorable features of Kerala, such as an early commitment to public education and especially education of girls (related to state policy in Travancore and Cochin, the two "native states" – formally outside the British empire), and a firm history of radical politics (originally getting dialectical strength from the fact that the hold of upper classes and castes, which was challenged by the new left-wing politics, was stronger in Kerala than in most parts of India).

However, there may be two difficulties in making the matrilineal property rights the central story. First, this system of property inheritance applies only to a part of Kerala's population and not to the whole of it. Of course, the Nairs (the most notable among the matrilineal communities) were influential in state policy and there is certainly a connection there, and also in the "demonstration effect" of women's property rights for a significant section of the state's population, but the picture is not as simple as it would have been if the system actually gave (as you say) "most women notable property rights and made daughters more sought after than sons." The contribution of matrilineal property rights for a part of the population has to be placed within a fuller picture, which must recognize several other favorable features of Kerala.

Second, to put great emphasis on historical luck (in having a "matrilineal tradition" of property rights over centuries) may well be unduly discouraging for what can be done here and now. That is one reason for highlighting state policy, as you rightly say I do, but state policy can be concerned not only with education and other measures of women's empowerment, but also with reforming ownership and inheritance rights in favor of women, which too can enhance the agency and power of women. I should perhaps mention in this context, that when India became independent in 1947, in the newly formed state of Kerala (based mainly on the ground of a shared language, Malayalam), the bulk of the population came from the two "native states" outside the British empire (Travancore and Cochin), but another bit came from the old province of Madras. Malabar – from British India – was immensely backward socially in comparison with Travancore and Cochin, including in the role of women. But a uniform state policy, with particular emphasis on helping Malabar to "catch up," has made, by now, the different parts of Kerala nearly indistinguishable from each other in terms of social development. To rely too heavily on the luck of having a "favorable history" can be unduly pessimistic.

BA, JH, IR: In what ways do you think gender analysis has had an impact on mainstream economics?

AS: Well, I don't think it has yet had the kind of impact it should have, and I am sure will eventually have. There is, however, already a very widespread recognition that in the apparently neutral and open-minded tradition of mainstream economics, there are implicit biases which lead to an over-concentration on some questions rather than others which are of particular interest to disadvantaged groups in general and to women in particular. So, in this sense, a significant contribution has already been made through questioning the complacency about neglecting some significant issues, and this is having the effect of broadening the agenda of investigation. When I had to organize, as President-elect of the American Economic Association, the annual meeting of the Association in 1994 I was very impressed by the number and quality of contributions that were submitted on inequality which were clearly influenced, in one way or another, by gender analysis, and broadly speaking, the feminist perspective.

The exact question you have posed is hard to answer for two distinct reasons. First, there is no agreed reading of what constitutes "mainstream economics." For example, is development economics a part of mainstream economics? If it is, then the impact of gender analysis is clearly well reflected in the kind of issues that have received attention in recent years, at least in a part of what is seen as development economics. Also, the economics of the family cannot but be influenced by gender analysis, and certainly in recent years there have been many contributions that take the interests of women and men within the family as distinct entities, rather than their being submerged in some uniform formulation of the undifferentiated interests of "the family." So the answer to your question will depend partly on whether the economics of the family is seen as lying firmly outside mainstream economics or not.

Second, gender analysis can have indirect effects as well as direct ones, and sometimes the indirect effects can be quite powerful even though there is no immediately visible gender connection. Let me illustrate. One of the lessons from the recent analyses of family economics (through seeing it as a "bargaining problem" or as some other form of "cooperative conflict") is the recognition that a family arrangement can be very inequitable and unjust even when the different parties gain something in comparison with having no cooperation at all. When there are gains from cooperation, there can be many alternative arrangements that benefit each party compared with no cooperation. It is necessary, therefore, to ask whether the distribution of gains is fair or acceptable, and not just whether there exist some gain for all parties (which would be the case for a great many alternative arrangements).

This elementary lesson from family economics, and its extensive relevance for feminist economics, has an immediate application in understanding the issues involved in the current debates about globalization. The defenders of the present system of globalized economic relations often argue that globalization cannot be bad since it improves the lot of all the countries – the poorer as well as the richer ones. However, as the analysis of cooperative conflict in family economics shows, that outcome, even if true, will not in itself establish anything about the fairness of the system of globalization. What has to be shown is not only that all parties gain something, which will hold for a great many alternative arrangements, but that the distribution of gains is, in some plausible sense, fair, or at least not grossly unfair. The analogy is with the understanding, from gender studies, that to recognize that a particular family arrangement is unequal and unfair, it does not have to be shown that women would have done comparatively better had there been no families at all ("if you don't like it, pray live on your own!"), but only that the sharing of the benefits of the family system is seriously unequal and unfair as things are typically organized.

Recent debates on globalization have generated much heat and comparatively little light by concentrating on the wrong question, with defenders (or apologists) of globalization claiming that all the parties have gained, while the detractors (or egg-throwers) claim that the poor have gotten poorer. The lesson to derive from gender studies is that concentrating on the question whether there has been some gain (anything at all) for all is not in itself the right focus of investigation. The poor do not have to get actually poorer for the distribution system to be thoroughly unjust; the issue is the relative sharing of gains, not the presence of an actual loss from the prevailing system of interrelations (which may or may not occur).

BA, JH, IR: You are a rare economist in your weaving of economics with politics and ethics. Most mainstream economists by contrast insistently separate the normative from the positive. Have you found yourself consistently battling mainstream economists as a result? And which thrust do you think will prevail?

AS: There is a long tradition in economics that takes normative issues as seriously as positive ones. That tradition includes not only Smith, Mill, Marx, Edgeworth, Marshall, Pigou, and many others, but also a number of contemporary economists. So in taking normative economics seriously, against the admonition of positivists, I do not feel particularly lonely or abandoned.

The issue of "separation" of normative and positive questions is, however, more difficult and also more complex. I do not take the view that in no sense does such a separation communicate anything useful: there is a difference between saying "the number of people laid off has increased this year" and "it is terrible that the number of people laid off has increased this year." It is, of course, possible to have a fine philosophical argument as to whether that separation is sustainable in terms of their respective epistemic and ethical contents (I am interested in that question, but it is not central to the practice of economics). On the other hand, it is actually quite important to insist that once our ethics lead us to the kind of questions that we ought to ask, we must then seek, in the case of mainly empirical questions, as factually sound answers as possible (within the limits of the nature of the questions asked). We can rightly grumble that it is a great pity that there is so little work on inequality and so much on efficiency and aggregate growth, but when we start looking at the empirical picture of inequality we should not be guided primarily by our morality, ignoring the evidence that can be found (often with hard empirical work). If I reacted with a little reserve to the very kindly meant remark of my friend Robert Solow that I was "the conscience of economics" (which is quoted quite often), it was because of my conviction that conscience alone could get us nowhere. For example, burning the midnight candle to make sense of unruly and awkward famine data to construct a coherent picture of what happened is not a matter of conscience, but of hard, empirical sweat.

329

AMARTYA SEN'S WORK AND IDEAS

In terms of the motivation for your question, if I judge it right, we must have some sense of: (1) the extent to which economic analysis can actually help ethical reasoning, and (2) the extent to which ethics can be useful in economic investigations. I have taken a rather interlinked view in claiming that ethics and economics make substantial contributions to each other (and have argued for that perspective in such writings as *On Ethics and Economics*). To state briefly the argument for (1), since values are fact-dependent, factual economic analysis of a relevant kind is central to ethical assessment of situations and policies. Regarding (2), policies need values and thus economic policies do need ethics. Also, facts are endless, and to decide what to look at in empirical economics, we need to have a sense of what is important and valuable. Further, since people's behavior responds to ethical arguments, we have to understand ethical arguments to follow economic reasoning. Even though I have not had a great many followers, neither have I found a great sense of hostility to what I have tried to do. I should be content with that.

BA, JH, IR: You take a rather negative view of identity politics. But for the women's movement, identity politics based on common gender interests has brought some obvious gains, without women necessarily having to deny their other identities. Could you comment?

AS: I quite agree that the identity of being a woman – or for that matter of being a feminist (whether female or male) – can be very important in pursuing gender justice. And it has certainly tended to work that way. My complaint about identity politics is not meant to question, in any way, the contributions that the sense of identity of deprived groups can make in changing the predicament of those groups. Gender or class or caste can be taken up from the perspective of deprivation and can then be an important part of resisting inequality and injustice.

Part of my unease with identity politics lies in the use that is made of the bonds of identity by privileged groups to act against the interest of others. Identity is invoked not only by impoverished groups seeking redress, but also by privileged groups that try to suppress and terrorize the others. For example, the targeting – even genocide – of vulnerable communities is often organized through incitement based on invoking and cultivating the belligerent identity of powerful communities (White supremacists, anti-Semitic "Aryans," and so on). To take another kind of example, the solidarity of land-owning castes in northern Bihar has been responsible for assaulting and murdering cultivating laborers seeking liberation.

However, more foundationally – and this is the central issue – it is appalling to insist that identity is a matter of "discovery" (to quote a favorite phrase of "identity" activists), rather than its being a matter of choice – and of ethics – for us to determine what importance we want to (and have reason to) attach to one or other of the many identities that we simultaneously have. It is one thing for, say, a woman activist to decide that the identity of being a woman is overwhelmingly important, given her own values and the nature of the unjust world in which she lives, and quite another for people being led like herds in an organized direction to pursue some intolerant cause or an orchestrated program. People can be suddenly made to feel that they are not really what they took themselves to be: not Rwandans, but Hutus ("we hate Tutsis"), or not Yugoslavs but Slavs ("you and I don't like Albanians"). "Any kiddie in school can love like a fool," Ogden Nash had claimed, "but hating, my boy, is an art." That art is widely practiced by skilled artists and instigators and the weapon of choice often is the imposition of a unique identity that has to be "discovered." I protest against both (1) the failure to see that we belong to many different groups, so that the identities that we choose to focus on is a matter of our decision, and (2) the incendiary use that is made of identity politics to terrorize the nonmembers of a privileged identity. I am actually writing a book on all this (tentatively called *Identity and Innocence*), but you will not find me grumbling there about choosing to give priority to one's identity as a member of an underprivileged group.

BA, JH, IR: One field of growing importance in which there are few references to Amartya Sen is environmental economics. Are there aspects of your theoretical work that would illuminate environmental concerns? And are you planning to address such concerns more explicitly in future work?

AS: I have written a certain amount about environmental economics, but I am not surprised that I have not been particularly influential. I think environmental problems often need a more radical formulation, taking note of their interdependences with other aspects of social choice. For example, the literature on "contingent valuation" asked questions about how much will you be willing to pay to remove some environmental disaster. The answer must depend on many implicit presumptions, regarding what others will do, and what difference I can credibly believe will my own contribution make. The question as posed can be interpreted as either being partly unformulated ("you assume about the others what you like") or being strangely presumptive in assuming that a socially integrated problem can be seen as an atomistic *as if* market choice ("if your paying $10 will eliminate – on its own without anyone else paying anything at all – that entire disaster resulting from Exxon Valdez spill, will you be willing to 'buy' it?"). The question under the former interpretation is altogether unclear, and under the latter interpretation, it strains one's imagination too much ("would I spend $10 if it would, on its own, clear up the entire sound befouled by the Exxon Valdez spill – come again?"). It also, by the way, violates what Arrow called "the independence of irrelevant alternatives." A proper statement of the problems calls for a fuller "social choice formulation," as I tried to discuss in a paper (called "Environmental Evaluation and Social Choice") in the *Japanese Economic Review* (1995). This argued for eschewing the implicit market models underlying many environmental formulations, and for using instead a broader social choice structure.

A similar difficulty arises in following the powerful reasoning presented by Gro Brundtland and Robert Solow on "sustainable development." Solow has argued in his monograph *An Almost Practical Step towards Sustainability* (1992) that we can see sustainability as the requirement that the next generation must be left with "whatever it takes to achieve a standard of living at least as good as our own and to look after their next generation similarly." This is an excellent formulation (dealing with future generations recursively), but we can ask whether the overall standard of living is the only thing we may be concerned with. There are several difficulties here.

First, it is a very anthropocentric concept. Indeed, the preservation of human living standards need not be the only concern that human beings themselves have. To use a medieval European distinction, we are not merely "patients" preoccupied with just our own standard of living, but also responsible and active "agents" who are capable of judging the world around us and undertaking wider commitments. As Buddha argued in *Sutta Nipata*, since we are enormously more powerful than the other species, we human beings have some responsibility towards them that arises from this asymmetry of power. We can indeed make a significant distinction between (1) our ability to preserve the quality of our human lives and (2) our ability to preserve what we think is worth preserving (perhaps including other species), not just to the extent that they impinge on the quality of human lives.

Second, the Brundtland-Solow approach may be too aggregative if we have reason to attach importance to particular freedoms, even when there is no loss in the overall standards of living. To illustrate the difference (with an example that does not involve future generations – only a contemporary confrontation), if it is thought that a person has the right not to have smoke blown on to her face by a heavy – and indiscriminate – smoker, the right to be free of secondary smoking need not be compromised merely because the person thus affected happens to be very rich and endowed with an outstanding standard of living (particularly compared with the miserable smoker). Similarly a fouled environment in which the future generations are denied the presence of fresh air (say, because of some specially nasty emission) will remain foul even if the future generations are so very rich and so tremendously well served in terms of other amenities of good life that their *overall* standards of living are well sustained. The loss of particular freedoms matters, even when overall living standards are preserved.

Third, exactly *how* the environment and living standards are preserved can itself make a difference in a fuller social choice formulation. If environmental policies lead to the loss of human freedom in the cause of preserving or promoting living standards, then that loss has to be specifically acknowledged, rather than being "submerged" in an aggregative accounting of the standard of living. To illustrate, even if it turns out that restricting human freedoms through draconian policies of coercive family planning (as in, say, the "one-child family" in China) helps to sustain living standards (this is, in fact, empirically far from clear, as I have tried to discuss in "Fertility and Coercion," *University of Chicago Law Review*, 1996), it must nevertheless be unequivocally acknowledged that something of importance is sacrificed – rather than sustained – through these policies themselves.

One way of putting all these concerns into an integrated formulation is to argue that what we must be concerned with is not just sustaining living standards, but sustaining human freedoms. Indeed, I would argue that the idea of "sustainable freedoms" can add something substantial to the living-standard-based notion of sustainable development. It can combine the very important concept of sustainability – rightly championed by Brundtland and Solow – with a view of human beings as agents whose freedoms matter, rather than seeing people simply as patients who are no greater than their living standards. So I do want to see quite a big advance in environmental economics. However, I would be extremely surprised if this campaign proves to be easy. I am certainly not holding my breath!

REFERENCES

Bentham, Jeremy. [1843] 1994. *Anarchical Fallacies: Being an Examination of the Declaration of Rights Issued During the French Revolution* in *The Works of Jeremy Bentham*, Vol. 2. London: Thoemmes Press.

Boserup, Ester. 1970. *Women's Role in Economic Development.* London: Allen & Unwin.

De Beauvior, Simone. 1953. *The Second Sex.* H. M. Parshley (ed.). Trans. H. M. Parshley. New York: Knopf.

Drèze, Jean and Amartya Sen. 1989. *Hunger and Public Action.* New York: Clarendon Press.

—— 1995. *India: Economic Development and Social Opportunity.* New York: Oxford University Press.

Sen, Amartya. 1987. *On Ethics and Economics.* New York: Blackwell.

—— 1990. "Gender and Cooperative Conflict," in Irene Tinker (ed.) *Persistent Inequalities: Women and World Development.* New York: Oxford University Press.

—— 1995. "Environmental Evaluation and Social Choice." *Japanese Economic Review* 46(1): 23 – 37.

—— 1996. "Fertility and Coercion." *University of Chicago Law Review* 63(3): 1035 – 1061.

—— 1999. *Development as Freedom.* New York: Anchor.

Solow, Robert. [1992] 1997. *An Almost Practical Step Toward Sustainability: An Invited Lecture on the Occasion of the Fortieth Anniversary of Resources for the Future.* Washington, DC: Resources for the Future.

Universal Declaration of Human Rights. 1948. United Nations General Assembly Resolution 217 A (III), December 10, 1948. On-line. Available http://www.un.org/Overview/rights.html (May 2003).

Wollstonecraft, Mary. [1972] 1988. *A Vindication of the Rights of Woman: An Authoritative Text; Backgrounds; The Wollstonecraft Debate; Criticism (Norton Critical Editions).* 2d ed. Carol H. Poston (ed.). New York: Norton.

CAPABILITIES, LISTS, AND PUBLIC REASON: CONTINUING THE CONVERSATION

Amartya Sen

This contribution furthers the exchange, "Continuing the Conversation: Amartya Sen Talks with Bina Agarwal, Jane Humphries, and Ingrid Robeyns," which appeared in *Feminist Economics*, Vol. 9, No. 2/3, July/ November, 2003, "A Special Issue on Amartya Sen's Work and Ideas: A Gender Perspective," guest edited by Bina Agarwal, Jane Humphries, and Ingrid Robeyns.

BA, JH, IR: In your writings on the capability approach you provide no list of capabilities. Is that because you think such a list cannot be drawn?

AS: The problem is not with listing important capabilities, but with insisting on one predetermined canonical list of capabilities, chosen by theorists without any general social discussion or public reasoning. To have such a fixed list, emanating entirely from pure theory, is to deny the possibility of fruitful public participation on what should be included and why.

I have, of course, discussed various lists of capabilities that would seem to demand attention in any theory of justice and more generally in social assessment, such as the freedom to be well nourished, to live disease free lives, to be able to move around, to be educated, to participate in public life, and so on. Indeed, right from my first writings on using the capability perspective (for example in my 1979 Lectures "Equality of What?"), I have tried to discuss the relevance of many specific capabilities. The 1979 lecture went into the relevance of "the ability to move about" (and discussed why disabilities can be a central concern in a way that an income-centered approach may not be able to grasp), along with other basic capabilities, such as "the ability to meet one's nutritional requirements, the wherewithal to be clothed and sheltered, the power to participate in the social life of the community" (see Sen 1982: 367–8). The contrast between lists of capabilities and commodities was a central concern in *Commodities and*

Capabilities (Sen 1985). The relevance of many capabilities that are often neglected was discussed in the second set of Tanner Lectures (Sen 1987), given at Cambridge University, and published under the title *The Standard of Living*.

What I am against is the fixing of a cemented list of capabilities, which is absolutely complete (nothing could be added to it) and totally fixed (it could not respond to public reasoning and to the formation of social values). I am a great believer in theory. The theory of evaluation and assessment does, I believe, have the exacting task of pointing to the relevance of what we are free to do and free to be (the capabilities in general), as opposed to the material goods we have and the commodities we can command. But pure theory cannot "freeze" a list of capabilities for all societies for all time to come, irrespective of what the citizens come to understand and value. That would be not only a denial of the reach of democracy, but also a misunderstanding of what pure theory can do, completely divorced from the particular social reality that any particular society faces.

Along with the exercise of listing the relevant capabilities, there is also the problem of determining the relative weights and importance of the different capabilities included in the relevant list. Even with a given list, the question of valuation cannot be avoided. There is sometimes a temptation not only to have one fixed list, but also to have the elements of the list ordered in a lexicographic way. But this can hardly work. For example, the ability to be well nourished cannot in general be put invariably *above* or *below* the ability to be well sheltered, so that the tiniest improvement of one will always count as more important than a large change in the other. We may have to give priority to the ability to be well nourished when people are dying of hunger in their homes, whereas the freedom to be sheltered may rightly receive more weight when people are in general well fed, but lack shelter.

Some of the basic capabilities (with which my 1979 Tanner Lecture was particularly concerned) will no doubt figure in every list of relevant capabilities in every society. But the exact list to be used will have to take note of the purpose of the exercise. There is often good sense in narrowing the coverage of capabilities for a specific purpose. An example is the use of a selected list of very elementary capabilities for assessing the extent of poverty in some countries. Jean Drèze and I did try to do that in *Hunger and Public Action* (Drèze and Sen 1989), and *India: Participation and Development* (Drèze and Sen 2002). I see Martha Nussbaum's use of a given list of capabilities for some minimal rights against deprivation as being extremely useful in the same practical way. For another practical purpose, we may have another list.

For example, when my friend Mahbub ul Haq asked me, in 1989, to work with him on indicators of human development, and in particular to help develop a general index for global assessment and critique, it was clear to me that we were involved in a particular exercise of specific relevance. So the "human development index" (the HDI) was based on a very minimal listing of capabilities, with a particular focus on getting at a minimally basic quality of life, calculable from available statistics, in a way that the GNP or GDP failed to capture. Lists of capabilities have to be used for various purposes, and so long as we understand what we are doing (and in particular that we are getting a list for a particular reason, related to a particular assessment, evaluation, or critique), we do not put ourselves against other lists that may be relevant or useful for other purposes.

All this has to be contrasted with insisting on one "final list of capabilities that matter." To decide that some capability will not figure in the list of relevant capabilities at all amounts to putting a zero weight on that capability for every exercise, no matter what the exercise is concerned with, and no matter what the social conditions are. This could be very dogmatic, for many distinct reasons.

First, we use capabilities for different purposes. What we focus on cannot be independent of what we are doing and why (e.g., whether we are evaluating poverty, specifying certain basic human rights, getting a rough and ready measure of human development, and so on).

Second, social conditions and the priorities that they suggest may vary. For example, given the nature of poverty in India as well as the nature of available technology, it was not unreasonable in 1947 (when India became independent) to concentrate on elementary education, basic health, and so on, and not worry too much about whether everyone can effectively communicate across the country and beyond. However, with the development of the Internet and its wide-ranging applications, and the advance made in information technology (not least in India), access to the web and the freedom of general communication are now parts of a very important capability that is of interest and relevance to all Indians.

Third, even with given social conditions, public discussion and reasoning can lead to a better understanding of the role, reach, and the significance of particular capabilities. For example, one of the many contributions of feminist economics has been precisely to bring out the importance of certain freedoms that were not recognized very clearly – or at all – earlier on, for example freedom from the imposition of fixed and time-honored family roles, or immunity from implicit derogation in social communication. To insist on a fixed forever list of capabilities would deny the possibility of progress in social understanding and also go against the productive role of public discussion, social agitation, and open debates.

I have nothing against the listing of capabilities but must stand up against a grand mausoleum to one fixed and final list of capabilities.

REFERENCES

Drèze, Jean and Amartya Sen. 1989. *Hunger and Public Action.* Oxford: Oxford University Press.

Drèze, Jean and Amartya Sen. 2002. *India: Development and Participation.* Oxford: Oxford University Press.

Sen, Amartya. 1979. "Equality of What?" Tanner Lectures on Human Values, Stanford University. http://www.tannerlectures.utah.edu (accessed October 18, 2004).

——. 1982. *Choice, Welfare, and Measurement.* Cambridge, MA: The MIT Press.

——. 1985. *Commodities and Capabilities.* New York: Elsevier Science Publishing Company.

——. 1987. *Tanner Lectures in Human Values: The Standard of Living.* Cambridge, UK: Cambridge University Press.

NOTES ON CONTRIBUTORS

Bina Agarwal is Professor of Economics at the Institute of Economic Growth, University of Delhi. She is also Vice-President of the International Economic Association, and President-elect of IAFFE. She has published extensively on environment and development; the political economy of gender; land, livelihoods, and property rights; collective action and community forestry; poverty and inequality; and agriculture and techno-logical change. Her most recent book *A Field of One's Own: Gender and Land Rights in South Asia* (Cambridge University Press, 1994) was awarded the A. K. Coomaraswamy Book Prize 1996; the Edgar Graham Book Prize 1996; and the K. H. Batheja Award 1995–96. She also received the Malcolm Adhiseshiah award 2002 for distinguished contributions to Development Studies. She is now working on some theoretical and empirical aspects of gender, environment, and collective action.

Elizabeth Anderson is Professor of Philosophy and Women's Studies at the University of Michigan, Ann Arbor. She is the author of *Value in Ethics and Economics* (Harvard University Press, 1993) and has written extensively on ethics, democracy, rational choice, philosophy of the social sciences, and feminist theory.

Stanley L. Engerman is John H. Munro Professor of Economics and Professor of History at the University of Rochester, Rochester, NY, USA. He is co-author (with Robert W. Fogel) of *Time on the Cross: The Economics of American Negro Slavery,* and more recently has co-edited (with the late Robert Gallman) *The Cambridge Economic History of the United States* and (with Seymour Drescher and Robert L. Paquette) *Slavery: A Reader.*

Sakiko Fukuda-Parr is a development economist and advocate of people-centered approaches to development. She is Director of the UNDP's Human Development Reports. She has written and spoken widely on a broad range of policy issues, particularly human rights, gender, poverty, technology, and capacity development. She is co-editor of *Capacity for Development: Old Problems, New Solutions;* and *Readings in Human Development: Concepts, Measures and Policies for a Development Paradigm.* She is editor of the *Journal of Human Development: Alternative Economics in Action* and is on the editorial board of *Feminist Economics.*

Des Gasper is Associate Professor in Public Policy at the Institute of Social Studies in The Hague. He works on topics in evaluation, policy argumentation, and ethics and development.

Marianne Hill is Senior Economist with the Center for Policy Research and Planning in Jackson, Mississippi, and editor of the *Mississippi Economic Review and Outlook,* where she publishes the state economic forecast. A longtime activist, she began the Mississippi Coalition for Women, which worked successfully with the state legislature to create a Women's Commission in 2001. Her recent research focuses on power, gender, race, and economic development. She has written on public policy issues in Puerto Rico and Bangladesh, as well as in the US. She was on the IAFFE Board of Directors from 1999 to 2001.

Jane Humphries taught in the faculty of Economics at Cambridge University for eighteen years before moving to Oxford where she is the Reader in Economic History and Fellow of All Souls College. She has worked on issues to do with women, the family, and the economy for many years. She is currently working on a book on child labor in the British industrial revolution.

Vegard Iversen is Lecturer in Economics and Director of the Masters Programme in Development Economics at the School of Development Studies, University of East Anglia, UK. His research experience includes studies of the environmental impacts of structural adjustment policies in sub-Saharan Africa undertaken while a researcher at the Agricultural University of Norway. He has also worked as a Programme Officer for the United Nations Development Programme in New Delhi. He completed his PhD from the University of Cambridge in 2000. Titled *Child Labor and Theories of the Family,* the dissertation focused on child labor migration in south India, developed new theory, and presented new evidence challenging received wisdom about families, children, and children's agency.

Stephan Klasen is Professor of Economics at the University of Munich. He holds a PhD in economics from Harvard University where he wrote a dissertation on gender bias in mortality, supervised by Amartya Sen. His current research focuses on issues of poverty and inequality in developing countries, with particular emphasis on the extent, the causes, and the consequences of gender bias in developing countries.

Christine M. Koggel is Associate Professor in the Philosophy Department at Bryn Mawr College. She is the author of *Perspectives on Equality: Constructing a Relational Theory* (Rowman & Littlefield, 1998); editor of *Moral Issues in Global Perspective* (Broadview, 1999); and co-editor (with Wesley Cragg) of the fourth edition (McGraw-Hill Ryerson, 1997) and the fifth edition (McGraw-Hill Ryerson, forthcoming) of *Contemporary Moral Issues*. Her current work is on poverty and, specifically, on inequalities of wealth within and across borders.

Martha C. Nussbaum is Ernst Freund Distinguished Service Professor of Law and Ethics at the University of Chicago, appointed in the Philosophy Department, Law School, and Divinity School. She is Associate in the Political Science Department and the Classics Department, Affiliate of the Committee on Southern Asian Studies, Board Member of the Human Rights Program, and the founder and coordinator of the Center for Comparative Constitutionalism. Her most recent books are *Women and Human Development: The Capabilities Approach* (2002) and *Upheavals of Thought: The Intelligence of Emotions* (2001).

Fabienne Peter is Assistant Professor of Economics at the University of Basel. Her research explores issues at the intersection of economics and philosophy, with particular emphasis on normative theories of social evaluation and on the methodology of the social sciences. Before joining the University of Basel, she was a research fellow at the Harvard Center for Population and Development Studies, where she worked on health equity. *Public Health, Ethics, and Equity*, a volume she has co-edited with Sudhir Anand and Amartya Sen, is forthcoming from Oxford University Press.

Ingrid Robeyns received her PhD from the Faculty of Economics and Politics at Cambridge University. She is now a post-doctoral research fellow in the Department of Political Science at the University of Amsterdam, working on Amartya Sen's capability approach and distributive justice in welfare states. Her research interests include social and distributive justice, inequality, social policy, the intersection of political philosophy and welfare economics, feminist theory, and methodological and epistemological discussions.

Irene van Staveren is Senior Lecturer in Labor Economics of Developing Countries at the Institute of Social Studies in The Hague. Her PhD dissertation at Erasmus University Rotterdam on the values of freedom, justice, and care in economics won the 2000 Gunnar Myrdal Prize.

Claudia Wink is Investment Manager at DEG-Deutsche Investitions und Entwicklungsgesellschaft mbH, Cologne, an enterprise of the KfW Group, which finances investments of private companies in developing and transition countries. As one of Europe's largest institutions for long-term project and company financing, it promotes private business structures to contribute to sustainable economic growth and improved living conditions.

At DEG she is in charge of implementing Public – Private Partnerships in China and Mongolia. She graduated from the University of Munich in Economics where she wrote her thesis on "missing women" in developing countries, supervised by Stephan Klasen.

INDEX